Trade Liberalisation and International Co-operation

For Andrew, Max and Zoe

Trade Liberalisation and International Co-operation

A Legal Analysis of the Trans-Pacific Partnership Agreement

Edited by

Tania Voon

Melbourne Law School, The University of Melbourne, Australia

Edward Elgar

Cheltenham, UK • Northampton, MA, USA

Published by
Edward Elgar Publishing Limited
The Lypiatts
15 Lansdown Road
Cheltenham
Glos GL50 2JA
UK

Edward Elgar Publishing, Inc.
William Pratt House
9 Dewey Court
Northampton
Massachusetts 01060
USA

A catalogue record for this book
is available from the British Library

Library of Congress Control Number: 2013946815

This book is available electronically in the ElgarOnline.com
Law Subject Collection, E-ISBN 978 1 78254 678 8

MIX
Paper from
responsible sources
FSC® C013056

ISBN 978 1 78254 677 1

Typeset by Columns Design XML Ltd, Reading
Printed and bound in Great Britain by T.J. International Ltd, Padstow

Contents

List of contributors vii
Acknowledgments xiv

1 Introduction: national regulatory autonomy and the Trans-Pacific Partnership Agreement 1
Tania Voon
2 Coping with proliferating preferential rules of origin and the TPP's role in their harmonisation 11
Won-Mog Choi
3 The Trans-Pacific Partnership Agreement and development 28
Meredith Kolsky Lewis
4 The TPP as a case study of changing dynamics for international intellectual property negotiations 50
Kimberlee Weatherall
5 Plain packaging for the Pacific Rim – tobacco control and the Trans-Pacific Partnership 75
Matthew Rimmer
6 Agriculture and the Trans-Pacific Partnership negotiations 106
Deborah Elms
7 Services in the TPP: a case study of telecommunications 131
Danny Kotlowitz and Tania Voon
8 State–state dispute settlement under the Trans-Pacific Partnership Agreement 156
Andrew Mitchell and James Munro
9 Investor–state dispute settlement under the Trans-Pacific Partnership Agreement 179
Leon E. Trakman
10 The Trans-Pacific Partnership Agreement, the environment and climate change 207
Joshua P. Meltzer

11 The Trans-Pacific Partnership Agreement and regulatory coherence 231
Rodrigo Polanco

Bibliography 262
Index 273

Contributors

Won-Mog Choi
Professor, Ewha Woman's University Law School

Won-Mog is a professor of law of Ewha Law School and director of the WTO Law Center, Ewha Woman's University at Seoul. He serves as the President of the Korean Society of International Economic Law and the editor-in-chief of the *Korean Journal of International and Comparative Law*. He is also a member of the editorial board of many journals, including the *Journal of International Economic Law* (Oxford), the *Law and Development Review* (Sydney), the *Indian Journal of International Economic Law* (Bangalore), the *Beijing Law Review* (Beijing) and the *Journal of Korea Trade* (Seoul). Won-Mog received his legal education in the United States (Georgetown Law, SJD and LLM) and Korea (Seoul National University, MPA and LLB). He is also a member of the New York Bar. Prior to joining the faculty of Ewha, he worked for the Ministry of Foreign Affairs and Trade of Korea for 11 years as a diplomat and legal officer in charge of numerous trade issues, including WTO dispute settlements, trade remedy issues and FTAs. Currently advising the Korean Government on trade law and policy issues and working as a columnist of major newspapers in Seoul, Professor Choi has actively published books and articles. His recent publications include 'Defragmenting Fragmented Rules of Origin of RTAs: A Building Block to Global Free Trade' (*JIEL* 2010), 'Aggressive Regionalism in Korea-US FTA: The Present and Future of Korea's FTA Policy' (*JIEL* 2009), 'The Present and Future of the Investor-State Dispute Settlement Paradigm' (*JIEL* 2007), 'To Comply or Not To Comply? – Non-implementation Problems in the WTO Dispute Settlement System' (*JWT* 2007) and 'Legal Analysis of Korea-ASEAN Regional Trade Integration' (*JWT* 2007). He is the winner of eight academic prizes.

Deborah Elms

Head, Temasek Foundation Centre for Trade & Negotiations and Senior Fellow of International Political Economy, S. Rajaratnam School of International Studies, Nanyang Technological University

Deborah participates in teaching, research and networking. Her research interests are negotiations and decision-making, particularly in trade. Her current research topic is the Trans-Pacific Partnership negotiations. She also conducts a range of teaching and training for government officials from around Asia, for members of parliament, for business leaders and for graduate students. She has provided consulting to the governments of Abu Dhabi, Sri Lanka, Cambodia, Taiwan and Singapore on a range of trade issues. Deborah received a PhD in political science from the University of Washington, an MA in international relations from the University of Southern California, and a BA and BS from Boston University in international relations and journalism.

Danny Kotlowitz

Legal Counsel, Corporate Affairs, Telstra Corporation

Danny has worked in communications law since 1995 across several jurisdictions including Australia, South Africa and Hong Kong. His current practice focuses on competition law, radiofrequency spectrum regulation and commercial agreements for spectrum use, regulation in several Asian nations, and advice to Telstra on telecommunications aspects of trade agreements. Prior to joining Telstra's legal group, Danny was employed by Mallesons Stephen Jaques in Melbourne and Edward Nathan & Friedland in Johannesburg. His research papers include an analysis of the US Trade Representative's conduct of its Section 1377 process, for the Communications Policy Research Forum in Sydney in 2006; and an examination of Australia's spectrum licensing approach to enabling passenger use of mobiles aboard commercial aircraft, for the Telecommunications Policy Research Conference in Washington, DC, in 2010. Danny studied trade law at the University of Toronto, where he completed an LLM and was awarded the WCG Howland Graduate Prize for overall best achievement. He also holds BBusSci (Hons) and LLB degrees from the University of Cape Town.

Meredith Kolsky Lewis

Associate Professor, SUNY Buffalo Law School

Meredith is Associate Professor and Director of the Canada–US Legal Studies Centre at the SUNY Buffalo Law School. She is also Associate

Professor and Associate Director of the New Zealand Centre of International Economic Law at the Victoria University of Wellington Law School. She was a Visiting Professor of Law at Georgetown Law in 2010–11. Her research focuses on international economic law, with a particular emphasis on free trade agreements and the WTO. Meredith is Co-Executive Vice President and a founding member of the Society of International Economic Law. She is one of New Zealand's two representatives to the International Law Association's International Trade Law Committee; a member of the Asian WTO Research Network; co-chair of the Law in the Pacific Rim Region Interest Group of the American Society of International Law; a board member of the Asian International Economic Law Network and co-founder and previous co-chair of the International Economic Law interest group of the Australia–New Zealand Society of International Law. Her publications include Meredith Kolsky Lewis and Susy Frankel (eds) *International Economic Law and National Autonomy* (Cambridge University Press 2010); a co-authored textbook published with Oxford University; and articles in numerous journals including the *Stanford Journal of International Law*, the *Journal of International Economic Law* and the *University of Chicago Journal of International Law*. Meredith wrote the first law review article to examine the TPP – 'Expanding the P-4 Agreement into a Broader Trans-Pacific Partnership: Implications and Opportunities' (2009) 4 *Asian Journal of WTO & International Health Law and Policy* 401 – and has since published 'The Trans-Pacific Partnership: New Paradigm or Wolf in Sheep's Clothing?' (2011) 34 *Boston College International and Comparative Law Review* 27 and 'Achieving a Free Trade Area of the Asia-Pacific: does the TPP present the most attractive path?' in C.L. Lim, Deborah K. Elms and Patrick Low, eds, *The Trans-Pacific Partnership – A Quest for a Twenty-first Century Trade Agreement* (Cambridge 2012). Meredith received her BA from Northwestern University and her MSFS and JD degrees from Georgetown University.

Joshua P. Meltzer
Fellow, Brookings Institution

Joshua is a fellow in the Global Economy and Development programme at the Brookings Institution and an adjunct professor at Johns Hopkins School of Advanced International Studies and Georgetown Law School. He is an expert on international trade law and policy issues relating to the World Trade Organization and free trade agreements. His research includes the intersection between climate change, energy and international trade and the role of the trade policy and law in supporting Internet access and data flows. He also writes on the legitimacy of the

WTO. Joshua has testified on international trade issues before the United States Congress and the US International Trade Commission. Prior to joining Brookings in November 2010, Joshua was first secretary for trade policy at the Australian Embassy in Washington, DC. At the Australian Embassy, he focused on climate change and energy issues, particularly with respect to their trade-related aspects. He was also responsible for intellectual property and the trade and environment issues in the Doha Round. Joshua has also worked in the Office of Trade Negotiations in the Australian Department of Foreign Affairs and Trade, where he was a trade negotiator for Australia's free trade agreement negotiations with Malaysia and ASEAN/New Zealand. He was also responsible for providing the Australian government with legal advice on its commitments under its FTAs, including the Australia–US FTA. Joshua has also interned in the Legal Affairs Division at the WTO and the United Nations International Law Commission. Joshua has been published in a range of peer-reviewed legal and policy journals such as the *Journal of International Economic Law* and the *Georgetown Journal of International Affairs*. Joshua is a regular commentator in international print media including the *New York Times*, the *Wall Street Journal*, the *Washington Post* and the *Asahi Shimbun*. Joshua has also appeared on television news media outlets such as the BBC, CNN and Fox News. Joshua holds degrees from Monash University in Melbourne, Australia as well as an SJD and LLM from the University of Michigan Law School in Ann Arbor.

Andrew D. Mitchell
Professor, Melbourne Law School

Andrew joined the faculty at Melbourne Law School in 2006. In 2007, following a nomination by the Australian government, the WTO's Dispute Settlement Body added him to the Indicative List of Governmental and Non-Governmental Panellists to hear WTO disputes. He has law degrees from Melbourne Law School, Harvard Law School and the University of Cambridge. His previous employers include the IMF, the OECD, Davis Polk & Wardwell, and Allens Arthur Robinson. Andrew also consults for the private sector and governmental and non-governmental organisations including Telstra and the World Health Organization (WHO). He has over 80 academic publications and has taught at numerous other law schools in Canada, the US and Australia.

James Munro
Researcher and PhD Candidate, Melbourne Law School

James has worked for a number of years in international trade and investment law as a Legal Officer in the Office of International Law, Attorney-General's Department. He has provided legal advice in the negotiations for free trade agreements with China, Malaysia, Japan and the Trans-Pacific Partnership Agreement; has worked on WTO disputes including third party submissions in *US – Anti-Dumping and Countervailing Duties* and *Canada – Renewables*; and has provided general advice to government on WTO law and bilateral investment treaties. He has also spent time in the Office of International Climate Law, where he provided advice to government on legal issues relating to the Kyoto Protocol, international carbon markets, international law issues relating to the carbon pricing mechanism, and various climate-related treaties under negotiation. James is currently undertaking graduate research into the consistency of the *Clean Energy Act 2012* with international trade and investment law, and is working as a research assistant on the Australian National Preventive Health Agency Preventive Health Research Grants Program on the relationship between non-communicable diseases and international law.

Rodrigo Polanco
Assistant Professor, University of Chile Law School

Rodrigo is an Assistant Professor of International Economic Law at the University of Chile, where he has been teaching foreign investment law, international environmental law and international trade law, both at the law school and the Institute of International Studies. Until February 2013, he also served as the Director of International Affairs at the same law school, where he was in charge of academic relations with foreign universities and international organisations. He holds a Bachelor of Laws and Social Sciences and a Master of Laws from the University of Chile and an LLM in International Legal Studies from New York University. He is also a published scholar (*Foreign Investment: Legal Regime and Dispute Settlement*, co-author LexisNexis Chile) and legal practitioner with experience in both the public and private sectors. Rodrigo specialises in investment law, environmental law, trade law, and air and space law. In 1998 he co-founded the Fiscalía del Medio Ambiente – a non-profit that does pro bono work in public interest environmental cases before domestic and international tribunals, and teaches environmental law to communities and members of the judiciary. He is also editor of environmental law journal *Justicia Ambiental*. In February 2013, Rodrigo joined the World Trade Institute of the University of Bern as a Researcher and PhD Fellow, under the SECO Project, which supports development of Regional Competence Centres for Trade Law and Policy in Peru, South Africa, Vietnam, Indonesia and Chile.

Matthew Rimmer
Associate Professor, Australian National University College of Law

Dr Matthew Rimmer is an Australian Research Council Future Fellow, working on intellectual property and climate change. He is an Associate Professor at the ANU College of Law, and an Associate Director of the Australian Centre for Intellectual Property in Agriculture (ACIPA). He holds a BA (Hons) and a University Medal in literature, and an LLB (Hons) from the Australian National University. Rimmer received a PhD in law from the University of New South Wales for his dissertation on *The Pirate Bazaar: The Social Life of Copyright Law*. He is a member of the ANU Climate Change Institute. Rimmer has published widely on copyright law and information technology, patent law and biotechnology, access to medicines, clean technologies and traditional knowledge. Rimmer is a researcher and commentator on the topic of intellectual property, public health and tobacco control. He has undertaken research on trade mark law and the plain packaging of tobacco products, and given evidence to an Australian parliamentary inquiry on the topic.

Leon E. Trakman
Professor, University of New South Wales Faculty of Law

Leon is Professor of Law and Past Dean of the Faculty of Law at the University of New South Wales. He holds master's and doctorate degrees in law from Harvard Law School. He is author or editor of eight books and over one hundred articles on contract law, international commercial arbitration and investment law. His academic appointments include, amongst others, Distinguished Visiting Professor at the University of California (Davis), Visiting Professor at Wisconsin Law School, Tulane Law School and the University of Cape Town, Professor of Law at Dalhousie University and Bolton Visiting Professor at McGill University. He has served extensively as an international commercial arbitrator, and as a panellist appointed by the US, Canadian and Mexican governments to decide anti-dumping and countervailing duty disputes under the NAFTA. He has also acted as a constitutional consultant to the Canadian Government and the African National Congress.

Tania Voon
Professor, Melbourne Law School

Tania is Professor and Associate Dean (Research) at Melbourne Law School. A former Legal Officer of the Appellate Body Secretariat of the WTO, she has previously practised law with Mallesons Stephen Jaques and the Australian Government Solicitor, and taught law at Georgetown University, the University of Western Ontario, the Australian National University, Monash University, and Bond University. Tania undertook her Master of Laws at Harvard Law School and her PhD in Law at the University of Cambridge. She has published widely in the areas of public international law and international economic law. She is the author of *Cultural Products and the World Trade Organization* (Cambridge University Press 2007), a member of the editorial board of the *Journal of International Economic Law*, and a member of the Indicative List of Governmental and Non-Governmental Panellists for resolving WTO disputes. Tania has provided expert advice and training to entities such as Telstra, the Australian Department of Foreign Affairs and Trade, the European Parliament, the WTO, the WHO, and NGOs such as the Cancer Council Victoria and the Canadian International Development Agency.

Kimberlee Weatherall
Associate Professor, Sydney Law School

Kimberlee is an Associate Professor of Law at the University of Sydney. Prior to joining the Law School in 2012, Kimberlee held positions at the University of Queensland, the University of Melbourne and the Intellectual Property Research Institute of Australia. She holds degrees from the University of Sydney, Yale University and Oxford University. Kimberlee teaches and researches in intellectual property law, with a particular interest in digital copyright, and the relationship between international trade and intellectual property. She has spoken and published widely about intellectual property in international agreements, including earlier agreements such as the Australia–US Free Trade Agreement and the Anti-Counterfeiting Trade Agreement. She has given presentations on the potential impacts of the Trans-Pacific Partnership in Taiwan, Japan, the US, Europe and Australia, and has provided detailed analysis and advice to negotiators from Australia and elsewhere. She is a member of the Law Council of Australia's IP Subcommittee, and is a member of the Board of the Australian Digital Alliance and the Arts Law Centre of Australia.

Acknowledgments

I gratefully acknowledge the funds provided by the University of Melbourne, Melbourne Law School, and the Australian Research Council pursuant to the Discovery Project scheme (project number DP130100838), which assisted in various aspects of the research and editing involved in the production of this volume. I am also grateful to Vesna Stefanovski, Di Otto and the Institute for International Law and the Humanities for assistance in bringing many of the authors together. The excellent Law Research Service at Melbourne Law School also provided valuable research assistance in the conceptual stages. My sincere thanks to Devon Whittle for his extensive editorial assistance in relation to many of the chapters, and to Catherine Gascoigne and Sarah Crouch for their editorial assistance with other chapters. Finally, thanks go to Andrew Mitchell, Clarissa Terry and the Global Economic Law Network for ongoing support.

1. Introduction: national regulatory autonomy and the Trans-Pacific Partnership Agreement

Tania Voon

As the Doha Round of multilateral trade negotiations within the World Trade Organization (WTO) continues to flounder, all eyes have turned to a series of plurilateral trade agreements being negotiated around the world, with the Trans-Pacific Partnership Agreement (TPP) at the centre. The core group of countries negotiating this agreement has expanded well beyond the initial members of the *Trans-Pacific Strategic Economic Partnership Agreement* ('P4'): New Zealand,[1] Singapore,[2] Brunei Darussalam[3] and Chile.[4] Negotiations with the additional TPP partners of Australia, Malaysia, Peru, the United States and Vietnam began in Melbourne in 2010,[5] with Canada and Mexico joining discussions in 2012[6] and Japan most recently joining in 2013,[7] bringing the number of

[1] Signed 18 July 2005 (provisionally entered into force 1 May 2006; officially entered into force 28 May 2006).

[2] Ibid.

[3] Signed 2 August 2005 (entered into force 12 July 2006).

[4] Signed 18 July 2005 (entered into force 8 November 2006).

[5] See, e.g., *Update on the first round of Trans-Pacific Partnership (TPP) negotiations – a strong start*, Australian Government, Department of Foreign Affairs and Trade <http://www.dfat.gov.au/fta/tpp/100326-tpp-stakeholder-update-1.html>. See also, e.g., Meredith Kolsky Lewis, 'Expanding the P-4 Trade Agreement into a Broader Trans-Pacific Partnership: Implications, Risks and Opportunities' (2009) 4 *Asian Journal of WTO and International Health Law and Policy* 401.

[6] See, e.g., Office of the United States Trade Representative, 'Trans-Pacific Partnership Leadership Statement' (Press Release, 9 September 2012) <http://www.ustr.gov/about-us/press-office/press-releases/2012/september/tpp-leadership-statement>; International Centre for Trade and Sustainable Development, 'Mexico, Canada Receive Invite to Trans-Pacific Trade Talks' (20 June 2012) 16(24) *Bridges Weekly Trade News Digest* (online).

negotiating countries to 12. At the time of writing in May 2013, the 17th round of negotiations is taking place in Peru.[8]

The global significance of the agreement is reflected not only in the already burgeoning literature on the subject,[9] but more importantly in its potential economic benefits. The current negotiating countries in the TPP in 2012 had a collective GDP of more than US$27,500 billion and a population of more than 790 million.[10] Existing trade between TPP partners is extensive, with the United States a dominant partner.[11] According to one study, adding Japan to the agreement (as is under way at the time of writing) will extend the global benefits of an agreement from $75 billion to $223 billion per year, and adding Korea (as may happen in the future) would further increase benefits to $295 billion per year.[12]

The potential economic scope of the agreement means that, at a broader strategic level, the TPP could realistically provide a 'pathway'

---

[7] See, e.g., Office of the United States Trade Representative, 'Joint Statement of TPP Ministers: Trans-Pacific Partnership Ministers Chart Path Forward on Key Issues and Confirm Next Steps on Japan's Entry' (Press Release, 20 April 2013) <http://www.ustr.gov/about-us/press-office/press-releases/2013/april/joint-statement-tpp-ministers>; International Centre for Trade and Sustainable Development, 'Japan Gets TPP Invite, as APEC Calls for Faster WTO Talks' (25 April 2013) 17(14) *Bridges Weekly Trade News Digest* (online).

[8] See, e.g., *Trans-Pacific Partnership (TPP): 17th Round of TPP Negotiations Set for Lima, Peru – May 15–24, 2013*, Office of the United States Trade Representative <http://www.ustr.gov/tpp>.

[9] See, e.g., C.L. Lim, Deborah Elms and Patrick Low (eds), *The Trans-Pacific Partnership: A Quest for a Twenty-first Century Trade Agreement* (Cambridge University Press, 2012); Jane Kelsey (ed.), *No Ordinary Deal: Unmasking the Trans-Pacific Partnership Free Trade Agreement* (Allen & Unwin, 2010); Jeffrey Schott, Barbara Kotschwar and Julia Muir, *Understanding the Trans-Pacific Partnership* (Peterson Institute for International Economics, 2013).

[10] *Trans-Pacific Partnership Agreement negotiations*, Australian Government, Department of Foreign Affairs and Trade <http://www.dfat.gov.au/fta/tpp/>. See also Brock Williams, 'Trans-Pacific Partnership (TPP) Countries: Comparative Trade and Economic Analysis' (CRS Report for Congress R42344, Congressional Research Service, 29 January 2013) 3.

[11] Williams, above n 10, 5, 20–21.

[12] Peter Petri, Michael Plummer and Fan Zhai, *Adding Japan and Korea to the TPP* (7 March 2013) Asia-Pacific Trade <http://asiapacifictrade.org/wp-content/uploads/2013/03/Adding-Japan-and-Korea-to-TPP.docx>.

towards further economic integration[13] among the current and additional parties, particularly through the possibility of a 'Free Trade Area of the Asia-Pacific' as envisaged by the Asia-Pacific Economic Cooperation (APEC) forum[14] and as discussed further in Chapter 3 of this volume. The TPP negotiating parties already have a complex web of preferential trade agreements (PTAs) between them.[15] At the same time, other major plurilateral trade and investment negotiations are taking place in various contexts.

The Regional Comprehensive Economic Partnership (RCEP) negotiations commenced in late 2012 among 16 countries (that is, the 10-member Association of Southeast Asian Nations (ASEAN) plus the six countries with existing PTAs with ASEAN).[16] The goal of the RCEP negotiations is 'to achieve a modern, comprehensive, high-quality and mutually beneficial economic partnership agreement among the ASEAN Member States and ASEAN's FTA Partners', covering a broad range of areas including trade in goods and services, investment, technical cooperation, intellectual property, competition and dispute settlement.[17]

In February 2013, President Obama announced the intention of launching negotiations between the United States and the European Union towards a Transatlantic Trade and Investment Partnership (TTIP), 'envisioned as an ambitious, high-standard trade and investment agreement' between parties that already account for 'one third of total goods and

---

[13] See generally, e.g., Meredith Kolsky Lewis, 'Achieving a Free Trade Area of the Asia-Pacific: does the TPP present the most attractive path?' in C.L. Lim, Deborah Elms and Patrick Low (eds), *The Trans-Pacific Partnership: A Quest for a Twenty-first Century Trade Agreement* (Cambridge University Press, 2012) 223; Peter Petri, Michael Plummer and Fan Zhai, 'The Trans-Pacific Partnership and Asia-Pacific Integration: A Quantitative Assessment' (East-West Center Working Papers: Economic Series No 119, East-West Center, 24 October 2011).

[14] See, e.g., APEC Secretariat, 'Regional initiatives boost pursuit of APEC-wide free trade area' (News Release, 22 November 2012).

[15] Ian Fergusson et al., 'The Trans-Pacific Partnership Negotiations and Issues for Congress' (CRS Report for Congress No R42694, Congressional Research Service, 15 April 2013) 6.

[16] The ASEAN members are Brunei Darussalam, Cambodia, Indonesia, Laos, Malaysia, Myanmar, Philippines, Singapore, Thailand and Vietnam. The additional countries are Australia, China, India, Japan, the Republic of Korea and New Zealand.

[17] *Guiding Principles and Objectives for Negotiating the Regional Comprehensive Economic Partnership* (2012) ASEAN <http://www.asean.org/images/2012/documents/Guiding%20Principles%20and%20Objectives%20for%20Negotiating%20the%20Regional%20Comprehensive%20Economic%20 Partnership.pdf>.

services trade and nearly half of global economic output'.[18] Already some stumbling blocks have started appearing in the initial talks, such as European concerns about the treatment of audiovisual products in the agreement.[19]

Negotiations are also continuing among more than 20 WTO Members including the European Union (representing 27 countries) towards an extensive plurilateral agreement on services, variously termed the 'International Services Agreement'[20] and the 'Trade in Services Agreement'.[21] As discussed further in Chapter 7 of this volume, these negotiations similarly aim for an ambitious, high-quality agreement in the specific context of trade in services.

The simultaneous negotiation of a range of novel, broad-reaching plurilateral agreements affecting matters including trade in goods, trade in services, intellectual property and investment raises a number of questions and potential problems. In particular, what impact will these different negotiations have on the TPP? To what extent will success, failure, trade-offs or conclusions reached in one forum affect others? Debate exists, for example, as to the compatibility of the TPP and the RCEP, and whether these are properly regarded as alternative or concurrent tracks towards the goal of deeper integration in the Asia-Pacific.[22] These numerous ongoing negotiations, not to mention moves towards additional bilateral treaties, may lend an urgency to the TPP discussions, providing an additional impetus to reach agreement in the TPP given the competing demands and opportunities.

---

[18] *Fact Sheet: United States to Negotiate Transatlantic Trade and Investment Partnership with the European Union* (13 February 2013) Office of the United States Trade Representative <http://www.ustr.gov/about-us/press-office/fact-sheets/2013/february/US-EU-TTIP>.

[19] See, e.g., 'EU Parliament Resolution Backs Audiovisual Exclusion in U.S.-EU Talks' (3 May 2013) 31(18) *Inside US Trade* (online). See also 'A transatlantic tipping-point', *The Economist* (online), 27 April 2013 <http://www.economist.com/news/united-states/21576704-historic-trade-pact-between-america-and-europe-needs-saving-transatlantic>.

[20] Office of the United States Trade Representative, 'Interagency Trade Policy Group Holds Public Hearing on Negotiating Objectives for International Services Agreement Negotiations' (Press Release, 12 March 2013) <http://www.ustr.gov/about-us/press-office/press-releases/2013/march/tpsc-services-hearing>.

[21] *Trade in Services Agreement (TISA)*, Australian Government, Department of Foreign Affairs and Trade <http://www.dfat.gov.au/trade/negotiations/services/trade-in-services-agreement.html>.

[22] 'TPP Officials See RCEP as Complementary, but U.S. Businesses Worried' (23 November 2012) 30(46) *Inside US Trade* (online).

All of these negotiations, and the steps being taken towards the TPP in particular, have given rise to an overarching concern about the impact of additional trade and investment agreements on national regulatory autonomy. Questions about the extent to which international trade and investment agreements constrain state sovereignty are not new. Even bilateral agreements between only two parties can create major problems for future governments in implementing their preferred policies, as was feared and arguably eventuated in the case of the *Australia–United States Free Trade Agreement* (AUSFTA),[23] with Australia losing out.[24] Concerns about the impact of international trade and investment law on public policy are frequently exacerbated by the processes by which international agreements are reached, which in many countries are non-transparent and impenetrable by external stakeholders.[25]

In the case of the TPP, an additional element of conspiracy was added by the negotiating partners' pact of secrecy. As explained by the Office of the United States Trade Representative:

> Major trade and investment negotiations address a broad range of often complex and commercially sensitive sectors and issues and often take many months or even years to conclude. In order to reach agreements that each participating government can fully embrace, negotiators need to communicate with each other with a high degree of candor, creativity, and mutual trust. … [W]hen the TPP negotiations got underway in 2009, the United States and its TPP negotiating partners entered into a confidentiality arrangement reflecting the customary understanding between countries engaged in trade negotiations that the negotiations should be carried out in private.[26]

---

[23] Signed 18 May 2004, [2005] ATS 1 (entered into force 1 January 2005).

[24] See, e.g., Andrew Mitchell and Tania Voon, 'Australia – United States Free Trade Agreement' in Simon Lester and Bryan Mercurio (eds), *Bilateral and Regional Trade Agreements: Case Studies* (Cambridge University Press, 2009) 6, 42–43. See also Linda Weiss, Elizabeth Thurbon and John Mathews (eds), *How to Kill a Country: Australia's Devastating Trade Deal with the United States* (Allen & Unwin, 2004).

[25] See, in the context of Australia, the WTO and the AUSFTA, Hilary Charlesworth et al., *No Country Is an Island: Australia and International Law* (UNSW Press, 2006) 112–140.

[26] *FACT SHEET: Transparency and the Trans-Pacific Partnership* (June 2012) Office of the United States Trade Representative <http://www.ustr.gov/about-us/press-office/fact-sheets/2012/june/transparency-and-the-tpp>.

The broad contents and framework of the confidentiality agreement between the TPP partners were released in 2011.[27] The partners agree to hold negotiating documents 'in confidence for four years after entry into force of the Trans Pacific Partnership Agreement, or if no agreement enters into force, for four years after the last round of negotiations'.[28]

The continued refusal of parties to release draft texts or proposals through official channels has understandably increased fears among the various national communities involved that an agreement would be reached without fully taking account of their particular interests. Uncertainty and pessimism have not been alleviated by the occasional leaking of draft texts and proposals, without the necessary context surrounding the origins of the texts and proposals or their reception in negotiations. Opportunities to make submissions to negotiating governments in writing and in periodic stakeholder meetings have offered little comfort in the absence of any assurance that negotiators are taking such views into account and without the possibility of meaningful responses from negotiators.

Against that background, one purpose of this volume is to provide timely input into the negotiations and qualitative principles for assessing a final TPP agreement. Rather than focusing on a close interrogation of the specific wording of leaked texts, which may or may not represent conclusions reached by the TPP partners in negotiations, the authors reflect on broader, enduring questions raised by the TPP and fundamental implications of the TPP for the future of international trade, investment, law and public policy. Most chapters in this volume were finalised in March or April 2013,[29] and negotiations have progressed since then. The volume nevertheless presents a broad and deep analysis of many of the primary legal and policy issues arising through the TPP negotiations, which will continue to be of concern upon the conclusion of the negotiations. In particular, each chapter explores different dimensions of the relationship between the TPP and national regulatory autonomy, taking account of legal, economic, political and sectoral perspectives.

---

27 Mark Sinclair, *TPP Talk: Content of confidentiality letters* (29 November 2011) New Zealand Ministry of Foreign Affairs & Trade <http://mfat.govt.nz/Trade-and-Economic-Relations/2-Trade-Relationships-and-Agreements/Trans-Pacific/1-TPP-Talk/0-TPP-talk-29-Nov-2011.php>.

28 Ibid., linking to model letter: <http://mfat.govt.nz/downloads/trade-agreement/transpacific/TPP%20letter.pdf>.

29 Chapter 6 was finalised in February 2013, and Chapters 1, 5 and 7 in May 2013.

In Chapter 2, Won-Mog Choi explains the TPP within the broader context of the proliferation of PTAs and the implications of the agreement for the harmonisation of rules of origin, which are used to identify the origin of a given product and hence the conditions under which preferential treatment may be granted under a PTA. Highlighting the different models for rules of origin adopted across the world, Choi emphasises the potential distortions that may arise from the use of particular rules of origin, as well as the significant business costs arising from divergent rules of origin. While multilateral harmonisation may not yet be possible, the TPP offers an opportunity for significantly increasing the consistency of rules of origin globally by harmonising rules on intra-TPP trade, thereby multiplying the benefits of unilateral, regional and multilateral trade liberalisation.

In Chapter 3, Meredith Kolsky Lewis tackles an equally significant, cross-cutting issue, namely the relationship between the TPP and development. The TPP's importance for development lies in the unusual diversity of its parties and breadth of its coverage. Comparing PTAs with the WTO, including the WTO's concept of 'special and differential treatment' for developing countries, Lewis identifies differences in bargaining structures that may weaken the negotiating strength of developing countries in bilateral and plurilateral trade negotiations and environments. However, she explains that the TPP presents novel circumstances, as 'the first plurilateral FTA to be negotiated amongst several developed and several developing countries from non-congruent parts of the world', and because the negotiators have specifically identified development as one of the cross-cutting issues to be addressed. Developing countries may derive significant benefits from the agreement simply by virtue of its potential for deeper integration and market access, but other TPP areas are more problematic, including heightened intellectual property protections, the introduction of binding commitments on labour and the environment, and strict rules of origin. The outcomes on these issues may set a precedent for other PTAs and the WTO itself, increasing the significance of the TPP from a development perspective.

In Chapter 4, Kimberlee Weatherall examines in greater detail the implications of the TPP for intellectual property. Like other aspects of the TPP, intellectual property negotiations in the TPP present new challenges – such as the broad regional trade aspirations underlying the TPP – alongside old concerns – such as the ambitions of the United States for higher levels of intellectual property protection. Weatherall clarifies how these different factors may influence the outcome of the intellectual property negotiations. For example, 'the RCEP … represents a possible future competitor for a regional framework: one which is likely to contain provisions on IP more palatable to regional powers than anything the US might push in the TPP'. Thus, ongoing negotiations towards the RCEP may dampen efforts towards stringent intellectual property provisions in the TPP. As Weatherall demonstrates, broader public unease about increasing intellectual property protections through international agreements may have a similar tendency to the extent that such sentiments influence the TPP negotiations. Intellectual property thus provides a clear case study of the potential for actual and perceived conflict between public policy and the TPP.

Chapter 5 presents a more concrete case study of that same issue, with Matthew Rimmer addressing the intersection between tobacco control and the TPP, with specific reference to Australia's law mandating the standardised packaging of tobacco products. Rimmer highlights procedural problems with the TPP negotiations in the context of tobacco, including the influence of the tobacco industry on proceedings. Having regard to the legal disputes concerning so-called 'plain' packaging within Australia and internationally, Rimmer also draws connections between the TPP, health and intellectual property such as trade marks on tobacco packages. Rimmer considers related developments in New Zealand and the United States, focusing in particular on the United States' proposal regarding tobacco in the TPP.

In Chapter 6, Deborah Elms discusses the pervasive problem of agriculture in the TPP, against the background of the treatment of agriculture in the WTO and existing PTAs. As always, agriculture raises highly sensitive issues and sectors, yet Elms notes that some of the difficulties of agricultural negotiations are alleviated in the TPP, for example due to the existing PTAs between the TPP partners and the absence of competition between them in relation to some agricultural products. But sugar and dairy remain sticking points in the agricultural negotiations, along with how to address tariff rate quotas and rules of origin in the TPP. Elms concludes that success in the agricultural talks is imperative in reaching the ambitions of the TPP partners for a high-quality agreement.

Danny Kotlowitz and I take telecommunications as a case study of services in the TPP, in Chapter 7. Placing the TPP negotiations within the context of other developments concerning the international regulation of telecommunications services, we reflect on the plurilateral services negotiations already mentioned as well as the revised International Telecommunications Regulations adopted by some Member States of the International Telecommunication Union. We then emphasise the opportunity presented by the TPP and similarly ambitious trade negotiations to create a new breed of telecommunications chapter in PTAs, breaking with outdated approaches to classification of telecommunications services and related obligations. Finally, we offer a brief critique of the suggestion that the TPP might be used to address international mobile roaming charges through plurilaterally agreed regulations.

The next two chapters deal with different forms of dispute settlement that may emerge through the TPP: first in Chapter 8, where Andrew Mitchell and James Munro explore the implications of the TPP for state–state dispute settlement, and then in Chapter 9, where Leon Trakman outlines the options for investor–state dispute settlement in the TPP. Mitchell and Munro consider how a new dispute settlement mechanism in the TPP for resolving TPP-related disputes among TPP partners would relate to existing dispute settlement fora under PTAs and the WTO, taking into account the rules regarding treaty interpretation and conflicts of norms or jurisdiction under public international law. Trakman addresses the rather more controversial question of whether and in what terms investors might be permitted to bring claims against host governments under the TPP. For Australia, as he discusses in detail, the issue appeared closed, at least for the government led by Julia Gillard, which had already indicated its general opposition to investor–state dispute settlement in the TPP and more generally. Trakman goes on to analyse the nuanced pros and cons of the position taken by Australia, including the relevance of the investment claim already brought against Australia in connection with plain tobacco packaging, as discussed in Chapter 5.

In Chapter 10, Joshua Meltzer returns to a core site of potential conflict between public policy, trade and investment, reflecting on the TPP's significance for the environment and climate change. Acknowledging the power of the United States in the TPP negotiations, he first provides a detailed examination of that country's approach to the environment in its existing PTAs, as a basis for determining the likely preferences and interests of the United States in the TPP context. Meltzer then describes two specific environmental problems that may need to be addressed in the TPP: trade in illegally harvested timber, and fisheries subsidies. Meltzer demonstrates that the environmental implications of the TPP are not limited to the environment chapter or specific references to the environment in particular provisions. Trade in environmental goods, for example, will be significantly affected by the potential tariff cuts and reduction in non-tariff barriers to be offered in the TPP. The chapter concludes by highlighting the potential positive impact of the TPP on the environment.

Finally, in Chapter 11, Rodrigo Polanco addresses the stated goal of achieving 'regulatory coherence' through the TPP negotiations, including through a dedicated chapter of the agreement designed to enhance transparency and coherence of regulations both within and between TPP partners. Polanco considers approaches to the concept of regulatory coherence adopted in other institutions such as the Organisation for Economic Co-operation and Development, pondering the utility of regulatory coherence in resolving a central question of this book: 'How can we secure the benefits of trade liberalisation without infringing the freedom of governments to pursue legitimate regulatory objectives?' Polanco ends on a cautionary note about the choice of instruments open to TPP negotiators in striving for regulatory coherence.

Together, the authors in this volume tackle the question posed by Polanco in various ways, recognising both the importance of the TPP in securing cross-global welfare benefits through an ambitious, market-opening deal, and the real potential for the TPP to disconnect sovereign governments from their policy goals and people. On the one hand, for example, deep and broad integration through the TPP and successor agreements – including in agriculture – may proffer lasting benefits for developed and developing countries alike. Harmonisation of rules of origin through the TPP and beyond similarly has the potential to greatly facilitate trade for the benefit of countries around the world. The framework for the negotiations and the countries involved mean that the parties have the chance to try new techniques in relation to a whole range of sectors including, for example, telecommunications. On the other hand, the potential for egregious errors to be made in areas such as health, the environment and intellectual property is high, with correspondingly high risks to the regulatory autonomy of TPP parties. These risks may be somewhat reduced by the parties taking a balanced approach to provisions on dispute settlement and regulatory coherence, and could be further mitigated by increasing the level of transparency in the course of negotiations. But, in the end, the TPP will be judged as a whole, and the world must wait to see with hindsight whether the negotiators have got it right.

2. Coping with proliferating preferential rules of origin and the TPP's role in their harmonisation[1]

Won-Mog Choi

INTRODUCTION

It is fair to say that the most important trade policy development in the world trading system in the last decade is the spread of regional trade agreements (RTAs). The chief factors that spurred this development are the slow progress of the World Trade Organization (WTO) Doha Round of trade talks and the economic integration processes in North America and Europe. Governments have increasingly realised that integration must be accelerated in order to improve international competitiveness through the exploitation of scale economies, strengthen their bargaining power, and make their voice heard in global trade issues in the age of economic rivalry between Europe and North America, the two giant blocs.

The 1997–98 Asian financial crises and the current global economic downturn have underscored the need for national economies to work together in trade and investment; only by addressing common challenges can they sustain growth and stability. The Asia-Pacific is no exception to this awakening process and, indeed, it is now actively pursuing an 'aggressive regionalism' policy.[2] In 2000, there was little RTA activity in

[1] This chapter is based on Won-Mog Choi, 'Defragmenting Fragmented Rules of Origin of RTAs: A Building Block to Global Free Trade' (2010) 13(1) *Journal of International Economic Law* 111.

[2] Countries negotiating an RTA plan to use treaty rules as a large-scale problem-solving process. That is, they intend to use RTAs to counter any unreasonable acts, requests, and practices of their trading partners and to increase the benefits of trade integration. This new trend may be called '*aggressive regionalism*'. See Won-Mog Choi, 'Aggressive Regionalism in Korea–U.S. FTA: The Present and Future of Korea's FTA Policy' (2009) 12(3) *Journal of International Economic Law* 595–615.

the region. One decade later, the Asia-Pacific region has emerged at the forefront of global RTA activity, with 185 RTA initiatives signed, under negotiation, or proposed by the Asia-Pacific economies as of 2012.[3]

In the absence of a Doha trade deal, comprehensive well-designed RTAs may be a means of achieving regional liberalisation and structural reforms, which can constitute a building block to multilateral liberalisation. On the other hand, different tariffs and rules of origin (ROOs) in multiple RTAs have resulted in the trade phenomenon called the 'spaghetti bowl',[4] which increases the burden for doing business. The 'noodle bowl' phenomenon[5] caused by the recent proliferation of RTAs in Asia has created specific costs for the region, as well as for the world economy. In this light, problems created by fragmented RTAs in the Asia-Pacific need to be thoroughly examined by economies in the region. Indeed, offering policy suggestions for how fragmented RTAs should be treated and reducing the costs of such fragmentation is becoming an increasingly urgent task.

With this background in mind, the leaders of the nine Trans-Pacific Partnership (TPP) countries (today increased to 11) announced in November 2011 that 'TPP countries have agreed to seek a common set of rules of origin to determine whether a product originates in the TPP region'.[6] By having these common rules, enterprises in the Asia-Pacific

---

[3] According to the Asian Development Bank (ADB), there were only 26 RTAs signed, under negotiation, or proposed by Asia-Pacific countries in 2000. This number dramatically increased to 185 in 2012: Asia Regional Integration Center, *Table 5: Plurilateral FTAs by WTO Notification and Status, 2000 and 2013* ADB <http://aric.adb.org/ftatrends.php>.

[4] See generally Jagdish Bhagwati, 'Regionalism and Multilateralism: An Overview' in Jaime de Melo and Arvind Panagariya (eds), *New Dimensions in Regional Integration* (Cambridge University Press, 1993); Jagdish Bhagwati and Arvind Panagariya (eds), *The Economics of Preferential Trade Agreements* (AEI Press, 1996).

[5] ADB president Haruhiko Kuroda (in a speech delivered to the Jeju Summer Forum in Korea in July 2006) referred to the phenomenon of spaghetti bowls in Asia as the Asian noodle bowl effect of FTAs and warned that it could pose future challenges to broader regional and global integration. See Masahiro Kawai and Ganeshan Wignaraja, 'The Asian "Noodle Bowl": Is It Serious for Business?' (Working Paper No 136, Asian Development Bank Institute, April 2009).

[6] The outlines were agreed by Australia, Brunei Darussalam, Chile, Malaysia, New Zealand, Peru, Singapore, Vietnam, and the United States on 12 November 2011: *Enhancing Trade and Investment, Supporting Jobs, Economic Growth and Development: Outlines of the Trans-Pacific Partnership Agreement* (November 2011) Office of the United States Trade Representative

region could certainly reduce the costs of doing business. These common rules will also contribute to any global efforts to harmonise preferential ROOs by showing how existing bilateral rules of origin in the region and their related interests could be successfully adjusted to produce a single set of preferential ROOs. This chapter examines the extent to which different ROOs are spread worldwide and in the Asia-Pacific region, why ROOs need to be harmonised through the TPP negotiation, and what are the core elements in harmonising ROOs of TPP.

I TYPES AND FAMILIES OF PREFERENTIAL ROOS

There are many different types of preferential ROOs. For most of the live animals or primary products, the wholly obtained or produced rule applies and, for other products, change in tariff classification (CTC), regional value content (RVC), and/or technical requirements apply. Accordingly, claiming the benefit of RTAs requires compliance with a complicated set of rules. Each RTA's rules differ according to the relevant product's Harmonized System Code classification. For example, the *North American Free Trade Agreement* (NAFTA) has the most restrictive rules for manufactured goods,[7] whereas the Pan-Euro model places more restrictions on primary products. Even the tariff classification criteria tend to vary among RTAs.

Despite marked divergences across ROOs regimes around the world, there are clear ROOs 'families' centred in the United States, the European Union (EU), and the Association of Southeast Asian Nations (ASEAN). This means that there is a potential for some form of regional ROOs convergence. Moreover, there are some signs of a de facto cross-regional stylistic harmonisation of ROOs, as NAFTA and EU-style agreements are spreading into other regions via the recent trans-continental agreements.

<http://www.ustr.gov/about-us/press-office/fact-sheets/2011/november/outlines-trans-pacific-partnership-agreement>.

[7] See generally Antoni Estevadeordal and Kati Suominen, 'Rules of Origin: A World Map' (Paper presented at the seminar 'Regional Trade Agreements in Comparative Perspective: Latin America and the Caribbean and Asia-Pacific', Washington, DC, 22–23 April 2003) 22–24 <http://www.pecc.org/publications/papers/trade-papers/4_ROO/1-estevadeoral.pdf>.

A Pan-Euro ROOs

The European Commission's drive to harmonise the EU's ROOs in the 1990s has created highly homogeneous ROOs in the European region. Commencing in the early 1970s, the Commission endeavoured to harmonise ROOs with European Free Trade Association (EFTA) countries, and similar efforts were made in the context of the European Agreements with Bulgaria, the Czech Republic, Estonia, Hungary, Latvia, Lithuania, Poland, Slovakia, and Romania.[8] The concerted push for harmonisation culminated in 1997 with the launch of the Pan-Euro system, which established identical ROOs protocols across the EU's existing RTAs. The Commission's Regulation No 46 of January 1999 sets out the harmonised protocols, outlining the so-called Single List ROOs. These ROOs combine the change in chapter or heading in tariff classification rule with the RVC and/or some technical requirements, as well as allowing for a certain optional way of meeting the ROOs for about 25 per cent of the products. The most frequently used alternate ROOs are a stand-alone import content criterion. This Single List was incorporated into the Euro-Mediterranean Association Agreements between the EU and various southern Mediterranean countries. The system of accumulation operates among countries that have signed regional bilateral agreements with each other. This list forms the basis of the harmonised ROOs of the so-called Pan-Euro-Med Accumulation Zone covering the 27 EU members and 17 other territories.[9]

Beyond this zone, the Pan-Euro ROOs model is incorporated in the EU's RTAs with South Africa, Mexico, and Chile as well as the EU's Stabilization and Association Agreements with Albania, Bosnia and Herzegovina, Croatia, the former Yugoslav Republic of Macedonia, and Serbia and Montenegro. Meanwhile, the EU's Generalized System of Preferences and the 2000 Cotonou Agreement with the African, Caribbean, and Pacific (ACP) economies are adopting virtually identical ROOs

---

[8] For the background and details, see Bart Driessen and Folkert Graafsma, 'EC's Wonderland: An Overview of the Pan-European Harmonized Origin Protocols' (1999) 33 *Journal of World Trade* 19, 33–34.

[9] The Pan-Euro-Med Accumulation system operates between the EU, the member states of the EFTA (Iceland, Liechtenstein, Norway, and Switzerland), Turkey, and countries that signed the Barcelona Declaration: Algeria, Egypt, Israel, Jordan, Lebanon, Morocco, Syria, Tunisia. The Palestinian Authority of the West Bank and Gaza Strip and the Faroe Islands have also joined the system.

to the Pan-Euro model's rules.[10] EFTA's recently concluded RTAs with Mexico and Singapore also follow the model, albeit providing an alternative rule in selected sectors, such as plastics, rubber, textiles, iron and steel products, and some machinery products.[11]

B NAFTA, Latin America, and P4[12]

Unlike Europe, which has agreed to a policy of harmonising ROOs, the Americas are slowly progressing into a de facto harmonisation. At the centre of this gradual process is the NAFTA, whose ROOs have become the reference points of subsequent RTAs made by the United States (US), Canada, and Mexico. The ROOs in the newer agreements require many products to change their chapter, heading, subheading, or even item, combined with exceptions, RVC, or technical requirements.

As the initial set of revised NAFTA ROOs took effect on 1 January 2003,[13] NAFTA model ROOs regimes have progressively adopted liberal frameworks that have been used as a reference point by many RTAs: for example, US–Chile, US–Colombia, US–Peru, Chile–Canada, Canada–Costa Rica, US–Central America–Dominican Republic, Mexico–Costa Rica, Mexico–Chile, Mexico–Bolivia, Mexico–Nicaragua, Mexico–Northern Triangle (El Salvador, Guatemala, and Honduras), and Mexico–Colombia–Venezuela.[14]

This NAFTA model is distinct from: (i) other ROOs employed by Latin American RTAs, including the Latin American Integration Association (LAIA), the Andean Community (CAN) and Mercado Común del Sur (Mercosur); (ii) the agreements between its members and with Chile, which uses a change in tariff classification at the heading level applicable across the board to all tariff items; or, alternatively, a regional value added of at least 50 per cent of the Free on Board (FOB) export value of

[10] Antoni Estevadeodal, Jeremy Harris and Kati Suominen, 'Multilateralizing Preferential Rules of Origin around the World' in Richard Baldwin and Patrick Low (eds), *Multilateralizing Regionalism: Challenges for the Global Trading System* (Cambridge University Press, 2009) 6.

[11] Ibid.

[12] *Trans-Pacific Strategic Economic Partnership Agreement*, Brunei Darussalam–Chile–New Zealand–Singapore, signed 18 July 2005 (Brunei Darussalam signed 2 August 2005) (entered into force: 28 May 2006 (New Zealand and Singapore), 12 July 2006 (Brunei Darussalam), 8 November 2006 (Chile)) (P4).

[13] 'Regulations Amending the NAFTA Rule of Origin Regulations' in Canada, *Canada Gazette*, 137(2), 15 January 2003.

[14] See Estevadeodal, Harris and Suominen, above n 10, 6–7.

the final good, plus a handful of rules applicable to specific products; (iii) the Central American Common Market (CACM), which uses mostly a CTC rule at either the chapter, heading, or subheading level, depending on the product in question; and (iv) US bilateral RTAs with non-American countries such as Jordan, Israel, Morocco, Bahrain, Oman, and Korea, wherein RVC rules are heavily used.[15]

Despite the divergence in the Americas, it is likely that the NAFTA model, with appropriate adjustments, will play a converging role, as the three North American countries strive to integrate their economies into the Northern Hemisphere and with the world. For example, the US Free Trade Agreements (FTAs) with Singapore, Australia, and Korea incorporate ROOs that are similar to the US–Central America–Dominican Republic RTA. Peru–Thailand, Chile–Japan, the P4 (Brunei, Chile, New Zealand, and Singapore), and Mexico–Japan RTAs are based on ROOs models inherited from these Latin American countries' RTAs with the United States.[16]

P4 in particular uses a change in tariff classification at the chapter, heading, and subheading level, depending on the product in question. In some product categories, as an alternative to the CTC rule, a business may use an RVC of at least 45 per cent for such products including certain vegetables, cereals, flour, fruits, nuts, tobacco, oils, chemicals, metals, fertilisers, rubber, iron, tools, machinery and equipment, vehicles, clocks and toys. This 45 per cent RVC level is increased to 50 per cent for textile and textile articles. An interesting feature of P4 ROOs is that they take into consideration outward processing as an integral part of modern manufacturing processes, given the long list of exceptions to the principle of prohibition of outward processing.[17]

It seems that an effort to converge or harmonise ROOs in the Americas has started cautiously. The August 2007 joint declaration of the Montebello Summit among the three NAFTA countries' heads of state endorsed 'an analysis of the free trade agreements that each country has negotiated subsequent to the NAFTA, beginning with those in the western hemisphere, including opportunities for innovative provisions on rules of origin.'[18]

---

15 Ibid.
16 Ibid.
17 See P4 annex 4B.
18 See Estevadeodal, Harris and Suominen, above n 10, 27.

C ASEAN ROOs Model

RTAs established among ASEAN members and between the ASEAN and non-member economies (e.g., ASEAN–China and ASEAN–Korea RTAs) carry an across-the-board RVC rule (40 per cent) with relatively few exceptions. The ASEAN Free Trade Area (AFTA) is also moving towards more liberal alternatives, i.e., allowing traders to choose certain CTC rules instead of RVC rules in many sectors.[19] The Bangkok Agreement, the Australia–Singapore FTA, and the South Pacific Regional Trade and Economic Cooperation Agreement (SPARTECA) also use this approach.

However, the ASEAN model will likely not play a significant converging role in Asia. As the North American countries enter into more RTAs with Asia-Pacific economies, the NAFTA-type ROOs may spread widely in Asia. This trend was manifested when the Australia–New Zealand Closer Economic Relations Trade Agreement (ANZCERTA) recently replaced its across-the-board RVC rule with a set of rules that closely resembles those of the US–Australia FTA regime.[20] Australia and New Zealand have also adopted a similar variety of rules in their respective RTAs with Thailand.[21] European countries will also endeavour to integrate with Asian economies in order to counterbalance the US engagement policy in Asia, thereby introducing the Pan-Euro model to the region as well.[22]

D The Africa–Middle East Model

Relatively simple ROOs are in place in many African RTAs. The Common Market for Eastern and Southern Africa (COMESA), the Economic Community of West African States (ECOWAS), and the Gulf Cooperation Council (GCC) in the Middle East are based on an across-the-board RVC rule that ranges from 30 per cent (ECOWAS) to 40 per cent (COMESA).[23] Some of the agreements allow or, indeed, require the calculation of ROOs to be based on import content. Most of these regimes also specify alternative ROOs that apply the CTC criterion.[24]

---

[19] Choi, above n 1, 122.

[20] Estevadeodal, Harris and Suominen, above n 10, 8.

[21] Ibid.

[22] For example, the Korea–EU FTA uses CTC rule at chapter or heading levels and RVC (mostly 20, 30, 40, 50 per cent) rules, influenced largely by the Pan-Euro model.

[23] See Estevadeodal, Harris and Suominen, above n 10, 27.

[24] Ibid.

The alternative often involves a change in heading or subheading, as in the case of ECOWAS, which has a relatively low RVC requirement.[25] However, the ROOs of the Southern African Development Community (SADC) approximate the Pan-Euro model, both in their sectoral types and sectoral selectivity.[26] Moreover, there have been some initiatives to renegotiate COMESA ROOs, and such attempts may eventually lead to regimes of greater complexity.[27]

Table 2.1 Rules of origin in existing free trade and preferential trade agreements of EU, in comparison with those of major countries

	Change of Tariff Classification	Value Added (Domestic or Import Content)	Specific Manufacturing Process
A. Agreements involving the EU			
EU – PanEuro	Yes (4, 2)	Yes – Import (50%–30%)	Yes
EU – GSP	Yes (4, 2)	Yes – Import (50%–30%)	Yes
EU – Contonou	Yes (4, 2)	Yes – Import (50%–30%)	Yes
EU–Chile	Yes (4, 2)	Yes – Import (50%–30%)	Yes
EU–Mexico	Yes (4, 2)	Yes – Import (50%–30%)	Yes
EU–South Africa	Yes (4, 2)	Yes – Import (50%–30%)	Yes
B. Others			
NAFTA	Yes (6, 4, 2)	Yes – Domestic (60%–50%)	Yes
AFTA		Yes – Import (60%)	
ANZERTA		Yes – Domestic (50%)	
Singapore–Japan	Yes (4)	Yes – Domestic (60%)	Yes
Singapore–US	Yes (6, 4, 2)	Yes – Domestic (55%–35%)	Yes
Korea–US	Yes (6, 4, 2)	Yes – Domestic (generally 35%) / Import (generally 45%)	Yes
Korea–EU	Yes (4, 2)	Yes – Import (50% –20%)	Yes

Source: Won-Mog Choi, 'Aggressive Regionalism in Korea–U.S. FTA: The Present and Future of Korea's FTA Policy' (2009) 12(3) *Journal of International Economic Law* 595, 612.

25 Ibid.
26 Ibid.
27 Ibid.

II SPAGHETTI/NOODLE BOWL COSTS

Preferential ROOs heighten the disadvantage of economies that cannot utilise the benefit of such ROOs in the proliferating RTA era. Since ROOs determine the scope of products that are eligible for preferential treatment under an RTA, they are crucial in determining the magnitude and recipients of the economic benefits that accrue from the trade agreements. It is no secret that preferential ROOs have been used as a trade policy instrument for offsetting the benefits of tariff liberalisation. ROOs can be used to favour intra-RTA industry linkages over those between an RTA and the rest of the world, thereby indirectly protecting RTA-based input producers *vis-à-vis* their extra-RTA rivals. As such, ROOs are akin to a tariff on the intermediate product levied by the country importing the final good.[28]

Driven by such political-economic dynamics, ROOs distort economic outcomes. Restrictive and selective ROOs discourage trade flows, engendering trade diversion. ROOs stifle the incentive to qualify for tariff preferences, as preference margins of 10 per cent would be needed to compensate for the costs of complying with a typical regional value content rule of origin.[29] A study shows that NAFTA's ROOs-related administrative costs are approximately 2 per cent of the value of Mexican exports to the US market.[30] According to other studies, ROOs can affect utilisation of FTA preferences in a direct manner. Canada's utilisation rates of preferences to the US market declined in sectors where NAFTA ROOs became more stringent than the Canada–US FTA ROOs.[31] The

---

[28] Several empirical studies provide grounds for believing that ROOs are indeed used for political-economic purposes – the same dynamics behind tariffs and the restrictiveness of ROOs are driven by the same political-economic dynamics – and that ROOs play an independent role in arbitrating preferential tariff liberalisation. See Antoni Estevadeordal, 'Negotiating Preferential Market Access: The Case of the North American Free Trade Agreement' (2000) 34(1) *Journal of World Trade* 141; Kati Suominen, *Rules of Origin in Global Commerce* (PhD Dissertation, University of California, San Diego, 2004).

[29] Celine Carrere and Jaime de Melo, 'Are Rules of Origin Equally Costly? Estimates from NAFTA' in Oliver Cadot et al. (eds), *The Origin of Goods* (Oxford University Press, 2006) 191.

[30] Oliver Cadot et al., 'Assessing the Effect of NAFTA's Rules of Origin' (Research Unit Working Paper No 0306, Laboratoire d'Economie Appliquée, National Institute for Agricultural Research, 2002) 12–20.

[31] Antoni Estevadeordal and Eric Miller, 'Rules of Origin and the Pattern of Trade between U.S. and Canada' (Integration, Trade and Hemispheric Issues Division, Inter-American Development Bank, 2002).

mere 64 per cent utilisation rate of NAFTA preferences was due in part to restrictive ROOs.[32] Low utilisation rates of the EU's trading partners in the textile sector arise from the excessive stringency of EU ROOs.[33]

Even to economies that are eligible to claim certain preferential ROOs benefits, divergent ROOs are one of the main causes of rising costs of doing business. If the numerous agreements carry widely distinct ROOs, they can impose undue transaction costs on traders, investors, and governments dealing in several RTA markets simultaneously – in sum, the spaghetti bowl costs. In the case of Korea, which succeeded in ratifying RTAs with the US as well as the EU, a large automobile firm had to undertake at least three tasks to deal with multiple ROOs: (i) creating a dedicated team to handle ROOs; (ii) building a computer system for sourcing inputs, and analysing production processes and ROOs; and (iii) constructing a verification system to check compliance with ROOs.[34]

Most Asian economies rely heavily on foreign source materials, and export their final products all over the world. As a result, the spaghetti bowl costs will become more damaging and onerous as the Asian region negotiates more RTAs. Since the 1990s, spaghetti bowls have occurred in major regions around the world. In Asia, China's approach to ASEAN for an RTA in 2001 stimulated rivalry relationships among China, Japan, and Korea towards ASEAN.[35] This triggered a domino effect,[36] creating so-called 'noodle bowl costs'. India recently joined this phenomenon by pursuing an active regionalism approach. In this sense, the domino effect of the 'noodle bowl' phenomenon has a distinctly Asian flavour.

Ten years ago 'spaghetti bowls' were heavily drawn in America but were less intense between Asia and America across the Pacific. Increasingly, however, 'noodle bowls' have become trans-Pacific, as North

---

32 Cadot et al., above n 30, 12, 13, 25–27.

33 Paul Brenton and Miriam Manchin, 'Making EU Trade Agreements Work: The Role of Rules of Origin' (CEPS Working Document No 183, Centre for European Policy Studies, 2003) 6–7.

34 See Inkyo Cheong and Jungran Cho, 'The Impact of Free Trade Agreements on Korea's Business Activity' (Working Paper Series No 156, ADB Institute, 2009) 18.

35 See Choi, above n 1, 119.

36 Richard Baldwin, 'The Domino Theory of Regionalism' in Richard Baldwin, Pertti Haaparanta and Jaakko Kiander (eds), *Expanding Membership of the European Union* (Cambridge University Press, 1995) 25.

American countries try to engage with Asia-Pacific economies.[37] Accordingly, this trans-Pacific version of criss-crossing FTAs may be called a 'Spaghetti-Noodle bowl' or 'Noodle-Spaghetti bowl' effect.

This noodle-spaghetti bowl cost is one of the most important reasons why the FTA utilisation ratio in the Asia-Pacific remains so low, making the need for solutions to this issue particularly pressing. Many firms that have been hurt by this complexity tend to push governments to untangle RTAs. Naturally, regional policies strive to simplify the ROOs and link FTAs to one another. How to multilateralise RTAs through the harmonisation of ROOs has become a major concern for the Asia-Pacific as well as for the world more generally.[38]

III HARMONISATION OF ROOS IN THE TPP

A Implications of the Pan-Euro Case

The Pan-Euro ROOs system harmonised different rules of origins into the single set of rules by amending all existing RTAs in the region. These common rules were extended even to the Northern African and Middle East region. The Pan-Euro ROOs system is quite a successful harmonising case that should be replicated by TPP countries. Of course, it will be difficult to duplicate the European example in other regions, not only because of the variety in cultural and historical backgrounds amongst the Asia-Pacific region, but also because of the region's significant territorial disputes. Nonetheless, this process of harmonising or at least reconciling different rules of origin must begin anyway in other regions as it is the only way to reduce the cost generated from the fragmented RTA phenomenon.

Notwithstanding the 2011 announcement by the leaders of TPP countries, it is unclear whether the ROOs of TPP will supersede and replace those of existing agreements or exist alongside ROOs of various bilateral agreements, allowing industry to pick and choose ROO criteria. If the latter approach is taken, business in TPP countries could ultimately opt for the ROOs contained in either the TPP or any other FTAs between them. This means that the TPP will hardly serve the goal of solving the

---

[37] The TPP is one of the typical examples, and the United States and Canada are making an effort to conclude a significant number of bilateral RTAs with Asian economies, not to mention Mexico.

[38] See Richard Baldwin, 'Multilateralizing Regionalism: Spaghetti Bowls as Building Blocks on the Path to Global Free Trade' (2006) 29(11) *The World Economy* 1451.

overlapping problems of multiple free trade arrangements in the region. By allowing states to continue to use the provisions of existing bilateral agreements – alongside the TPP rules – the agreement merely adds another layer of pasta to the spaghetti bowl.

Already, such voices are heard from the industries that: (i) the National Association of Manufacturers (NAM) explicitly conditioned their support on allowing existing FTA agreements to remain in force, as they argued that their supporters should not be worse off as a result of the TPP negotiations; (ii) the American Sugar Industry insisted that all previous concessions remain intact, without being subject to any further modifications; and (iii) US Dairy will push hard to ensure that ROOs for the dairy industry are country-specific in order to prevent dairy from being trans-shipped through various TPP member states before reaching their ultimate destination in the United States.[39]

B Harmonising ROOs in the TPP and Beyond

Preferential ROOs ultimately need to be subjected to the multilateral process of regional regulation at some point in time. Current WTO rules are imposing so many disciplines on non-preferential rules while there are a handful of mere procedural disciplines, such as a transparency requirement applicable against preferential rules of origins. As a result, preferential ROOs are consistent with the WTO agreements as long as they are clearly specified and published, based on a positive standard, applied in a timely and non-retroactive manner, subject to a review procedure, and applied in a manner that allows business secrets to remain confidential (see Table 2.2).

Theoretically, it is desirable that WTO Members produce harmonised preferential ROOs and make decisions to adopt these rules globally. However, complete harmonisation at the multilateral level would be technically difficult given the diversity of ROOs around the world. Moreover, it might be politically unfeasible due to resistance by the sectors that are benefiting from the *status quo*. Having said this, it is more likely that harmonisation or convergence efforts at the regional level will bring some results, as seen from the European case. In this sense, the TPP is the best forum for this long-term project given the size and diversity of economies covered by the agreement.

---

[39] Deborah Elms, 'From the P4 to the TPP: Explaining Expansion Interests in the Asia-Pacific' (Paper prepared for the Asia-Pacific Trade Economists' Conference, Bangkok, 2–3 November 2009) <http://www.unescap.org/tid/artnet/mtg/Deborah%20Elms.pdf>.

Table 2.2 WTO disciplines on ROOs

	Non-preferential ROOs		Preferential ROOs
	Before Harmonisation	After Harmonisation	
Clearly specified	O	X	O
Not used as instruments to pursue trade objectives	O	X	X
Do not create restrictive, distorting, or disruptive effects on trade	O	X	X
Do not discriminate	O	O	X
Consistent administration	O	O	X
Based on a positive standard	O	X	O
Published	O	O	O
No delay in determination	O	O	O
No retroactive application of changes	O	O	O
Review procedure	O	O	O
Confidential treatment of information	O	O	O
Applied equally for all purposes	X	O	X
Apply the last substantial transformation criteria	X	O	X

Notes

O = existent, X = non-existent
Compare Part II and Annex II of WTO *Agreement on Rules of Origin*.

As a first step to harmonising ROOs, a work program to research how such harmonisation might occur is in order. The program could run in-depth comparisons of preferential ROOs included in the RTAs of TPP countries and produce 'best practices' to use as a benchmark. Alternatively, as soon as the harmonised non-preferential ROOs are adopted by WTO Members, these rules could also be used as the benchmark for preferential rules with some modifications. At any rate, in order to establish a certain benchmark, it is necessary to develop a TPP map of ROOs, graded by different levels of trade restrictiveness among the TPP countries.

It may be difficult to comply with RVC thresholds that are set too high, particularly in low-wage, low-income economies. Therefore, it is important to require reasonable levels of RVC and allow alternative ways of using CTC rules. Currently, various ROOs regimes are employing a variety of RVC criteria across sectors. The most complex of the agreements is NAFTA's, which requires a 30–80 per cent RVC across many sectors using the build-up method, followed by the two agreements most closely modelled on it: RTAs of Canada (30–65 per cent) and the US (40–65 per cent) with Chile.[40] Agreements patterned after NAFTA and EU agreements are generally the most complex. For example, the EU's agreements with Chile and Mexico require an RVC of 20–50 per cent and 20–60 per cent respectively, using the factory cost method.

Agreements within South America, Africa, and Asia are generally the simplest.[41] For example, Paraguay's agreement with Columbia, Ecuador, Peru, and Venezuela has adopted a 50 per cent maximum imported content rule, and this rule is also applied to Uruguay's agreement with those countries. The agreements of Argentina and Brazil with Latin American countries are employing 40–55 per cent maximum imported content criteria. Japan's agreements with Malaysia, Singapore, and Thailand apply a 40–60 per cent RVC rule using the build-up method. Korea's agreements use a 30–50 per cent RVC rule and Japan's agreements, a 50–60 per cent RVC rule.

The most common level of RVC is 40–50 per cent, whether defined as maximum import content or as an RVC. Therefore, a maximum RVC level of 50 per cent, for example, could generally be imposed across most sectors. Only a small percentage of the sectors that are sensitive to a substantial number of TPP countries or less developed economies may be excepted from this RVC capping so that a higher RVC threshold could be set up to protect their domestic industries.

In developing these benchmarks, co-equality arrangements between the CTC and RVC rules need to be made as far as possible. According to a series of surveys asking for Asian firms' opinions about their preferred ROOs, 52 per cent of 143 respondents wanted to have the option to choose between an RVC rule and a CTC rule with regard to the origin determination of a specific product.[42] Around 29 per cent preferred the CTC rule and 19 per cent the RVC rule.[43] Giant firms are particularly in favour of being able to choose between ROOs because they use RTAs

---

40 See Estevadeodal, Harris and Suominen, above n 10, 14.

41 Ibid.

42 Kawai and Wignaraja, above n 5, 21–22.

43 Ibid.

more and encounter multiple rule issues.[44] The surveys suggest that firms are supportive of alternative ROOs (or co-equal rules) for the same product for several reasons: (i) if they cannot reach the RVC requirement, having another ROO enables them to avail themselves of their RTA preference; (ii) the application for the RVC rule may require the disclosure of confidential information on costs, and suppliers together with many firms are often reluctant to divulge such information; and (iii) some ROOs may be better aligned with the technology and production process of particular industries. Given these results and observations, co-equality between the CTC and RVC rules needs to be adopted in origin rules for as many relevant sectors as possible. Note in this regard that AFTA recently allowed a comprehensive listing of co-equal product-specific rules.[45] Note as well that the benefits from co-equal ROOs could be increased significantly with the adoption of extended accumulation policies. At any rate, having a single RVC criterion across sectors and simplified CTC rules in the Asia-Pacific will greatly reduce transaction costs. The China–Chile FTA is an example of far more simplified ROOs than others, as it is based on only two CTC criteria (change of chapter and change of heading) and a single 50 per cent VC rule.[46]

This process of harmonising ROOs, if successful, will enable TPP members to tackle other harmonisation issues over the longer term. More complex customs rules will be harder to administer, and administering various institutional or systemic provisions of RTAs will require customs authorities to spend a larger portion of their time and budgets identifying the correct rules and their proper application. Such customs costs are also relevant for traders. Complications at customs can result in shipment delays and increase the time needed for marketing goods. Inventory costs go up when the delayed shipments are intermediates.

When overlapping regimes become more complex, there is a greater possibility that the rules for a given product or service will vary across regimes, forcing firms to adjust their production and marketing strategies to accommodate different rules. If the different agreements carry widely differing rules of trade, they can impose undue transaction costs on traders and investors dealing in several RTA markets simultaneously. Firms tackling several RTA fronts may need to alter their production and marketing patterns to meet the varying requirements of each RTA. These

---

44 Ibid.

45 See Choi, above n 1, 122.

46 *Free Trade Agreement between the Government of the People's Republic of China and the Government of the Republic of Chile*, signed November 2005 (entered into force October 2006) annex 3 (*Product Specific Rules*).

problems can increase the uncertainty for traders and investors, and they will likely hit traders in developing economies disproportionately because the customs services of developing economies are more likely to be unprepared to handle the complicated administrative tasks associated with divergent trade rules.

Overall, discriminatory trade liberalisation, occurring under multiple, criss-crossing FTAs which subject the same commodity to different tariffs, tariff reduction trajectories, and systemic rules for obtaining preferences, tends to increase transaction costs and uncertainties. Reducing these costs and uncertainties should be one of the goals of the TPP process. Undoubtedly, all of these efforts and experiences made by the initiatives of the TPP will ultimately contribute to any serious endeavour and realisation of broader economic integration, as well as to any global integration efforts.

CONCLUSION

The spread of RTAs in the Asia-Pacific has sparked systemic concerns about criss-crossing RTAs. Due to the growing number of fragmented RTAs, coping with increasing transaction costs is becoming an unavoidable burden for the international trading system in the region. Divergent preferential ROOs are one of the main causes of rising costs – a cost-ineffective and non-transparent means of protection. Simple, consistent, and predictable ROOs are more likely to foster the growth of cross-country production networks in the world trading system.

The Pan-European Cumulation System is a good example of harmonising ROOs on a regional basis. Therefore, the TPP needs actively to pursue the goal of harmonising ROOs in the region. The adoption of co-equality in CTC and RVC rules can also offer flexibility to trading firms. If the TPP countries are able to set up certain best practice or benchmark ROOs, this process of harmonisation could be facilitated. This benchmark could also be used to check for any deviation that might be placed in the ROOs of future RTAs involving TPP countries.

In the longer term, other systemic rules in addition to ROOs need to be converged or harmonised across RTAs on a regional basis. These efforts for harmonisation should continue well beyond the conclusion of a round of tariff reductions that bind Most Favoured Nation tariffs at zero or very low levels for nearly all products. Although all preferential origin regimes would become irrelevant with zero global tariffs (as there would be no meaningful tariff preferences for which to qualify), varying rules and procedures still need to be coordinated and harmonised across RTAs in the region. For example, customs rules, trade remedy provisions, the *Agreement on the Application of Sanitary and Phytosanitary Measures* and the *Agreement on Technical Barriers to Trade* each create standards that require further convergence and harmonisation.

This endless effort to defragment fragmented RTAs is worthwhile if only to bring the diverging regimes up to date with the commercial and technological realities of the contemporary world. Our ultimate path to global free trade will be determined by the concerted will to solve these issues, both regionally and globally.

3. The Trans-Pacific Partnership Agreement and development

Meredith Kolsky Lewis

INTRODUCTION

Differential treatment for developing countries has long been a feature of the World Trade Organization (WTO) and the *General Agreement on Tariffs and Trade 1947* (GATT)[1] before it. Developing countries may avail themselves of myriad provisions within the WTO agreements that permit them to make lesser concessions than developed countries; to engage in activities not permitted for developed countries; and to take longer to implement commitments than developed countries. In addition, within the WTO negotiating framework, developing countries can join together to attempt to influence the negotiating agenda consistent with their interests. Free trade agreements (FTAs) have generally presented a different environment for developing countries. Special and differential treatment is less consistently a feature of FTAs than it is of the GATT and WTO agreements. Furthermore, in the context of negotiating an FTA, developing countries are often not as able to negotiate on an even footing with developed country partners as they are in the WTO. The Trans-Pacific Partnership (TPP) is a free trade agreement, but a somewhat unusual one. Most FTAs are bilateral; in contrast, the TPP is a plurilateral agreement currently being negotiated amongst 11 countries. In addition, the TPP partners comprise multiple developed and multiple developing countries. Furthermore, the TPP participants have sought to create a 'high

[1] *Marrakesh Agreement Establishing the World Trade Organization*, opened for signature 15 April 1994, 1867 UNTS 3 (entered into force 1 January 1995), annex 4 (GATT 1947).

standards, twenty-first century'[2] trade agreement with more broad-reaching coverage than any FTA to date. The TPP therefore has various implications for developing countries, some of which mirror those relevant to developing countries in the context of bilateral FTA negotiations, and some of which are more particular to this agreement. This chapter will address both sets of considerations. In Part I, this chapter first addresses the approach to developing countries reflected in the WTO agreements. Part II identifies ways in which developing countries' interests are differently impacted by WTO and by FTA negotiations. Part III highlights the particularities of the TPP as they relate to developing countries. Lastly, Part IV sets out implications of the TPP's approach to developing countries.

I THE WTO AND DEVELOPING COUNTRIES

The number of developing countries participating in the GATT/WTO has steadily increased over time. While relatively few developing countries were original signatories to the GATT upon its creation in 1947, today the bulk of the WTO's 159 members[3] comprises developing and least developed countries.[4] Although developing country participation has grown significantly over time, these members have never had the same package of obligations as the developed country members. Initially, developing countries were exempted from making certain commitments at all. Later, developing countries were expected to provide some concessions, but their entitlement to 'special and differential treatment' also became more formalised. On the whole, developing countries are, in numerous ways, not subjected to the same most-favoured-nation (MFN) obligations as developed country WTO Members.

---

[2] See, e.g., Office of the US Trade Representative, *TPP Statements and Actions to Date*, December 2009, <http://www.ustr.gov/about-us/press-office/fact-sheets/2009/december/tpp-statements-and-actions-date> (quoting President Obama's 14 November 2009 announcement that 'The United States will also be engaging with the Trans-Pacific Partnership countries with the goal of shaping a regional agreement that will have broad-based membership and the high standards worthy of a 21st century trade agreement').

[3] As at 23 March 2013.

[4] The WTO website indicates that over two-thirds of its Members are developing countries. See World Trade Organization, *Trade and Development* (2013) <http://www.wto.org/english/tratop_e/devel_e/devel_e.htm>.

A Developing Country Participation: No Initial Commitments

The earliest negotiation rounds of the GATT were focused almost exclusively on converting quotas and other trade barriers to tariffs, and then negotiating reductions in those tariff levels. During these initial years, there were relatively few GATT signatories. In 1960, there were 37 signatories, of which 16 were developing countries and 21 developed.[5] For the first several years of the GATT, almost all of the signatories, both developed and developing countries, were restricting imports on the basis of balance-of-payments concerns. These restrictions were sufficiently significant to minimise the perceived need for, and therefore use of, other types of protectionist measures.[6] In addition, it became clear by the late 1950s that developing country tariff rates were not subject to much discipline. The developing countries had not bound the majority of their tariffs and therefore could raise the tariffs on their unbound tariff lines if they so desired.[7]

The dynamics between developing and developed countries in the GATT changed significantly during the early 1960s. Developing countries' bargaining position was bolstered by the formation of the United Nations Conference on Trade and Development (UNCTAD) in 1964. The Soviet Union had long supported the creation of an international trade organisation within the United Nations (UN) to rival the GATT. Western developed countries were concerned that developing countries might leave the GATT in favour of what they might perceive as a more development-friendly forum, and be more susceptible to Soviet influence. The Western developed countries were willing to make concessions in order to keep the developing countries from doing so.[8] In addition, developing countries began joining together in this period, forming the 'Group of 77' in the UNCTAD context, which likely enhanced their bargaining power and negotiating positions within the GATT.[9] Thus the die was cast for developing countries to seek – and for developed countries to grant – preferential treatment.

---

[5] *General Agreement on Tariffs and Trade: Basic Instruments and Selected Documents*, 8th Supp (GATT Secretariat, 1960) (*GATT BISD*) 99–100. For a discussion of this period, see Robert Hudec, *Developing Countries in the GATT Legal System* (Cambridge University Press, 1987) 39–46.

[6] Hudec, above n 5, 40.

[7] Hudec, above n 5, 44.

[8] Hudec, above n 5, 51.

[9] Hudec, above n 5, 51–52.

Later in the 1960s, many more countries became contracting parties, with developing countries comprising the majority of the newcomers. In 1970, the GATT had 77 signatories, of which 25 were developed and 52 were developing countries.[10] Since that time, developing countries have always significantly outnumbered developed countries in the GATT and, thereafter, the WTO.

B Special and Differential Treatment in the GATT

In the Kennedy Round, the previous requirements of reciprocity in the granting of concessions gave way to a new understanding that, while developing countries would be expected to contribute in some way, that contribution 'should be considered in the light of the development and trade needs of these countries'.[11] During the negotiations, it became clear that the 'contribution' did not have to be in the form of developing countries lowering their tariffs. And by and large developed countries did not push hard to obtain concessions from the developing countries.[12] In addition, one of the outcomes of the Kennedy Round was the adoption by GATT contracting parties of Part IV of the GATT, entitled 'Trade and Development'. Part IV provides, inter alia, that developed countries 'do not expect reciprocity for commitments made by them in trade negotiations to reduce or remove tariffs and other barriers to the trade of less-developed contracting parties'.[13] It also recognises a need for developed countries to prioritise reducing trade barriers affecting developing countries.[14] In the Tokyo Round, developing countries again made only minor trade concessions while the developed countries made rather substantial tariff reductions.[15] Further, in 1979 the GATT contracting

---

[10] *GATT BISD*, 17th Supp (GATT Secretariat, 1970) vii. See also Hudec, above n 5, 40.

[11] *GATT BISD*, 12th Supp (GATT Secretariat, 1964), 48.

[12] Hudec, above n 5, 56.

[13] *Marrakesh Agreement Establishing the World Trade Organization*, opened for signature 15 April 1994, 1867 UNTS 3 (entered into force 1 January 1995) annex 1A (GATT 1994), art XXXVI (8).

[14] GATT 1994 art XXXVI (4). Developing countries have complained that they have experienced minimal benefit from Part IV of GATT because the provisions are hortatory rather than mandatory. See World Trade Organization, *Work on Special and Differential Provisions* <http://www.wto.org/english/tratop_e/devel_e/dev_special_differential_provisions_e.htm>.

[15] Hudec, above n 5, 78.

parties adopted the Enabling Clause,[16] which effectively permits GATT signatories to grant preferential treatment to developing countries under Generalized System of Preferences (GSP) schemes.[17] Developing countries have discounted the value of much of this favourable treatment due to developed countries erecting new trade barriers (such as voluntary export restraints) and excluding key products from GSP programmes.[18] Nonetheless, developing countries did succeed, over the history of the GATT, in embedding special and differential treatment as a norm for developed/developing country trading relations.

C Differential Treatment for Developing Countries in the WTO

The various forms of special and differential treatment developing countries attained in the GATT years have remained since the transition to the WTO. In addition, the WTO has additional ways in which it provides special treatment to developing countries.

The WTO treats developing countries as different from developed countries in three main ways: (1) by holding developing countries to different commitments from developed countries; (2) through the work of committees dedicated to developing country issues; and (3) by providing technical assistance.[19]

1 Different commitments

In numerous places, the WTO agreements provide developing countries with different commitments from developed countries. This special treatment, usually referred to as 'special and differential treatment', most commonly consists of longer time periods to implement commitments; less stringent obligations than those required of developed countries; terms permitting developed countries to provide developing countries

---

16 *Differential and More Favorable Treatment Reciprocity and Fuller Participation of Developing Countries*, GATT Doc L/4903 (28 November 1979) (Decision) GATT BISD 26S/203.

17 GSP originated from the UNCTAD in 1968: see Gerhard Erasmus, 'Accommodating Developing Countries in the WTO: From Mega-Debates to Economic Partnership Agreements' in Debra Steger (ed.), *Redesigning the World Trade Organization for the Twenty-first Century* (Centre for International Governance Innovation, 2010).

18 Hudec, above n 5, 78.

19 See World Trade Organization, *Understanding the WTO: Developing Countries* <http://www.wto.org/english/thewto_e/whatis_e/tif_e/dev1_e.htm>.

with better treatment than non-developing countries; as well as terms designed to enhance export opportunities for developing countries.[20]

Although developing countries have consistently sought preferential treatment in GATT and WTO negotiations, and have succeeded in negotiating numerous instances of special and differential treatment (by one count, there are 145 such provisions throughout the WTO agreements),[21] it is far from clear whether these preferences have in fact been beneficial for developing countries.[22] Nonetheless, to the extent that developing countries have sought differential treatment, they have often been successful. While WTO negotiations operate to a degree under a principle of reciprocity, the commitments expected from developing countries are often not one-to-one exchanges with developed countries. As an example, in the Uruguay Round negotiations over agricultural tariff levels, the participants agreed that developed and developing countries would make different levels of commitments. Developed countries agreed to cut their agricultural tariffs by an average of 36 per cent over six years, whereas developing countries committed to reducing their agricultural tariffs by an average of 24 per cent over ten years.[23] Where substantive commitments are the same for developed and developing countries, developing countries are often given longer periods of time to implement those obligations.

The current round of WTO negotiations, the Doha Round, was intended to be a round focused on development. It is sometimes called the Doha Development Round, and the agenda established for the round at the 2001 Ministerial Conference held in Doha, Qatar is known as the Doha Development Agenda or 'DDA'. The Doha Round remains indefinitely stalled, and it remains to be seen whether any of the development-focused items in the DDA will ever be fully realised. Nonetheless, it

---

[20] Ibid.

[21] Hunter Nottage, 'Trade and Development' in Daniel Bethlehem et al. (eds), *The Oxford Handbook of International Trade Law* (Oxford University Press, 2009) 481, 488. See also Erasmus, above n 17, 363. The WTO has prepared a number of compilations of the various special and differential treatment provisions. See World Trade Organization, *Work on Special and Differential Provisions* <http://www.wto.org/english/tratop_e/devel_e/dev_special_differential_provisions_e.htm>.

[22] See, e.g., Hudec, above n 5, 176–179 (arguing that developing countries had not fared well in the GATT era under the preferential treatment schemes then in place).

[23] World Trade Organization, *Tariff Negotiations in Agriculture: Reduction Methods* <http://www.wto.org/english/tratop_e/agric_e/agnegs_swissformula_e.htm>.

reflects the power that developing countries have in the WTO that they were able to achieve a consensus that the round would be development-focused.

2 Committee work

The WTO has committees dedicated to representing the interests of developing countries, including the Committee on Trade and Development and a Subcommittee on Least-Developed Countries. In addition, a number of committees have been established to address issues relating to the Doha Development Agenda.[24]

3 Technical assistance

The WTO also provides special treatment to developing countries in the form of technical assistance. This takes many forms. One example is legal assistance for developing countries participating in WTO dispute settlement. The WTO Secretariat has dedicated legal advisors to provide developing countries with legal advice and assistance in participating in WTO dispute settlement. In addition, the WTO supported the creation in 2001 of the Advisory Centre on WTO Law, which provides free legal advice on WTO matters and discounted legal services in assisting its developing country members in WTO dispute settlement proceedings.[25]

In addition, an initiative known as Aid for Trade was launched at the 2005 Hong Kong Ministerial Conference.[26] Aid for Trade is focused on helping developing countries develop their capacities on the supply side so that they will be better equipped to expand their export flows.

Furthermore, the WTO has an extensive training and technical assistance program that includes seminars, workshops and other training activities provided in developing countries around the world.

II NEGOTIATING WITHIN THE WTO VERSUS NEGOTIATING FREE TRADE AGREEMENTS

It is generally believed that the WTO presents opportunities for better negotiating outcomes for developing countries than do FTAs. There are a number of reasons for this view. First, the WTO operates on a consensus

---

24 See World Trade Organization, *Understanding the WTO: Committees* <http://www.wto.org/english/thewto_e/whatis_e/tif_e/dev2_e.htm>.

25 See Advisory Centre on WTO Law <http://www.acwl.ch/e/index.html>.

26 *Doha Work Programme*, WTO Doc WT/MIN(05)/DEC (22 December 2005, adopted 18 December 2005) (Ministerial Declaration) [57].

basis; second, developing countries can negotiate together in blocs in the WTO context; and third, the power imbalance between developed and developing countries is particularly acute in the context of bilateral, rather than multilateral, negotiations.

A WTO Negotiating Structure

Developing countries likely will be better able to achieve their objectives through the WTO's multilateral negotiating process than through bilateral FTA negotiations. This is not to suggest that developing countries have had optimal experiences within the GATT/WTO framework. Indeed, developing countries historically experienced significant challenges in participating meaningfully in the GATT negotiations for a variety of reasons, including the frequent practice of developed countries negotiating the agreements largely without consulting the developing countries or allowing them to participate.[27] Some of the difficulties faced by developing countries in the GATT era have remained challenges under the WTO regime and have contributed to the collapse of the Cancun Ministerial[28] as well as the difficulties in completing the Doha Round. Nonetheless, for all of its imperfections, the WTO is viewed as a better negotiating forum for developing countries than the FTA context.

One of the reasons the WTO is seen as a preferable forum for developing countries is that it operates on a consensus basis. Unlike the World Bank and International Monetary Fund (IMF), the WTO does not formally provide larger economies with more voting power than smaller economies.[29] This means that, in theory, even a small developing country could prevent the conclusion of a round of trade negotiations. In practice, this is unlikely to happen. However, it is the case that developing countries cannot be ignored within the WTO simply because of their size

---

27 See Gilbert Winham, *International Trade and the Tokyo Round Negotiation* 354 (Princeton University Press, 1986), describing the practice of the developed countries negotiating an agreement and then presenting it to the developing countries as a *fait accompli* as 'pyramidal bargaining'. See also Hudec, above n 5.

28 See, e.g., James Thuo Gathii, 'Process and Substance in WTO Reform' (2004) 56 *Rutgers Law Review* 885, 893–904.

29 The World Bank and IMF both employ a weighted system of voting based on countries' contributions to the organisations, which are in turn based on economic size. See generally World Bank, *Voting Powers* (12 November 2012) <http://web.worldbank.org/WBSITE/EXTERNAL/EXTABOUTUS/ORGANIZATION/BODEXT/0,,contentMDK:21429866~menuPK:64020035~pagePK:64020054~piPK: 64020408~theSitePK:278036,00.html>.

or lack of economic clout. Their buy-in will need to be obtained before a negotiation can be concluded, even if the developing countries did not have as much opportunity as they might have liked to participate in the substance of the negotiations.[30] While developing countries face many challenges in advancing their agendas in the WTO, the WTO's consensus-based structure is a positive weight on the scale. In FTA negotiations, however, smaller and weaker countries may feel less able to object to the terms presented by *demandeur* developed countries.

B Safety in Numbers?

Second, developing countries can join together to form negotiating blocs within the WTO, something that is not possible when a nation is negotiating on its own in the context of a bilateral FTA. While some of the difficulties faced by developing countries remain, the practice of joining together with like-minded members in forming collective negotiating positions has been seen as a positive and effective development.[31] Even if developing countries do not align with each other with respect to every issue, their sheer numbers make it very difficult for negotiating issues to gain traction if the developing countries are opposed. For example, at the Singapore Ministerial in 1996, working groups were established to pursue new commitments with respect to transparency in government procurement, trade facilitation, trade and investment, and trade and competition. These work programs were known as the Singapore issues. Developing countries largely objected to the Singapore issues, particularly the investment and competition agenda items. All of these issues, except for government procurement, were ultimately dropped from the Doha agenda in 2004 because consensus could not be

[30] Traditionally, GATT and WTO negotiations on contentious issues have been resolved through so-called 'green room' negotiations in which only a small subset of members participate. The resulting consensus is then presented to the larger membership, in what is generally considered to be a *fait accompli*. In recent years 'green room' negotiations have been expanded to include more developing countries than in the past. See generally Jeffrey Schott and Jayashree Watal, 'Decision-Making in the WTO' (Policy Brief No 00-2, Peterson Institute for International Economics, March 2000) <http://www.iie.com/publications/pb/print.cfm?ResearchId=63&doc=pub>.

[31] See, e.g., Pedro da Motta Veiga, 'Brazil and the G20 Group of Developing Countries' in Peter Gallagher, Patrick Low and Andrew Stoler (eds), *Managing the Challenges of WTO Participation* (Cambridge University Press, 2005), providing a largely positive critique of Brazil's experience creating and leading the G20 group of developing countries in WTO negotiations.

reached – due to developing country opposition – as to how or whether to proceed with negotiations.[32]

C Power Politics

As alluded to above, the dynamics of a single developed country negotiating with a single developing country are inherently imbalanced. Outside the trading relationship, the developing country may rely upon the developed country for military or financial assistance, which may de facto limit the negotiating power of the developing country. In addition, the developing country is likely to perceive the FTA as providing it with significant opportunities and will therefore be more concerned about negotiations breaking down and failing. Developing countries have more limited financial and human resources to devote to negotiations, particularly if they were to become contentious and protracted. In practice, developing countries negotiating FTAs with developed countries are often expected to largely accept the terms presented to them by the developed country partner. For example, the United States (US) has developed a template of sorts for its FTAs and generally expects its FTA partners – to date mostly developing countries – to agree to the template. Although more economically strong US FTA partners such as Australia have had some minor success in diverging from the template, developing countries have generally been less successful in doing so.[33]

The large number of countries participating in WTO negotiations provides somewhat more of a buffer for developing countries from the economic and political clout of the developed countries. Because developing countries significantly outnumber developed countries in the WTO, the interests and objectives of the developing countries cannot simply be ignored. Part of the reason for the current Doha Round impasse is the inability of the largest developed countries and major developing countries to reach consensus as to what would constitute a fair and desirable

---

[32] See World Trade Organization, *Understanding the WTO: The Doha Agenda* <http://www.wto.org/english/thewto_e/whatis_e/tif_e/doha1_e.htm#singapore>.

[33] Australia succeeded in getting the US to agree to exclude investor–state dispute settlement from the FTA between the two countries: *Australia–United States Free Trade Agreement*, signed 18 May 2004, [2005] ATS 1 (entered into force 1 January 2005). Nonetheless, even Australia was not able to avoid the heightened intellectual property protections and agricultural exclusions demanded by the US.

package of concessions.[34] This reflects the fact that developing countries have the power, collectively, to reject agreements they do not feel are sufficiently in their interests.

III THE TPP'S APPROACH TO DEVELOPING COUNTRIES

The discussion of FTAs above assumed negotiations between two partners – that is, bilateral agreements. While most FTAs are bilateral, a few, such as the *North American Free Trade Agreement* (NAFTA)[35] and the Association of Southeast Asian Nations (ASEAN) FTA[36] are not.[37] Generally though, agreements comprising more than two countries have either been: customs unions rather than FTAs; FTAs between a customs union and another country; or FTAs between a larger FTA such as ASEAN and another country. In all of these cases, the core group of countries has been geographically linked. For example, ASEAN members are all based in Southeast Asia and the NAFTA countries are all part of North America. The TPP therefore presents a strikingly unusual dynamic. It is the first plurilateral FTA to be negotiated amongst several developed and several developing countries from non-congruent parts of the world.[38] We therefore cannot assume that the TPP presents the same dynamics for developing countries as a bilateral FTA negotiation. In addition, development is an explicit part of the TPP negotiating agenda, which is highly unusual for an FTA.

A Negotiating Dynamics

As a plurilateral agreement, the TPP presents some of the same disadvantages for developing countries – relative to the WTO – as do

---

[34] See, e.g., 'The Doha Round: Dead Man Talking', *The Economist* (London), 30 April 2011, 35.

[35] *North American Free Trade Agreement*, signed 17 December 1992, 32 ILM 289 (entered into force 1 January 1994) (NAFTA).

[36] *Agreement on the Common Effective Preferential Tariff Scheme for the ASEAN Free Trade Area*, signed 28 January 1992, 31 ILM 513 (entered into force 28 January 1992).

[37] NAFTA comprises Canada, Mexico and the US. ASEAN's member states are Brunei, Cambodia, Indonesia, Laos, Malaysia, Myanmar, the Philippines, Singapore, Thailand and Vietnam.

[38] The TPP members are all broadly a part of the Asia-Pacific, but the reach from Chile to New Zealand to Brunei to the US is broad indeed.

traditional bilateral FTAs. Even though there are multiple developing countries negotiating, there are also multiple developed country participants. To the extent that terms are being dictated within the TPP, it seems that the draft language is coming in large part from the US. Just as it is difficult for a developing country to overcome such language in a bilateral negotiation, it remains a challenge in the plurilateral context.

Another concern is that the outcomes of the TPP may be replicated in later agreements. Thus if there are provisions the developing country participants have to accept largely unwillingly, such as heightened intellectual property (IP) protections, the countries favouring such provisions may then seek to have them adopted in their subsequent FTA negotiations. As one commentator has explained:

> The problem with plurilateralism, apart from not being representative enough, is that it encourages selectivity and exclusivity where like-minded countries negotiate and agree on rules that best suit their interests and goals. The danger is that those rules could subsequently find their way into bilateral agreements between developed and developing countries, through negotiations in which the developing countries will, in all likelihood, have less leverage than they would have had in the multilateral setting.[39]

This concern also applies in the other direction: some of the outcomes of the TPP could ultimately be *multilateralised* by being placed successfully on a WTO negotiating agenda.

Nonetheless, it seems that while the TPP is in many ways likely not as positive a negotiating forum for the developing country participants as the WTO, it is likely more positive than negotiating a bilateral FTA with a developed country, particularly the US. To the extent that there are terms in the TPP which the developing countries favour, they may themselves be more successful in 'spreading' these provisions to later negotiations with other trading partners, or indeed to within the WTO. In addition, the developing country participants are forming coalitions on certain issues, sometimes with each other, but in other instances with some of the developed countries. For example, the US is urging various TRIPS-plus IP protections;[40] these draft provisions have been met with concern not just from some of the developing country participants such

---

[39] Edward Kwakwa, 'Reflections on "Development," "Developing Countries" and the "Progressive Development" of International Trade and Intellectual Property Law' (2011–12) 40 *Denver Journal of International Law and Policy* 221, 228–29.

[40] See Chapter 4 of this volume for a discussion of IP and the TPP. See also below n 50 and corresponding text.

as Malaysia and Vietnam, but also from New Zealand, a developed country.[41] It is likely helping the positions of Malaysia and Vietnam that they are both raising concerns, but also that they can ally with New Zealand in negotiating some of these issues. Furthermore, the developing country participants that already have FTAs with the US (Chile, Peru and Mexico) appear more willing to stick to their positions as to certain provisions. For example, Chile – which has FTAs with *all* the other TPP participants – has threatened to abandon the negotiations if the US does not drop some of its IP-related demands. Because Chile does not feel it 'needs' the TPP due to its existing FTAs, it can be more aggressive in its negotiating positions. This is in contrast to the way most negotiations between the US and a single developing country play out. In that context, the developing country tends to largely accept the terms dictated by the US (for example, Peru), or, if it objects too much, the US will terminate the negotiations (for example, Malaysia). Because the TPP is about more than market access, and incorporates geopolitical strategic goals as well as economic ones, there is an incentive for the traditional *demandeur* – the US – to keep all the participants in the negotiation if possible. This is likely to redound to the benefit of the developing countries in the final analysis.

B Development within the TPP: How Significant?

As noted above, the TPP participants have built development issues into the negotiating framework. But what will this actually mean for the developing country members? This section will examine the TPP's approach to development. It will then address some reasons why the TPP may not be as development-friendly as the framework might seem.

1 Development in the TPP negotiating structure

According to the United States Trade Representative's (USTR) website, the negotiating officials have identified five defining features of the TPP that will make it a '21st Century agreement'.[42] They are:

---

41 Although many of the other participants would, at one time, have preferred not to adopt TRIPS-plus IP protections, for the countries that already have FTAs with the US (Australia, Canada, Chile, Mexico, Peru and Singapore), they have already agreed to such provisions in their bilateral negotiations.

42 See Office of the United States Trade Representative, *Outlines of the Trans-Pacific Partnership Agreement* <http://www.ustr.gov/about-us/press-office/fact-sheets/2011/november/outlines-trans-pacific-partnership-agreement>.

a. comprehensive market access;
b. fully regional agreement, including development of production and supply chains;
c. addressing new trade challenges (such as the digital economy);
d. creating a living agreement that will enable updating and adding new members; and
e. coverage of cross-cutting trade issues.

With respect to the last of these, coverage of cross-cutting trade issues, again from the USTR website, it is stated that in the TPP framework there are four cross-cutting issues on work being done in the Asia-Pacific Economic Cooperation and other, and these are:

a. regional coherence;
b. competitiveness and business facilitation;
c. small and medium enterprises; and
d. development.

In describing the 'Development' issue, the USTR's website states:

> Comprehensive and robust market liberalization, improvements in trade and investment-enhancing disciplines, and other commitments – including a mechanism to help all TPP countries to effectively *implement* the Agreement and fully realize its benefits, will serve to strengthen institutions important for economic development and governance and thereby contribute significantly to advancing TPP countries' respective economic development priorities.[43]

In addition, the website refers to an area under negotiation as being 'Cooperation and Capacity Building', which is described as follows:

> The TPP countries agree that capacity building and other forms of cooperation are critical both during the negotiations and post-conclusion to support TPP countries' ability to implement and take advantage of the Agreement. They recognize that capacity building activities can be an effective tool in helping to address specific needs of developing countries in meeting the high standards the TPP countries have agreed to seek. In this spirit, several cooperation and capacity building activities have already been implemented in response to specific requests, and additional activities are being planned to assist developing countries in achieving the objectives of the Agreement. The TPP countries are also discussing specific text that will establish a demand-driven and flexible institutional mechanism to effectively

---

43 Ibid. (emphasis added).

> facilitate cooperation and capacity building assistance after the TPP is implemented.[44]

It therefore appears that there are plans for capacity-building and cooperation, but none of the plans outlined on the USTR website seem to resemble special and differential treatment of the sort seen either in the WTO, or even in other FTAs. In many FTAs featuring one or more developing countries, development is dealt with through mechanisms such as providing longer phase-out periods for developing countries and requiring less comprehensive commitments from developing country partners.

The information available on the TPP seems to suggest that developing countries are likely to receive assistance in implementing the commitments, but that they will have to commit to the same so-called 'high standards' terms as all the other participants. However, although draft texts are not yet available, it does appear that the TPP negotiating countries have been open to providing the developing country participants with additional time to phase in their commitments under the agreement. This would entail longer time periods than those applicable to the developed country members, but would not be akin to 'special and differential treatment' provisions exempting developing country participants from assuming particular obligations.[45] In addition, there is speculation that the US will ultimately propose a form of 'special and differential treatment' for the developing country members in the context of at least some IP commitments. In particular, there is talk that the US might propose that developing countries need only satisfy the IP protections agreed to within the US Congress, in the so-called 'May 10 standards',[46] which were applied in the US FTAs with Colombia, Panama and Peru. The speculation then would be that the developed country members would need to meet the higher IP standards found in the Korea–US FTA.[47]

Press releases following the conclusion of the 16th round of negotiations, held in Singapore in early March 2013, indicate that progress on,

---

[44] Ibid.

[45] 'U.S., TPP Countries Open to Phasing in Developing Country Commitments' (6 July 2012) 30(27) *Inside US Trade*.

[46] See, e.g., Sungjoon Cho, 'The Bush Administration and Democrats Reach a Bipartisan Deal on Trade Policy' (2007) 11(15) *ASIL Insight* (online) <http://www.asil.org/insights070529.cfm>.

[47] 'TPP Countries Slowly Restart Formal Talks on Pharmaceutical IP Protections' (15 March 2013) 31(11) *Inside US Trade*.

inter alia, development issues was sufficiently significant that the negotiating groups tasked with these issues 'will not meet again to discuss the legal texts in future rounds and any remaining work in these areas will be taken up in late-stage rounds as the agreement is finalized'.[48]

2 The substantive coverage of the TPP: attractive or unattractive for developing countries?

Certain aspects of the TPP are likely to be especially appealing to the developing country participants. One example is the potential market access gains from completely open markets, particularly if there are no exclusions for sensitive sectors or products. Of course it remains to be seen whether the market access commitments do end up being fully comprehensive, but for agricultural exporters such as Chile, and textiles exporters such as Vietnam, it would be attractive to have markets – particularly the US market – fully open to these exports.[49] In addition, the TPP provides a unique opportunity to engage in a deeper form of integration than other trade agreements. While the developing country participants may not be comfortable with all aspects of this plan, emphasis on regulatory coherence and small and medium enterprises could lead to more efficient trading patterns and more streamlined supply chains for their exporters.

However, there are other aspects of the TPP that have proven to be less attractive to the developing country participants, and would likely be unattractive as well to other developing countries that might consider joining the TPP in the future (for example, Thailand and the Philippines). The list below is intended to be indicative rather than comprehensive.

C TRIPS-plus IP Provisions

As discussed elsewhere in this volume, the leaked draft IP chapter, understood to have been drafted by the US, provides for numerous forms of IP protection that go far beyond that provided for in the *Agreement on*

---

48 Office of the United States Trade Representative, *TPP Negotiations Shift into Higher Gear at 16th Round* (13 March 2013) <http://www.ustr.gov/about-us/press-office/press-releases/2013/march/tpp-negotiations-higher-gear>.

49 If Japan joins the TPP, as it has recently indicated its intention to, this would also likely provide additional market access for the participants to Japan's markets, especially for rice, dairy products, and meat. See Reiji Yoshida, 'Abe Declares Japan Will Join TPP Free-Trade Process', *The Japan Times* (Tokyo), 16 March 2013 <http://www.japantimes.co.jp/news/2013/03/16/business/abe-declares-japan-will-join-tpp-free-trade-process>.

Trade-Related Aspects of Intellectual Property Rights (TRIPS).[50] Chile and Peru have already agreed to high-level IP protection in their FTAs with the US and are not keen to sign onto even higher levels of protection as contemplated in the leaked IP text. In fact, Chile is reportedly considering walking away from the agreement over the IP issues. Malaysia is also very concerned, in particular that the proposed IP provisions would increase its cost of medicines significantly. These provisions are likely to be unattractive to other developing countries that are currently outside the TPP but that could join in the future.

D Binding Labour and Environmental Provisions

The TPP will have chapters addressing labour and the environment. Many FTAs do not include such chapters. To the extent they are included, in most cases the language is in the nature of hortatory 'best endeavours' commitments. In the TPP, however, the provisions will be substantive in that the chapters will each be included within the scope of commitments subject to binding dispute settlement. Developing countries generally do not wish to commit to labour and environmental provisions, much less to ones that will be subject to formal dispute settlement mechanisms. Indeed, when Malaysia and the US previously attempted to negotiate a bilateral FTA, one of the main reasons the negotiations broke down was that Malaysia did not want to commit to a stringent labour chapter. As with TRIPS-plus IP protections, outsiders looking in will be concerned about agreeing to binding labour and environmental provisions.

E Strict Rules of Origin

Rules of origin (ROO) are an important feature of trade agreements.[51] ROO are the rules that are applied to determine the country of origin for an imported product. Customs officials apply these rules to determine origin. The origin of the product will then dictate which tariff rate will be applied – the MFN rate, the rate applicable under a relevant FTA, or perhaps a preferential rate pursuant to a GSP scheme. ROO can have the effect of helping developing countries, but if the rules are very strict it may mean a developing country will be unable to meet the required thresholds. Thus, for example, a ROO requiring 60 per cent local content would be harder to satisfy than one requiring only 40 per cent local

---

[50] *Marrakesh Agreement Establishing the World Trade Organization*, opened for signature 15 April 1994, 1867 UNTS 3 (entered into force 1 January 1995), annex 1C (*Agreement on Trade-Related Aspects of Intellectual Property Rights*).

[51] See further the detailed discussion in Chapter 2 of this volume.

content. In addition, the more complicated ROO are, the less likely exporters will be to complete all of the necessary documentation to qualify for the preferential tariff rate.[52]

Rumours about the TPP negotiations include that the US is demanding a yarn forward ROO for textiles, which would effectively preclude Vietnam's textiles exports from qualifying as a product of Vietnam (because the yarn used primarily comes from China). Similarly, it is understood that the US may be seeking a high local content requirement for automotive ROO, which would be a negative for Mexico.

To the extent that developing countries not currently participating in the TPP negotiations may consider joining in the future, issues such as rules of origin will be of concern. Developing countries often have a limited range of significant exports. If rules of origin may be employed to effectively prevent a developing country from benefitting from the FTA tariff rate for its key export or exports, it will be less interested in joining the TPP.

IV IMPLICATIONS OF THE TPP'S APPROACH

This final section will discuss certain strategic implications of the TPP's appeal, or lack thereof, for developing countries. It will explain why it matters if the TPP is not particularly development-friendly or attractive to developing countries, offering a few implications of the current state of affairs.

A The Strategic Objective for Negotiating the TPP

The origins of the TPP lie with the *Trans-Pacific Strategic Economic Partnership Agreement*,[53] also known as the P4 Agreement, formed by Brunei, Chile, New Zealand and Singapore in 2005. Those disparately located countries decided to form a high standards FTA because they wanted their agreement to serve as a potential model for an ultimate Free Trade Agreement of the Asia-Pacific (FTAAP).[54]

---

52 See, e.g., Lorand Bartels, 'The Trade and Development Policy of the European Union' (2007) 18 *European Journal of International Law* 715, 747–8.

53 Signed 18 July 2005 (entered into force 1 May 2006).

54 See, e.g., New Zealand Ministry of Foreign Affairs and Trade, *Trans-Pacific Strategic Economic Partnership (P4) Agreement* (25 July 2012) <http://www.mfat.govt.nz/Trade-and-Economic-Relations/2-Trade-Relationships-and-Agreements/Trans-Pacific/2-P4.php>; Meredith Kolsky Lewis, 'Achieving a Free

The FTAAP concept has been discussed for some time, with a number of different potential models having been suggested by Asia-Pacific countries over the years. At one stage it was thought that such an agreement could grow out of, and with the leadership of, the Asia-Pacific Economic Cooperation. More recently, the models discussed included an agreement with ASEAN at its hub, with the addition of Japan, China and South Korea (ASEAN + 3); an agreement with ASEAN at its hub plus Japan, China, South Korea, Australia, New Zealand and India (ASEAN + 6); or an agreement centring around an East Asian FTA between Japan, China and South Korea.

It did not escape the United States' notice that the above-mentioned FTAAP models all contained China, while none of them featured the US. The P4 Agreement – which contains an open accession clause to facilitate the addition of new members – therefore caught the United States' eye as a potential avenue to include itself in a FTAAP contender.[55]

Thus from the beginning, one of the aspirations of the TPP countries has been for the agreement to ultimately expand, ideally until it encompasses enough countries and trade to be considered an FTAAP.

Unsurprisingly, China has not sat idly by while the TPP has been under negotiation. Instead, it has pushed harder for one of the alternate FTAAP visions to be pursued. These efforts have borne fruit. Recently, steps have been taken towards pursuing an ASEAN + 6 arrangement, which is being called the Regional Comprehensive Economic Partnership, or 'RCEP'.[56] Initially, the RCEP will be negotiated amongst the ten members of

---

Trade Area of the Asia-Pacific: Does the TPP Present the Most Attractive Path?' in C.L. Lim, Deborah K. Elms and Patrick Low (eds), *The Trans-Pacific Partnership: A Quest for a Twenty-first-Century Trade Agreement* (Cambridge University Press, 2012) 223, 224–25.

[55] Although the TPP is formally being negotiated as a new agreement rather than an expansion of the P4, the historical link is clear. The US initially attended negotiations to extend the P4 Agreement to include new investment and financial services chapters; when these talks appeared sufficiently attractive, the US indicated its intent to join. Shortly thereafter, it became evident that a new agreement would in fact be created (the TPP), though obviously building upon the P4 model. See generally Meredith Kolsky Lewis, 'Expanding the P-4 Agreement into a Broader Trans-Pacific Partnership: Implications and Opportunities' (2009) 4 *Asian Journal of WTO and International Health Law and Policy* 401.

[56] ASEAN, *ASEAN and FTA Partners Launch the World's Biggest Regional Free Trade Deal* (20 November 2012) <http://www.asean.org/news/item/asean-and-fta-partners-launch-the-world-s-biggest-regional-free-trade-deal?category_id=27>.

ASEAN, together with China, Japan, South Korea, Australia, India and New Zealand. While ASEAN already has FTAs with each of the other six members of the RCEP negotiations, these are hub-and-spoke linkages, created without forming bonds amongst the spokes (so-called ASEAN + 1 agreements). In contrast, the RCEP would create new linkages between the six non-ASEAN members, most importantly amongst China, Japan and South Korea, the three largest economies in Asia. At present there are no FTAs between any two of these three countries. The RCEP would link all three to each other, which – if successful – would be a significant development. In addition, the RCEP will apparently be open for accession by other countries following the creation of the initial agreement.[57]

It therefore appears that the TPP and the RCEP could be in a competition of sorts to expand into an ultimate FTAAP. In order for the TPP to be the agreement that grows into an FTAAP, it will be necessary to attract more developing countries at a later stage, including perhaps Thailand, Indonesia and the Philippines. However, the nature of the TPP commitments – particularly those pertaining to intellectual property, labour and the environment – may mean that these countries and others decide against participating.[58] It may be more attractive for them merely to stick with the 'ASEAN +' model, of which they are already a part. If the Asia-Pacific developing countries that are not currently participating in the TPP negotiations do not find the agreement attractive enough to seek to join, it would be less likely that it will be the TPP that becomes the basis for an FTAAP.

B Systemic Implications of the TPP for Developing Countries

The substance of the TPP commitments will have implications for developing countries that go beyond the confines of the agreement itself.

First, if a plurilateral agreement of 11 or more countries features TRIPS-plus provisions and other 'high standards' terms, there is a potential for these provisions to become 'the new normal' and ultimately to be multilateralised in the WTO context. If more and more WTO Members agree to these sorts of terms, either by joining the TPP directly

---

[57] Murray Hiebert and Liam Hanlon, *ASEAN and Partners Launch Regional Comprehensive Economic Partnership* (7 December 2012) Center for Strategic and International Studies <http://csis.org/publication/asean-and-partners-launch-regional-comprehensive-economic-partnership>.

[58] See generally Meredith Kolsky Lewis, 'The Trans-Pacific Partnership: New Paradigm or Wolf in Sheep's Clothing?' (2011) 34 *Boston College International and Comparative Law Review* 27.

or by agreeing to them in future FTAs with TPP participants, these provisions may become prevalent enough for the US or others to seek to place them on the WTO negotiating table with the aim of raising the standards bar across the WTO.

Secondly, a plurilateral agreement such as the TPP may mean that developing countries need to recalibrate their expected outcomes in WTO negotiations. By failing to reach agreement thus far in Doha, developing countries have not received what they wanted. But with FTAs continuing to proliferate and with an agreement such as the TPP achieving very high standards across a group of countries, it may be that when the parties return to the WTO negotiating table there will have been a shift in what is offered by whom, and not in favour of the developing countries.

By attaining high standards outcomes from a group of trading partners, there is less for the US and other participants to gain from traditional WTO market access negotiations. At the same time, the level of concessions the US will demand with respect to the current WTO agenda items is likely to go up, as there may be a critical mass of countries in the TPP making higher levels of commitment than before.

However, the TPP may also present new opportunities in the WTO context. Because the scope of the TPP is broader than that of the WTO, the US and other TPP parties may seek to multilateralise some of the novel aspects of the TPP into the WTO. If this is the case, the TPP will result in more issues coming into play in WTO negotiations. With additional and more varied items on the negotiating agenda, members may have enough on the table to enable a fruitful give-and-take (which does not seem to be the case at present). Developing countries still may face a situation where they are asked to make more concessions to achieve a deal than has been the case in the Doha Round negotiations thus far. However, if the range of potential concessions is broadened, developing countries may have some success in offering concessions in some of the new agenda items that come into play, resulting in less of a need to make concessions in more sensitive areas.

CONCLUSION

Developing countries have generally felt the WTO presents a better negotiating forum to accomplish their goals than do bilateral FTA negotiations. The ability to negotiate in blocs, the system of negotiating by consensus, and the fact that developing countries significantly outnumber developed countries all make the WTO a more attractive option than the bilateral context, where power politics are often brought into play.

While the TPP presents some of the same disadvantages for its developing country participants as traditional FTAs, as a large plurilateral agreement pursuing a high-standards agenda it also raises unique considerations. Developing countries can have more success in negotiating within a plurilateral agreement such as the TPP than in a bilateral FTA, because they can join together – sometimes even with certain developed countries – to oppose terms sought primarily by one country, the US. On the other hand, it appears that a part of the TPP's high-standards agenda will be that developing countries will not receive the type of special and differential treatment currently available within the WTO and often featuring in bilateral FTAs between a developed and a developing country.

Strategically, developing countries within the TPP may find that the concessions they make within this trade agreement will ultimately be multilateralised, applying to the vast majority of their trading relationships. This prospect, as well as the general concern over the nature of some of the commitments, may make other developing countries less likely to want to join the TPP in the future. This reluctance may in turn have implications for the TPP and its objectives. If the TPP is to expand into an FTAAP, its current participants will want more developing countries from the Asia-Pacific region to join the agreement in the future. Yet the very provisions drafted by the current participants may undermine that ultimate objective.

4. The TPP as a case study of changing dynamics for international intellectual property negotiations

Kimberlee Weatherall

INTRODUCTION

It is not surprising that the intellectual property (IP) chapter has proven to be one of the most contentious in the negotiations for the Trans-Pacific Partnership Agreement (TPP).[1] Observers of international IP law could have predicted that the chapter would involve sticking points requiring high-level political resolution towards the end of the discussions. IP negotiations are controversial in the second decade of the twenty-first century. This is true whether they occur in bilateral trade negotiations, at a multilateral level in the World Intellectual Property Organization (WIPO) or World Trade Organization (WTO), or in that shadowy and variegated world in between: the plurilateral or regional agreement.

There are however some aspects of the negotiation dynamics for the TPP that are different from what has gone before. Its regional aspirations, a new hostility in the public policy environment for international IP lawmaking, and the increased fragmentation of the international IP legal environment all cast shadows over these negotiations and will colour both the eventual outcomes and the implications of any resulting text. This chapter explores how the negotiating environment for the IP chapter in the TPP differs from past IP negotiations, what this could mean for the likely outcomes, and the implications for the impact of the IP chapter that emerges at the other end.

---

1 See, e.g., 'Business Lobbyist Sees Strong Objections to US IPR Demands in TPP' (25 May 2012) 30(21) *Inside US Trade* (online); 'USTR Faces Resistance on Variety of Copyright Issues in TPP Talks' (23 March 2012) 30(12) *Inside US Trade* (online).

I SAME OLD, SAME OLD: ONGOING THEMES FOR THE TPP IP NEGOTIATIONS

The period since the 1990s has seen the rapid development of IP as a core subject in trade negotiations. Although IP has been included in some trade negotiations since the nineteenth century,[2] IP as a modern trade issue was firmly established by the conclusion of the *Agreement on Trade Related Aspects of Intellectual Property Rights* (TRIPS) as part of the WTO suite of treaties in the mid-1990s.[3] Subsequent to TRIPS, IP has been an important part of an integrated European Union (EU) and has become a topic frequently dealt with in bilateral trade agreements, particularly those involving either Europe or the United States (US). There has been enough activity that certain common patterns or themes have emerged: themes we see repeated in the TPP negotiations.

A Divergent Interests

The first factor affecting the TPP IP dynamics that is neither new nor surprising is the parties' divergent interests. A state's interests in framing domestic IP law will depend on a variety of factors: its development status; the level of indigenous research and innovation; the local mix of industries (a country with a strong export industry in education, for example, may have an interest in copyright exceptions for educational uses); and other issues such as the health status of the population (a country suffering an AIDS or other pandemic, for example, may wish to make use of flexibilities in patent law to reduce the cost of, and increase access to, essential medicines). In trade negotiations today, divergent interests in IP are the rule rather than the exception.

Thus the fact that the parties commenced the TPP IP negotiations a long way apart is no novelty. Among the negotiating countries are those with highly developed IP systems reflecting the most IP-protective international standards (the US, Australia, and Singapore), and, at the other extreme, developing countries that have brought their laws into

---

[2] See, e.g., the discussion of the early history of IP agreements in Europe that preceded the multilateral era ushered in through the *Berne Convention on the Protection of Literary and Artistic Works* in 1886: Sam Ricketson, *The Berne Convention for the Protection of Literary and Artistic Works: 1886–1986* (Kluwer, 1987) 25–38.

[3] *Marrakesh Agreement Establishing the World Trade Organization*, opened for signature 15 April 1994, 1867 UNTS 3 (entered into force 1 January 1995), annex 1C (*Agreement on Trade-Related Aspects of Intellectual Property Rights*).

compliance with TRIPS only very recently, such as Vietnam. There are countries in the region with significant pharmaceutical industries (in particular the US) and others, such as Peru, Vietnam, Malaysia and Brunei, for whom pricing of pharmaceuticals, and access to essential medicines, are pressing public policy issues. The US is a net exporter of IP with an interest in ensuring protection for its innovators and creators in other countries; other parties to the negotiations are net importers with an economic interest in lesser levels and/or shorter terms of protection.

Further, internationally, states' positions regarding the optimal scope and shape of IP law and the balance of interests between owners and users vary considerably. The TPP parties' divergence thus does not reduce to a simple disagreement based on gross domestic product or level of development. New Zealand and Canada, in particular, maintain strong and well-developed IP systems but with unique features not shared by other developed nations, based on different local public policy positions. Canada, for example, in 2011 passed significant revisions to its copyright law following many years of consultations and proposals; the law creates an internationally unique system for managing IP infringement online that does not involve automatic takedown of allegedly copyright infringing material.[4] It would be difficult for Canada to revisit that law, as it 'struck a delicate domestic political balance and took a number of years to hammer out'.[5] New Zealand has systems for the recognition and protection of traditional symbols as part of its trade mark law. In the area of pharmaceuticals, many of the negotiating countries, including Australia, New Zealand, and Canada, have systems for pricing control and/or subsidies which the US considers inconsistent with patent protection. These differences all complicate the IP negotiations.

The presence of diverse interests has meant that the parties have come to the table with a series of competing priorities and concerns. The US commenced negotiations with a long list of demands spanning IP in the digital environment, pharmaceutical patents, protection for trade secrets and IP enforcement. But other countries have raised their own priorities: such as recognition and protection for traditional knowledge, traditional cultural expressions and genetic resources.[6] Peru tabled proposals that

---

[4] *Copyright Modernization Act 2012* (Canada), in force November 2012, amending the *Copyright Act* RSC 1985 c C-42.

[5] 'In Shadow of ACTA, EU Drops Criminal IPR Provisions in CETA Talks' (2 November 2012) 30(43) *Inside US Trade* (online).

[6] 'U.S. Mulls Strategy on TPP Medicines Proposal in Light of Stiff Resistance' (27 April 2012) 30(17) *Inside US Trade* (online); 'Peru, N.Z. Still Pushing Traditional Knowledge, Genetic Resources in TPP' (9 March 2012)

would require pharmaceutical companies to obtain prior consent for use, and ultimately share benefits from, the development of commercial products based on traditional knowledge and genetic resources.[7] New Zealand proposed that members may provide protection against the unauthorised disclosure of traditional knowledge and traditional cultural resources, among other provisions.[8] The US has historically been opposed to such proposals, agreeing only to low-level 'recognition' of such interests in its free trade agreement (FTA) with Peru.[9]

But all this is old hat for IP negotiations in a trade context. The parties' interests, systems and priorities are different, and some compromises within the chapter and trade-offs with other areas of trade will be required.

B The United States' Ambitions

A second factor that is not new is the high ambition of the US negotiators. As one of the world's few net IP-exporting states, with significant IP-dependent industries including in entertainment and pharmaceutical manufacturing,[10] the US has high levels of domestic IP

30(10) *Inside US Trade* (online) (noting that 'Peru and New Zealand are continuing to push other parties involved in the Trans-Pacific Partnership (TPP) negotiations to agree to provisions that would better protect traditional knowledge and genetic resources used to make commercial products, an effort the U.S. opposes').

7 'Peru, N.Z. Still Pushing Traditional Knowledge, Genetic Resources in TPP' (9 March 2012) 30(10) *Inside US Trade* (online).

8 Ibid.

9 Ibid. This recognition is contained in the *Understanding Regarding Biodiversity and Traditional Knowledge* (the '*Understanding*'), part of the *Trade Promotion Agreement*, Peru–United States, signed 12 April 2006 (entered into force 1 February 2009). There are no substantive binding obligations in the *Understanding*, in which the parties 'recognize' the importance of traditional knowledge and biodiversity, and undertake to 'endeavor to seek ways to share information that may have a bearing on the patentability of inventions based on traditional knowledge or genetic resources' by providing publicly accessible databases with relevant information, and 'opportunities' (but no obligation) to cite prior art relevant to patentability in patent examination.

10 There have been disputes regarding whether promoting strong IP protection is in fact in the United States' national interest, given both the high proportion of foreign ownership of firms in the United States' IP-owning industries, and the fact that the US is also the home to many industries that rely on exceptions and flexibilities in IP. See e.g. Jonathan Band and Jonathan Gerafi, *Foreign Ownership of Firms in IP-Intensive Industries* (March 2013)

protection and enforcement, and considers most other countries to have inadequate systems. In fact, in 2012 the US had active disagreements regarding IP law with a majority of the TPP negotiating parties: of the eleven countries, the US singled out six on its 2012 annual 'Priority Watch List' or 'Watch List' as having markedly inadequate IP laws or enforcement by US standards.[11]

A leaked US proposal dated February 2011 shows that the US approached the TPP negotiations the same way it has approached its bilateral negotiations since the earliest years of the twenty-first century: presenting a detailed template for an IP chapter based closely on US law and developed through past bilateral negotiations.[12] The United States' starting point for negotiation[13] was that the TPP should adopt the strongest standards from the most recent US bilateral with South Korea – and then add some innovations not previously seen in the US template,[14]

<infojustice.org/foreignownrep>. At present, however, it seems that the USTR and Congress take the position that stronger international IP law is a US negotiating goal.

[11] Ambassador Ronald Kirk, '2012 Special 301 Report' (Office of the United States Trade Representative, April 2012) <http://www.ustr.gov/sites/default/files/2012%20Special%20301%20Report_0.pdf>. This is not entirely coincidental. As Drahos and Braithwaite have pointed out, inclusion of countries on the USTR's Watch List is itself a mechanism for putting pressure on countries with which the US has ongoing trade negotiations: Peter Drahos with John Braithwaite, *Information Feudalism: Who Owns the Knowledge Economy?* (Earthscan, 2002).

[12] For a description of this approach, see Peter Yu, 'Six Secret (and Now Open) Fears of ACTA' (2011) 64 *Southern Methodist University Law Review* 975; Andrew Christie, Sophie Waller and Kimberlee Weatherall, 'Exporting the DMCA Through Free Trade Agreements' in Christopher Heath and Anselm Kamperman Sanders (eds), *Intellectual Property and Free Trade Agreements* (Hart Publishing, 2007) 220.

[13] For a full analysis of the implications of the leaked TPP draft proposal from the United States for Australian law, in the area of copyright and enforcement mechanisms, see Kimberlee Weatherall, *An Australian Analysis of the February 2011 Leaked US TPPA IP Chapter Text – Copyright and Enforcement* (July 2011) SelectedWorks <http://works.bepress.com/kimweatherall/22>; Sean Flynn et al., 'The US Proposal for an Intellectual Property Chapter in the Trans-Pacific Partnership Agreement' (2012) 28 *American University International Law Review* 105; Susy Frankel, 'IP in New Zealand and the TPPA', in Jane Kelsey (ed.), *No Ordinary Deal. Unmasking the Trans-Pacific Partnership Free Trade Agreement* (Bridget Williams Books, 2010), 163.

[14] See the leaked United States proposal: *Trans-Pacific Partnership: Intellectual Property Rights Chapter* (10 February 2011) Knowledge Ecology International <http://keionline.org/sites/default/files/tpp-10feb2011-us-text-ipr-chapter.pdf> (US Draft TPP IP Chapter). Examples include: mandatory provision

including provisions previously rejected by some TPP parties.[15] For example, the US proposed:

- limits on parallel importation;[16]
- extension of the copyright term for films and sound recordings to 95 years;[17]
- a presumption of validity for patents and trade marks;[18] and
- detailed regulations governing the management of geographical indications and their relationship with trade marks.[19]

Subsequently, the US added more proposals which are new to the template, that is, they are not found even in the strongest of the recent US FTAs, such as one relating to trade secret protection.[20] Most controversial of the early US proposals was that relating to patents and pharmaceuticals, a summary of which was publicly released in the form of a White Paper entitled 'Trans-Pacific Partnership Trade Goals to Enhance Access to Medicines'.[21] This document talked in general language about the United States' 'new strategic initiative' called 'Trade Enhancing

---

for customs authorities to seize allegedly infringing in-transit goods (an idea rejected in the recent *Anti-Counterfeiting Trade Agreement* (ACTA) negotiations (art 14.4.)) – this proposal appears to come from early drafts of ACTA, although in-transit seizure became optional in the final ACTA text; and statutory damages for breaches of the anti-circumvention provisions (art 12.12.) – according to reports, the United States has subsequent to this document proposed that all TPP partners agree to put in place criminal penalties for government officials who wilfully disseminate trade secrets that are provided to them in confidence: 'Group Urges Joint Government, Business Response to Trade Secrets Theft' (22 June 2012) 30(25) *Inside US Trade* (online).

[15] Such as statutory damages for copyright infringement and trade mark counterfeiting: ibid., art 12.4. This proposal was not accepted by Australia in its FTA with the United States: *Australia–US Free Trade Agreement*, signed 18 May 2004, [2005] ATS 1 (entered into force 1 January 2005) (AUSFTA).

[16] Ibid., art 4.2. No similar limitation presently exists in Australia's FTA with the United States.

[17] US Draft TPP IP Chapter, above n 14, art 4.5. In AUSFTA, the copyright term for these items was extended to 75 years (from a previous 50 years): AUSFTA art 17.4.4.

[18] US Draft TPP IP Chapter, above n 14, art 10.2.

[19] US Draft TPP IP Chapter, above n 14, art 2, especially art 2.14–2.22.

[20] 'Group Urges Joint Government, Business Response to Trade Secrets Theft' (22 June 2012) 30(25) *Inside US Trade* (online).

[21] Office of the United States Trade Representative, *Trans-Pacific Partnership Trade Goals to Enhance Access to Medicines* (11 September 2011)

Access to Medicines' (TEAM), which, according to the document, was 'designed to deploy the tools of trade policy to promote trade in, and reduce obstacles to, access to both innovative and generic medicines, while supporting the innovation and intellectual property protection that is vital to developing new medicines'.

Prior to the release of the White Paper, the US had a differentiated approach to the relationship between patents and pharmaceuticals in trade agreements depending on the level of development of the partner country. The model for *developed* countries, reflected in its most stringent form in the *South Korea–United States Free Trade Agreement*,[22] requires patent term extensions to compensate for unreasonable delays that occur in granting a patent[23] or in obtaining marketing approval for pharmaceutical patents,[24] data exclusivity granting monopolies in clinical test data submitted for marketing approval for five years (requiring generic companies to wait to seek approval or re-do expensive clinical trials),[25] and an obligation to refuse drug marketing approval to a company seeking to rely on clinical test data submitted by another without the consent of the previous patent owner during the patent term (known as 'patent linkage').[26] For *developing* countries, these obligations were relaxed, pursuant to an agreement known as the 'May 10, 2007 Bipartisan Trade Agreement',[27] negotiated between Democrats and Republicans in order to secure Congressional approval for trade agreements with

---

<http://www.ustr.gov/about-us/press-office/press-releases/2011/september/trade-enhancing-access-medicines>.

[22] *Republic of South Korea–United States Free Trade Agreement*, signed June 30, 2007; further legal texts signed 10 February 2011 (entered into force 15 March 2012).

[23] Ibid., art 18.8.6(a).

[24] Ibid., art 18.8.6(b).

[25] Ibid., art 18.9.1(a). In addition the agreement provides for three years of data exclusivity for data relating to a chemical entity previously approved for marketing in another pharmaceutical product.

[26] Ibid., art 18.9.5.

[27] The genesis of these provisions is discussed in detail in I.M. Destler, 'American Trade Politics in 2007: Building Bipartisan Compromise' (Policy Brief Number PB07-5, Peterson Institute for International Economics, May 2007). The detail of the agreement may be found in a document published by the House Committee on Ways and Means, United States Congress: Peru & Panama FTA Changes (10 May 2007) <http://waysandmeans.house.gov/Media/pdf/110/05%2014%2007/05%2014%2007.pdf>. A more general introduction may be found in the Office of the United States Trade Representative, *Trade Facts: Bipartisan Trade Deal* (May 2007). <http://www.ustr.gov/sites/default/files/uploads/factsheets/2007/asset_upload_file127_11319.pdf>.

Panama, Peru, Colombia and South Korea.[28] Under the agreement, developing countries were entitled to apply exceptions to protection for clinical test data, protect test data only as long as it was protected in the US, only optionally provide for patent term extensions to compensate for delays in the patent or marketing approval process, and were not required to 'link' drug regulatory agencies' approval processes and patent issues.

Under the TEAM approach, it was proposed that the flexibilities accorded to developing countries under the May 10, 2007 Bipartisan Trade Agreement to deny the various special protections for pharmaceutical patents would no longer apply. Instead, 'pharmaceutical-specific IP protections' would be available in all TPP countries, but conditional on the pharmaceutical patent holder bringing medicine to TPP markets within an agreed window of time (the 'TPP access window').[29] The US proposal was subject to strong criticism from groups interested in access to medicines[30] and was opposed by the other TPP negotiating countries.[31] The abandonment of a differentiated approach towards developing and developed countries also represented a departure from past bilateral and multilateral agreements relating to IP. The White Paper demonstrated clearly that the US was approaching the TPP as it had past IP negotiations – taking its existing agreements as a baseline and coming up with new, more IP-protective innovations. At the time of writing, the US was considering how to amend its proposals on patents and pharmaceuticals in light of opposition from both industry (who considered the proposals

---

28 The IP provisions of the May 10, 2007 Bipartisan Trade Agreement were not applied to South Korea, which was considered a developed country less in need of these balancing provisions. Other aspects of the agreement did apply to South Korea.

29 This would be coupled with a series of other proposals relating to medicines: such as the elimination of tariffs on medicines, reducing customs obstacles, taking steps to curb trade in counterfeits, reducing internal barriers to distribution of medicines, and promoting 'transparency and procedural fairness' in the operation of government healthcare reimbursement programs: Office of the United States Trade Representative, above n 21.

30 See, e.g., Médecins Sans Frontières, *Trading Away Health: How the U.S.'s Intellectual Property Demands for the Trans-Pacific Partnership Agreement Threaten Access to Medicines* (August 2012), <http://aids2012.msf.org/wp-content/uploads/2012/07/TPP-Issue-Brief-IAC-July2012.pdf>.

31 'TPP Countries Signal New Proposals to Counter U.S. SOE, IPR Demands' (14 December 2012) 30(49) *Inside US Trade* (online); 'U.S. Mulls Strategy on TPP Medicines Proposal in Light of Stiff Resistance' (27 April 2012) 30(17) *Inside US Trade* (online); 'U.S. TPP Access to Medicines Proposal Faces Strong Opposition' (16 March 2012) 30(11) *Inside US Trade* (online).

as potentially too weak or too onerous for industry) and other negotiating countries (who considered them to be too strong).

At first glance, dropping 30 or more pages of detailed IP provisions based on idiosyncratic domestic law on the negotiating table, and then proposing new, more stringent IP provisions in the single most controversial area of international IP law, is a strange way to commence discussions aimed at producing a regional framework agreement involving multiple parties, even assuming that the proposals represent no more than an ambit claim. Recent experience of plurilateral negotiations suggests that the US could not expect to prevail in imposing such detailed provisions: as discussed further below, the US approached the plurilateral *Anti-Counterfeiting Trade Agreement*[32] (ACTA) proposal in 2008 with a similarly detailed template, which was considerably watered down over the course of negotiations.[33] The circumstances of the ACTA were very different from those surrounding the TPP.[34] ACTA involved Europe, which has its own strong but different system, and because ACTA was solely concerned with IP enforcement, there was no opportunity to trade off IP against gains in other trade areas such as agriculture. Nevertheless, as the ACTA negotiations illustrated, there is strength in numbers: the nine or more other countries in the room can band together to oppose US demands and/or propose alternatives.

The US stance is explicable by reference to the domestic environment in which the United States Trade Representative (USTR) operates. The USTR faces pressure, both from IP stakeholders and from members of Congress, to achieve strong protection for IP rights. Coverage of the TPP negotiations in publications like *Inside US Trade* has been full of references to the demands of interest groups ranging from the pharmaceutical industry, the movie and music industries, and the US Chamber of Commerce for the TPP to include IP provisions stronger even than the United States' existing bilateral agreements. As noted above, even the United States' new proposals on patents and pharmaceuticals – which were much stronger than anything found in past US FTAs and which faced universal resistance from the other parties – were opposed by US

---

32 *Anti-Counterfeiting Trade Agreement*, Opened for signature 1 October 2011, [2011] ATNIF 22 (not yet in force).

33 See generally Kimberlee Weatherall, 'ACTA as a New Kind of International IP Lawmaking' (2011) 26(3) *American University International Law Review* 839.

34 ACTA was concluded in late 2010. As of the time of writing only Japan had ratified the agreement. The agreement will enter into force once six countries ratify the agreement.

industry on the basis that they could be too weak or would create onerous burdens for pharmaceutical companies wanting the highest levels of patent protection.[35]

More generally, there are institutional and bureaucratic constraints that dictate the USTR approach. The *Trade Act of 2002* requires, as a US negotiating objective, that 'the provisions of any multilateral or bilateral trade agreement governing intellectual property rights that is entered into by the United States reflect a standard of protection similar to that found in United States law'[36] – a provision that appears to have been interpreted as requiring treaty provisions which themselves largely match US law. Further, the USTR's goal is an agreement that will achieve the Congressional approval required for new trade agreements.[37] The coalition in support of FTAs in the US Congress is fragile,[38] as evidenced by the difficulties the executive faced in passing the most recent batch of bilateral FTAs, which took five years to pass.[39] IP lobby groups make significant contributions to political campaigns, and these lobby groups take a dim view of IP chapters that are in any respect weaker than past agreements. The Industry Trade Advisory Committees (ITACs), constituted by industry stakeholders, that review and report on proposed trade agreements have a history of drawing comparisons between the text of any proposed agreement and past trade agreements, with less IP-protective provisions attracting significant negative comment. Given these political considerations, an FTA will have a more realistic chance of obtaining the necessary approval if it follows – or better still, strengthens – an already established model.

In summary, as in previous arenas, the US has started from an ambitious base in its IP negotiations, generating considerable controversy, but no real surprise, among observers. Although the US has been relatively successful with this approach in bilateral trade negotiations, the plurilateral context of ACTA discussed further below proved more of a

---

35 'U.S. Mulls Strategy on TPP Medicines Proposal in Light of Stiff Resistance' (27 April 2012) 30(17) *Inside US Trade* (online); 'U.S. TPP Access to Medicines Proposal Faces Strong Opposition' (16 March 2012) 30(11) *Inside US Trade* (online).

36 19 USC § 2802(b)(4)(A)(i)(II) (2011).

37 19 USC § 3805(a)(1)(D) (2011).

38 See generally Destler, above n 27; I.M. Destler, *American Trade Politics* (Peterson Institute for International Economics, 2005).

39 Binyamin Applebaum and Jennifer Steinhauer, 'Congress Ends 5-Year Standoff on Trade Deals in Rare Accord', *The New York Times* (online), 12 October 2011 <http://www.nytimes.com/2011/10/13/business/trade-bills-near-final-chapter.html>.

challenge. The TPP negotiations, however, are different; not least, it will be possible to trade off concessions in other areas to achieve goals in IP. The extent to which the United States' ambitions can be fulfilled will depend on a series of other features of the dynamics for the negotiation – the subject of the next section of this chapter.

II WHY THE TPP IP NEGOTIATIONS ARE INTERESTING: NEW DYNAMICS AND NEW IMPLICATIONS

Although certain old and well-worn themes in international IP law-making have recurred in the TPP negotiations, there are other dynamics that are new. These new factors will have implications both for the likely outcome of the negotiations and for the significance of any concluded agreement.

A Regional Aspirations and Regional Competition

The first new factor is the overall aim of creating a regional trade framework. The goal of the TPP negotiations is not merely to manage, and consolidate, the 'noodle bowl' of extant trade agreements between the negotiating parties.[40] The parties hope that other countries in the region will accede to the TPP over time, extending its membership and creating a 'Free Trade Area for the Asia-Pacific' (FTAAP). Indeed, as many commentators have noted, the economic benefits of a TPP between the negotiating parties would be limited; only if bigger regional economies participate, such as India, South Korea, and China, will these negotiations generate a real payoff.[41]

---

[40] Ann Capling and John Ravenhill, 'Multilateralising Regionalism: What Role for the Trans-Pacific Partnership?' (Paper presented at the Australian Political Science Association Conference 2011, Australian National University, 26 September 2011) 5; John Ravenhill, 'Extending the TPP: the Political Economy of Multilateralization in Asia' (Paper presented at the Asia-Pacific Trade Economists' Conference, Bangkok, 2–3 November 2009) 24–25: as Ravenhill points out, an enlarged TPP including the current negotiating parties would duplicate a number of existing trade agreements: in fact, of the 21 bilateral preferential arrangements that an expanded TPP would create, only eight are not already covered by some existing agreement.

[41] Mireya Solis, 'Last Train for Asia-Pacific Integration? US Objectives in the TPP Negotiations' (Working Paper No 201102, Organization for Japan–US Studies, Waseda University, July 2011) 9–10; Meredith Kolsky Lewis, 'The

Australia has clearly indicated that regional integration is the ultimate goal. In 2012, in its White Paper 'Australia in the Asian Century', the government reiterated its support for the ambition of an FTAAP, and cited the TPP as one possible pathway to achieve that ambition.[42] The US also sees the TPP as the potential basis for broader regional integration,[43] in particular, one that follows the United States' preferred model of binding trade commitments. The TPP model may be a compromised version of regional integration. Whereas Australia and other countries initially talked about the 'multilateralisation of regionalism' by replacing or harmonising existing bilateral agreements between TPP parties, the United States' vision – which prevailed – involves the retention of existing bilateral arrangements, rolled into the TPP together with new market access arrangements between countries which do not have existing bilateral agreements.[44] Nevertheless, all agree on the goal of expanding the TPP's membership in the long term, an ambition reflected in the proposal for open accession provisions.

Regional aspirations must logically affect the negotiations and the kind of text being proposed. Importantly too the TPP has competition for the role of regional trade framework from initiatives based in the Association of Southeast Asian Nations (ASEAN). As of early 2013, the latest of these is the Regional Comprehensive Economic Partnership (RCEP), launched in November 2012, involving the ten ASEAN member states and countries which have existing FTAs with ASEAN – Australia, China, India, Japan, the Republic of Korea and New Zealand. Like the TPP, the RCEP aims to create a modern, comprehensive, high-quality and mutually beneficial economic partnership agreement covering intellectual property as well as trade in goods, trade in services, investment, economic and technical cooperation, competition, dispute settlement and

---

Trans-Pacific Partnership: New Paradigm or Wolf in Sheep's Clothing?' (2011) 34 *Boston College International and Comparative Law Review* 27, 35–36; Deborah Elms, 'From the P4 to the TPP: Explaining Expansion Interests in the Asia-Pacific' (Paper prepared for the Asia-Pacific Trade Economists' Conference, Bangkok, 2–3 November 2009) 4–5.

[42] Department of Prime Minister and Cabinet, 'Australia in the Asian Century' (White Paper, October 2012) 187 <http://asiancentury.dpmc.gov.au/sites/default/files/white-paper/australia-in-the-asian-century-white-paper.pdf>.

[43] See, e.g., Ian Fergusson and Bruce Vaughn, 'The Trans-Pacific Partnership Agreement' (CRS Report for Congress No R40502, Congressional Research Service, 12 December 2011) 3 <http://www.fas.org/sgp/crs/row/R40502.pdf>, noting that '[i]t is envisaged that the TPP will add members in successive tranches'.

[44] Kolsky Lewis, above n 41; Capling and Ravenhill above n 40.

other issues.[45] Also like the TPP, it is envisaged that the RCEP will include open accession provisions to enable the participation of any future ASEAN FTA partner or other external economic partner in the future. Even if the RCEP were to fall by the wayside, there are other possible groupings involving ASEAN and its neighbours that have been mooted as providing a pathway to an FTAAP.[46]

Whether the TPP fulfils its potential will depend, in part, on its text. As the Australian Trade Minister recognised, 'if we're to encourage others to dock on to the agreement, we want to make sure we've got the foundations right.'[47] Or, as Kolsky Lewis put it:

> For the TPP to serve as a model for a future FTAAP, it will have to be an agreement that other countries are interested in joining. The TPP agreement is not the only option available for Asia-Pacific regionalism, and if the TPP is not sufficiently attractive, one of the other visions for regional economic integration may instead fill the role as FTAAP model.[48]

How does this impact on the IP negotiations? It is unlikely that the substance of an IP chapter will, on its own, be a deal-breaker either for the TPP negotiations themselves or for any country considering joining a TPP in the future. First, other areas in the TPP negotiations are of equal or greater controversy – for example, issues such as the role of state-owned enterprises, the presence or absence (and scope) of investor–state dispute settlement mechanisms, the freedom of countries to institute capital controls, and US proposals for an overarching chapter on regulatory coherence. Secondly, for many countries in the region, there are traditional trade issues of far greater immediate economic salience than IP – for example, access for agricultural products (such as dairy, sugar, rice and beef), or textiles and footwear, are much more likely to be of immediate concern. Thirdly, even a 'TRIPS-plus-plus'[49] TPP IP chapter is less of a step from present IP standards than it would have been had

---

45 'Study shows TPP would boost U.S. Income, Divert Trade from China' (11 January 2013) 31(2) *Inside US Trade* (online).

46 Kolsky Lewis, above n 41.

47 The Hon. Simon Crean, Minister for Trade, 'The Trans Pacific Partnership: Australia to Join Efforts to Promote Free Trade in the Asia Pacific' (Ministerial Statement, 26 November 2008) <http://trademinister.gov.au/speeches/2008/081126_tpp.html>.

48 Kolsky Lewis, above n 41, 50–51 (citations omitted).

49 The first generation of post-TRIPS IP chapters in bilateral trade agreements – such as those found in the United States FTAs concluded between 2000 and 2007 – have been described as 'TRIPS-plus' as they affirm the TRIPS

countries not already been obliged to implement high standards of IP protection as a result of their membership of the WTO and TRIPS. If the choice confronting a state was between developed country IP standards in a TPP on the one hand, and a highly idiosyncratic, nationally tailored innovation system on the other, the TPP would be a much more daunting (and perhaps deal-breaking) commitment.

Nevertheless, the content of any IP chapter will affect the attractiveness of a finalised TPP both for negotiating parties and future potential members. These regional aspirations are therefore one factor impacting on the negotiations that trade negotiators have not had to consider in past international IP deal-making.

It seems likely that ASEAN-based competition for a pathway to an FTAAP, such as the RCEP, would have an IP chapter very different from anything likely to emerge from negotiations involving the US. Although countries like Australia and Singapore might propose aspects of the US model (because they have already adopted these laws), without the US prioritising such provisions they seem unlikely to be adopted. In addition, China and India would likely be involved in an ASEAN-based initiative. It is difficult to see these major powers as being willing to accept strong, detailed IP standards. Current arrangements between ASEAN and India, and between ASEAN and China, do not include commitments on IP beyond general agreements to consult and cooperate.[50] US proposals for criminal enforcement would be inconsistent with China's domestic law

---

standards and then add additional protections for IP rights. More recent agreements, which take these bilateral standards and then add still more, have been described as 'TRIPS-plus-plus' to differentiate them from the earlier agreements.

50 See *Framework Agreement on Comprehensive Economic Cooperation Between the Republic of India and the Association of Southeast Asian Nations*, signed 8 October 2003 (entered into force 1 July 2004), which includes a general agreement to cooperate in art 3; *Protocol to Amend the Framework Agreement on Comprehensive Economic Cooperation between the Association of Southeast Asian Nations and the Republic of India*, signed 13 August 2009 (entered into force 1 January 2010), which contains no provisions on intellectual property; *Agreement on Trade in Goods Under the Framework Agreement on Comprehensive Economic Cooperation between the Association of Southeast Asian Nations and the Republic of India*, signed 8 October 2003 (entered into force 1 July 2004), which contains no provisions on intellectual property. In 2009 China and ASEAN signed a *2009 Memorandum of Understanding between the Governments of the Member States of the Association of Southeast Asian Nations and the Government of the People's Republic of China on Cooperation in the Field of Intellectual Property*, signed 21 December 2009 (not yet in force), consisting of several articles to increase cooperation, consultation and coordination but containing no new standards or obligations on IP rights or enforcement.

and would roll back the recognition for its laws won in a WTO dispute.[51] US proposals on patents and pharmaceuticals, even at the level of the *South Korea–United States Free Trade Agreement*, let alone as envisaged in TEAM, would require significant legal changes and be devastating to the significant Indian generic pharmaceutical industry. Both China and India have also expressed concern about heightened IP enforcement.[52] Further, ASEAN cooperation on IP has historically focused on voluntary measures, practical cooperation and proposals for more integration of IP registration offices rather than trying to set new IP standards.[53] The IP chapter of the *ASEAN–Australia–New Zealand Free Trade Agreement* (AANZFTA),[54] which was concluded in 2009 and came into force in 2012, could be some guide to what might be expected in an RCEP. Chapter 13 of the AANZFTA includes a few short obligations relating to copyright and trade marks, affirms existing international agreements such as TRIPS, but is mostly focused on cooperation of various kinds: for example, capacity building, and cooperation on administration, IP registration systems, education, enforcement, border measures and the implementation of multilateral agreements. The chapter also establishes an IP Committee to monitor the agreement – effectively, to monitor these various forms of cooperation.

In summary, although the RCEP is far less advanced than negotiations on the TPP, it represents a possible future competitor for a regional framework: one which is likely to contain provisions on IP more palatable to regional powers than anything the US might push in the TPP. Detailed provisions of the kind that the US favours would be very difficult, politically and economically, for regional powers like China and India, at least for the short to mid-term. Whether the TPP negotiators will

---

51 Panel Report, *China – Measures Affecting the Protection and Enforcement of Intellectual Property Rights*, WTO Doc WT/DS362/R (26 January 2009). The Panel found that China was entitled to maintain numerical minimum thresholds for criminal prosecutions.

52 Both countries made critical statements concerning IP enforcement moves including ACTA at the July 2010 meeting of the TRIPS Council. A summary of the meeting and discussion is published on the WTO's website, see World Trade Organization, *Council Debates Anti-counterfeiting Talks, Patents on Life* (8–9 June 2010) <http://www.wto.org/english/news_e/news10_e/trip_08jun10_e.htm>.

53 Discussed from various angles in the assorted chapters in Christoph Antons, Michael Blakeney and Christopher Heath (eds), *Intellectual Property Harmonisation with ASEAN and APEC* (Kluwer Law International, 2004).

54 *Agreement Establishing the ASEAN–Australia–New Zealand Free Trade Area*, signed Thailand 27 February 2009, [2010] ATS 1 (entered into force 1 January 2010).

be able to overcome the pressures to reach an agreement that will satisfy the existing negotiating countries and domestic constituencies for now, in the interests of creating a truly open framework that can accommodate other countries and other interests, is a very interesting question.

B A New Hostility in the Public Policy Environment

A second new dynamic affecting the TPP IP negotiations arises out of public and international controversies in 2011–12 over proposals to strengthen IP enforcement. In itself, controversy regarding stronger IP law is not new. Software protection in the 1980s, digital and online copyright issues in the 1990s, and access to medicines issues around the AIDS pandemic in the late 1990s and early 2000s have all given rise to considerable debate. Nor is controversy over the relationship between IP law and trade and the implications of setting domestic IP standards in trade agreements a new development. When Australia concluded an FTA with the US in 2004, the IP chapter was criticised by a strikingly broad cross-section of interest groups, commentators and the public.[55]

However, the period 2011–12 saw IP laws and enforcement take on a new salience, even to the level of massed public demonstrations. There were two key catalysts for popular concern. The first was the proposed Stop Online Piracy Act,[56] or SOPA, in the US. SOPA would have increased copyright and trade mark enforcement in the online environment by requiring the domain name system, search engines, and financial services providers like credit card companies to cut off services and access to alleged pirate sites.[57] Concern about SOPA entered the general public consciousness on 18 January 2012 as a result of an internet 'blackout', where many sites, most notably Wikipedia, 'went dark' entirely or posted notices protesting the legislation, generating considerable US and global media coverage and millions of signatures on

---

55 Robert Burrell and Kimberlee Weatherall, 'Exporting Controversy? Reactions to the Copyright Provisions of the US–Australia Free Trade Agreement: Lessons for US Trade Policy' (2008) 2 *University of Illinois Journal of Law, Technology and Policy* 259.

56 Stop Online Piracy Act (SOPA), H.R. 3261, 112th Cong. (2011).

57 For a description of this legislation, see generally Yochai Benkler, 'Wikileaks and the PROTECT-IP Act: A New Public–Private Threat to the Internet Commons' (2011) 140 *Daedelus* 154; Kimberlee Weatherall, 'Evaluating SOPA: Who Should Enforce IP Online?' (2012) 62(4) *Telecommunications Journal of Australia* 59.1.

petitions.[58] Prior to these events, SOPA had strong bipartisan support in both chambers of Congress and was expected to pass.[59] Afterwards, Congressional support collapsed.[60]

The second flashpoint was an international plurilateral agreement on IP enforcement, ACTA. Although ACTA was concluded and published in late 2010, it was signed by many countries in late 2011, and debates over its ratification and implementation in Europe occurred in early 2012, when opponents could capitalise on the immediate aftermath of SOPA to raise public awareness of, and opposition to, the treaty. Mass protests were organised across Europe,[61] and a petition calling on Members of the European Parliament to reject ACTA attracted more than 2 million signatures.[62] In response, the European Parliament overwhelmingly rejected the agreement.[63] Through 2012 ACTA struggled to gain acceptance internationally – 12 months after its conclusion only Japan had ratified the agreement and an Australian Parliamentary Committee, the Joint Standing Committee on Treaties, expressed considerable reservations.[64]

The public outcry over both SOPA and ACTA is relevant to the TPP negotiations at two levels. First and most obviously, it suggests that an IP chapter that strengthens IP enforcement in any significant way, particularly one that includes provisions similar to those in SOPA or in ACTA,

---

58 Kimberlee Weatherall, 'Three Lessons from ACTA and its Political Aftermath' (2012) 35 *Suffolk Transnational Law Review* 575, 584–585 (for details on the public response to SOPA).

59 Yochai Benkler, 'Seven Lessons from SOPA/PIPA/Megaupload and Four Proposals on Where We Go from Here' on *TechPresident* (25 January 2012) <http://techpresident.com/news/21680/seven-lessons-sopapipamegauplaod-and-four-proposals-where-we-go-here>.

60 By 20 January 2012, two days after the Internet blackout, it had been announced that PIPA would not go to the floor of the Senate: ibid. See also Jim Abrams, 'Lawmakers Try to Keep Anti-Piracy Bills on Track', *Associated Press* (Washington), 19 January 2012. PIPA, or the Preventing Real Online Threats to Economic Creativity and Theft of Intellectual Property Act, S. 968, 112th Cong. (2011), was the Senate equivalent SOPA, which was a House bill.

61 Dave Lee, *ACTA: Europe Braced for Protests Over Anti-Piracy Treaty* (6 February 2012) BBC News <http://www.bbc.co.uk/news/technology-16906086>.

62 Don Melvin, 'European Parliament Rejects ACTA Anti-Piracy Pact', *Associated Press* (Brussels), 5 July 2012.

63 The parliamentary vote on ACTA saw 478 against and 39 in favour, with 165 abstentions: ibid.

64 Joint Standing Committee on Treaties, Parliament of Australia, *Report 126: Treaty Tabled 21 November 2011: Anti-Counterfeiting Trade Agreement (Tokyo on 1 October 2011)* (2012).

could engender another negative public response and undermine support for the TPP. Secondly, the objections to both SOPA and ACTA have been partly driven by their substance, but also by the perception that they were drafted for the benefit of corporate interests with little consideration of, or input from, user interests or civil society generally.[65] ACTA was condemned as a 'secret treaty' negotiated without transparency; SOPA too was perceived as having been written by IP-owning interests with no user input and presented to the United States Congress as an unbalanced *fait accompli*. Despite later publication of draft text and considerable watering-down of its provisions, ACTA has never shaken its image as a secret, draconian treaty. As a trade agreement negotiated behind closed doors with no opportunity for public commentary on text – but with corporate input via the United States' advisory committee system – any IP chapter in the TPP will almost inevitably be subject to similar criticism. The substance of the chapter may affect the vehemence of the reaction, but some criticism is inevitable.

The course of the TPP negotiations in 2012 appeared to make some concession to this new dynamic, with the US proposing provisions in copyright described as promoting 'balance' and protecting user interests through copyright exceptions.[66] According to the USTR, the proposal would obligate parties to seek to achieve an appropriate balance in their copyright systems in providing copyright exceptions and limitations.[67] The significance of this proposal should not be underestimated. It represents a first for the US, which has in the past been criticised for exporting only the IP-protective aspects of its law in its bilateral

---

[65] This criticism has been widely made, see, e.g., David Levine, 'Transparency Soup: the ACTA Negotiating Process and "Black Box" Lawmaking' (2011) 26 *American University Law Review* 811; Yu, above n 12.

[66] See 'U.S. Tables New Proposal in TPP Outlining Broader Copyright Exceptions' (6 July 2012) 30(27) *Inside US Trade* (online), noting that 'U.S. trade officials may be hoping that this incremental step may build goodwill in the negotiations, thereby helping to unlock other tough areas in the IPR chapter later on', and also noting that the proposal has been seen as a response to developments in relation to ACTA. The copyright exceptions proposal is also a culmination of significant lobbying efforts by United States' internet industries: 'Internet Groups Push USTR For More Exceptions in TPP IPR Proposals' (9 March 2012) 30(10) *Inside US Trade* (online). As this story notes, events relating to ACTA and SOPA including public concern about the same may well have galvanised these lobbying efforts.

[67] Office of the United States Trade Representative, 'USTR Introduces New Copyright Exceptions and Limitations Provision at San Diego TPP Talks' (Press Release, 3 July 2012).

negotiations, without extending its own relatively generous and at times anomalous exceptions. Regardless of whether there are good theoretical reasons to leave exceptions out of international agreements,[68] the resulting lack of balance has made it easy for opponents to generate concern about IP chapters in the broader community.[69]

The concession was limited, however: it was clear from public announcements (and even more clear once the text was leaked) that the language proposed for promoting 'balance' was aspirational or exhortatory, and would create no binding obligations, in stark contrast to the numerous, specific rights granted to right-holders. In addition, the right to introduce exceptions would be 'subject to' the three-step test: a model for limiting exceptions found in existing multilateral copyright agreements such as the *Berne Convention* and TRIPS.[70] The three-step test has been perceived, in recent times, to be unduly limiting on copyright exceptions, at least as interpreted in the one international decision to consider it,[71] and, as commentators pointed out, the leaked text suggested that even exceptions which are not currently subject to the test would be rolled in, meaning that copyright exceptions well established in domestic law could become open to challenge.[72]

In summary, a significant number of commentators and a not insubstantial number of members of the general public have responded with scepticism or even downright hostility to recent proposals to strengthen IP law and IP enforcement. The potential for such protests in response to a TPP IP chapter must have played on the minds of the negotiators, as suggested by the unprecedented US proposal for balancing provisions. However, this limited concession to the need for balance in IP sits beside

---

68 Jane Ginsburg, 'International Copyright: From a "Bundle" of National Copyright Laws to a Supranational Code?' (2000) 47 *Journal of the Copyright Society of USA* 265, 287.

69 See, for example, the reaction of Australian Parliamentarians and the broader community to the IP chapter of AUSFTA: Burrell and Weatherall, above n 55. See also my discussion of the need for international agreements to affirm copyright exceptions in Weatherall, above n 33.

70 *Berne Convention for the Protection of Literary and Artistic Works*, as amended and opened for signature 24 July 1971, 1161 UNTS 31 (entered into force 15 December 1972) art 9(2); TRIPS art 13.

71 Panel Report, *United–States – Section 110(5) of the US Copyright Act*, WTO Doc WT/DS160/R (15 June 2000).

72 William New, 'US Proposes 3-Step Test for Copyright Exceptions in Trans-Pacific Trade Talks' on *Intellectual Property Watch* (4 July 2012) <http://www.ip-watch.org/2012/07/04/us-proposes-3-step-test-for-copyright-exceptions-in-trans-pacific-trade-talks/>.

other US proposals to strengthen IP even in developing countries, as embodied in its suggestions regarding patents and pharmaceuticals mentioned earlier in this chapter. Thus whether the negotiators will do enough to stave off a hostile public response must be considered doubtful.

C Increased Complexity and an Uncertain Multilateral Future

A third new factor impacting on the TPP IP negotiations is the increased complexity and fragmentation of the international IP legal environment, which creates uncertainty regarding the future for any TPP IP provisions and complicates the potential impact of any IP chapter and hence the calculus of a country's interests in the negotiations.

It used to be that commentators could tell a tale of ever-rising international IP obligations. They would point to detailed IP chapters in bilateral trade agreements and argue that they represented the first stage of a conscious strategy on the part of countries like the US aiming at the eventual incorporation of these higher IP standards into multilateral treaties. TRIPS-plus provisions in multiple FTAs would become at least a starting point, and possibly even a floor, for future multilateral negotiations.[73] As evidence of this 'ratcheting-up' process, commentators have pointed to the negotiation of TRIPS, where bilateral mechanisms were used to break down developing country resistance to stronger IP protections prior to the Uruguay round of negotiations for the WTO.[74]

But it is important to note certain features of the pre-TRIPS period. Many of the obligations in TRIPS were based on existing multilateral conventions: in particular, the *Berne* and *Paris Conventions* dealing with copyright and industrial IP rights respectively. Although the parties to these conventions prior to TRIPS largely comprised developed countries and their (former) colonies, nevertheless they represented a broad baseline agreed by multiple countries. Insofar as TRIPS went further, differences between the major developed country players were ironed out so that TRIPS represented the compromise text. The bilateral agreements

---

[73] Bryan Mercurio, 'TRIPS-Plus Provisions in FTAs: Recent Trends' in Lorand Bartels and Federico Ortino (eds), *Regional Trade Agreements and the WTO Legal System* (Oxford University Press, 2006) 215, 223.

[74] Drahos with Braithwaite, above n 11; Peter Drahos, 'BITs and BIPs: Bilateralism in Intellectual Property' (2001) 4 *Journal of World Intellectual Property* 791.

reached prior to TRIPS were focused on bringing developing countries up to the *Berne* and *Paris Convention* standards.[75]

The picture has, however, become much more complicated in recent times as compared with the 1990s. IP chapters in trade agreements of the kind the US has negotiated (and proposed for the TPP) embody standards so technology-specific, and based so closely on US law, that they are highly unlikely ever to be 'multilateralised' in the way that pre-TRIPS bilateral agreements were. As a colleague and I have previously noted, given the state of the EU *acquis communautaire* on IP, there is little chance of the EU signing up to the United States' standards on digital copyright, criminal enforcement, or the United States' insistence that all IP rights be freely transferable by contract.[76] Indeed, as the ACTA negotiations revealed, there are many other differences on the appropriate rules for IP enforcement between the EU and US (and other, generally IP-friendly countries involved in those negotiations) that could only be resolved by adopting high-level and general language with many optional provisions. ACTA tells us as much about the differences between developed nations on the details of IP law as it does about common ground.[77] In addition, no meaningful new international standard could emerge without the support of countries such as China, India, and Brazil, and they are equally unlikely to sign up to the United States' detailed standards.[78]

Whether provisions are, or are likely to be, adopted multilaterally or not matters, and the risk that the TPP IP provisions will not be acceptable at a multilateral level should give parties to the TPP negotiations some pause. Countries that are not net exporters of IP – which is most of the world – can suffer real competitive disadvantage from adopting stronger or longer IP laws than competitor countries. For example, if a country is required to recognise more and longer patent protection for pharmaceuticals, it may become a less attractive base for generic pharmaceutical manufacture, since generics companies will prefer to manufacture in countries where patents expire earliest. Signing up, therefore, to higher standards that will *not* be multilateralised risks locking in a long-term competitive disadvantage in attracting certain industries.

Further, differences between the major powers coupled with detailed provisions in trade deals leads to a multiplicity of different – and

---

75 Drahos with Braithwaite, above n 11.

76 Burrell and Weatherall, above n 55, 314–315.

77 Weatherall, above n 33.

78 Burrell and Weatherall, above n 55, 315.

potentially inconsistent – IP standards. Signing up to one set of (US-oriented) IP standards in the TPP could preclude, or at least complicate, trade deals with other major players or other multi-party IP negotiations such as those occurring in WIPO. The US and EU have pursued standards in bilateral agreements that may not be consistent, particularly in areas such as geographical indications. Signing up to detailed standards in an agreement with the United States could actually render a later trade deal with the EU more difficult. It may not be possible to predict even now which detailed provisions will cause such conflict. Detailed IP enforcement provisions in the TPP could also complicate negotiations occurring in WIPO around exceptions for the visually impaired and for institutions such as educational institutions and libraries.[79] Thus, again, a negotiating country should pause before signing up to detailed chapters that will either prevent other countries joining the TPP, prevent the signatory country from entering other trade deals with countries in other regions, or block other multilateral initiatives.

Even if the TPP does not create IP provisions that are in direct conflict with those negotiated in other trade agreements or other multilateral fora, the multiplication of IP standards in different agreements must complicate the role of bureaucrats and policymakers responsible for ensuring that domestic law and practice complies with these varying standards.

In sum, the international environment for IP standard-setting has become exceedingly complicated. Instead of a 'one-way global IP ratchet' we now have 'an every-which-way global IP ratchet'.[80] This fragmentation significantly complicates the calculus for negotiating parties, particularly those other than the US. The fact that detailed provisions are unlikely to be able to be elevated to a multilateral level, and the potential for conflict with other trade partners would suggest that most parties to the negotiations would be better served by a more general,

---

[79] For example, it is not clear how prescriptive anti-circumvention provisions such as those found in the Australia–US FTA or South Korea–US FTA are consistent with any potential obligation, under a WIPO Instrument on Limitations and Exceptions for Visually Impaired Persons, to ensure that beneficiaries of such an instrument can get access to material otherwise subject to technological locks: compare article F of the *Draft Text for an International Instrument/Treaty on Limitations and Exceptions for Visually Impaired Persons/ Persons with Print Disabilities,* SCCR/25/2 Rev. (22 February 2013) to AUSFTA art 17.4.7.

[80] Weatherall, above n 33, 871.

abstract, high-level text focused on cooperation rather than standard-setting. Whether this can be achieved in the face of the factors driving the US negotiators and the pressure to reach an overall deal remains to be seen.

IMPLICATIONS AND CONCLUSIONS

Despite the challenges and the 'currents and cross-currents'[81] described here, any TPP which emerges from the present negotiations will have an IP chapter. IP has become a fixture of comprehensive 'twenty-first century' trade agreements of the kind to which the TPP negotiators aspire. Even the document setting out the likely framework for the rival ASEAN initiative, the RCEP, names IP as an issue to be dealt with. The real question, therefore, is what kind of IP chapter can be negotiated in a TPP, and the significance and implications of any resulting text.

For all the usual reasons, the TPP IP negotiations have proved to be contentious. The parties started far apart in their interests and priorities; the US, as usual, entered the negotiating room with an extraordinarily detailed, idiosyncratic and ambitious plan. But, as this chapter has also sought to demonstrate, there are new factors that have complicated the environment within which the TPP negotiations have occurred. The negotiators have had to consider whether proposed text will stand in the way of the regional aspirations for the TPP, and whether the short-term gains from reaching an agreement that is acceptable to the parties in the room will be outweighed by the barrier such a text will pose to other important regional countries. They have had to consider the potential public fallout of IP-protective provisions in light of heightened public sensitivity in a post-SOPA, post-ACTA world. And they have had to consider the potential impact of TPP provisions on goals they, as individual countries, may have of negotiating further trade deals with other major players and the long-term implications of being locked into a heightened IP position that will not be multilateralised and that could create competitive disadvantage.

The dynamic affecting these negotiations might, therefore, be described as a conflict between short-term interests and long-term interests, and between the achievements of the past and the new political reality. The new dynamics affecting these particular negotiations all

---

[81] To borrow a phrase from Peter Yu, 'Currents and Cross-Currents in the International Intellectual Property Regime' (2004) 38 *Loyola of Los Angeles Law Review* 323.

suggest that the best IP chapter would be one that is relatively high level and abstract – affirming existing consensus standards, affirming the need for balance in IP law, accommodating the particular interests of developing countries, and perhaps building in mechanisms for ongoing cooperation. Such a chapter would be more palatable for the existing negotiating parties (other than the US) but, more importantly, it would be more attractive to other potential regional partners. It would also be less objectionable to the public, which has become interested in international IP negotiations, and it would not stand in the way of other trade deals for the negotiating parties with, for example, Europe. However, such a chapter would inevitably be inconsistent with the USTR's more immediate goal of achieving an IP chapter that can be accepted by the US Congress. And given USTR's need to conclude such an agreement, efforts to push for a more high-level chapter are likely to stand in the way of the immediate goal of all negotiators of reaching a deal.

Predictions are odious, but the most likely outcome of such a complicated set of negotiations with so many countervailing dynamics must be a messy compromise IP text of the kind we saw come out of the (also plurilateral) ACTA negotiations. It will likely contain 'blurry text', the meaning of which is unclear, allowing various parties to claim a 'victory'.[82] It will likely contain provisions that offer a series of alternatives rather than one specific choice.[83] It will likely also, like ACTA, include detailed provisions but framed as optional, rather than compulsory, reflecting areas where the parties have been unable to agree. Since the short-term aims of concluding an agreement seem likely to prevail over longer-term considerations relevant to creating a true regional framework, the chapter is likely to contain more IP-protective provisions than would be optimal in order to give the TPP the best chance of becoming a pathway to an FTAAP.

---

82 See Kimberlee Weatherall, 'Politics, Compromise, Text, and the Failures of the Anti-Counterfeiting Trade Agreement' (2011) 33 *Sydney Law Review* 229, 243–261 (outlining various aspects of the ACTA text that are unclear as to their intended meaning and effect).

83 For an example, see art 9 of ACTA, which addresses damages and statutory damages, discussed ibid., 254–259. The provision sanctions statutory damages, presumptions as to damages, and 'additional' damages as acceptable alternatives. The fact that these systems are quite different, with different results and different goals, makes the intended effect of ACTA unclear and could in the future lead to some conflict between ACTA parties if the agreement ever comes into effect.

What are the implications of such an IP chapter? Such a chapter will, first and foremost, contribute to, rather than help to control, the increasing fragmentation of international IP lawmaking. Assuming the detail in the TPP IP chapter is different from that found in other bilateral deals and any future multilateral agreements, the complexities facing both bureaucrats and businesses seeking to ascertain their rights and obligations will be considerable. Uncertainty will be increased, not decreased, by such a text. Domestic lawmaking will be complicated by questions of what is permissible under the multiple sources of obligation to which individual countries are subject. And, it has to be said, all this legislative and bureaucratic complexity may well distract from what ought to be the overall goal of IP – finding ways to encourage creativity and innovation. This would not, however, be the first time that bureaucratic and institutional imperatives and political realities have stood in the way of the best possible trade agreement.

5. Plain packaging for the Pacific Rim – tobacco control and the Trans-Pacific Partnership

Matthew Rimmer

> Kids today don't just start smoking for no reason. They're aggressively targeted as customers by the tobacco industry. They're exposed to a constant and insidious barrage of advertising where they live, where they learn, and where they play.[1] (United States President Barack Obama)

INTRODUCTION

Big Tobacco has been engaged in a dark, shadowy plot and conspiracy to hijack the Trans-Pacific Partnership Agreement (TPP) and undermine tobacco control measures – such as graphic health warnings and the plain packaging of tobacco products. The tobacco industry has long considered the use of trade agreements as a means of delaying, blocking and frustrating the introduction of tobacco control measures.[2] In the 1990s, internal documents highlight that the tobacco industry considered whether the use of trade actions under the World Trade Organization (WTO) may delay the introduction of measures, such as the plain packaging of tobacco products. However, there was an admission in the internal memos that such action would provide 'little joy' for the tobacco companies.[3] A number of countries allied to the tobacco industry have

[1] President Barack Obama, 'Remarks by the President' (Speech delivered at the signing of the *Family Smoking Prevention and Tobacco Control Act*, White House Rose Garden, 22 June 2009) <http://www.whitehouse.gov/the-press-office/remarks-president-signing-family-smoking-prevention-and-tobacco-control-act>.

[2] Becky Freeman, Simon Chapman and Matthew Rimmer, 'The Case for the Plain Packaging of Tobacco Products' (2008) 103(4) *Addiction* 580.

[3] British American Tobacco, *DB Presentation to GM's Conference* (21 July 1994) Legacy Tobacco Documents Library <http://legacy.library.ucsf.edu/tid/hpp34a99>.

challenged Australia's plain packaging of tobacco products regime under the *Agreement on Trade-Related Aspects of Intellectual Property Rights* (TRIPS)[4] and the *Agreement on Technical Barriers to Trade*.[5] British American Tobacco has lobbied the United States Trade Representative on intellectual property and trade.[6] In the course of the *Anti-Counterfeiting Trade Agreement* (ACTA)[7] discussions, British American Tobacco argued: 'We would strongly advocate tobacco and tobacco products being prioritized in the course of the negotiations when specific areas of concern are being addressed.'[8]

The TPP is a blockbuster, plurilateral free trade agreement, spanning the Pacific Rim.[9] There has been concern that tobacco companies have been seeking to use this trade agreement to undermine tobacco control measures – such as graphic health warnings and the plain packaging of tobacco products – and the implementation of the *WHO Framework Convention on Tobacco Control*.[10] Philip Morris made a submission to the United States Trade Representative on the TPP, emphasising: 'We strongly support U.S. participation in the TPP negotiations, and welcome the future expansion of this initiative to include additional countries in

---

4 *Marrakesh Agreement Establishing the World Trade Organization*, opened for signature 15 April 1994, 1867 UNTS 3 (entered into force 1 January 1995) annex 1C ('*Agreement on Trade-Related Aspects of Intellectual Property Rights*').

5 *Marrakesh Agreement Establishing the World Trade Organization*, opened for signature 15 April 1994, 1867 UNTS 3 (entered into force 1 January 1995) annex 1A ('*Agreement on Technical Barriers to Trade*').

6 See, e.g., Office of the United States Trade Representative, *Vol. 1 Anti-Counterfeiting Trade Agreement Public Comments* (7 August 2008) 18.

7 *Anti-Counterfeiting Trade Agreement*, signed 1 October 2011, [2011] ATNIF 22, not yet in force.

8 Office of the United States Trade Representative, above n 6, 18.

9 See *Enhancing Trade and Investment, Supporting Jobs, Economic Growth and Development: Outlines of the Trans-Pacific Partnership Agreement* (November 2011) Office of the United States Trade Representative <http://www.ustr.gov/about-us/press-office/fact-sheets/2011/november/outlines-trans-pacific-partnership-agreement>; *The Trans-Pacific Partnership Agreement Negotiations*, Australian Government, Department of Foreign Affairs and Trade <http://www.dfat.gov.au/fta/tpp/index.html>. For an overview, see Ian Fergusson et al., 'The Trans-Pacific Partnership Negotiations and Issues for Congress' (CRS Report for Congress No R42694, Congressional Research Service, 15 April 2013) <http://www.fas.org/sgp/crs/row/R42694.pdf>.

10 *WHO Framework Convention on Tobacco Control*, opened for signature 21 May 2003, 2302 UNTS 166 (entered into force 27 February 2005).

the Asia-Pacific region.'[11] The company has even sponsored a trade reception, involving many of the participants in the negotiations.[12] The treaty negotiations have included members of the Pacific Rim – such as Australia, New Zealand, Brunei Darussalam, Malaysia, Singapore, Vietnam, Peru, Chile, Canada, Mexico and the United States. In April 2013, Japan was included in the TPP negotiations.[13] Thailand has been approached by the United States Government to join the negotiations. In this context, there has been concern about the extent to which tobacco control measures of negotiating nations will be affected by the TPP (see Table 5.1).

There has been debate as to whether the TPP has undermined democratic decision-making processes by elected representatives – particularly in respect of public health.[14] There has been much concern about the lack of transparency, due process, and public participation in the TPP.[15] Lori Wallach of Public Citizen has described the proposed agreement as 'NAFTA on Steroids', saying: 'Think of the TPP as a stealthy delivery mechanism for policies that could not survive public scrutiny.'[16] A number of those with inside access to the TPP have an interest in tobacco and tobacco control – including Roger Quarles of the Burley Tobacco Growers Cooperative Association Inc, Clyde N. Wayne Jr. of Tobacco Associates Inc, and Monique Muggli of the Campaign for

---

[11] Philip Morris International, Submission No USTR-2009-0041-0016 to Office of the United States Trade Representative, *Request for Comments Concerning the Proposed Trans-Pacific Partnership Trade Agreement*, 22 January 2010, 2.

[12] Hayden Donnell, 'Ambassador to US "Should be Sacked"', *The New Zealand Herald* (online), 27 February 2012 <http://www.nzherald.co.nz/nz/news/article.cfm?c_id=1&objectid=10788367>.

[13] Office of the United States Trade Representative, 'Obama Administration Notifies Congress of Intent to Include Japan in Trans-Pacific Partnership Negotiations' (Press Release, 24 April 2013) <http://www.ustr.gov/about-us/press-office/press-releases/2013/april/congressional-notification-japan-tpp>.

[14] Inside Story Americas, 'Will the Pacific Trade Deal Protect Workers?', *Al-Jazeera*, 5 December 2012 <http://www.aljazeera.com/programmes/inside storyamericas/2012/12/2012125101118819500.html>.

[15] Carolina Rossini, 'Congress Members Demand USTR Tell the American People What's Going on with the Trans-Pacific Partnership and its Impact on Digital Freedom' on *Deeplinks Blog* (5 September 2012) <https://www.eff.org/deeplinks/2012/09/congress-demand-ustr-reveal-tpp>.

[16] Lori Wallach, 'NAFTA on Steroids', *The Nation* (New York), 16 July 2012 <http://www.thenation.com/article/168627/nafta-steroids>.

Table 5.1 World Health Organization Tobacco Control Profiles for Participants in the TPP

Country	Ratification of *WHO Framework Convention on Tobacco Control*	Adult prevalence, smoking current	Health warnings	Health warnings include picture or graphic	Plain packaging
United States	Not ratified	27.0%	Yes	Yes (under review)	No
Canada	26 November 2004	19.5%	Yes	Yes	No
Mexico	28 May 2004	15.9%	Yes	Yes	No
Peru	30 November 2004	NA	Yes	Yes	No
Chile	13 June 2005	35%	Yes	Yes	No
Australia	27 October 2004	16.6%	Yes	Yes	Yes (as of 2012)
New Zealand	27 January 2004	19.9%	Yes	Yes – cigarettes	Yes (agreed 2013)
Malaysia	16 September 2005	26%	Yes	Yes – cigarettes	No
Singapore	14 May 2004	21%	Yes	Yes	No
Vietnam	17 December 2004	23.8%	Yes	No	No
Brunei Darussalam	3 June 2004	18 %	Yes	Yes – cigarettes	No
Japan	8 June 2004	27%	Yes	No	No
Thailand (possible member)	8 November 2004	24%	Yes	Yes – cigarettes large warnings	No
The Philippines (possible member)	6 June 2005	28%	Yes	No	No

Source: Data compiled from World Health Organization country profiles: see World Health Organization, *Tobacco Control Country Profiles* <http://www.who.int/tobacco/surveillance/policy/country_profile/en/index.html>.

Tobacco-Free Kids.[17] Although trade officials and members of trade committees have had access to the texts, the texts have not been made available to politicians, civil society, or the wider public. Wallach has argued that civil activists should pursue a 'Dracula' strategy to bring the TPP out of the twilight and into the sunshine of public debate.[18]

The Kentucky delegation in the United States Congress has lobbied the United States Trade Representative on behalf of tobacco companies.[19] In October 2011, a number of United States Congressmen and women from Kentucky – led by Representative Geoff Davis and Senator Mitch McConnell – wrote to Ambassador Kirk, expressing their 'strong opposition to requests to exclude products, specifically tobacco, from the Trans-Pacific Partnership Agreement … negotiations'.[20] The submission emphasised: 'Excluding specific products from the TPPA could have a serious impact on future trade agreement negotiations and significantly damage Kentucky's economy.'[21] The Kentucky delegation made a crude slippery slope argument that the exclusion of tobacco would lead to the exclusion of other products, such as alcohol and dairy products: 'Excluding tobacco from the TPP would establish a broad and possibly economically debilitating precedent potentially applicable to any industry.'[22] The Kentucky politicians maintained that there was a need to include tobacco trade in the TPP in order to protect American jobs:

---

[17] *Agricultural Technical Advisory Committee for Trade,* Office of the United States Trade Representative <http://www.ustr.gov/about-us/intergovernmental-affairs/advisory-committees/agricultural-technical-advisory-committee-tra>.

[18] Lori Wallach, 'Can a "Dracula" Strategy Bring Out the Trans-Pacific Partnership into the Sunlight' on *Truthout* (30 November 2012) <http://truth-out.org/news/item/13061-can-a-dracula-strategy-bring-trans-pacific-partnership-into-the-sunlight>.

[19] See, for instance: *Tobacco's Status in the Trade Transaction is Disputed* (14 March 2012) Tobacco Facts <http://www.tobacco-facts.net/2012/03/tobaccos-status-in-the-trade-transaction-is-disputed>; Paul Hornback and Wilson Stone, 'Plan to Exclude Tobacco from Trade Pact Unfair to State of Kentucky: Farm Families Deserve Level Playing Field', *Kentucky.com*, 2 April 2012 <http://www.kentucky.com/2012/04/02/2135891/plan-to-exclude-tobacco-from-trade.html>.

[20] Letter from Representatives Geoff Davis, Harold Rogers, Ed Whitfield, Ben Chandler, John Yarnruth and Ben Guthrie and Senators Mitch McConnell and Rand Paul to the United States Trade Representative (7 October 2011) <http://waysandmeans.house.gov/uploadedfiles/sfr_tpp_david.pdf>.

[21] Ibid.

[22] Ibid.

> As over eighty percent of tobacco grown in Kentucky is exported to other countries, the exclusion of tobacco products from the TPPA threatens our growers' business and could harm the communities where they live and employ Kentuckians.[23]

Similarly, Congressman Sanford Bishop from Georgia – along with other representatives and senators for Georgia – wrote a letter to Ambassador Kirk, urging him to 'ensure that Georgia's tobacco farmers are not excluded from taking advantage of trade protections offered under the Trans-Pacific Partnership Agreement'.[24]

In May 2012, Congresswoman Renee Ellmers, a Republican from North Carolina, also published in support of trade in tobacco under the TPP.[25] She maintained that the tobacco industry had been the victim of unfair prejudice: 'Tobacco farmers deserve the same recognition and consideration as any other legal agricultural commodity.'[26] Congressman Mike McIntyre, also from North Carolina, argued: 'Including a safe harbor provision in the trade deal will treat tobacco unfairly, and the Administration needs to hear from the farming and business community that opposes this effort.'[27]

In the context of this heavy lobbying by Big Tobacco and its proxies, this chapter provides an analysis of the debate over trade, tobacco, and the TPP. This discussion is necessarily focused on the negotiations of the free trade agreement – the shadowy conflicts before the finalisation of the text. This chapter contends that the trade negotiations threaten hard-won gains in public health – including international developments such as the *WHO Framework Convention on Tobacco Control*, and domestic measures, such as graphic health warnings and the plain packaging of tobacco

---

23 Ibid.

24 Congressman Sanford D. Bishop, Jr, 'Bishop Seeks Trade Protections for Georgia's Tobacco Farmers' (Press Release, 2 December 2011) <http://bishop.house.gov/press-release/bishop-seeks-trade-protections-georgias-tobacco-farmers>.

25 Tom Doheny, *Ellmers Calls for Responsible Treatment of Tobacco Farmers in Trans-Pacific Partnership* (15 May 2012) Congresswoman Renee Ellmers <http://ellmers.house.gov/latest-news/ellmers-calls-for-responsible-treatment-of-tobacco-farmers-in-transpacific-partnership/>.

26 Ibid.

27 Congressman Mike McIntyre, 'USTR Heeds McIntyre's Call, Holds off Introduction of Tobacco Text in TPP to Gather Input from Tobacco Community' (Press Release, 15 May 2012) <http://mcintyre.house.gov/index.php?option=com_content&view=article&id=627:-ustr-heeds-mcintyres-call-holds-off-introduction-of-tobacco-text-in-tpp-to-gather-input-from-tobacco-community&catid=1:2010-press-releases&Itemid=26>.

products. It maintains that there is a need for regional trade agreements to respect the primacy of the *WHO Framework Convention on Tobacco Control*. There is a need both to provide for an open and transparent process regarding such trade negotiations, as well as a due and proper respect for public health in terms of substantive obligations. Part I focuses on the debate over the intellectual property chapter of the TPP, within the broader context of domestic litigation against Australia's plain tobacco packaging regime and associated WTO disputes. Part II examines the investment chapter of the TPP, taking account of ongoing investment disputes concerning tobacco control and the declared approaches of Australia and New Zealand to investor–state dispute settlement. Part III looks at the discussion as to whether there should be specific text on tobacco control in the TPP, and, if so, what should be its nature and content. This chapter concludes that the plain packaging of tobacco products – and other best practices in tobacco control – should be adopted by members of the Pacific Rim.

I INTELLECTUAL PROPERTY

In a number of contexts, the tobacco companies and their confederates have argued that the plain packaging of tobacco products amounts to a violation of their intellectual property rights.[28] Such arguments have been framed in terms of constitutional law, trade law, and investment law. The United States Chamber of Commerce's statements about the plain packaging of tobacco products are typical in this regard:

> We believe that the lack of distinguishing trade dress and labelling may ultimately result in an increased risk of consumer deception and confusion; may paradoxically result in unintended harm to public health; and would deny the property rights of companies and their workers who have invested in building their brand's reputation.[29]

This position represents an extremely aggressive form of intellectual property maximalism, which presumes that intellectual property rights can block government health regulation. Such a stance fails to recognise

---

[28] Freeman, Chapman and Rimmer, above n 2.

[29] United States Chamber of Commerce, Submission to the Department of Health and Ageing, *Public Consultation on the Exposure Draft of the Tobacco Plain Packaging Bill 2011*, 26 May 2011 <http://www.health.gov.au/internet/yourhealth/publishing.nsf/Content/Myron-Brilliant>.

that intellectual property law is intended to serve larger public objectives – including the protection of public health.

A The High Court of Australia

Professor Tania Voon has observed: 'Plain packaging of cigarettes and other tobacco products represents a crucial focal point for industry, government, and public health across the world today.'[30]

In order to support the *WHO Framework Convention on Tobacco Control*, the Australian Parliament passed the *Tobacco Plain Packaging Act 2011* (Cth), with the support of all the main political parties. In response, Japan Tobacco International[31] and British American Tobacco[32] brought legal action in the High Court of Australia, complaining that the *Tobacco Plain Packaging Act 2011* (Cth) amounted to an acquisition of property on less than just terms under s 51(xxxi) of the *Australian Constitution* 1901. Philip Morris Ltd and Imperial Tobacco intervened in the case, supporting their fellow tobacco companies. The Australian Government defended the constitutionality of the *Tobacco Plain Packaging Act 2011* (Cth).[33] The Australian Government was supported by the Cancer Council Australia and the governments of the Australian Capital Territory, the Northern Territory, and Queensland.

Having announced its ruling in August 2012, the High Court of Australia published the reasons for its decision on the tobacco companies' challenge to Australia's regime for the plain packaging of tobacco products in October 2012.[34] By a majority of six to one, the High Court of Australia rejected the arguments of the tobacco companies that there

---

[30] Tania Voon, 'Introduction' in Tania Voon et al. (eds), *Public Health and Plain Packaging of Cigarettes: Legal Issues* (Edward Elgar Publishing, 2012) 1, 1.

[31] *Case S409/2011: JT International SA v Commonwealth of Australia*, High Court of Australia <http://www.hcourt.gov.au/cases/case-s409/2011>.

[32] Case S389/2411: *British American Tobacco Australasia Limited and Ors v The Commonwealth of Australia*, High Court of Australia <http://www.hcourt.gov.au/cases/case-s389/2011>.

[33] Matthew Rimmer, 'Big Tobacco's Box Fetish: Plain Packaging at the High Court', *The Conversation* (20 April 2012) <http://theconversation.edu.au/big-tobaccos-box-fetish-plain-packaging-at-the-high-court-6518>.

[34] *JT International SA v Commonwealth of Australia* (2012) 291 ALR 669 ('*JT International*'). This discussion draws upon my piece: Matthew Rimmer, 'The High Court and the Marlboro Man: The Plain Packaging Decision', *The Conversation* (18 October 2012) <http://theconversation.edu.au/the-high-court-and-the-marlboro-man-the-plain-packaging-decision-10014>.

had been an acquisition of property under the *Australian Constitution* 1901. After listening to extensive arguments, the court closely considered the public health objectives of the *Tobacco Plain Packaging Act 2011* (Cth) and related regulations. Hayne and Bell JJ observed: 'Legislation that requires warning labels to be placed on products, even warning labels as extensive as those required by the *Plain Packaging Act*, effect no acquisition of property.'[35] The judges ruled that 'The *Plain Packaging Act* is not a law by which the Commonwealth acquires any interest in property, however slight or insubstantial it may be.'[36] The judges concluded: 'The *Plain Packaging Act* is not a law with respect to the acquisition of property.'[37]

Kiefel J emphasised: 'Many kinds of products have been subjected to regulation in order to prevent or reduce the likelihood of harm.'[38] Her Honour noted that labelling is required for medicines, poisonous substances as well as some food 'to both protect and promote public health'.[39] Discussing the history of tobacco regulation in Australia, she summarised the cumulative impact of public health measures and suggested plain packaging was but the latest of a long line of tobacco control measures in Australia.

Noting the links between smoking tobacco and fatal diseases, Crennan J observed that the regime implemented international health law: 'The objects of the *Packaging Act* are to improve public health and to give effect to certain obligations that Australia has as a party to the *WHO Framework Convention on Tobacco Control*.'[40] She insisted: 'Legislative provisions requiring manufacturers or retailers to place on product packaging warnings to consumers of the dangers of incorrectly using or positively misusing a product are commonplace.'[41]

French CJ emphasised the public policy dimensions of intellectual property law, noting that trade mark legislation has 'manifested from time to time a varying accommodation of commercial and the consuming public's interests'.[42]

---

35 *JT International* (2012) 291 ALR 669, 713.
36 Ibid., 714.
37 Ibid.
38 Ibid., 746.
39 Ibid.
40 Ibid.
41 Ibid., 729.
42 Ibid., 679, quoting *Campomar Sociedad, Limitada v Nike International Ltd* (2000) 202 CLR 45, 65.

Gummow J commented that 'trade mark legislation, in general, does not confer a "statutory monopoly" in any crude sense'.[43] The judge emphasised that the *Trade Marks Act 1995* (Cth) did not confer 'a liberty to use registered trade marks free from restraints found in other statutes'.[44]

In his dissent, Heydon J complained generally about the government encroaching upon the acquisition of property clause.[45]

The decision of the High Court of Australia will encourage other countries to join an 'Olive Revolution', introducing plain packaging of tobacco products.[46] New Zealand, Scotland, India, Uruguay, and Norway are particularly keen to follow Australia's lead.[47] Under the leadership of David Cameron's Conservative Party, England and Wales have equivocated upon whether they will adopt the plain packaging of tobacco products.[48]

---

43 Ibid.

44 Ibid.

45 Ibid.

46 Matthew Rimmer, 'The Olive Revolution: Australia's Plain Packaging Leads the World', *The Conversation* (15 August 2012) <https://the conversation.edu.au/the-olive-revolution-australias-plain-packaging-leads-the-world-8856>.

47 On New Zealand, see New Zealand Ministry of Health, *Proposal to Introduce Plain Packaging of Tobacco Products in New Zealand: Consultation Document* (23 July 2012) <http://www.health.govt.nz/publication/proposal-introduce-plain-packaging-tobacco-products-new-zealand>; Tariana Turana, 'Government Moves Forward with Plain Packaging of Tobacco Products' (19 February 2013) New Zealand Government <http://www.beehive. govt.nz/release/government-moves-forward-plain-packaging-tobacco-products>; International Centre for Trade and Sustainable Development, 'New Zealand Confirms Plans for Introducing Cigarette Packaging Law' (27 February 2013) 17(7) *Bridges Weekly Trade News Digest* <http://ictsd.org/i/news/bridgesweekly/156105/>. On Scotland, see *Ministers Aim to Make Scotland "Tobacco Free" by 2034* (27 March 2013) BBC News <http://www.bbc.co.uk/news/uk-scotland-scotland-politics-21954909>.

48 On England and Wales, see *Standardised Packaging of Tobacco Products* (2012) The United Kingdom Department of Health <http://consultations.dh.gov.uk/tobacco/standardised-packaging-of-tobacco-products/consult_view>; Patrick Wintour, 'Government to Legislate for Plain Cigarette Packaging this Year', *The Guardian* (online), 5 March 2013 <http://www.guardian.co.uk/society/2013/mar/05/government-legislate-plain-cigarette-packaging>; Marita Hefler and Stan Shatenstein, 'UK: Government Condemned for Bowing to Tobacco Industry Over Plain Packs' on *Tobacco Control* (7 May 2013) <http://blogs.bmj.com/tc/2013/05/07/uk-government-condemned-for-bowing-to-tobacco-industry-over-plain-packs/>; Tanya Gold, 'Death is Tobacco Companies' Business', *The*

B The WTO

Australia's Minister for Trade in 2012, Craig Emerson, stressed that the victory in the High Court of Australia will strengthen Australia's defence of the plain packaging of tobacco products in international fora.[49] He emphasised that the Australian Government would vigorously defend challenges against the regime brought by Ukraine, Honduras and the Dominican Republic through the World Trade Organization.[50] Emerson maintained: 'Australia will strongly defend its right to regulate to protect public health through the plain packaging of tobacco products.'[51] Both TRIPS and the *Agreement on Technical Barriers to Trade* have long recognised that WTO Members can take measures necessary to protect public health. Emerson has also stressed that Australia will defend plain packaging in other arenas: 'Australia will strongly defend its plain packaging legislation in all forums.'[52] Cuba and Indonesia have announced in 2013 that they will join the challenges to Australia's plain packaging regime in the World Trade Organization.[53]

Guardian (online), 5 May 2013 <http://www.guardian.co.uk/commentisfree/2013/may/05/death-tobacco-companies-business-packaging>.

49 Craig Emerson, 'High Court Ruling Bolsters Australia's WTO Case for Plain Packaging' (Media Release, 20 August 2012) <http://trademinister.gov.au/releases/2012/ce_mr_120820.html>.

50 World Trade Organization, *Australia – Certain Measures Concerning Trademarks and Other Plain Packaging Requirements Applicable to Tobacco Products and Packaging* (18 December 2012) <http://www.wto.org/english/tratop_e/dispu_e/cases_e/ds434_e.htm>; World Trade Organization, *Australia – Certain Measures Concerning Trademarks, Geographical Indications and Other Plain Packaging Requirements Applicable to Tobacco Products and Packaging* (20 November 2012) <http://www.wto.org/english/tratop_e/dispu_e/cases_e/ds435_e.htm>; World Trade Organization, *Australia – Certain Measures Concerning Trademarks, Geographical Indications and Other Plain Packaging Requirements Applicable to Tobacco Products and Packaging* (18 December 2012) <http://www.wto.org/english/tratop_e/dispu_e/cases_e/ds441_e.htm>.

51 Craig Emerson, 'High Court Ruling Bolsters Australia's WTO Case for Plain Packaging' (Media Release, 20 August 2012) <http://trademinister.gov.au/releases/2012/ce_mr_120820.html>.

52 Ibid.

53 David Jolly, 'Cuba Challenges Australian Tobacco Rules', *The New York Times* (online), 6 May 2013 <http://www.nytimes.com/2013/05/07/business/global/07iht-smoke07.html>; World Trade Organization, 'Cuba Files Dispute Against Australia on Tobacco Plain Packaging' (News Item, 3 May 2013)

C The TPP

There has also been concern that Big Tobacco is trying to use the TPP as a Trojan horse to attack tobacco control measures.[54] In a revealing submission to the United States Trade Representative, Philip Morris expressed concern about 'government-sponsored initiatives that would effectively cancel or expropriate valuable trademark rights'.[55] The company supported 'the inclusion of a comprehensive "TRIPs-plus" intellectual property chapter that includes a high standard of protection for trademarks and patents'.[56] In particular, Philip Morris objected to Australia's regime of plain packaging of tobacco products: 'The consequences of the introduction of plain packaging in Australia are far-reaching and should be examined in the broader context of U.S.–Australia trade relations and in the upcoming TPP negotiations.'[57] The company also made objections to Singapore's *Smoking (Control of Advertisements & Sale of Tobacco) Act*.[58]

There has been concern about the intellectual property chapter of the TPP.[59] There was a leak of the draft text of the intellectual property chapter of the TPP in 2011.[60] The United States has promoted an ambitious intellectual property chapter with standards above and beyond those in TRIPS, the *Australia–United States Free Trade Agreement*,[61] and even ACTA.[62] The chapter will cover copyright law, trade mark law,

---

<http://www.wto.org/english/news_e/news13_e/ds458rfc_03may13_e.htm; 'Indonesia Becomes Fifth to File WTO Case Against Australia Tobacco Plain-Packaging', *Intellectual Property Watch*, 22 September 2013, <http://www.ip-watch.org/2013/09/22/indonesia-becomes-fifth-to-file-wto-case-against-australia-tobacco-plain-packaging/>.

54 Peter Martin, 'Plain Packs: The New Lines of Attack. Big Tobacco tries the WTO and TPPA', *The Sydney Morning Herald* (Sydney), 20 August 2012.

55 Philip Morris International, above n 11.

56 Ibid.

57 Ibid.

58 Ibid.

59 Matthew Rimmer, 'A Mercurial Treaty: The Trans-Pacific Partnership and the United States', *The Conversation* (15 June 2012) <http://theconversation.edu.au/a-mercurial-treaty-the-trans-pacific-partnership-and-the-united-states-7471>.

60 'The Complete Feb 10, 2011 Text of the US Proposal for the TPP IPR Chapter' on *Knowledge Ecology International* (10 March 2011) <http://keionline.org/node/1091>.

61 *Australia–United States Free Trade Agreement*, signed 18 May 2004, [2005] ATS 1 (entered into force 1 January 2005).

62 See above n 7.

patent law, customs and border measures, and intellectual property enforcement. There have been particular concerns about tight parallel importation restrictions, the evergreening of drug patents, and draconian penalties for piracy and counterfeiting.

Sean Flynn and his colleagues provided a comprehensive analysis of the text, observing:[63]

> The U.S. proposals, if adopted, would create the highest intellectual property protection and enforcement standards in any free trade agreement to date. If adopted, the TPP would predictably lead to higher prices and decreased access to a broad range of consumer products in many TPP member countries, from medicines to textbooks to information on the internet, with little or no benefit to any TPP member in the form of increased innovation, creativity or local economic activity.[64]

The leaked version of the intellectual property chapter lacks appropriate safeguards with respect to public health – particularly with regard to tobacco control measures contemplated under the *WHO Framework Convention on Tobacco Control.*

Inside US Trade has reported that Australia, New Zealand, and Singapore have proposed replacing some elements of the United States proposal on intellectual property enforcement with language drawn from ACTA.[65] This is also disturbing. The European Parliament and its various committees overwhelmingly rejected ACTA.[66] The United Nations Special Rapporteur on the Right to Health, Anand Grover, applauded this decision: 'ACTA's defeat in Europe is a welcome blow to the flawed agreement that has failed to address numerous concerns related to access to medicines.'[67]

---

63 Sean Flynn et al., 'Public Interest Analysis of the US TPP Proposal for an IP Chapter' (Research Paper No 21, Program on Information Justice and Intellectual Property, American University Washington College of Law, 6 December 2011) 54–55 <http://digitalcommons.wcl.american.edu/research/21/>.

64 Ibid.

65 'Countries Offer ACTA Language To Replace U.S. IPR Proposal' (18 May 2012) 30 *Inside US Trade* (online).

66 Stephanie MacDonald, 'ACTA Dead and Buried', *Computerworld* (5 July 2012) <http://www.computerworld.com.au/article/429588/acta_dead_buried_europe/>.

67 'UN Expert on Health Hails European Parliament's Rejection of Anti-Counterfeiting Agreement' on *United Nations Regional Information Centre for Western Europe* (9 July 2012) <http://www.unric.org/en/latest-un-buzz/27676-un-expert-on-health-hails-european-parliaments-rejection-of-anti-counterfeiting-agreement->.

In June 2012, the Australian Parliament's Joint Standing Committee on Treaties recommended delaying and postponing ratification of ACTA.[68] The Committee recommended:

> that the *Anti-Counterfeiting Trade Agreement* not be ratified by Australia until the:
>
> - Joint Standing Committee on Treaties has received and considered the independent and transparent assessment of the economic and social benefits and costs of the Agreement referred to in Recommendation 2;
> - Australian Law Reform Commission has reported on its Inquiry into *Copyright and the Digital Economy*; and
> - the Australian Government has issued notices of clarification in relation to the terms of the Agreement as recommended in the other recommendations of this report.[69]

There were concerns about the impact of the treaty upon Australia's healthcare system – particularly in respect of tobacco control and access to essential medicines.[70] It is notable that ACTA did not provide proper recognition for the *WHO Framework Convention on Tobacco Control*.

Comparing ACTA and the TPP, Professor Peter Yu has written about the 'alphabet soup of transborder intellectual property enforcement'.[71] He contended that the United States has greater political and economic leverage in the TPP: 'Without the European Union at the negotiation table, the United States is able to rely more on its sheer economic and geopolitical strengths to push for provisions that are in the interest of its intellectual property industries.'[72] Yu worries: 'Because of the different value negotiating parties place on trade and trade-related items, some parties may be willing to concede more on intellectual property protection and enforcement in exchange for greater benefits in other trade or trade-related areas.'[73] He fears that the 'TPP, therefore, could include more stringent obligations in the intellectual property area'.[74]

---

68 Joint Standing Committee on Treaties, Parliament of Australia, *Report 126: Treaty Tabled on 21 November 2011* (2012).

69 Ibid., x.

70 Matthew Rimmer, 'Opening Pandora's Box: Secret Treaty Threatens Human Rights', *The Conversation* (4 April 2012) <http://theconversation.edu.au/opening-pandoras-box-secret-treaty-threatens-human-rights-6092>.

71 Peter Yu, 'The Alphabet Soup of Transborder Intellectual Property Enforcement' (2012) 60 *Drake Law Review Discourse* 16.

72 Ibid., 26.

73 Ibid., 27.

74 Ibid.

There is a need for the TPP to instead support a development agenda – which allows for countries to take measures to address public health concerns, such as tobacco control.

II INVESTMENT

There has been controversy over Big Tobacco using investor–state dispute resolution mechanisms to challenge public health measures – such as graphic warnings and the plain packaging of tobacco products.

A Ongoing Investment Challenges

After moving the shares of its Australian subsidiary to Hong Kong, Philip Morris has brought a contrived investor–state arbitration claim under the *Australia–Hong Kong Agreement on the Promotion and Protection of Investments*.[75] The economist, Peter Martin, notes:

> The almost comic attempt to get mileage out of the treaty (moving from Australia to Hong Kong in order to complain that it was being discriminated against because it was from Hong Kong) masks a broader, more serious attempt to turn trade treaties into instruments that allow corporations to sue governments.[76]

There has been much academic criticism of the investment action by Philip Morris.[77]

---

[75] *Agreement between the Government of Hong Kong and the Government of Australia for the Promotion and Protection of Investments*, signed 15 September 1993, 1748 UNTS 385 (entered into force 15 October 1993); *Philip Morris Asia Limited (Hong Kong) v The Commonwealth of Australia* <http://www.pca-cpa.org/showpage.asp?pag_id=1494>; Attorney-General's Department, *Investor*–State Arbitration – Tobacco Plain Packaging <http://www.ag.gov.au/Internationalrelations/InternationalLaw/Pages/Tobaccoplainpackaging.aspx>.

[76] Martin, above n 54.

[77] Tania Voon and Andrew Mitchell, 'Time to Quit? Assessing International Investment Claims Against Plain Tobacco Packaging in Australia' (2011) 14(3) *Journal of International Economic Law* 1; Mark Davison, 'Big Tobacco vs. Australia: Philip Morris Scores an Own Goal', *The Conversation* (20 January 2012) <http://theconversation.edu.au/big-tobacco-vs-australia-philip-morris-scores-an-own-goal-4967>; Kyla Tienhaara, 'Government Wins First Battle in Plain Packaging War', *The Conversation* (13 August 2012) <https://theconversation.edu.au/government-wins-first-battle-in-plain-packaging-war-8855>; Thomas Faunce,

Philip Morris has also used international investment rules to challenge Uruguay's restrictions on cigarette marketing.[78] In particular, the tobacco company has complained about graphic health warnings being used by the Uruguayan Government, lamenting that: 'The 80 per cent health warning coverage requirement unfairly limits Abal's right to use its legally protected trademarks, and not to promote legitimate health policies.'[79] Benn McGrady provides a thoughtful analysis of the ramifications of the dispute.[80]

In the context of the TPP discussions, there has been concern that tobacco companies would use investment clauses to challenge public health measures – such as tobacco control.

B Australian Policy

In a trade policy, the Australian Labor Party Government has disavowed the inclusion of investor–state dispute resolution clauses in any future free trade agreements – including the TPP.[81] The statement notes:

> Some countries have sought to insert investor–state dispute resolution clauses into trade agreements. Typically these clauses empower businesses from one country to take international legal action against the government of another country for alleged breaches of the agreement, such as for policies that allegedly discriminate against those businesses and in favour of the country's domestic businesses.[82]

The policy document states: 'The Government does not support provisions that would confer greater legal rights on foreign businesses than

---

'An Affront to the Rule of Law: International Tribunals to Decide on Plain Packaging', *The Conversation* (29 August 2012) <http://theconversation.edu.au/an-affront-to-the-rule-of-law-international-tribunals-to-decide-on-plain-packaging-8968>.

[78] *FTR Holding SA et al v Uruguay (Request for Arbitration)* (ICSID Arbitral Tribunal, Case No ARB/10/7, 19 February 2010).

[79] Ibid.

[80] Benn McGrady, 'Implications of Ongoing Trade and Investment Disputes Concerning Tobacco: *Philip Morris v Uruguay*' in Tania Voon et al. (eds), *Public Health and Plain Packaging of Cigarettes: Legal Issues* (Edward Elgar Publishing, 2012) 173.

[81] Department of Foreign Affairs and Trade, *Gillard Government Trade Policy Statement: Trading Our Way to More Jobs and Prosperity* (Commonwealth Government, 12 April 2011) <http://www.dfat.gov.au/publications/trade/trading-our-way-to-more-jobs-and-prosperity.html>.

[82] Ibid.

those available to domestic businesses.'[83] The trade statement emphasises that: 'The Government has not and will not accept provisions that limit its capacity to put health warnings or plain packaging requirements on tobacco products or its ability to continue the Pharmaceutical Benefits Scheme.'[84] Moreover, the policy document observes: 'If Australian businesses are concerned about sovereign risk in Australian trading partner countries, they will need to make their own assessments about whether they want to commit to investing in those countries.'[85]

A number of industry groups and trade lawyers have been irked by the policy of the Australian Government to refuse to sign trade agreements with state–investor dispute resolution clauses. The Australian Chamber of Commerce and Industry has lobbied for the inclusion of investment clauses in free trade agreements – including the TPP. The law firm Clifford Chance has argued: 'It is Australian companies investing off-shore that will perhaps suffer most from the Australian government's new approach.'[86] Trade lawyer Leon Trakman has protested: 'Australian investors abroad probably will suffer.'[87] Arbitrator Michael Pryles has observed that: 'We have the recent example of tobacco companies saying their trademarks have been expropriated, but it's unusual.'[88]

The Conservative Coalition won the Australian election in September 2013. The Minister for Foreign Affairs, Julie Bishop, has written that she will reconsider including investment clauses in the TPP.[89] The Minister for Trade and Investment, Andrew Robb, had emphasised that the Coalition is open to utilising investor–state dispute settlement clauses as part of Australia's negotiating position.

Such advocacy for investment clauses is weak and unconvincing. The abuse of investment clauses by tobacco companies is not unusual or exceptional. It is commonplace. The involvement of Philip Morris in the TPP highlights this problem.

---

83 Ibid.

84 Ibid.

85 Ibid.

86 Chris Merritt, 'Change in Treaty Policy Detrimental to Aussie Companies: Clifford Chance', *The Australian* (Australia), 7 September 2012.

87 Ibid.

88 Ibid.

89 Julie Bishop, 'Free Trade Focus', *Online Opinion* (28 March 2013) <http://www.onlineopinion.com.au/view.asp?article=14855>. For a critique, see Greens Senator Peter Whish-Wilson, 'Past is not the Future for Trade', *Online Opinion* (8 April 2013) <http://www.onlineopinion.com.au/view.asp?article=14879>.

C The TPP

A key chapter of the TPP relates to investment. Philip Morris has been a strong supporter of the inclusion of an investor–state dispute resolution mechanism in the TPP:

> Philip Morris International has made significant investments in many countries, including the identified U.S. TPP partners. For that reason, we believe strong investor protections must be a critical element of the TPP and any future U.S. Free Trade Agreements.
>
> PMI supports the inclusion in the TPP of an investor–state dispute settlement mechanism. The strong investment chapter of the yet-to-be ratified U.S.–South Korea Free Trade Agreement should be used as a model for negotiating a similar chapter in the TPP.
>
> PMI considers the availability of an investor–state dispute settlement mechanism, including the right for investors to submit disputes to independent international tribunals, a vital aspect of protecting its foreign investments.[90]

Under such a mechanism, Philip Morris would be able to challenge government regulations – much like they have done in disputes with Australia and Uruguay.

There has been much concern about the investment chapter of the TPP – especially since a draft of the text was leaked in 2012.[91] The regime provides that no party may expropriate or nationalise a covered investment except for a public purpose, and with prompt, adequate, and effective compensation. The chapter also establishes an investor–state dispute settlement system: one that enables corporations from one country to take legal action against the government of another country for alleged breaches of the agreement. Professor Thomas Faunce of the Australian National University has observed of this text: 'Such proposals give foreign investors (such as tobacco multinationals) greater rights than domestic investors.'[92] There are only vague safeguards in respect of public health – such as 'the parties recognise that it is inappropriate to encourage investment by relaxing its health, safety or environmental

---

[90] Philip Morris International, above n 11, 2–3.

[91] Zach Carter, 'Obama Trade Document Leaked, Revealing New Corporate Powers and Broken Campaign Promises', *The Huffington Post*, 13 June 2012 <http://www.huffingtonpost.com/2012/06/13/obama-trade-document-leak_n_1592593.html>.

[92] Faunce, above n 77.

measures'.[93] There is no specific, explicit recognition in this draft regime for the *WHO Framework Convention on Tobacco Control.*

With the leak of the investment chapter, the Obama Administration stands accused of breaking its 2008 campaign promise:

> We will not negotiate bilateral trade agreements that stop the government from protecting the environment, food safety, or the health of its citizens; give greater rights to foreign investors than to U.S. investors; require the privatization of our vital public services; or prevent developing country governments from adopting humanitarian licensing policies to improve access to life-saving medications.[94]

D New Zealand

Taking a principled stance, the Australian Government has thus far refused to submit to the investor–state dispute resolution clause. However, the New Zealand Prime Minister John Key has argued that there should not be special treatment for Australia: 'An exclusion solely for Australia, not for everybody else, is unlikely to be something that we would support.'[95] His position is misguided. Professor Jane Kelsey from the University of Auckland has commented: 'The global multi-billion-dollar commercial players that dominate the alcohol and tobacco industries can afford to fund lengthy and costly arbitration to stop precedent-setting policies, even where their legal case is weak.'[96] She has written a report on international trade law and tobacco control.[97] She has commented:

> The proposed TPPA poses the most serious imminent risk to New Zealand's ability to design, introduce and implement the innovative tobacco control

---

[93] Citizens Trade Campaign, *Investment* <http://www.citizenstrade.org/ctc/wp-content/uploads/2012/06/tppinvestment.pdf>.

[94] Faunce, above n 77.

[95] Radio New Zealand News, *NZ 'Unlikely' to Support Special TPP Deal for Australia* (14 June 2012) <http://www.radionz.co.nz/news/political/108189/nz-%27unlikely%27-to-support-special-tpp-deal-for-australia>.

[96] Jane Kelsey, 'New-Generation Free Trade Agreements Threaten Progressive Tobacco and Alcohol Policies' (2012) 107(10) *Addiction* 1719.

[97] Jane Kelsey, 'International Trade Law and Tobacco Control: Trade and Investment Law Issues Relating to Proposed Tobacco Control Policies to Achieve an Essentially Smoke Free Aotearoa New Zealand by 2025' (Report, New Zealand Tobacco Control Research Tūranga, May 2012) <http://www.turanga.org.nz/sites/turanga.org.nz/files/Kelsey%20Trade%20Law%20Tobacco%20Control%20Report.pdf>.

> policies needed to achieve the 2025 goal, as it would legally guarantee the tobacco industry and supply chain stronger, enforceable legal rights and the opportunity to influence domestic policy.[98]

The New Zealand Prime Minister John Key has struggled with questions on investment and the TPP in the New Zealand Parliament.[99] The New Zealand Greens co-leader, Metiria Turei, asked John Key: 'Will New Zealand open itself up to litigation from firms based in the Trans-Pacific Partnership countries should we sign up to the investor–State dispute settlement procedures, which Australia has rejected?'[100] In response, John Key mischaracterised the approach of the Australian Government to the question of investment:

> Well for a start-off, I do not think it is actually correct to say that Australia has rejected them. What is true to say is that there are different countries bringing different perspectives to the negotiation, but when a final Trans-Pacific Partnership agreement is agreed, all parties are likely to sign up.[101]

Under further questioning, Prime Minister Key was unfamiliar with a number of investment disputes – such as the action against Germany's environmental controls on coal-fired power stations;[102] the action by the Renco Group against Peru in respect of regulations designed to stop lead poisoning;[103] and the action by Chevron Oil under investor–state procedures against Ecuador in respect of clean-costs for toxic waste.[104] Prime Minister Key insists more generally upon the existence of 'safeguards' in the TPP: 'I can tell you the way that New Zealand legislates and goes about these free-trade agreements, and it is very careful to give itself the

---

98 Ibid., 62.

99 'The Trans-Pacific Partnership – Investor–State Dispute Provisions', New Zealand, *Parliamentary Debates*, House of Representatives, 4 December 2012, 6996 (John Key, Prime Minister) <http://www.parliament.nz/en-NZ/PB/Business/QOA/c/a/8/50HansQ_20121204_00000004-4-Trans-Pacific-Partnership-Investor-State.htm>.

100 Ibid.

101 Ibid.

102 *Vattenfall v Germany (Award)* (ICSID Arbitral Tribunal, Case No ARB/09/6, 11 March 2011).

103 The Renco Group, Inc, *Claimant's Notice of Intention to Commence Arbitration* (29 December 2010) Investment Treaty Arbitration <http://italaw.com/sites/default/files/case-documents/ita0713.pdf>.

104 See ChevronToxico, *About the Campaign* <http://chevrontoxico.com/about/>.

safeguards that we would think make sense.'[105] However, the leaked text from the draft investment chapter would suggest that such 'safeguards' are not particularly safe.

The New Zealand Prime Minister John Key was particularly non-plussed by questions over tobacco control and the TPP. The New Zealand Greens co-leader, Metiria Turei, asked John Key:

> Does the Prime Minister have any concerns that Philip Morris could use the investor–State procedures in the Trans-Pacific Partnership to sue New Zealand, given its actions in Australia and the veiled threats made by its spokesperson in New Zealand, Chris Bishop; if not, why not?[106]

In response, John Key argued:

> The member will be aware that Australia as of 1 December went into its programme of plain packaging. It is not in any way concerned about doing that and continuing to be part of the officials group and continuing to negotiate as part of the Trans-Pacific Partnership. That tells you that it must believe that the two policies are compatible.[107]

Again, the New Zealand Prime Minister is incorrect on this point. The Australian Government has indeed expressed concerns about interference by Big Tobacco in the TPP negotiations. Similarly, United States Members of Congress – like Henry Waxman – have also been concerned by the approach of the United States Trade Representative to the question of tobacco control and the TPP.

In 2013, the New Zealand Government announced that it would adopt the plain packaging of tobacco products in 2013 – while still pursuing the TPP.

---

105 Key, above n 99, 6996.

106 'The Trans-Pacific Partnership – Investor–State Dispute Provisions', New Zealand, *Parliamentary Debates*, House of Representatives, 4 December 2012, 6996 (Metiria Turei, Co-Leader, Greens) <http://www.parliament.nz/en-NZ/PB/Business/QOA/c/a/8/50HansQ_20121204_00000004-4-Trans-Pacific-Partnership-Investor-State.htm>.

107 Key, above n 99, 6998.

III TOBACCO CONTROL

The United States Trade Representative, Ambassador Ron Kirk, has been equivocal on the question of tobacco control and the TPP.[108] In February 2012, the Ambassador appeared before the United States Congress, and said: 'We have not tabled any proposal to exclude any product.'[109] Kirk has said: 'There are people who are fanatically opinionated on both sides.'[110] He observed: 'Our job is to follow U.S. law. Strike that balance. But on this one we'll sometime have to make a decision.'[111] There has been a concern that the United States Trade Representative has been willing to appease or placate the representatives of the tobacco industry. There has also been discussion of the United States Trade Representative having ties with the tobacco industry – having been a partner of Vinson & Elkins LLP which defended the tobacco industry, and a consultant to the tobacco company, Philip Morris.[112]

A The Family Smoking Prevention and Tobacco Control Act of 2009

In the TPP negotiations, the United States Trade Representative's objective is to create a 'safe harbour' for the United States Food and Drug Administration to regulate tobacco products under the *Family Smoking Prevention and Tobacco Control Act of 2009*. There is a need to understand the nature of the Obama Administration's tobacco control measures.

On 22 June 2009, President Barack Obama signed into law the *Family Smoking Prevention and Tobacco Control Act of 2009*. The President reflected upon the significance of the legislative reform: 'Since at least the middle of the last century, we've known about the harmful and often

---

108 Geoff Davis, *Congressman Davis Questions USTR Ron Kirk on Possible Tobacco Exclusions* (29 February 2012) YouTube <http://www.youtube.com/watch?v=n1mgsx3YcPs>.

109 Ibid.

110 Franco Ordonez, 'Tobacco Growers Fear Trade Deal Will Harm Exports', *McClatchy*, 28 February 2012 <http://www.mcclatchydc.com/2012/02/28/140249/tobacco-growers-fear-trade-deal.html>.

111 Ibid.

112 See *Ron Kirk* (19 December 2008) Source Watch <http://www.sourcewatch.org/index.php/Ron_Kirk>; Mark Drajem, 'Ex-Dallas Mayor Kirk Said to be Obama's Trade Pick', *Bloomberg*, 18 December 2008 <http://www.bloomberg.com/apps/news?pid=newsarchive&sid=aV1huzewQ4gY&refer=us>; Todd Gillman, 'Lobbyist Record of Texas Democratic Senate Hopeful Kirk Draws Scrutiny', *The Dallas Morning News* (Texas), 4 April 2002.

deadly effects of tobacco products.'[113] He lamented: 'More than 400,000 Americans now die of tobacco-related illnesses each year, making it the leading cause of preventable death in the United States.'[114] President Obama observed: 'This legislation will not ban all tobacco products, and it will allow adults to make their own choices.'[115] He noted that this legislation 'will force these companies to more clearly and publicly acknowledge the harmful and deadly effects of the products they sell'.[116]

The tobacco industry has brought a range of lawsuits against the *Family Smoking Prevention and Tobacco Control Act of 2009*.[117] President Obama reflected upon such litigation:

> Today, some big tobacco companies are trying to block these labels because they don't want to be honest about the consequences of using their products. Unfortunately, this isn't surprising. We've always known that the fight to stop smoking in this country won't be easy.[118]

There have been variations between how circuit courts in the United States have addressed the challenges by the tobacco industry to graphic health warnings – most notably between Kentucky,[119] which dismissed a challenge to graphic health warnings, and the District of Columbia, where the tobacco industry's challenge was upheld.[120]

In December 2012, the United States Court of Appeals denied the request by the United States Government for the full court or panel to rehear the case in the District Court of Columbia.[121] The United States

---

113 President Barack Obama, above n 1.

114 Ibid.

115 Ibid.

116 Ibid.

117 See *Discount Tobacco City & Lottery Inc v United States*, 674 F 3d 509 (6th Cir, 2012) and *RJ Reynolds Tobacco Co v Food and Drug Administration*, 696 F 3d 1205 (DC Cir, 2012).

118 Jim Kuhnhenn, 'Obama Scolds Tobacco Companies For Fighting New Cigarette Warning Labels', *The Huffington Post*, 17 November 2011 <http://www.huffingtonpost.com/2011/11/17/barack-obama-tobacco_n_1099274.html>.

119 *Discount Tobacco City & Lottery Inc v United States*, 674 F 3d 509 (6th Cir, 2012).

120 *RJ Reynolds Tobacco Co v Food and Drug Administration*, 696 F 3d 1205 (DC Cir, 2012).

121 Associated Press, 'Appeals Court Denies Rehearing on Decision Blocking Graphic Health Warnings on Cigarette Packets', *The Washington Post*, 6 December 2012 <http://www.washingtonpost.com/business/appeals-court-denies-rehearing-on-decision-blocking-graphic-health-warnings-on-cigarette-packs/2012/12/05/ec8e99f4-3ef1-11e2-8a5c-473797be602c_story.html>.

Government considered appealing the decision to the Supreme Court of the United States.[122] In the end, the Department of Justice sent a letter to the House Speaker, saying that it would not ask the Supreme Court of the United States to review the ruling.[123]

However, the tobacco industry's challenges to the *Family Smoking Prevention and Tobacco Control Act of 2009* have not necessarily been successful, either. In April 2013, the Supreme Court of the United States refused to hear a challenge to the regime by tobacco companies such as R.J. Reynolds Tobacco Co.[124]

Such domestic conflict may help explain the focus of the United States Trade Representative's proposal on tobacco control.[125] Such litigation demonstrates that the tobacco industry has increasingly tried to co-opt and appropriate the language of freedom of speech in legal debates. Professor Kevin Outterson has warned that 'powerful corporations are increasingly using an expanding definition of the First Amendment to challenge public health regulations'.[126] He has observed that: 'For public health advocates, one lesson is that the purpose and mechanism for new regulations must be carefully articulated and documented, especially if any conceivable First Amendment issue can be raised.'[127]

---

[122] Richard Craver, 'Successful Appeal of Graphic Cigarette Labels Likely Headed for U.S. Supreme Court', *Winston-Salem Journal*, 5 December 2012 <http://www.journalnow.com/news/local/article_751e2000-3f2e-11e2-b08c-001a4bcf6878.html>.

[123] Steve Almasy, *FDA Changes Course on Graphic Warning Labels for Cigarettes* (20 March 2013) CNN <http://edition.cnn.com/2013/03/19/health/fda-graphic-tobacco-warnings>.

[124] *American Snuff v United States*, 12-521 (2013); Greg Stohr, 'Tobacco Industry Spurned by Top Court on Package Warnings', *Bloomberg*, 22 April 2013 <http://www.bloomberg.com/news/2013-04-22/tobacco-industry-spurned-by-top-court-on-package-warnings.html>.

[125] *Fact Sheet: TPP Tobacco Proposal* (May 2012) Office of the United States Trade Representative <http://www.ustr.gov/about-us/press-office/fact-sheets/2012/may/tpp-tobacco-proposal>.

[126] Kevin Outterson, 'Smoking and the First Amendment' (2011) 365 *The New England Journal of Medicine* 2351.

[127] Ibid.

B The United States Trade Representative's Proposal on Tobacco Control

In 2012, the United States Trade Representative published a statement on its proposal on tobacco control on its website.[128] The statement notes that the Obama Administration sought input from 'health advocates, farmers, industry stakeholders, and others' on tobacco and the TPP.[129] The United States Trade Representative observed that: 'The [Obama] Administration also considered the increasing effort both in the United States and around the world over the past several years to regulate tobacco products.'[130] Particular reference is made to the *Family Smoking Prevention and Tobacco Control Act of 2009* (US).

While not making the draft proposal publicly available, the United States Trade Representative has published a limited summary, emphasising that the draft proposal has three elements. First, the proposal 'would explicitly recognize the unique status of tobacco products from a health and regulatory perspective'.[131] Second, 'the proposal would make tobacco products (like other products) subject to tariff phase-outs, thus avoiding putting U.S. tobacco products at a competitive disadvantage and avoiding a precedent for excluding tobacco or other products from future U.S. tariff negotiations'.[132] Third, the proposal would 'include language in the "general exceptions" chapter that allows health authorities in TPP governments to adopt regulations that impose origin-neutral, science-based restrictions on specific tobacco products/classes in order to safeguard public health'.[133]

Focusing upon the United States, the United States Trade Representative commented:

> This language will create a safe harbor for FDA tobacco regulation, providing greater certainty that the provisions in the TPP will not be used in a manner that would prevent FDA from taking the sorts of incremental regulatory actions that are necessary to effectively implement the *Tobacco Control Act*, while retaining important trade disciplines (national treatment, compensation for expropriations, and transparency) on tobacco measures.[134]

---

128 *Fact Sheet: TPP Tobacco Proposal*, above n 125.
129 Ibid.
130 Ibid.
131 Ibid.
132 Ibid.
133 Ibid.
134 Ibid.

A number of former United States Trade Representatives have written to the current United States Trade Representative, Ambassador Ron Kirk, urging him not to propose a tobacco-specific exception.[135] The authors portrayed the provisions creating policy space as open to abuse by recalcitrant trading partners. The authors stated:

> While we are confident that the United States would not adopt or impose measures that restrict trade or investment without a sound basis to do so, we have witnessed over the years other governments attempting to justify their protectionist measures in the name of health or safety, especially in agriculture.[136]

At the Auckland talks in November 2012,[137] the United States Trade Representative refused to table the proposal on tobacco control, because the agency was still apparently reviewing input from stakeholders. A spokeswoman for the office said: 'We are still reflecting on what we've heard from stakeholders on our TPP tobacco proposal, and will be continuing consultations beyond the December 3–12 Auckland round to determine the right balance on this issue.'[138] Matthew Myers, president of the Campaign for Tobacco-Free Kids, has been displeased by this prevarication: 'USTR consulted fully before it crafted its proposal. There is nothing that will satisfy the tobacco companies.'[139] His concern was that the United States Trade Representative was retreating from its proposal to protect tobacco control measures.

This proposal seems rather parochial, modelled upon United States domestic law and political exigencies. Benn McGrady comments: 'It seems worth adding that the proposal appears more responsive to the outcome of *US–Clove Cigarettes* and preserving the regulatory powers of the FDA than to contemporary developments, such as ongoing claims against Australia and Uruguay.'[140]

---

135 Benn McGrady, 'The Tobacco Specific Trans-Pacific Partnership Exception and Customary International Law' on O'Neill Institute for National and Global Health Law, *Trade, Investment & Health* (27 June 2012) <http://www.oneillinstitutetradeblog.org/the-tobacco-specific-tpp-exception-and-customary-international-law/>.

136 Ibid.

137 'USTR Holding Off on Tabling TPP Tobacco Proposal at Auckland Round' (22 November 2012) 30(46) *Inside US Trade* (online).

138 Ibid.

139 Ibid.

140 Benn McGrady, 'Tobacco in the Trans-Pacific Partnership: Trade, Tobacco, Health' on O'Neill Institute for National and Global Health Law, *Trade,*

By 2013, the USTR had retreated from its proposal for a safe harbour in respect of tobacco control, to the dismay of public health advocates.

C United States Congressman Henry Waxman's Critique

Senior United States Congressman Henry Waxman has raised significant reservations about the proposed text on tobacco control.[141] He commented:

> In light of recent trade challenges to U.S. and Australian tobacco control laws, I am concerned that the exemption contemplated in the U.S. proposal emphasizes regulatory measures and fails to also explicitly exempt statutory tobacco control measures that otherwise meet the origin-neutral and science-based criteria set forth in the Proposal.[142]

Congressman Waxman stressed that in his view: 'it is essential to safeguard countries' sovereign authority to take the most appropriate and most feasible action to protect the health of their citizens.'[143] Waxman was also 'deeply troubled that the U.S. Proposal fails to exclude tobacco products from tariff schedule reductions'.[144] He observed: 'This element of the Proposal is contrary to the intent and the spirit of the "Doggett Amendment" and Executive Order 13193 issued by President Clinton, both of which prohibit the U.S. government from promoting the sale or export of tobacco products.'[145] Congressman Waxman emphasised the need for the United States Trade Representative to respect local laws: 'In the case of the United States, this would safeguard the implementation of the *Tobacco Control Act*, legislation that is critically important in addressing our country's ongoing problem with tobacco addiction.'[146]

D Further Criticism of the Tobacco Control Text

In a letter to Ambassador Ron Kirk, United States health groups observed: 'There is a global consensus that governments should be doing

---

Investment & Health (29 November 2012) <http://www.oneillinstitute tradeblog.org/tobacco-in-the-trans-pacific-partnership-agreement/>.

[141] Letter from Representative Henry Waxman to the United States Trade Representative (22 May 2012) <http://democrats.energycommerce.house.gov/ sites/default/files/documents/Letter_Kirk_05.22.12.pdf >.

[142] Ibid., 2.

[143] Ibid.

[144] Ibid.

[145] Ibid.

[146] Ibid., 3.

everything possible to reduce consumption of tobacco products and the resulting harms from that consumption.'[147] The organisations maintain that 'Trade agreements should not undermine the authority of governments to [reduce tobacco use].'[148] The groups note that 'This consensus is reflected in the world's first public health treaty, the World Health Organization's Framework Convention on Tobacco Control, under which 175 countries have made legally binding commitments to enact effective tobacco control measures.'[149] The health groups comment that 'the global goal of reducing tobacco usage is in contrast to the usual free trade goal of expanding access to and consumption of products.'[150] The submission emphasised: 'Tobacco products killed 100 million people in the 20th century and will kill one billion people in the 21st century unless governments take urgent action.'[151]

Chris Bostic, deputy director for policy at the Action on Smoking and Health, has commented that the United States regime is parochial, and very focused upon domestic United States law.[152] He has noted that officials from the United States Trade Representative 'recognize the weaknesses … in that it won't apply to a lot of the ways that other countries do tobacco control regulations'.[153]

Dr Margaret Chan of the World Health Organization has warned: 'The incentive for industry to use international trade or investment agreements in lobbying or litigation is especially high when potentially trend-setting measures are at stake.'[154] She stressed: 'This is true for very large health

---

[147] Letter from the American Academy of Family Physicians, American Academy of Pediatrics, American Association for Cancer Research, American Association for Respiratory Care, American Cancer Society – Cancer Action Network, American Heart Association, American Lung Association, American Thoracic Society, Campaign for Tobacco-Free Kids, National Latino Tobacco Control Network, Oncology Nursing Society, and Partnership for Prevention to the United States Representative (22 May 2012) <http://www.prevent.org/data/images/public%20health%20letter%20to%20ustr%20re%20tpp.pdf>.

[148] Ibid., 1.

[149] Ibid.

[150] Ibid.

[151] Ibid.

[152] Ibid.

[153] Ibid.

[154] Margaret Chan, 'Global Governance of Tobacco in the 21st Century' (Speech delivered at the Harvard University Conference on Governance of Tobacco in the 21st Century: Strengthening National and International Policy for Global Health and Development, Cambridge, MA, 26 February 2013) <http://www.who.int/dg/speeches/2013/tobacco_20130226/en/index.html>.

warnings on packs in Uruguay, legislation mandating plain packaging in Australia, and a ban on point-of-sales advertising in Norway.'[155]

There is a failure to acknowledge or recognise the primacy of international law on tobacco control. Conspicuously, the summary of the proposed text on the TPP fails to mention the *WHO Framework Convention on Tobacco Control*, and its accompanying guidelines. This omission is regrettable and lamentable. There is a need to ensure that the TPP does not affect the comprehensive range of tobacco control measures contemplated by the *WHO Framework Convention on Tobacco Control* – such as the plain packaging of tobacco products. Furthermore, there is also a need to ensure that any future tobacco control initiatives under the *WHO Framework Convention on Tobacco Control* – or by any enterprising governments – are not stymied by the TPP.

CONCLUSION

In conclusion, there are deep concerns about both the process and the substance of the TPP – particularly as it pertains to public health. The pernicious secrecy surrounding the negotiations of the treaty has been unacceptable. The submissions of parties, the negotiating texts and the talks should be open and transparent. Politicians, health advocates, civil society groups, and the wider public should be able to participate in the discussions, particularly given the sweeping nature of the agreement. A number of the chapters of the TPP have implications for tobacco control measures – particularly graphic health warnings and the plain packaging of tobacco products. The intellectual property chapter should not adopt 'TRIPs-Plus' or 'TRIPS-Double Plus' standards. There is a need to ensure that member states can take a range of measures to address public health concerns, without interference from tobacco companies under the guise of intellectual property rights. The investment chapter of the TPP should be abandoned, especially given the weak protections for public health. There is a need to internationally address the abuse of state–investor dispute settlement clauses by tobacco companies. Technical barriers to trade could also be an issue.[156] The United States Trade

---

155 Ibid.

156 'International Trade and Standards: An Interview with Jeff Weiss, Office of the U.S. Trade Representative' (May/June 2011) *ASTM Standardization News* <http://www.astm.org/SNEWS/MJ_2011/provocative_mj11.html>; World Trade Organization, *World Trade Report 2012* (July 2012). Countries have raised issues on technical barriers to trade in a number of WTO disputes including: Panel

Representative's text on tobacco control is lamentably parochial. There is a need to ensure that the TPP in no way curtails, or confines, tobacco control measures as contemplated by the *WHO Framework Convention on Tobacco Control* – either in its present form or in future revisions. Moreover, there is a need to be wary that the TPP is a mercurial treaty – a 'living agreement' which can be updated to 'address trade issues that emerge in the future as well as new issues that arise with the expansion of the agreement to include new countries'.[157] Future iterations of the treaty must not undermine global efforts to combat the tobacco epidemic.

Laurent Huber, the executive director of Action on Smoking and Health in Washington, DC, makes an eloquent case for why tobacco should be excluded from the TPP altogether:

> Responsible trade policy acknowledges what we've known for decades: Tobacco is a uniquely dangerous product that causes death and disease from ordinary use. Tobacco is not just another agricultural product that deserves promotion through U.S. trade policy. It is the target of the world. The World Health Organization's first and only treaty – which all of the TPPA countries, except for the United States, have ratified – recognizes the devastating effects of tobacco and its increasing threat to global health and welfare. Including tobacco in the TPPA would undermine the success of this treaty in preventing tobacco-related disease around the world.[158]

Susan Liss, the executive director of the Campaign for Tobacco-Free Kids, reflects that: 'Reforms to specific parts of the TPPA such as the

---

Report, *United States – Measures Affecting the Production and Sale of Clove Cigarettes*, WTO Doc WT/DS406/R (2 September 2011); Appellate Body Report, *United States – Measures Affecting the Production and Sale of Clove Cigarettes*, WTO Doc WT/DS406/AB/R (4 April 2012). See also World Trade Organization, *Australia – Certain Measures Concerning Trademarks and Other Plain Packaging Requirements Applicable to Tobacco Products and Packaging* (18 December 2012) <http://www.wto.org/english/tratop_e/dispu_e/cases_e/ds434_e.htm>; World Trade Organization, *Australia – Certain Measures Concerning Trademarks, Geographical Indications and Other Plain Packaging Requirements Applicable to Tobacco Products and Packaging* (20 November 2012) <http://www.wto.org/english/tratop_e/dispu_e/cases_e/ds435_e.htm>; World Trade Organization, *Australia – Certain Measures Concerning Trademarks, Geographical Indications and Other Plain Packaging Requirements Applicable to Tobacco Products and Packaging* (18 December 2012) <http://www.wto.org/english/tratop_e/dispu_e/cases_e/ds441_e.htm>.

157 Rimmer, 'A Mercurial Treaty', above n 59.

158 Laurent Huber, 'Tobacco from all Nations Excluded in Trade Pact', *Kentucky.com*, 30 April 2012 <http://www.kentucky.com/2012/04/30/2169551/tobacco-from-all-nations-excluded.html>.

technical barriers to trade, intellectual property, or investment chapters may address part of the problem, but even that would not prevent second guessing of legitimate efforts as being more trade restrictive than necessary.'[159] She insists that: 'Anything other than exclusion of tobacco products may continue the chilling effect of threatened lawsuits, preventing countries from enacting public health protections for their citizens.'[160] As such, there is a need to ensure that the TPP is not hijacked by Big Tobacco for the purposes of encouraging the trade in tobacco, and warding off the introduction of tobacco control measures.[161]

The plain packaging of tobacco products – and other best practices in tobacco control – should be embraced by all members of the Pacific Rim.

---

[159] Susan Liss, *Campaign for Tobacco-Free Kids Urges Trans Partnership Agreement Negotiators to Exempt Tobacco Products from the Proposed Free Trade Agreement*, Campaign for Tobacco-Free Kids <http://www.tobaccofreekids.org/content/what_we_do/federal_issues/trade/TPP.pdf>.

[160] Ibid.

[161] Mike Bloomberg, 'Why is Obama Caving on Tobacco?', *The New York Times*, 22 August 2013, <http://www.nytimes.com/2013/08/23/opinion/why-is-obama-caving-on-tobacco.html>; The Editorial Board, 'The Hazard of Free-Trade Tobacco', *The New York Times*, 31 August 2013, <http://www.nytimes.com/2013/09/01/opinion/sunday/the-hazard-of-free-trade-tobacco.html>; Ellen Shaffer, 'Stop TPP Protections for Big Tobacco', *The Huffington Post*, 9 September 2013, <http://www.huffingtonpost.com/ellen-r-shaffer/stop-tpp-protections-for-big-tobacco_b_3886771.html> and Eric Mar, 'U.S. Must Take Tobacco Out of Global Trade Talks', *San Francisco Chronicle*, 24 September 2013, <http://www.sfgate.com/opinion/openforum/article/U-S-must-take-tobacco-out-of-global-trade-talks-4819528.php>.

6. Agriculture and the Trans-Pacific Partnership negotiations

Deborah Elms

INTRODUCTION

One of the more innovative aspects of the Trans-Pacific Partnership Agreement (TPP) negotiations has been an emphasis on granting full market access to member countries with 'no exceptions'. This statement has been made repeatedly from the earliest days of the negotiations in March 2010 and reiterated often throughout the talks. Even if – in the end – there are modest levels of protection remaining in a very limited number of agricultural sectors, the promises to open the market fully remain striking.

A willingness to open markets with no exceptions means putting the most sensitive areas up for discussion. For nearly all countries, this means agricultural products. For a variety of reasons, including history, culture, and politics, agriculture usually holds special significance to states. As this chapter highlights, unlike industrial goods, neither repeated commitments in multilateral fora like those created by the *General Agreement on Tariffs and Trade*[1] (GATT) or the World Trade Organization (WTO) nor promises made in regional or bilateral preferential trade agreements (PTAs) have resulted in similar low levels of protection for agricultural products. Yet officials have pledged in the TPP to put these highly sensitive areas up for liberalisation to the other partners.

I WHY INCLUDE AGRICULTURE?

Why are officials so prepared to take on this task in the TPP when they have been unwilling to do so in other venues? In part it was because of

1 Opened for signature 30 October 1947, 55 UNTS 187 (entered into force 1 January 1948) (GATT).

careful calculations about the economic benefits of the TPP. At the time that negotiations got under way in March 2010, the TPP membership included eight countries: Australia, Brunei, Chile, New Zealand, Peru, Singapore, the United States and Vietnam. These eight countries had relatively limited trade with one another and most trade was dominated by the United States, as shown in Chapter 1 of this volume. In addition, the eight countries were already relatively well connected by existing PTAs.

In preparing their calculations about the net benefits of the TPP, many officials realised that if agricultural trade were excluded from the final agreement (or if significant sectors were carved out of the final document), the net economic benefits from the TPP would be lower.[2] Because some agricultural sectors had not been liberalised or had not been fully liberalised in past agreements, there was still scope for improvement in the TPP. This chapter highlights some of the specific areas where this argument applied.

In addition, negotiators were extremely conscious of the precedent that would be set for the entire agreement if agricultural sectors could be excluded from the outset. If any one area could be carved out as too sensitive for inclusion it would establish the possibility that countries could carve out other highly sensitive issues from the text elsewhere. So, for example, parties might opt out of intellectual property provisions or labour or environmental rules. This was seen as undermining the 'high quality, 21st century' aspirational goals of the entire agreement, and therefore officials insisted from the beginning that all sectors had to be on the table for discussion and future liberalisation.

II TARIFFS AND HARMONISED SYSTEM CODES

The first order of business for officials interested in opening up markets to one another was to reduce tariff levels. Tariffs can be thought of as a tax on imported goods. Although the countries in the TPP negotiations have generally low tariff levels, some products are protected by a variety of mechanisms, including high tariffs for specific items or quantitative restrictions.

---

[2] Of course, under WTO rules, the TPP members could not simply carve out agriculture from the final agreement, as this would likely prevent the agreement from covering 'substantially all … trade' as required by WTO rules for PTAs. See Section IV below.

Goods are arranged into different categories using 'Harmonized System' (HS) codes.[3] HS codes can be thought of as a sorting system, with the greatest number of products bundled together at the two-digit level and more finely detailed information on products included as the number of digits increases. As an example, edible fruits and nuts are found at the two-digit level, at HS chapter 08. Citrus fruit, fresh or dried, are given the code 0805, at the four-digit level. Digging down further, at six digits, 080510, is fresh oranges. At this level of detail, goods are divided into over 5000 groups using six-digit HS codes.[4]

Each of these categories is assigned a particular tariff rate. For example, the tariff rate on code HS080510, fresh oranges, in the United States is 1.9¢ per kilogram. Oranges are subject to a most favoured nation (MFN) six per cent ad valorem duty for Peru,[5] but enter duty free (zero tariff) into Australia, Canada, Malaysia and Singapore.[6]

For agricultural products, the specific HS codes are contained in HS chapters 1–24.[7] Calculating the total number of tariff lines for agricultural products is surprisingly challenging. In part this is because every country has differing levels of existing tariff commitments in agriculture. Figure 6.1 shows the MFN applied tariff lines committed by the 11 TPP negotiating parties at the WTO and the wide variation among them – from Australia with only 755 lines to the United States with 1793.

Of course, it should be noted that commitments to bind tariffs at broader levels of specificity (at the six-digit level rather than the eight- or ten-digit level) actually includes more products. Recall the fresh oranges

---

3 The World Customs Organization manages the system and revises it periodically. For more information, see <http://www.wcoomd.org/en/topics/nomenclature.aspx>.

4 HS codes actually range from as few as two digits (where they aggregate into 99 product categories) to as many as 10 digits. All countries use six digits, but not all countries use the eight- or ten-digit level of specificity. In tariff negotiations, these are called domestic-level headings. The TPP negotiations are being conducted at the level of domestic headings, which will result in considerably more than 5000 tariff lines.

5 MFN rates are given to all WTO members. PTAs usually give a better deal to partners than the existing MFN tariff rates.

6 This example also shows the complexity of agricultural tariffs, something discussed in greater detail below.

7 The HS does not exactly match the divisions used by the WTO. In particular, agricultural products are counted differently. The WTO counts agriculture as HS chapters 1–24, except for chapter 3 (fish and crustaceans) plus a few other items like some chemicals, fur and fibres.

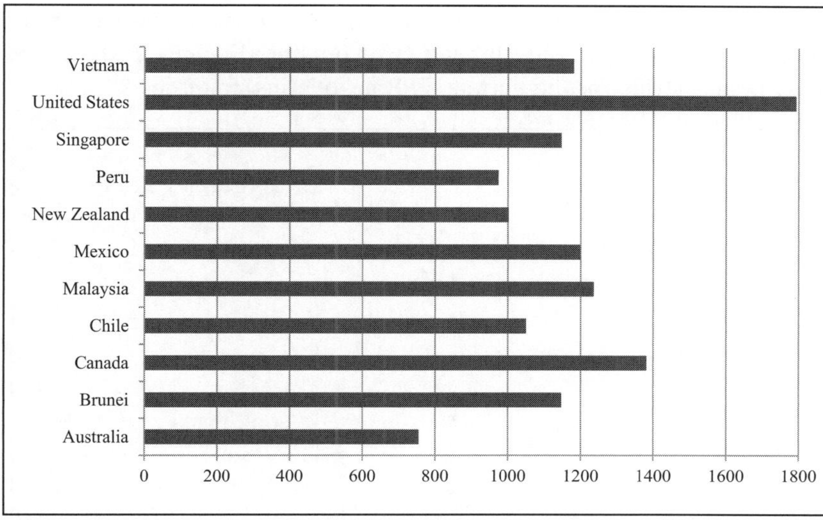

Figure 6.1 Number of MFN applied tariff lines in agriculture

example. If Country A were to bind tariffs at 3 per cent at the two-digit chapter heading, *all* edible nuts and fruits would be included.

III AGRICULTURAL TARIFF LEVELS AT THE WTO

It is one thing to argue in the abstract for no exclusions from trade agreements. It is another thing entirely to sit down with partners and hammer out details for opening markets. Agricultural liberalisation in various fora to date has been limited and piecemeal.

Although the GATT has been successively lowering tariff barriers to trade in goods since 1948, agriculture was specifically excluded from the early rounds. In fact, agriculture was not brought into the multilateral trade system in a sustained way until the Uruguay Round of negotiations from 1986–93. The Uruguay Round's[8] (*Agreement on Agriculture*) was the first attempt to improve market access and remove trade-distorting subsidies in agriculture. These commitments began in 1995 and were

[8] *Marrakesh Agreement Establishing the World Trade Organization*, opened for signature 15 April 1994, 1867 UNTS 3 (entered into force 1 January 1995), annex 1A (*Agreement on Agriculture*) 1867 UNTS 410.

phased in over a six- to ten-year period.[9] Even then, however, most members committed to only limited tariff binding. Figure 6.2 shows the WTO bound levels for the current TPP negotiating countries.[10]

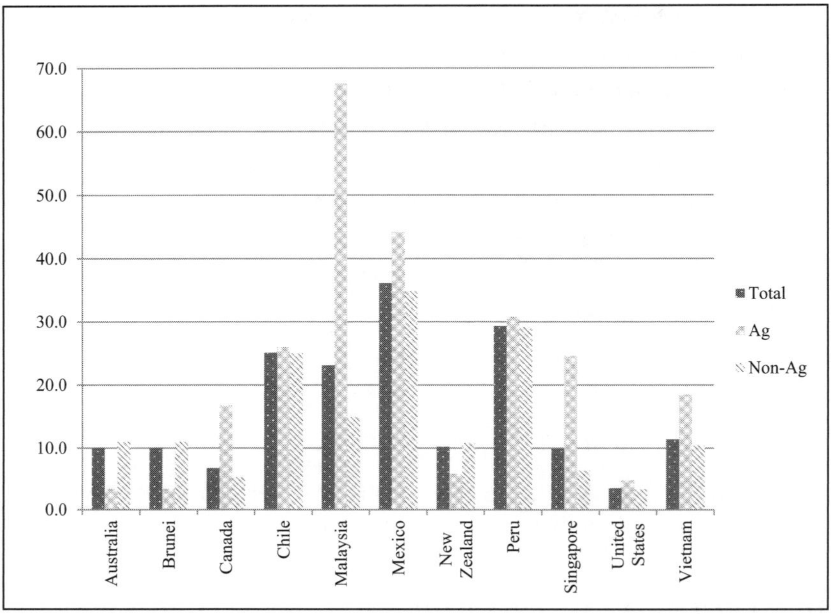

Figure 6.2 Simple average final WTO bound tariff (2010)

Applied tariffs – those tariffs actually used by countries on goods crossing their borders – are often substantially lower than the bound rate.[11] Figure 6.3 shows the applied tariff rates for TPP negotiating

[9] Ten years for developing countries, less for developed country members.

[10] Interestingly, Vietnam's bindings are lower than for many other TPP negotiating parties. This is because Vietnam joined the WTO much later than other WTO member states (in 2007) and was subject to much greater disciplines on tariff levels than older members. However, as Figure 6.3 shows, Vietnam's applied tariff levels are also higher than the rest on average, with levels nearly equal to the bound rates.

[11] The applied rate must be lower than the bound rate (except for in certain, exceptional circumstances). The gap between the two is known in WTO-speak as 'water'. A big part of the Doha Development Agenda negotiations is to reduce the 'water' currently in the system by lowering bound tariff rates.

countries. Note, however, how much higher, overall, the bound and applied rates are for agricultural goods versus industrial goods.[12]

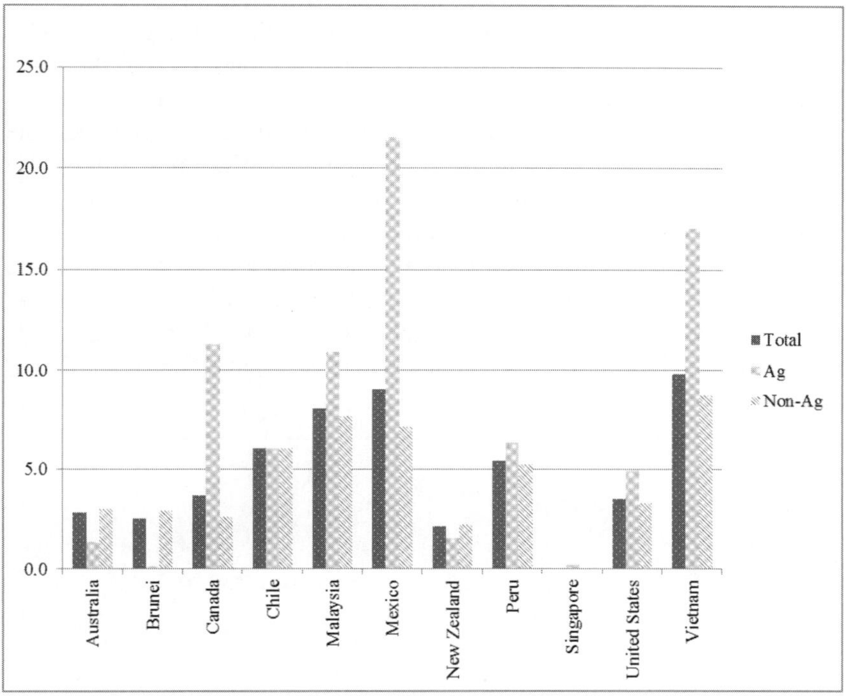

Figure 6.3 Simple average WTO MFN applied tariff (2009)

In fact, one of the 'built-in' agenda items for the current WTO negotiations in the Doha Development Agenda (DDA), started in November 2001, is agricultural trade, as WTO members recognised the limited extent of liberalisation in this area.[13] Because nearly every country protects agriculture, and because it is such a sensitive topic, more than a decade of tough talks have not led to a breakthrough at the multilateral system. With such limited progress in agriculture, the rest of the WTO's negotiating agenda has largely been stalled.

---

[12] Some items that most individuals would ordinarily consider to be agricultural, including fish and forestry products, are included under the category of industrial goods.

[13] The other 'built-in' item was services trade, as WTO Members also agreed that their early steps to open services trade were inadequate by the launch of the DDA in 2001.

In addition to overall high tariff rates, agricultural producers often face what are called 'tariff peaks'. This is where tariffs overall are generally low, but in one particular segment of trade, tariffs suddenly shoot up very high. Figures 6.4 and 6.5 offer two views of the same data of TPP members. A close examination of the figures shows clearly the tariff peaks for Canadian dairy and Mexican sugar products, which are discussed in greater detail below. In fact, these figures actually understate the tariff peaks, as both figures show applied tariff rates rather than bound rates, which are even higher.

Tariff peaks are much more significant in agricultural goods than for industrial goods, largely because eight prior rounds of tariff cuts via the GATT/WTO have brought down industrial goods tariffs quite substantially. As bound rates fall, applied rates also must fall to levels below bound rates. These tariff peaks, as we shall see, have been a particular challenge in the TPP negotiations.

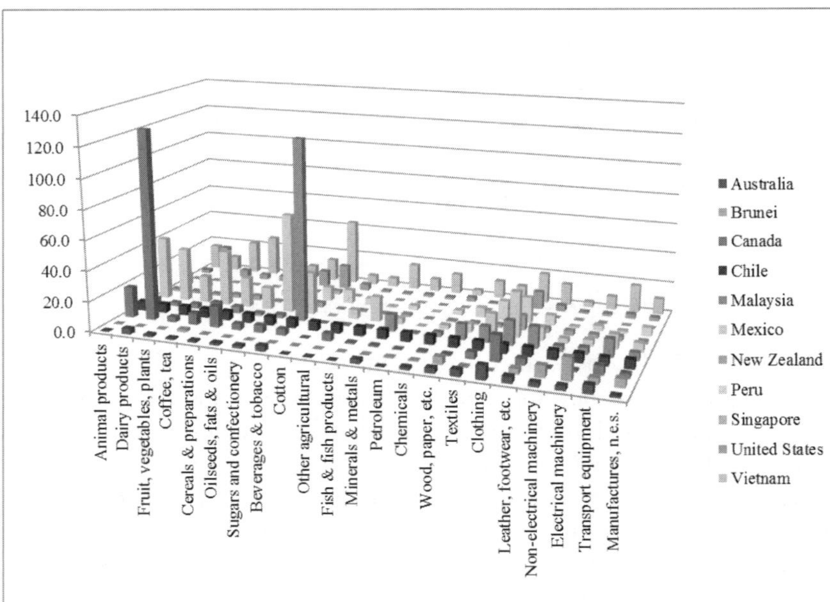

Figure 6.4 WTO applied tariff rates (2009)

Tariff peaks have also been vexing at the multilateral level. They are a big part of the stumbling block in the agricultural negotiations at the DDA negotiations. Because many governments were eager to create a system to reduce not just overall tariff levels but also begin to reduce

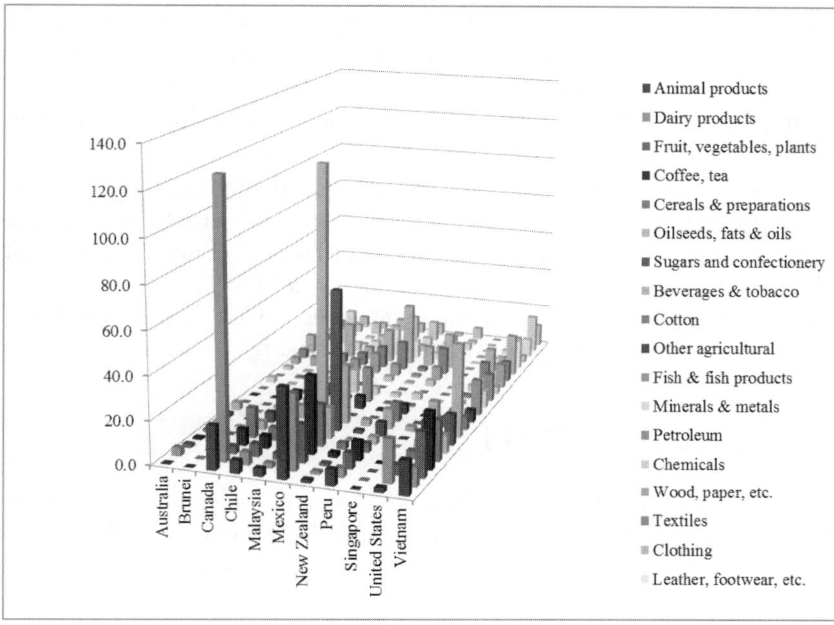

Figure 6.5 WTO applied tariff rates (2009)

these tariff peaks, officials in the WTO began to rethink their previous approaches to market access negotiations. In past rounds, countries bargained using what is called a 'request–offer' system. Simplified greatly, it meant that Country A would offer to reduce tariffs on, for example, chicken legs in exchange for tariff reductions on, for example, fresh oranges from Country B. If this deal was accepted by both parties, it was locked in and eventually extended to all WTO members using the MFN clause – granting all WTO members the same tariff rate on chicken legs from Country A and fresh oranges from Country B.

But request–offer is a poor mechanism for eliminating or significantly reducing tariff peaks. If a country maintained a tariff of something extremely high, like 500 per cent on an item, in request–offer it might be cut to only 450 per cent. So officials developed a new method for reducing tariffs called 'formula cuts'. This would have the advantage of mowing down tariff peaks substantially in one single process without the need to painfully negotiate each line separately. In fact, done right, it would actually reduce tariff peaks *more* substantially than remaining tariffs. So officials in Geneva spent years haggling over the exact formula needed to carry out this initiative. This was complicated by the need to ensure that developing countries maintained special and differential treatment from developed economies. It also needed to ensure that new members would not find themselves subject to new cuts soon after joining, since their tariffs were already bound at comparatively low levels.

In July 2008 the DDA negotiations came tantalisingly close to conclusion. Officials got close to agreement on a specific set of formulas that could be used in the agriculture talks of the DDA.[14] However, the round broke down before any country had to try to justify the use of the formula to their domestic audiences in detail, so we may never know whether or not it would have worked as promised.

IV AGRICULTURE IN PTAS

It is against this somewhat bleak background of failure that many countries have turned to regional and bilateral negotiations. The proliferation of PTAs has been explosive, particularly in Asia, as Chapter 1 of this volume notes.

Under WTO rules, PTAs are required to cover 'substantially all … trade' between partners.[15] Although members have never specified the thresholds for 'substantially all', in practice it means that PTAs that include at least one developed country member cannot simply carve out all of agricultural trade from an agreement; to do so would be to remove too great a percentage of trade between members. Instead, PTAs frequently avoid tariff reductions on some portion of trade in agricultural products. These sensitive sectors are 'carved out' of the final agreement that otherwise lowers barriers to trade between the parties.

As an illustration, Masahiro Kawai and Ganeshan Wignaraja have calculated that of the 58 PTAs concluded in Asia in 2010, only half had

---

14 See *The July 2008 Package* (2008) World Trade Organization <http://www.wto.org/english/tratop_e/dda_e/meet08_e.htm>. This document was later revised by Crawford Falconer, the chair of the agriculture negotiations, in December 2008: see *Chairperson's Texts 2008* (9 December 2008) World Trade Organization <http://www.wto.org/english/tratop_e/agric_e/chair_texts08_e.htm>.

15 *Marrakesh Agreement Establishing the World Trade Organization*, opened for signature 15 April 1994, 1867 UNTS 3 (entered into force 1 January 1995), annex 1A (*General Agreement on Tariffs and Trade 1994*) 1867 UNTS 187, art XXIV:8(b). An exception is possible for agreements between developing country members under the Enabling Clause of the Tokyo Round: *Decision on Differential and More Favourable Treatment, Reciprocity, and Fuller Participation of Developing Countries*, L/4903, BISD 26S/203 (28 November 1979).

what they called 'comprehensive' coverage of agricultural products.[16] Yet the definition of comprehensive is, itself, rather weak. Comprehensive coverage means that at least 85 per cent of all product lines are included or covered, or that not more than 150 product lines were excluded from coverage. Given the often low levels of trade between parties in PTAs, it is conceivable that the entire sum of agricultural trade between them might be located within a handful of tariff lines alone. If these are excluded from coverage, even a 'comprehensive' agreement will bring no market opening benefits.

Further, of the 58 PTAs examined, 21 per cent had excluded or limited agricultural coverage, where agriculture was either carved out completely or had less than a total of 100 lines included in the agreement.[17]

It is true that many of these 58 agreements under examination were not between TPP members or included only one TPP member. For example, the study included the agreement between the Republic of Korea (that is, South Korea – not party to TPP negotiations) and Chile (a TPP negotiating party). This 'comprehensive' agreement nevertheless excluded 21 products from the final agreement, including rice, apples and pears entering Korea and sugar and wheat entering Chile. Given the importance of these markets such exclusions could be significant. In 2010, Korea's sixteenth largest imported commodity was rice. Of all of Korea's top exports, refined sugar was third largest and sugar confectionary products were tenth largest.[18] For Chile, in 2010, apples were the third largest export market and pears were the seventeenth largest. On the import side, Chile relied on refined sugar from overseas (Chile's third largest imported commodity in 2010) and wheat (Chile's seventh largest imported commodity).

Similar patterns can be found throughout other PTAs – key commodity imports and exports can be limited to just a very few tariff lines of interest. If these lines or sectors are excluded from the final PTA, the value of the market opening for agricultural products overall drops off significantly.

---

16 Masahiro Kawai and Ganeshan Wignaraja, 'Asian FTAs: Trends, Prospects and Challenges' (Economics Working Paper No 226, Asian Development Bank, October 2010) 15–16 <http://www.un.org/esa/ffd/msc/regionalcooperation/ADB_WPs.pdf>.

17 This is possible because many of the agreements were between developing country members and thus subject to lower thresholds for overall coverage under WTO rules. See *Decision on Differential and More Favourable Treatment, Reciprocity, and Fuller Participation of Developing Countries*, above n 15.

18 See FAOSTAT, *Imports: Commodities by Country*, Food and Agricultural Organization <http://faostat.fao.org/site/342/default.aspx>.

In general, Jo-Ann Crawford has found that out of 65 PTAs studied, more than half of the agricultural chapters exclude one or more products from liberalisation.[19] The most frequently excluded products are HS chapters 17 (sugar), 21 (miscellaneous edible preparations),[20] 22 (beverages), 10 (cereals), 4 (dairy products) and 2 (meat). The extent to which countries exclude products from PTA coverage varies from agreement to agreement, so Crawford argues that it does not appear that countries routinely exclude the same sectors or lines.

V AGRICULTURAL NEGOTIATIONS IN THE TPP

Given the configurations of the partners in the TPP, agricultural negotiations have not entirely lived up to past experiences as highlighted by Crawford. In the TPP, two countries, Brunei and Singapore, are largely net agricultural importers.[21] Although several TPP negotiating parties have highly competitive agricultural export sectors, they do not compete fiercely between one another in markets for products such as rice, wheat, soybeans, corn or beverages. Thus, some of the typical areas of agricultural sensitivity were not going to be as challenging to negotiate.

In addition, the 11 TPP negotiating parties were already linked by a welter of existing PTA agreements, as noted in Chapter 1 of this volume. Although not all of these PTAs included complete – or even extensive – agricultural liberalisation, many of them did open markets further than existing WTO commitments. The previous negotiating experience also meant that for many TPP partners, officials already knew where the specific sensitivities were located.

This does not mean, of course, that agricultural negotiations in the TPP have been smooth. In addition to the highly contested issues of sugar and dairy, discussed in greater detail below, talks over agriculture have been structurally complex.

---

[19] See Jo-Ann Crawford, 'Market Access Provisions on Trade in Goods in Regional Trade Agreements' (Working Paper No ERSD-2012-20, World Trade Organization: Economic Research and Statistics Division, 31 October 2012) 19 <https://www.wto.org/english/res_e/reser_e/ersd201220_e.pdf> for an excellent review of all PTA provisions reported to the WTO Secretariat.

[20] Chapter 21 of the HS codes includes extracts of coffee and tea, yeasts, mustards, ketchup, soy sauce, soup, and ice cream.

[21] Singapore does have poultry and egg production for domestic consumption. It also exports some processed food products and beer.

Like the negotiations over market access in industrial goods, agricultural discussions have been taking place within the TPP in two parallel tracks. On one side are 'plurilateral' discussions between most of the TPP members.[22] On the other side are a set of bilateral discussions between the United States and Peru with those partners who do not already have existing bilateral PTAs.[23] These two separate tracks will cover goods commitments for each of the TPP partners from the date of entry into force of the agreement through the implementation period. Once the agreement has been fully phased in the two tracks should come into alignment.[24]

Under both tracks, officials were negotiating for 90 per cent of all lines for goods to fall to zero tariffs on entry into force. Roughly 8 per cent of the remaining tariff lines would go to zero by the end of implementation (10 years for developing countries). The remaining 1–2 per cent of the lines are still under discussion after three years of negotiations.[25] This formulation, however, applied to all goods trade. Agricultural goods are likely to make up a greater share of the transition lines.

This two-track approach to negotiations adds an extra layer of complexity to an already tricky situation. Why did the United States (in particular) insist on bilateral discussions? The reasoning, in brief, was

---

[22] Canada and Mexico joined the talks in late 2012 without making a formal decision about which market access 'track' they were planning to participate in.

[23] For the United States, the partner countries are Brunei, Malaysia, New Zealand, and Vietnam. In addition, because the United States was seeking additional market access commitments from Canada beyond what it received in the *North American Free Trade Agreement*, signed 17 December 1992, 32 ILM 289 (entered into force 1 January 1994) (NAFTA), bilateral talks in agriculture were also opened once Canada joined the talks in the 15th round in December 2012.

[24] This, at least, is the hope after three years of negotiating. As of the 15th round of talks, officials had not yet resolved the vexing issues of determining how to ensure that the two parallel tracks of market access commitments converge fully.

[25] Interviews with market access officials. This was the announced plan of both tracks. It was a bit trickier to assess the extent to which the bilateral tracks complied with the plan, particularly since the United States placed goods into 'baskets' for liberalisation. Only the first basket of goods was automatically designed to go to zero on implementation. The last basket of goods – containing most of the items of greatest interest to partners – remained 'undetermined' with limited details on scope and timing. Given the size of this basket, at nearly 1000 items, three years into negotiations, it was especially difficult to see whether the United States' offers for goods actually met the proposed plan of the plurilateral countries.

that this was deemed to give better benefits to firms already conducting business in TPP negotiating states.[26] In an environment of overlapping PTAs, many firms already receive preferential tariff rates, lower than WTO bound rates and often much lower than WTO applied rates. However, the TPP plurilateral track for market access started with WTO bound rates as the baseline for tariff reductions and cut down from there. This, argued the United States, would have severely disadvantaged firms in the interim period who could have seen tariff rates go up under the TPP in the early years instead of down. Using the bilateral track negotiations ensured that the United States' exporters would enjoy tariff advantages from the TPP from the very beginning of the agreement relative to the status quo under either any existing PTA agreements or no agreement at all. It also complicated the bargaining and ensured a more complex environment, overall, for businesses in the TPP in the transition period.

VI REMAINING SENSITIVE ISSUES

The bilateral track negotiations have largely been conducted behind closed doors, even within the TPP rounds. Only officials of countries actively engaged in the market access discussions with the United States have been privy to the content of the offers on the table. This means that there may be a few agricultural items of sensitivity to one or two TPP members that are not discussed here.

In general, however, the most contentious sectors for TPP members in agricultural trade have been sugar and dairy. This is not unusual. Linda Fulponi, Matthew Shearer and Juliana Almeida note that these two industries have almost never been completely liberalised in any of the 50 PTAs they studied.[27]

Sugar is a problem for the TPP in multiple ways. In general, the sector is highly sensitive. In the United States, protection of the industry began in earnest during the Depression and has never been relaxed. As a result, United States consumers have paid two to three times the world price for

---

[26] See Deborah Elms, 'The Trans-Pacific Partnership: The Challenges of Untangling the Noodle Bowl' (2013) 18 *International Negotiation* 25.

[27] Linda Fulponi, Matthew Shearer and Juliana Almeida, 'Regional Trade Agreements – Treatment of Agriculture' (Working Paper No 44, Organisation for Economic Co-operation and Development, 31 March 2011) <http://www.oecd-ilibrary.org/agriculture-and-food/regional-trade-agreements-treatment-of-agriculture_5kgg53fmnjxv-en>.

sugar for decades.[28] Yet efforts to roll back the various types of support for the sugar industry over the years have all been defeated.

In the 'P4 agreement' between Brunei, Chile, New Zealand and Singapore that formed the basis for the TPP,[29] sugar received the only sector-specific provision in the goods agreement. Chile got a special agricultural safeguard mechanism, 'the sugar treatment', to prevent disruptive surges in sugar imports.[30] Under the *North American Free Trade Agreement* (NAFTA),[31] one of the last items to be liberalised between the parties was sugar after a 14-year wait. Sugar is sensitive not only in the United States, but also in Mexico.[32]

There is also a specific problem for sugar rooted in the complex TPP negotiating environment. This is because sugar was completely carved out of the existing *Australia–United States Free Trade Agreement* (AUSFTA).[33] It was carved out of the agreement at the time as part of a grand bargain that allowed the United States to continue to protect its domestic sugar producers and Australia to opt out of the investor–state dispute mechanism. The former was an important objective for Australia,

---

28 See, for example, the estimates contained in 'Employment Changes in U.S. Food Manufacturing: The Impact of Sugar Prices' (Report, International Trade Administration, United States Department of Commerce, February 2006) <http://www.ita.doc.gov/media/Publications/pdf/sugar06.pdf>. The report goes on to note that 10 000 manufacturing jobs had been lost from sugar manufacturing jobs as well during the period 1997–2002 as a result of the high price of sugar.

29 *Trans-Pacific Strategic Economic Partnership*, Brunei Darussalam–Chile–New Zealand–Singapore, signed 18 July 2005 (Brunei Darussalam signed 2 August 2005) (entered into force 28 May 2006 (New Zealand and Singapore), 12 July 2006 (Brunei Darussalam), 8 November 2006 (Chile)).

30 New Zealand, however, noted that it only agreed to liberalisation of sugar products (in solid form, under HS code 1701) because it did not export such products to Chile. See New Zealand Ministry of Foreign Affairs and Trade, *Trans-Pacific Strategic Economic Partnership Agreement: National Interest Analysis* (July 2005) 8 <http://www.mfat.govt.nz/downloads/trade-agreement/transpacific/transpacific-sepa-nia.pdf>.

31 See above n 23.

32 The Mexican government, for example, provided over US$1 billion in loans to the domestic sugar industry in the early 2000s through the development bank, Financiera Nacional Azucarerara SA. See Gary Clyde Hufbauer and Jeffrey Schott, *NAFTA Revisited: Opportunities and Challenges* (International Institute for Economics, 2005) 295.

33 *Australia–United States Free Trade Agreement*, signed 18 May 2004, [2005] ATS 1 (entered into force 1 January 2005) (AUSFTA).

while the latter was a key issue for the Americans. In the end, both sides compromised by excluding these two items from the final agreement.[34]

Now, however, the sugar exclusion has presented a new challenge to negotiators in the TPP. If sugar is included in the TPP, it will, in practical terms, negate the AUSFTA. In what has been largely perceived as a response to this problem, the United States developed its strategy of refusing to negotiate for new market access with any country with an existing free trade agreement.[35]

But excluding sugar from the TPP is problematic. It is not just difficult for trade in agriculture. Doing so would allow other countries to argue for excluding their own most sensitive agricultural items. Given the relatively limited economic trade involved between many TPP members, carving out sectors, as previously mentioned, could seriously erode the potential economic gains from the final agreement. It also flies in the face of the 'no exclusions' mantra present from the earliest days of the negotiations.

Finally, carving out a sector like sugar could lead to similar behaviour elsewhere in the agreement. Like the AUSFTA example, the exclusion of sugar might result in the carving out of automobiles or investor protections or intellectual property protections for pharmaceutical products. If each of the 11 TPP members were allowed to exclude their 'favourite' sensitive product, sector or issue from the final agreement, the result could be a significant step back from the liberalising goals sought from the beginning.

The other particularly problematic sector for agriculture negotiators is dairy. Again, this is a historically sensitive industry for many countries with a poor track record of liberalisation across the board. In the context of the TPP, three of the original negotiating parties have highly competitive dairy industries, including Australia, New Zealand and the United States (the specific challenges of Canadian dairy are discussed below).

---

[34] For more detail on the history of the AUSFTA, see Ann Capling, *All the Way with the USA* (University of New South Wales Press, 2005).

[35] This policy was modified slightly with the addition of Canada and Mexico at the negotiating table. The United States announced that it would refuse to negotiate with countries with market access commitments that were 'not yet fully implemented'. See 'USTR Seeks to Negotiate on Goods Access with NAFTA Partners in TPP' (21 June 2012) 30(25) *Inside US Trade* (online). Since the AUSFTA has some tariffs on sugar and out-of-quota dairy commitments that remain until 2022, Australia was deemed to be ineligible for reopening market access commitments. Canadian concessions, however, could be sought, since the final NAFTA commitments were phased in by 2008.

New Zealand and the United States do not have an existing PTA. One of the biggest obstacles to completing a bilateral agreement in the past has been over issues in relation to dairy.[36] The United States has had a variety of measures in place to protect dairy farmers, including subsidies for milk production and price supports for dairy and dairy products. These programs have been backed up historically by high tariffs and by tariff rate quotas to limit imports of dairy products.

The primary issue for American milk producers in the TPP negotiations has been that New Zealand's dairy industry is viewed as a monopoly, with one firm (Fonterra) in control of 90 per cent of the market and substantial barriers to entry into the market.[37] If the United States' market were opened to competition through a PTA like the TPP, American dairy farmers have feared that New Zealand dairy producers will receive unfair competitive advantages.[38] In addition to problems of

---

[36] An earlier problem related to issues with New Zealand's refusal to allow American nuclear vessels into New Zealand waters for refueling.

[37] The WTO's review of New Zealand in 2003 found that dairy was no longer a monopoly, but the company had exclusive licenses to export to some markets from 2010 onwards, *Trade Policy Review: New Zealand*, WTO Doc WT/TPR/S/115 (14 April 2003) (Report of the WTO Secretariat) section IV, 2. See Fonterra (USA), Inc, Submission No USTR-2009-0002-0045 to the Office of the United States Trade Representative, *Request for Comments and Notice of Public Hearing Concerning Proposed Trans-Pacific Partnership Trade Agreement with Singapore, Chile, New Zealand, Brunei Darussalam, Australia, Peru and Vietnam*, 11 March 2009, in which Fonterra (USA), Inc argued that the market in New Zealand was open for competition, with no government subsidies, import tariffs or quota restrictions. It also argued that the entire New Zealand dairy industry was smaller than that of California and that it was no more globally competitive than American dairy in various export markets.

[38] The National Milk Producers Federation and US Dairy Export Council estimates that United States dairy producers would lose gross revenues of US$20 billion over the first ten years of a PTA: see National Milk Producers Federation, Oral Submission to the Office of the United States Trade Representative, 4 March 2009. Land O'Lakes was more careful, but urged the Office to look carefully at New Zealand's dairy industry for anti-competitive outcomes, see Land O'Lakes, Inc, Submission No USTR-2009-0002-0015 to the Office of the United States Trade Representative, *Request for Comments and Notice of Public Hearing Concerning Proposed Trans-Pacific Partnership Trade Agreement with Singapore, Chile, New Zealand, Brunei Darussalam, Australia, Peru and Vietnam*, 9 March 2009. The National Confectioners Association asked for immediate liberalisation of dairy from New Zealand, as it would bring about substantial benefits for their producers, who were forced to manufacture sweets with the highest-priced sugar and dairy in the world: National Confectioners Association, Submission No USTR-2009-0002-0024 to the Office of the United States Trade

direct competition,[39] a TPP agreement that included dairy would undermine some important gains from trade as, for example, New Zealand and Australia would become more competitive in the Peruvian market (with which neither state had a PTA in place).

These concerns were echoed by the US Dairy Export Council.[40] The Council noted its support for nearly all other PTAs, stemming from the experience with NAFTA, where Mexico became the single largest destination for United States' dairy exports. The United States' export market used to be driven primarily by the sale of government stockpiles and subsidised products, but export markets have become increasingly important for domestic producers. Given the export-oriented structure of the dairy industry in New Zealand, and the size of the United States' market, it is likely, the Council argued, that much of the New Zealand production would be directed at the United States.

Representative John McHugh wrote to the United States Trade Representative (USTR) that:

> the New Zealand dairy industry has the ability to flood our market with new imports, including such dairy products as cheese, milk proteins, butter fat, and dairy food preparations. These actions would likely result in the closure of thousands of small and medium-sized American dairy farmers, and negatively impact hundreds of rural manufacturers.[41]

After three years, the United States and New Zealand had made only the most limited steps towards resolving the issues over dairy in their bilateral market access talks.[42] Both sides acknowledged that dairy was likely to fall into the final end-game package for the TPP as a whole.[43]

Representative, *Request for Comments and Notice of Public Hearing Concerning Proposed Trans-Pacific Partnership Trade Agreement with Singapore, Chile, New Zealand, Brunei Darussalam, Australia, Peru and Vietnam*, 10 March 2009.

[39] This is happening in any case, as New Zealand dairy exports rose from $454 million in 2004 to $704 million in 2008. See US Dairy Export Council, Submission No USTR-2009-0002-0012 to the Office of the United States Trade Representative, *Request for Comments and Notice of Public Hearing Concerning Proposed Trans-Pacific Partnership Trade Agreement with Singapore, Chile, New Zealand, Brunei Darussalam, Australia, Peru and Vietnam*, 10 March 2009.

[40] Ibid.

[41] John McHugh, 'McHugh to Administration: Dairy Must Be Protected During FTA Negotiations' (Press Release, 25 September 2008).

[42] 'USTR Tables Initial TPP Dairy Proposal, Offers Little New to New Zealand' (23 March 2012) 30(12) *Inside US Trade* (online).

[43] 'U.S. Negotiator Sees New Zealand Dairy Talks as Part of TPP End Game' (13 September 2012) 30(37) *Inside US Trade* (online).

However, the calculus on dairy has changed somewhat with the addition of Canada and Mexico to the negotiating table with the 15th round of TPP negotiations in late 2012. In particular, United States dairy producers have the potential for greater market access into Canada, which might offset any losses inflicted by New Zealand farmers.

It was largely issues with dairy that derailed Canadian entry into the TPP for more than two years. Canadian officials originally approached TPP negotiating states in 2009–10 to request the bilateral consultations that precede any entry decision. Although officials have been coy about the results of these meetings, Canada was not granted entry at that time.[44] The primary reason for rejection centred on the obstacles posed by Canadian unwillingness to discuss its supply management systems for dairy and poultry in the context of the TPP.

Canada has a long-standing set of practices in place to encourage the growth and development of its domestic dairy, poultry and egg farmers.[45] This system was deemed necessary to protect Canadian farmers against competitive pressures from countries south of its border. The supply management system includes setting a floor price and tariff peaks on dairy that are as high as 300 per cent.

Under Canada's existing PTAs the supply management system for dairy (and poultry) has remained intact.[46] In fact, even under the fully implemented NAFTA, Canada continued to have less than free trade in dairy for American and Mexican producers. This has given rise to the potential for substantial changes in Canadian policy going forward that may have an impact on trade levels in dairy with other TPP partners.

VII TARIFF RATE QUOTAS

Unlike industrial goods, negotiators in agriculture also have to address another peculiarity in the system: the tariff rate quota (TRQ). Because

---

[44] Interviews with TPP officials.

[45] Approximately 13 000 dairy farmers participate in supply management, with the bulk of them located in Quebec and Ontario.

[46] Although a somewhat similar system for wheat was dismantled. TPP members were closely following the ongoing talks between Canada and the European Union (EU), under the assumption that supply management was likely on the table in that PTA, which was expected to conclude before the TPP.

agriculture has historically been so sensitive, repeated rounds of negotiations under the GATT largely left agricultural products uncovered. In the Uruguay Round talks, officials decided to include agriculture for the first time.

Up until this point, states had protected agriculture by a combination of high tariffs and non-tariff barriers, especially in the form of quotas. In order to properly address these barriers, officials created a system to translate non-tariff barriers into tariff terms. Over time, officials expected that barriers to trade in agricultural products would fall, just as other tariff barriers to trade have fallen in repeated rounds of negotiations.

Under the TRQ system, products were generally assigned two tariff rates and a specified quantity of imports allowed. The first, lower, tariff rate would apply for all imports of products up to the quota. A second rate (frequently much higher) would apply for all imports above the quota.[47] The *Agreement on Agriculture* established over 1425 TRQs, mostly used by developed economies. TRQs can be set up as 'supplier tariff quotas', or are country-specific rather than being open for imports from all WTO member states.[48]

TRQs have been used in PTA negotiations. For example, under the United States–Peru free trade agreement, the United States provided Peru with a 9000 ton sugar TRQ and an additional 2000 ton TRQ for specialty sugar.[49] This allows Peruvian exporters to ship up to 9000 tons of sugar per year to the United States, provided that Peru is a net exporter of sugar and that the United States does not choose to invoke its right to provide compensation in lieu of accepting imports.[50] The 9001st ton of sugar exported by Peru is subject to significantly higher tariff rates.

TRQs, in general, often cover the same sensitive issues as those sheltered by tariff peaks or subject to limited tariff reductions under

---

[47] If the second, out-of-quota, tariff is set high enough the entire formula effectively reduces to an import quota.

[48] This allows discrimination to take place within the WTO. Note that TRQs have been the subject of many disagreements and disputes in the WTO system, particularly about the methods of determining country-specific quotas and the non-transparent administration of some country's systems.

[49] The former quota also expands at 2 per cent simple annual growth per year, while the latter does not expand over time with growth. See United States Department of Agriculture, *Fact Sheet: U.S.–Peru Trade Promotion Agreement* (September 2009) <http://www.fas.usda.gov/info/factsheets/Peru/PeruTPA-09.pdf>.

[50] The exceptions to the TRQ shown in this example highlight both the complexity of the TRQ administration as well as some of the mechanisms that can be used to prevent imports.

PTAs, including dairy and sugar. After three years of negotiations, TPP officials had not yet gotten into the details of how to resolve the problems of existing TRQs; nor have they decided whether TRQs would be allowed in the TPP itself. Both of these issues are extremely difficult to resolve. If, for example, Peru has already been granted a TRQ of 9000 tons on sugar in the United States–Peru bilateral agreement, what will happen to this quota under the TPP? If the quota is altered under the bilateral TPP schedules between the United States and Peru, does it continue to exist into the future or will it get phased out over time? If it gets phased out, does it do so on the same schedule as the rest of the TPP agreement, or on a longer timetable?

In general, TRQs fly in the face of the '21st century, high quality'[51] rhetoric of the TPP. The explicit intention of the multilateral system from the outset was to make TRQs a temporary phenomenon, to be eliminated or converted to straight tariffs over time. To continue the practice of writing TRQs into the TPP suggests a path away from a 'gold standard' for future agreements, at least in this area.

VIII OTHER FACTORS AFFECTING TRADE IN AGRICULTURE

Tariffs are not the only issue of concern for assessing TPP outcomes in agriculture. For example, in any goods trade there is a tight connection between tariff levels and rules of origin (ROOs). As discussed in Chapter 2 in this volume, TPP officials have grappled with crafting an appropriate ROOs regime. It is possible to have completely open, duty-free access to the market for partner firms, but create such difficult ROOs that few products meet the criteria for origin. Thus, almost no firms will be able to claim the benefits originally promised by the duty-free access provisions. Conversely, it is possible to leave tariff levels relatively higher, but create liberal ROOs. Under this scenario, firms might find it easier to qualify their products as TPP-originating and be able to take advantage of the preferences offered to them in the agreement.

For agricultural products, ROOs often require goods to be 'wholly originating' in a member state. This means that the entire product must be 'from' a member country. Meeting this criterion is not difficult for commodities trade, as it involves products that are grown, harvested or

[51] C.L. Lim, Deborah Elms and Patrick Low (eds), *The Trans-Pacific Partnership: A Quest for a Twenty-first Century Trade Agreement* (Cambridge University Press, 2012).

extracted, or animals that were born and raised completely within one country. For example, wheat or tomatoes can easily be seen to be wholly originating as they are grown entirely in one country. Something like sheep meat can also be wholly originating, assuming that the animal was born, raised and slaughtered within a member country.

However, processed agricultural products face a more difficult challenge, depending on the ROOs selected.[52] Moving from raw agricultural products to finished goods such as biscuits or beer can make it harder to meet originating criteria. In part it depends on whether the rules require a change in the HS chapter heading used, which is often harder to reach for agricultural goods, particularly at the two-digit level. For example, to move from fresh oranges to orange juice is a shift from HS chapter 08 to chapter 02. However, if a firm wanted to peel imported fresh oranges and export the peels, this only shifts the HS code at the six-digit level from 080510 to 081400. It does not change the tariff code at the two-digit level and would not qualify for TPP partner preferential rates under these ROOs.

Another ROOs issue that applies particularly to processed agricultural goods is the level of cumulation allowed, as discussed in greater detail in Chapter 2 of this volume. Lower levels of cumulation make it easier, all else being equal, for firms to export agricultural products to other TPP member countries using the tariff preferences in the agreement.

Another area of deep concern for agricultural exporters is the extent to which the TPP sets new sanitary and phytosanitary (SPS) rules. SPS provisions ensure that countries are not using arbitrary health or safety concerns as disguised means of protecting markets. Generally, PTA members agree to abide by certain organisational standards for setting food safety, and animal and plant health rules. For instance, parties may pledge to use the Food and Agriculture Organization's *International Plant Protection Convention*[53] as the basis for plant health provisions. PTAs may also contain agreements on mechanisms for certifying that measures used in one partner are equivalent to measures in another partner.[54]

---

[52] The ROOs for goods can vary across agreements, but are most restrictive in agricultural and textile sectors. See, e.g., Antoni Estevadeoral and Kati Suominen, 'Rules of Origin in Preferential Trading Agreements: Is All Well with the Spaghetti Bowl in the Americas?'(2005) 5(2) *Economía* 63.

[53] Opened for signature 6 December 1951, 150 UNTS 67 (entered into force 3 April 1952).

[54] Other typical PTA provisions include risk assessment, risk management, border checks, laboratory testing, the development of enquiry points for transparency in regulations, and often cooperation agreements.

The WTO has rules in place for SPS measures, but TPP members have discussed going further and setting up new provisions beyond WTO commitments. These new provisions could include harmonising regulations between TPP members directly as well as greater scope in recognising equivalence and mutual recognition agreements.

Equally contentious in the TPP negotiations have been debates about whether or not any new SPS provisions ought to be legally binding and subject to enforcement under the TPP dispute settlement mechanism. For some exporters, new SPS provisions are only meaningful if they come with the 'teeth' of being legally binding. This is particularly true since new rules cannot be adjudicated in the WTO as they go beyond WTO commitments.

IX WHAT ABOUT JAPAN?

Conspicuously absent from the 11 TPP member list is any mention of Japan. This is in spite of several years of discussion of possible Japanese participation, Japan's bilateral dialogues with negotiating states, and even optimistic statements of membership from Japan's prime ministers.[55]

The payoffs from Japanese membership in the TPP are potentially very large. Although many of the current TPP members already have existing PTAs between themselves, many are not well connected to Japan. Bringing the world's third-largest economy into the agreement would have substantial economic benefits for participants. Japanese gains from TPP entry are also likely to be significant, as Peter Petri, Michael Plummer and Fan Zhai suggest.[56]

However, the single biggest obstacle to Japanese participation has been agricultural concerns within Japan. The most obvious impediment to joining has been the historically high levels of protection offered to

---

[55] Including, most notably, a statement of intent issued by Prime Minister Noda in November 2011 in conjunction with the Asia-Pacific Economic Cooperation Leader's Meeting, see Prime Minister Yoshihiko Noda, 'Opening Statement by Prime Minister Yoshihiko Noda' (Speech delivered at the 19th Asia-Pacific Economic Cooperation Economic Leaders' Meeting, Honolulu, 13 November 2011); Prime Minister Yoshihiko Noda, 'Policy Speech by Prime Minister Yoshihiko Noda to the 181st Session of the Diet' (Speech delivered at the 181st Session of the Japanese Diet, Tokyo, 29 October 2012).

[56] See their TPP track models in, Peter Petri, Michael Plummer and Fan Zhai, 'The Trans-Pacific Partnership and Asia-Pacific Integration: A Quantitative Assessment' (East-West Center Working Papers: Economic Series No 119, East-West Center, 24 October 2011).

Japanese farmers. The political structure is tilted to provide heavier representation of rural areas. Although farming does not contribute much to Japan's overall gross domestic product, the 2.5 million Japanese who farm full- or part-time are a formidable force, operating through the Japan Agriculture Group (JA Group).[57] The most potent symbol of Japan's protectionist farm policies is rice, which is sheltered behind rice tariffs that are higher than 700 per cent.

The JA Group has estimated that removal of tariff barriers to farm products would decimate Japan's agricultural sector. Given that most farmers manage very small plots that are economically uncompetitive with the large agribusinesses in Australia, New Zealand and the United States (in particular), the JA Group predicts that up to 90 per cent of Japanese rice production would be wiped out, as well as 99 per cent of wheat production, nearly all sugar production, and most beef.[58]

Many have argued that these figures are overblown. In addition, structural changes within Japanese agriculture are taking place regardless of whether Japan joins the TPP. The average age of Japan's farmers is 65, with few young people opting for farming as a career. Many of the current farmers lose money and work only part-time on their plots. Japan's consumers pay heavily for food protection and domestic farm support, including four times the average global price for rice; three times the global average for sugar, butter and beef; and twice the global average for wheat, according to government estimates.[59]

Japan levies a 252 per cent tariff on imported wheat, 360 per cent on butter, 328 per cent on sugar and 38.5 per cent for beef. These tariffs, as well as the politically charged rice tariff, would likely have to go in the TPP. If not completely removed (over a probable long transition period), they are going to be subject to significant modifications for the first time under a PTA.[60]

The debate within Japan about TPP membership has been heated. In the days leading up to the November 2011 Asia-Pacific Economic Cooperation (APEC) leaders' meeting, hundreds of farmers gathered in

---

57 Aya Takada and Yuriy Humber, 'Japan Wants Free Trade. Its Farmers Don't', *BusinessWeek* (New York), 6 August 2012.

58 Ibid.

59 Hiroko Tabuchi, 'Japan's Farmers Oppose Pacific Free Trade Talks', *New York Times* (New York), 10 November 2010.

60 However, Japan is also moving forward with PTA negotiations with the EU, where some of the same product tariffs are likely to be up for discussion. The rice tariff might be less problematic in the EU agreement, as the EU does not also produce rice, unlike the TPP negotiating parties.

Tokyo for noisy demonstrations. Several even drove their tractors down the Ginza district in Tokyo to protest the government's expected announcement of plans to join the TPP.[61] Over 11 million people signed a petition urging the government not to join the agreement.[62]

Japan is not alone in fearing the implications of far-reaching liberalisation in agriculture, however. The TPP is intended to expand to new members in the future. It is, officially, one of the paths to the future 'Free Trade Area of the Asia-Pacific' that could encompass the 21 member economies of APEC. Whether the TPP ever succeeds in reaching this goal, or indeed expands any further at all, depends in part on the final deal reached in agriculture. Since every country has historically protected this sector, few political leaders are eager to throw open the gates to the farm completely.

Convincing sceptical officials and members of the public of the benefits of joining the TPP in the future will involve a large measure of overcoming fears of agricultural liberalisation and market opening. It requires showing the benefits of trade, particularly in the form of lower prices and greater choices for consumers.[63] It may require help with building new export platforms. In the case of Japan, for example, it is likely that other TPP consumers would pay a premium price for the perfect apple or melon imported from Japan.

Opening up markets may also mean designing or modifying existing domestic level adjustment programs for the agriculture sector to move farmers into more competitive areas. The implementation periods granted under the TPP must be used wisely to help with the transition to more open markets.

---

[61] Chico Harlan, 'In Japan, Possible Free Trade Deal Comes With an Argument', *Washington Post* (Washington, DC), 30 October 2011.

[62] The petition was signed by 365 members of the Japanese Diet and presented to the government on 10 November 2011, with the collected signatures of 11 668 809. See a copy of the petition posted online at: *The Diet Petition for Opposing Japan's Joining the TPP Negotiations* (10 November 2011) Public Citizen <www.citizen.org/documents/japan-diet-petition-against-tpp.pdf>.

[63] Although Japanese consumers are frequently described as being unwilling to eat non-Japanese food, nearly 60 per cent of Japan's food needs are already imported: see Agriculture and Agri-Food Canada, *Agri-Food Consumer Profile: Japan* (May 2011) <http://www.ats-sea.agr.gc.ca/asi/pdf/4150-eng.pdf>.

CONCLUSION

Opening markets via the TPP depends on two factors. First, officials must demonstrate that the TPP opens agricultural markets in a way that is comprehensive, deep and fair. Second, they must do so in a way that manages the profound sensitivities that many countries have in their farm industries and ensure that consumers, producers, and farmers believe that the way forward will be broadly better.

Opening markets under the TPP is not the same, of course, as opening markets to the globe. It merely guarantees improved access to the markets in partner countries. It does not promise that each country will benefit, or will benefit equally, from this new access. In agriculture, like all areas of the TPP, there will be some sectors in some countries that are poised for significant economic growth. Other producers will not fare so well. Consumers, overall, ought to benefit from a greater range of available products at lower prices, once the entire agreement is fully implemented.

Reaching this end state will require courage of conviction on the part of political leaders. It is not only farmers in Tokyo who are threatening to drive tractors through the streets to maintain their historical levels of farm protections. Facing down these demands, nevertheless, is important. An inability to do so would represent the clearest example of failure to reach the '21st century, high quality' standard that leaders have promised to deliver in the Trans-Pacific Partnership Agreement.

7. Services in the TPP: a case study of telecommunications

Danny Kotlowitz* **and Tania Voon****

INTRODUCTION

The Trans-Pacific Partnership Agreement (TPP) has the potential to open services markets in numerous countries of differing levels of development, geographic regions and governance systems. This ambitious but defined effort may succeed where other attempts to liberalise services have failed. Specifically, advancements in the context of the *General Agreement on Trade in Services* (GATS)[1] have been limited since its creation in 1995 with the establishment of the World Trade Organization (WTO). Services liberalisation in preferential trade agreements (PTA) has been rather piecemeal, in many instances arguably falling short of the conditions applicable to the GATS Article V exception for economic integration agreements and containing significant 'GATS-minus' elements.[2]

TPP parties are faced with the challenge of harnessing and going beyond GATS and PTA obligations, while removing the 'water' between bindings regarding services trade and the domestic measures actually

* Email danny.kotlowitz@team.telstra.com. My thanks to Adela Woliansky for research assistance on foreign investment restrictions in several jurisdictions.

** Email tania.voon@unimelb.edu.au. I am grateful to Sarah Crouch and James Munro for research assistance in preparing this chapter.

1 *Marrakesh Agreement Establishing the World Trade Organization*, opened for signature 15 April 1994, 1867 UNTS 3 (entered into force 1 January 1995) annex 1B (*General Agreement on Trade in Services*).

2 Rudolf Adlung and Sébastien Miroudot, 'Poison in the Wine? Tracing GATS-Minus Commitments in Regional Trade Agreements' (2012) 46(5) *Journal of World Trade* 1045; cf. Sébastien Miroudot, Jehan Sauvage and Marie Sureau, 'Multilateralising Regionalism: How Preferential Are Services Commitments in Regional Trade Agreements?' (Trade Policy Papers No 106, Organisation for Economic Co-operation and Development, 2010) [81].

imposed on such trade.[3] In doing so, an important choice includes whether to adopt a 'negative list' approach – whereby a given commitment applies to all service sectors and modes of supply unless the party has scheduled a specific exemption (as is the approach to the most-favoured-nation (MFN) rule in GATS Article II) – or a 'positive list' approach, whereby a party agrees to certain obligations only with respect to nominated sectors and modes of supply (as is the approach to the national treatment rule in GATS Article XVII). PTAs of different TPP parties adopt different solutions to this choice.[4]

A more sophisticated approach to services trade regulation will also need to grapple with complex relationships between services and other areas to be covered by the TPP, including investment (given that the delivery of services via commercial presence (mode 3 in GATS) accounts for 55–60 per cent of trade in services[5] and simultaneously represents an investment in the country of delivery) and electronic commerce[6] (given that Internet-based commerce includes numerous services aspects including advertising, distribution, and financial services).[7] Telecommunications services also continue to converge with computer and audiovisual services.[8] These issues in turn raise potential concerns about intellectual property rights in traded goods and services and the privacy of data flowing across borders.[9]

---

[3] See, e.g., Craig VanGrasstek, 'The Political Economy of Services in Regional Trade Agreements' (Trade Policy Papers No 112, Organisation for Economic Co-operation and Development, 2011) 47.

[4] See, e.g., Stuart Harbinson and Aik Hoe Lim, 'Trade in Services' in C.L. Lim, Deborah Elms and Patrick Low (eds), *The Trans-Pacific Partnership: A Quest for a Twenty-first Century Trade Agreement* (Cambridge University Press, 2012) 133, 137.

[5] *Regulatory Issues in Sectors and Modes of Supply*, WTO Doc S/WPDR/W/48 (13 June 2012) (Note by the Secretariat) [269].

[6] See Andrew Mitchell, 'Towards Compatibility: The Future of Electronic Commerce Within the Global Trading System' (2001) 4 *Journal of International Economic Law* 663.

[7] See Panel Report, *China – Measures Affecting Electronic Payment Services*, WTO Doc WT/DS413/R (adopted 31 August 2012).

[8] *Regulatory Issues in Sectors and Modes of Supply*, WTO Doc S/WPDR/W/48 (13 June 2012) (Note by the Secretariat) [92]; Rolf Weber, 'Digital Trade in WTO-Law – Taking Stock and Looking Ahead' (2010) 5 *Asian Journal of WTO & International Health Law & Policy* 1, 10–13.

[9] See, e.g., *Regulatory Issues in Sectors and Modes of Supply*, WTO Doc S/WPDR/W/48 (13 June 2012) (Note by the Secretariat) [101]; 'TPP Countries to Discuss Australian Alternative to Data-Flow Proposal' (6 July 2012) 30(27) *Inside US Trade* (online).

Taking telecommunications services as a case study, this chapter examines the options available to TPP parties to create an ambitious new style of services agreement. We begin by examining the broader context for the TPP negotiations on telecommunications in the form of the ongoing talks towards an International Services Agreement among key WTO Members. We go on to note the recent controversy at the World Conference on International Telecommunications regarding revisions made to the International Telecommunication Regulations without the usual approach of negotiated consensus. We then turn to the telecommunications chapter in the TPP, exploring in general how a new architecture could be adopted to update telecommunications market access and competition regulation as envisaged in the GATS and current PTAs, and then considering more specifically how the TPP could work towards resolving the perceived problem of high international mobile roaming charges across the world. We conclude by calling for a constant evaluation of and adaptation to new technologies and developments in telecommunications, beyond the conclusion of the TPP and the International Services Agreement.

I DEVELOPMENTS IN THE REGULATION OF TELECOMMUNICATIONS SERVICES IN INTERNATIONAL AGREEMENTS

A International Services Agreement

The TPP has been described as a 'complementary approach for a far-reaching services agreement outside the WTO'.[10] A broader plurilateral services agreement could extend beyond the TPP parties, either by allowing non-parties to join the TPP services chapter only, or through a broader agreement on services liberalisation within, outside or linked to the WTO. Negotiations towards an 'International Services Agreement' have already commenced among at least 21 WTO Members (counting the European Union (EU) as a single Member): Australia, Canada, Chile, Chinese Taipei, Colombia, Costa Rica, the EU, Hong Kong, Iceland, Israel, Japan, Mexico, New Zealand, Norway, Pakistan, Panama, Peru, South Korea, Switzerland, Turkey, and the United States (US).[11] These 'Really Good Friends' of

---

[10] Gary Hufbauer, J. Bradford Jensen and Sherry Stephenson, 'Framework for the International Services Agreement' (Policy Brief No PB12-10, Peterson Institute for International Economics, April 2012) 24.

[11] ICTSD, 'Services Liberalisation Talks Among Group of WTO Members Move Forward' (10 October 2012) 16(34) *Bridges Weekly Trade News Digest*

Services alone account for 70 per cent of global trade in services[12] and represent seven of the current eleven TPP negotiating parties.

Initially, negotiations towards an International Services Agreement will be closed,[13] but ultimately such an agreement could be acknowledged in the WTO as a plurilateral agreement akin to the plurilateral trade agreements contained in Annex 4 to the *Marrakesh Agreement Establishing the World Trade Organization*,[14] or alternatively pursuant to the exception in GATS Article V for economic integration agreements, or on the basis of a waiver under Article IX: 3 of the *Marrakesh Agreement*.[15] Subsequently, the agreement could also be 'multilateralised' and open to all WTO Members – a position favoured by the EU and South Korea.[16] To some extent, non-parties to the plurilateral agreement would benefit in any event, as services obligations in modes 1 (cross-border supply), 2 (consumption abroad) and 3 (commercial presence) are typically implemented on an MFN basis – that is, without discriminating based on the origin or nationality of the relevant foreign service supplier.[17] Thus, all suppliers benefit from the increased liberalisation.

Talks on the International Services Agreement are under way at the time of writing. Following a series of discussions in 2012,[18] formal market access talks are expected to commence in 2013.[19] A range of broad

---

(online); ICTSD, 'Formal plurilateral services negotiations may be launched in March' (20 December 2012) 1(6) *Bridges Africa Review* (online).

12 'Officials' Services Debate Shows Fault Lines Over ISA Multilateralization' (21 September 2012) 30(37) *Inside US Trade* (online); Daniel Pruzin, '"Really Good Friends" Group to Meet for Technical Talks on Services Pact' *International Trade Daily* (online), 19 January 2013.

13 'EU to Seek New Mandate for Potential Services Plurilateral Negotiations' (2 November 2012) 30(43) *Inside US Trade* (online).

14 This approach would require a decision by consensus of the WTO Ministerial Conference: *Marrakesh Agreement Establishing the World Trade Organization* art X:9.

15 Hufbauer et al., above n 10, 23–24.

16 'EU to Seek New Mandate for Potential Services Plurilateral Negotiations' (2 November 2012) 30(43) *Inside US Trade* (online); 'Korean Minister Stresses Need for Clear Path to Multilateral Services Deal' (21 September 2012) 30(37) *Inside US Trade* (online).

17 Hosuk Lee-Makiyama, *The International Services Agreement (ISA) – from the European Vantage Point*, European Centre for International Political Economy (ECIPE) Working Paper (6 March 2012) 9.

18 See, e.g., 'U.S., Other WTO Members Begin Technical Work on Services Plurilateral' (27 January 2012) 30(4) *Inside US Trade* (online).

19 'Market Access Talks for Services Plurilateral Unlikely to Start Until 2013' (6 July 2012) 30(27) *Inside US Trade* (online).

principles and specific issues must be debated and agreed. In particular, will the agreement take a 'negative list' or 'positive list' approach, or some sort of 'hybrid'?[20] How much beyond 'locking in' existing GATS and PTA obligations will the agreement go?[21] Australia has been leading the talks to date and has announced agreement on a framework for the negotiations, including that no sector or mode of supply will be subject to an a priori exclusion, a negative list approach will apply to national treatment (that is, going beyond the GATS, national treatment will apply to all service sectors and modes unless the relevant party has scheduled an exemption), and a 'ratcheting up' provision will ensure that additional liberalisation is extended to all parties to the agreement.[22] Details of any discussion of telecommunications have not been publicised. However, these general questions and principles raise issues examined further below in the specific context of telecommunications sector regulation to be governed by the TPP. Other areas that could be addressed in the International Services Agreement, with particular significance for telecommunications, include stronger disciplines on State-Owned Enterprises (SOEs) and competition policy, and provision for free movement of data across borders.[23] The TPP negotiation may already be laying the groundwork for such objectives in respect of SOEs and competition policy, and to address protectionist restraints on cross-border data flow.[24]

The likelihood of reaching agreement among around 21 WTO Members on an International Services Agreement is relatively high, at least in comparison with the failure to make progress to date within the WTO's Doha Round of negotiations in relation to services or more generally. Whether that agreement can then be successfully multilateralised is more uncertain. The sensitive nature of particular service industries such as health and education (and telecommunications, to some extent) makes an ambitious agreement across the WTO membership unlikely. Parallel progress on services including telecommunications in the TPP may assist both the

---

[20] 'U.S., Other WTO Members See "Hybrid" Approach on Services Plurilateral' (21 September 2012) 30(37) *Inside US Trade* (online).

[21] 'Mexican WTO Official Advocates Two Stages for New Services Agreement' (21 September 2012) 30(37) *Inside US Trade* (online).

[22] Daniel Pruzin, 'Australia Reports Agreement on Framework for Talks on Global Services Trade Next Year' (7 December 2012) *International Trade Daily* (online).

[23] Hufbauer, Jensen and Stephenson, above n 10, 38–41.

[24] Kanishka Jayasuriya, 'Trans-Pacific Partnership at the frontlines of new geo-economic contests' (18 April 2013) *The Conversation* <http://theconversation.com/trans-pacific-partnership-at-the-frontlines-of-new-geo-economic-contests-13236>.

conclusion of an International Services Agreement and any subsequent broader discussion of services liberalisation in the WTO, providing additional perspectives and solutions to the difficult problems of removing discrimination and barriers in behind-the-border services regulation.

B International Telecommunications Regulations

Several developments in international regulations concerning telecommunications took place within the International Telecommunication Union (ITU) in 2012. The ITU, a specialised United Nations agency, has 193 Member States and more than 700 members from the private sector and academic institutions.[25] In November 2012, the four-yearly World Telecommunication Standardization Assembly was held in Dubai, adopting resolutions on matters including call-back, caller identification and other issues that may create privacy concerns,[26] cybersecurity[27] and non-discriminatory access to Internet resources.[28] The latter resolution resolves to invite ITU Member States 'to refrain from taking any unilateral and/or discriminatory actions that could impede another Member State from accessing public Internet sites'.[29]

In December 2012, the World Conference on International Telecommunications was held, also in Dubai. Only 89 of the ITU's 193 Member States signed the Final Acts of the Conference, including revised International Telecommunication Regulations, with many developed countries (including Australia, Canada, the US and European countries) and others (including India and several African and Latin American countries) declining to do so.[30] The revised regulations include a statement that 'Member States shall endeavour to promote competition in the provision of international roaming services and are encouraged to

---

[25] *Overview*, ITU <http://www.itu.int/en/about/Pages/default.aspx>.

[26] ITU-T, World Telecommunication Standardization Assembly, *Resolution 29 – Alternative calling procedures on international telecommunication networks* (20–29 November 2012); ITU-T, World Telecommunication Standardization Assembly, *Resolution 65 – Calling party number delivery, calling line identification and origin identification* (20–29 November 2012).

[27] ITU-T, World Telecommunication Standardization Assembly, *Resolution 50 – Cybersecurity* (20–29 November 2012).

[28] ITU-T, World Telecommunication Standardization Assembly, *Resolution 69 – Non-discriminatory access and use of Internet resources* (20–29 November 2012).

[29] Ibid., [1].

[30] *Signatories of the Final Acts: 89*, ITU <http://www.itu.int/osg/wcit-12/highlights/signatories.html>.

develop policies that foster competitive roaming prices for the benefit of end users'.[31] A transparency requirement regarding roaming prices is also included.[32] Some contentious issues were ultimately settled by consensus, for example in the case of roaming through the use of generalised text espousing desirable regulatory principles but dropping a controversial proposal for direct wholesale price regulation.[33]

A key reason for the division on the new treaty related to the perceived role of the Internet, with many countries refusing to sign on the basis that the Internet should remain subject to 'multi-stakeholder' governance[34] rather than falling within the scope of the ITU, and that governments may wish to censor Internet expression and impose charges on Internet data flows.[35] Disagreement over Internet governance exemplifies the deep ideological differences and varied regulatory perspectives found across the ITU Member States, creating a barrier to progress within that organisation. Again, the limited and 'like-minded' membership of the TPP, in contrast, may allow creative approaches to more ambitious and meaningful obligations and commitments in the telecommunications sector.

II TELECOMMUNICATIONS REGULATION THROUGH THE TPP

A A 'Smart' Telecommunications Chapter

The TPP and similar agreements currently being contemplated or negotiated offer an opportunity to adopt a new approach to services chapters

---

31 *Final Acts: World Conference on International Telecommunications* (Dubai, 2012), International Telecommunication Regulations, art 4.7.

32 Ibid., art 4.4.

33 Inês Nolasco, 'WCIT-12: a post-mortem' (Briefing Paper, Cullen International, 14 January 2013).

34 See, e.g., Philip Verveer, US Coordinator for International Communications and Information Policy, 'U.S. Engagement at the World Conference on International Telecommunications' on *DipNote: US Department of State Official Blog* (21 December 2012) <http://blogs.state.gov/2012/12/article/us-engagement-world-conference-international-telecommunications>; Senator the Hon. Stephen Conroy, 'Australia does not sign ITRs' (Media Release, 14 December 2012); David Fidler, 'Internet Governance and International Law: The Controversy Concerning Revision of the International Telecommunication Regulations' (2013) 17(6) *ASIL Insights* (online).

35 'Difference Engine: Nobbling the Internet', *The Economist* (online), 10 December 2012 <http://www.economist.com/blogs/babbage/2012/12/online-privacy>.

in PTAs. In particular, the history of telecommunications chapters and their current content and structure demonstrate a pressing need for revision and revitalisation. Parties to the TPP have a rare chance to develop a new architecture for commitments in the telecommunications sector in the form of a 'smart' telecommunications chapter, charting the path for other bilateral and plurilateral agreements.

1 Classification difficulties in telecommunications

The classification of telecommunications services in the GATS forms the basis for telecommunications obligations in some PTAs. That classification system distinguishes between 'basic telecommunication services' – which may be defined as services that 'involve end-to-end transmission of customer-supplied information between two or more points without any change being added to the information' – and 'value-added telecommunications services', namely 'services that employ computer processing applications to enhance the form or content of a customer's information or provide for its storage and retrieval'.[36] Yet this distinction is no longer easily applicable to today's technical and regulatory environment, creating uncertainty and difficulty in interpreting GATS commitments in connection with services such as broadband.[37]

Even apart from the blurring of the underlying distinction between basic and value-added telecommunications services, the typical classification of specific services in WTO Members' GATS Schedules is problematic. Many Members based their services schedules on 'document W/120',[38] which the GATT Secretariat prepared to assist in drafting schedules during the Uruguay Round negotiations. The WTO Appellate Body has characterised this document as offering a 'supplementary means' for interpreting GATS and

---

[36] Philip Raworth, *Trade in Services: Global Regulation and the Impact on Key Service Sectors* (Oceana Publications, 2005) 300.

[37] See Tania Voon and Andrew Mitchell, 'International Trade Law Implications of Australia's National Broadband Network' (2011) 35(2) *Melbourne University Law Review* 578, 611–614, discussing the characterisation of universal services obligations in general and broadband telecommunications services in the US. See also Lee Tuthill and Martin Roy, 'GATS classification issues for information and communication technology services' in Mira Burri and Thomas Cottier, *Trade Governance in the Digital Age* (Cambridge University Press, 2012) 157, especially 160–163; Rolf Weber and Mira Burri, *Classification of Services in the Digital Economy* (Springer, 2012) 61–81.

[38] *Services Sectoral Classification List*, WTO Doc MTN.GNS/W/120 (10 July 1991) (Note by the Secretariat).

its Schedules[39] pursuant to Article 32 of the *Vienna Convention on the Law of Treaties* (VCLT).[40] Document W/120 classifies telecommunications services as shown in Table 7.1.

Table 7.1 Document W/120 classification of telecommunications services

Sectors and Sub-sectors		Corresponding CPC[41]
2.	COMMUNICATION SERVICES	
. . .		
C.	Telecommunication services	
a.	Voice telephone services	7521
b.	Packet-switched data transmission services	7523**
c.	Circuit-switched data transmission services	7523**
d.	Telex services	7523**
e.	Telegraph services	7522
f.	Facsimile services	7521**+7529**
g.	Private leased circuit services	7522**+7523**
h.	Electronic mail	7523**
i.	Voice mail	7523**
j.	On-line information and data base retrieval	7523**
k.	Electronic data interchange (EDI)	7523**
l.	Enhanced/value-added facsimile services, incl. store and forward, store and retrieve	7523**
m.	Code and protocol conversion	n.a.
n.	On-line information and/or data processing (incl. transaction processing)	843**
o.	Other	

[39] Appellate Body Report, *United States – Measures Affecting the Cross Border Supply of Gambling and Betting Services*, WTO Doc WT/DS285/AB/R (adopted 20 April 2005) [196]. See also Panel Report, *China – Measures Affecting Trading Rights and Distribution Services for Certain Publications and Audiovisual Entertainment Products*, WTO Doc WT/DS363/R and Corr.1 (adopted 19 January 2010) [7.1222] (*China – Publications and Audiovisual Products*); Appellate Body Report, *China – Publications and Audiovisual Products*, WTO Doc WT/DS363/AB/R (adopted 19 January 2010) [411].

[40] Opened for signature 23 May 1969, 1155 UNTS 331 (entered into force 27 January 1980).

[41] 'CPC' refers to the United Nations' Central Product Classification, updated to version 2.0 on 31 December 2008: see <http://unstats.un.org/unsd/cr/registry/cpc-2.asp>. According to document W/120, 'The (**) indicates that the service specified constitutes only a part of the total range of activities covered by the CPC concordance (e.g. voice mail is only a component of CPC item 7523)'. See also WTO Council for Trade in Services, *Telecommunication Services: Background Note by the Secretariat*, S/C/W/74 (8 December 1998) annex.

Many of these services (e.g. telegraph, telex, facsimile, voicemail) are obsolete or in decline or do not provide a viable basis for commercial operations. Conversely, more recent technologies and products do not fit easily into this list. Even mobile telecommunications services are not listed in the document W/120 classification system, subjecting them to the following complicated analysis. Core mobile telecommunications services such as voice and text are typically regarded as basic telecommunications services falling within sub-sector 2.C(o) ('other') in the above list.[42] A reference to a basic telecommunications service in a GATS Schedule is generally agreed to cover the service as 'provided through any means of technology (e.g., cable, wireless, satellites)'. Accordingly:

> It should not be necessary to list cellular or mobile services as a separate subsector. However, a number of Members have done so … Therefore, in order to avoid extensive changes in schedules, it would seem appropriate for Members to maintain separate entries for these subsectors.[43]

As telecommunications technology and applications develop over time, the rigidity of the current classification template will tend to distribute newly emerging and evolved forms of telecommunications services in three ways:

- first, they may be subsumed in an ever increasing category of 'other' services;
- second, the new and evolved services may potentially fall by the wayside if Members can successfully argue that the wording of their Schedules does not extend to these services, which were unheard of or at least not taken into account at the time of drafting the GATS. This will depend on the specific wording of particular Schedules and the way they are interpreted. We consider an analogous example of attempted use of this strategy by a WTO Member below; and

---

[42] *Telecommunications Services*, WTO Doc S/C/W/74 (8 December 1998) (Background Note by the Secretariat) 2–3.

[43] *Note by the Chairman*, WTO Doc S/GBT/W/2/Rev.1 (16 January 1997) (Revision). See also *Telecommunications Services*, WTO Doc S/C/W/299 (10 June 2009) (Background Note by the Secretariat) [7], [10].

- third, the new and evolved services may find a home in other template PTA chapters such as the Electronic Commerce chapter.[44] For example, the rapidly growing category of 'cloud' services bundles a range of previously distinct services such as telecommunications carriage, remote storage, online security, transaction processing and process outsourcing. The US in particular has advocated that restrictions on the provision of cloud services across national borders should be addressed in the TPP negotiation, and appears to regard these services as a form of electronic commerce.[45]

Looking more closely at the second option, the WTO dispute *China – Publications and Audiovisual Products* provides an analogous situation where China contended that the reference in its GATS Schedule to 'Sound recording distribution services' covers distribution of sound recordings in physical form such as compact discs and not electronic distribution via the Internet.[46] In support of its contention, China maintained that 'electronic distribution of sound recordings as an established business and the legal framework for such business emerged only after the negotiation of its GATS Schedule and its accession to the WTO'.[47] This kind of reasoning, if successful, would suggest that WTO Members' GATS commitments will be constantly eroded as new technologies develop, because the commitments are restricted to services in existence at the time of drafting. In the *China – Publications and Audiovisual Products* dispute, the first instance Panel made a legal finding that technical feasibility and commercial reality at the time of making a commitment *may* be relevant in interpreting that commitment pursuant to VCLT Article 32.[48] (However, the Panel made a factual finding with respect to the circumstances before it that electronic distribution of sound recordings was technically feasible and a commercial reality well before

[44] See, e.g., *Australia–United States Free Trade Agreement*, signed 18 May 2004, [2005] ATS 1 (entered into force 1 January 2005) ch 16.

[45] See Joshua Meltzer, 'The Internet, Cross-Border Data Flows and International Trade' (Issues in Technology Innovation Number 22, Center for Technology Innovation at Brookings, February 2013); Jeffrey Bleich, 'Cloud agreement can bring blue skies', *The Sydney Morning Herald* (online), 12 December 2012 <http://www.smh.com.au/it-pro/government-it/cloud-agreement-can-bring-blue-skies-20121211-2b77f.html>.

[46] Panel Report, *China – Publications and Audiovisual Products*, [7.1161].

[47] Ibid., [7.1235].

[48] Ibid., [7.1237].

China's accession to the WTO.)[49] Fortunately, on appeal, the Appellate Body emphasised the evolutionary nature of treaty terms, such that the meaning of 'sound recording' and 'distribution' in China's GATS Schedule was not determined by their meaning at the time China joined the WTO.[50]

The Appellate Body's evolutionary approach to interpreting these kinds of words provides the basis for a more flexible reading of GATS Schedules in order to maintain their force, particularly in dynamic sectors such as telecommunications and audiovisual services. However, that interpretative approach is likely to be insufficient to redress the fundamental disjuncture between the GATS approach to telecommunications services classification and commitments on the one hand and current technologies and practice in the telecommunications sector on the other hand. The need for the trade framework to catch up with technology developments is illustrated by the 'Trade Principles for Information Communication Technology Services' jointly developed by the EU and the US. Released in April 2011, these principles attempt to address more recent domestic regulatory concerns such as 'net neutrality'[51] and cross-border information flow,[52] while reiterating enduring concerns in regard to market access, regulatory independence and interconnection that were first expressed in the GATS telecommunications instruments. The principles are not binding but provide a more contemporary baseline to be used by the EU and the US in their trade negotiations with third countries.

2 The 1997 PTA model based on the GATS and its Reference Paper

Many PTAs today adopt a standard format for the telecommunications chapter, with origins in the GATS Annex on Telecommunications and the Reference Paper[53] adopted by more than 82 WTO Members[54] as an

---

49 Ibid., [7.1247].

50 Appellate Body Report, *China – Publications and Audiovisual Products*, [396]–[397].

51 *European Union–United States Trade Principles for Information and Communication Technology Services* (4 April 2011) U.S. Department of State, principle 2 <http://www.state.gov/p/eur/rt/eu/tec/171020.htm>.

52 Ibid., principle 3.

53 WTO Negotiating Group on Basic Telecommunications, *Reference Paper* (24 April 1996). The Reference Paper is attached to WTO, *The WTO Negotiations on Basic Telecommunications* (Press Release, 6 March 1997) <http://www.wto.org/english/news_e/pres97_e/refpap-e.htm>. It is also reproduced in WTO, *World Trade Organization: Agreement on Telecommunications Services (Fourth Protocol to General Agreement on Trade in Services)* (1997) 36 ILM

additional commitment pursuant to the GATS: the '1997 model'. Not surprisingly, this model and the underlying GATS approach to telecommunications are outdated and unhelpful in certain respects. The GATS Annex on Telecommunications ensures access by suppliers of any services (not just telecommunications services) to 'public telecommunications transport networks and services'. The Reference Paper includes principles for: preventing anti-competitive practices in telecommunications (such as anti-competitive cross-subsidisation); ensuring interconnection on reasonable and non-discriminatory terms and conditions and at cost-oriented rates; maintaining transparency in allocation of scarce resources (such as radio communications frequency spectrum) and in licensing; and providing an independent, impartial regulator separate from telecommunications suppliers.

For example, the Reference Paper states, under the heading 'Prevention of anti-competitive practices in telecommunications':

> Appropriate measures shall be maintained for the purpose of preventing suppliers who, alone or together, are a major supplier from engaging in or continuing anti-competitive practices.[55]

This provision is mirrored, for instance, in the *Agreement between Japan and the Republic of Singapore for a New-Age Economic Partnership* as follows:

> Each Party shall maintain appropriate measures for the purpose of preventing suppliers, who alone or together are a major supplier, from engaging in or continuing anti-competitive practices.[56]

Other PTAs incorporate the relevant GATS provisions and commitments as a whole. For example, the *China–Singapore Free Trade Agreement*

354, 367. For background on the negotiations leading to its creation see Marco Bronckers and Pierre Larouche, 'Telecommunications Services' in Patrick F.J. Macrory, Arthur E. Appleton and Michael G. Plummer (eds), *The World Trade Organization: Legal, Economic and Political Analysis* (Springer, 2005) vol 1, 989, 992–994.

[54] *Regulatory Issues in Sectors and Modes of Supply*, WTO Doc S/WPDR/W/48 (13 June 2012) (Note by the Secretariat) [89] (counting EU states individually).

[55] Reference Paper, above n 53, section 1.1.

[56] *Agreement between Japan and the Republic of Singapore for a New-Age Economic Partnership*, signed 13 January 2002 (entered into force 30 November 2002) annex IVB, art II:1.

incorporates the GATS Annex on Telecommunications as an 'integral part' of the agreement.[57]

The Reference Paper and corresponding PTA provisions reflect the conventional wisdom of the mid-1990s in the US and leading European jurisdictions regarding best practice pro-competitive domestic regulation, particularly for fixed-line telecommunications services. The shared view of policymakers at the time was to unbundle access to incumbent operators under strong regulatory oversight – so-called 'access-based competition'.[58] Following extensive litigation in the US, the approach of the Federal Communications Commission altered to favour 'facilities-based competition' between telecommunications and cable operators.[59] The United Kingdom pioneered a model of functional separation of the former incumbent BT, with the creation of the Openreach business unit to provide wholesale services.[60] In Australia, the National Broadband Network represents a policy preference for long-term structural separation, facilitated through the creation of a new government-owned wholesale provider, NBN Co, with a functional separation regime imposed on the dominant operator Telstra in the interim.[61] A more creative approach is now needed to accommodate different regulatory pathways to the same claimed goal of domestic pro-competitive regulation.[62]

---

[57] *China–Singapore Free Trade Agreement*, signed 23 October 2008 (entered into force 1 January 2009) art 76.

[58] For example, the declared services and access regime introduced in 1997 in Australia, contained in Part XIC of the *Trade Practices Act 1974* (Cth) (now the *Competition and Consumer Act 2010* (Cth)), as well as interim pro-competitive regulation such as the pre-selection scheme in Part 17 of the *Telecommunications Act 1997* (Cth).

[59] Robert Litan and Hal Singer, *The Need for Speed – a New Framework for Telecommunications Policy for the 21st Century* (Brookings Institution Press, 2013) 20–21; Susan Crawford, *Captive Audience – The Telecom Industry and Monopoly Power in the New Gilded Age* (Yale University Press, 2013) 48–56. For a more detailed examination of withdrawal of unbundling obligations in the US until 2006, see Danny Kotlowitz, 'Is the United States Trade Representative's monitoring and enforcement of its trading partners' obligations on telecommunications market access still credible?' (Paper presented at the Communications Policy & Research Forum, Sydney, 26 September 2006) 8, 25–26, 33–35, 49 <www.networkinsight.org/verve/_resources/Kotlowitz_paper.pdf>.

[60] Mike Conradi (ed.), *Communications Law Handbook* (Bloomsbury Professional, 2009) 93–119.

[61] Martyn Taylor, 'National Broadband Network Overview' in *Australian Competition and Consumer Legislation 2012* (CCH, 2012) 17, 17–23.

[62] For a summary of the various forms of separation see Peter Waters and Oliver Damian, 'Separation regulation of dominant telecommunications operators

Some PTAs do go beyond the 'Reference Paper' model of 1997,[63] but they do so by incorporating on an ad hoc basis additions to the telecommunications chapter to reflect typical competition measures adopted domestically in the telecommunications sector up to the mid-2000s. For example, the *United States–Chile Free Trade Agreement* contains typical provisions on number portability and dialling parity:

> Each Party shall ensure that major suppliers in its territory provide number portability to the extent technically feasible, on a timely basis, and on reasonable terms and conditions.[64]
>
> Each Party shall ensure that major suppliers in its territory provide dialing parity to suppliers of public telecommunications services of the other Party and afford suppliers of public telecommunications services of the other Party non-discriminatory access to telephone numbers and related services with no unreasonable dialing delays.[65]

Other common additions, found in the recent *Malaysia–Australia Free Trade Agreement*,[66] provide for non-discriminatory access to submarine cable systems,[67] reasonable access to telecommunications services for the purpose of resale,[68] an express obligation regarding the unbundling of network elements,[69] flexibility in the choice of technologies,[70] and general provisions on enforcement,[71] dispute settlement[72] and transparency.[73] Some of these provisions find parallels in the GATS, but the

---

in today's legacy networks and tomorrow's next generation networks' (Report, Gilbert + Tobin) <http://www.gtlaw.com.au/wp-content/uploads/Separation-regulation.pdf>.

63 See the discussion in Lee Tuthill and Laura Sherman, 'Telecommunications: can trade agreements keep up with technology?' in Juan Marchetti and Martin Roy (eds), *Opening Markets for Trade in Services: Countries and Sectors in Bilateral and WTO Negotiations* (Cambridge University Press, 2008) 151, 170–177. See also Harbinson and Lim, above n 4, 142.

64 *United States–Chile Free Trade Agreement*, signed 6 June 2003 (entered into force 1 January 2004) art 13.4.6.

65 Ibid., art 13.4.7.

66 *Malaysia–Australia Free Trade Agreement*, signed 22 May 2012, [2013] ATS 4 (entered into force 1 January 2013).

67 Ibid., art 9.8.

68 Ibid., art 9.12.

69 Ibid., art 9.13.

70 Ibid., art 9.26.

71 Ibid., art 9.23.

72 Ibid., art 9.24.

73 Ibid., art 9.25.

GATS provisions are somewhat open to interpretation. For example, New Zealand previously regarded the reference to unbundling in the Reference Paper[74] as not requiring unbundling of the 'local loop'.[75] Similarly, in relation to the choice of technologies, as Tuthill and Sherman have pointed out,[76] the Chairman's Note on Scheduling already indicates that, unless otherwise noted in a WTO Member's GATS Schedule, 'any basic telecom service listed in the sector column … may be provided through any means of technology (e.g., cable, wireless, satellites)'.[77] However, the significance of the Chairman's Note in interpreting GATS Schedules is debatable,[78] meaning that provisions such as that included in the *Malaysia–Australia Free Trade Agreement* can provide further clarity and certainty. This ambiguity inherent in a number of GATS obligations may reflect a deliberate solution to a failure to reach agreement on key issues.

Other PTA provisions reflect that the role of regulation in the telecommunications sector may change over time as competition develops and existing interventions can be retired:

> Each Party may, in accordance with its laws and regulations, determine the appropriate level of regulation required to promote fair competition.[79]

---

[74] Reference Paper, above n 49, section 2.2(b).

[75] Foreign-owned telecommunications operators in New Zealand argued on the strength of prior views expressed by the Office of the United States Trade Representative that Article 2.2(b) of the Reference Paper should be interpreted to require unbundling of the local loop. However, in May 2004 the Communications Minister accepted the recommendation of the Commerce Commission against introduction of local loop unbundling. The Minister had received advice that New Zealand would not breach its trade commitments by refusing to unbundle the local loop. See Marta Steeman, 'TelstraClear tried scare tactics, documents show', *The Press* (Christchurch), 13 December 2005; Paul Brislen, 'International pressure on unbundling grows', *Computerworld* (online), 13 February 2004 <http://computerworld.co.nz/news.nsf/nl/CEB9F8D75515E5D2CC256E3800130 BEA>; the Hon. Paul Swain, *Decision on Telecom network recommendations* (19 May 2004) New Zealand Ministry of Communications and Information Technology <http://www.beehive.govt.nz/release/decision-telecom-network-recommendations>.

[76] Tuthill and Sherman, above n 63, 175.

[77] WTO Group on Basic Telecommunications, *Note by the Chairman: Revision*, WTO Doc S/GBT/W/2/Rev.1 (16 January 1997) [1].

[78] See, e.g., Panel Report, *Mexico – Measures Affecting Telecommunications Services*, WTO Doc WT/DS204/R (adopted 1 June 2004) [7.64].

[79] *Agreement between Japan and the Republic of Singapore for a New-Age Economic Partnership* annex IVB, art II:3.

> The Parties recognize the importance of relying on market forces to achieve wide choices in the supply of telecommunications services. To this end, where provided for under domestic law, each Party may forbear from applying regulation to a telecommunication service that the Party classifies as a public telecommunications service if its telecommunications regulatory body determines that:
>
> (a) enforcement of such regulation is not necessary to prevent unreasonable or discriminatory practices;
> (b) enforcement of such regulation is not necessary for the protection of consumers; and
> (c) forbearance is consistent with the public interest, including promoting and enhancing competition among suppliers of public telecommunications services.[80]

However, there is no accepted benchmark for the point at which 'sufficient' competition exists. A key limitation of all these provisions, and the approach to telecommunications in PTAs generally, is that they are based on existing domestic and international (GATS) obligations and therefore simply describe the way that things already work in the telecommunications sectors of the respective PTA parties. While some of the additions are welcome developments, increasing the extent of bound liberalisation compared with WTO Members' GATS commitments, because they are based on existing practice they contain no ambition or future direction for addressing 'behind-the-border' barriers in the telecommunications industry or the regulation of its participants. Rather, they simply reflect the lowest common denominator in terms of the degree of liberalisation that negotiating parties to particular PTAs have achieved in the telecommunications sector.

3 A new architecture in the TPP

In negotiating the TPP, countries have the opportunity to develop a new architecture for the telecommunications chapter, addressing the outmoded approach to classification of telecommunications services, the narrow competition principles in the context of telecommunications, and the changes that have taken place in the last decade and a half in relation to international regulation of services generally and telecommunications in particular.

Rather than attempting to provide a current-day snapshot of the telecommunications sector and its regulation, simply updating the obligations under the GATS and existing PTAs, the TPP could provide a vision

---

[80] *United States–Chile Free Trade Agreement*, signed 6 June 2003 (entered into force 1 January 2004) art 13.15.

to which parties could aspire. Specifically, the TPP telecommunications chapter could contain a set of agreed best practice principles for domestic regulation of telecommunications. (Even reaching agreement on such principles would be a valuable achievement, made more feasible in the context of the TPP than in the context of the WTO or the ITU because of the smaller number of parties.) Then, rather than requiring each party to adhere immediately to those principles without exception, parties could provide an initial statement of compliance indicating areas and reasons for non-compliance and a timetable for achieving compliance in the future (effectively a modified 'negative list' approach within the telecommunications sector). In some instances, non-compliance would be expected to endure for jurisdiction-specific reasons, whereas in other instances non-compliance would be only temporary. Regular reviews of the underlying principles and domestic adherence could be conducted, for example on a staggered three- or five-yearly basis, to encourage progress and reflection on domestic regulatory policies and practice.

Similar to the Trade Policy Review Mechanism, this approach would impose institutional pressure for change without the costs associated with formal dispute settlement, while also providing investors and others with information about the system of telecommunications regulation in the relevant country. Legitimate reasons for departure from agreed best practices would be acknowledged, in recognition of regulatory diversity and political and cultural differences between TPP parties. Such an approach would also encourage policy experimentation using different approaches to achieve competition outcomes as being acceptable and legitimate, rather than requiring domestic policymakers to rely on the intentional ambiguity of the existing obligations.

This proposed new architecture would go some way towards eliminating the gap between 'bound' and 'applied' services measures and increasing transparency about the latter in particular:

> It is widely recognized that the 'scheduling technology' used in the GATS does not greatly promote transparency. A fundamental need is to improve the available information on status quo policies. This will facilitate national reform efforts and help identify where the multilateral process can support such efforts. Unfortunately, there is nothing in the GATS or the WTO that encourages and assists countries in generating comprehensive information on applied policies and evaluating the impact of these policies.[81]

---

[81] Bernard Hoekman and Aaditya Mattoo, 'International Trade: Trade in Services' in Andrew Guzman and Alan Sykes (eds), *Research Handbook in International Economic Law* (Edward Elgar Publishing, 2007) 113, 136.

What kinds of principles could be agreed as part of this new architecture, and how would they relate to developments in other fora? Given the trade-liberalising focus of the TPP (like the GATS), TPP parties could agree not to introduce trade-diminishing measures in the telecommunications sector, regardless of whether the GATS or the ITU or other agreements allow or even endorse such measures. Specifically, TPP parties could agree to the aspirational foreign ownership limit of 100 per cent, removing all foreign ownership restrictions on the supply of telecommunications services via mode 3 (commercial presence). Foreign ownership restrictions remain of significant concern in the telecommunications industry, often protecting domestic interests at the expense of greater innovation, competition, and consumer benefits. Some PTAs have already increased foreign ownership limits, increasing the level of services trade liberalisation mandated by the GATS.[82] The TPP could provide an additional means of locking in these gains and enforcing existing commitments, since the uncertainty and complexity of the GATS and PTAs covering services sometimes increase the risk of non-compliance in the telecommunications arena.[83] As the Australian Productivity Commission has indicated, '[w]hile immediate reductions in services trade and investment barriers may be limited, agreements can create certainty by binding existing arrangements and can provide scope for future reductions in barriers'.[84]

For example, an exposition of the TPP parties' current compliance with the target of allowing 100 per cent foreign ownership of telecommunications suppliers operating through mode 3 could provide a basis for gradual progression towards the 100 per cent target, generating momentum for change by requiring governments to explain publicly why foreign ownership restrictions are required. Although some industries may claim strategic or national security reasons to justify sector-specific foreign ownership restrictions, in the case of telecommunications services the general screen for foreign ownership (for example, that applied by

---

[82] Tuthill and Sherman, above n 63, 166.

[83] See, e.g., Voon and Mitchell, above n 37 (analysing the consistency of Australia's National Broadband Network with its GATS obligations) and Tania Voon and Andrew Mitchell, 'Open for Business? China's Telecommunications Service Market and the WTO' (2010) 13(2) *Journal of International Economic Law* 321 (analysing the consistency of China's telecommunications regulation with its WTO obligations).

[84] Australian Productivity Commission, 'Bilateral and Regional Trade Agreements' (Research Report, Australian Government, November 2010) 89.

Australia's Foreign Investment Review Board)[85] is sufficient. Moreover, foreign ownership has the potential to reinvigorate the telecommunications industry, promoting productivity and increasing the scope and quality of service supply. For example, foreign investment in Australia (permitted to 100 per cent since 1997 except for the incumbent Telstra) has significantly contributed to a 130 per cent mobile penetration rate by the end of 2011.[86] In contrast, restrictions in Canada have protected vested domestic interests, increasing the capital cost for new entrants, and resulting in poor outcomes for consumers. The Canadian mobile sector, by comparison, had a penetration rate of 77.8 per cent at end-2011,[87] which was far lower than comparable developed nations such as the US, the United Kingdom, France, Germany, Italy, Japan, and Australia, all of which had passed the 100 per cent penetration mark.

Another example of a 'best practice' telecommunications principle would be to require functional or structural separation of wholesale and retail telecommunications service providers, which has already been embraced in Australia,[88] New Zealand[89] and Singapore.[90] Countries such as the US and Canada would need to explain why separation of this kind

---

[85] Australia's Foreign Investment Review Board (FIRB) is the federal agency responsible for making recommendations under the *Foreign Acquisitions and Takeovers Act 1975* (Cth). See <http://www.firb.gov.au>.

[86] Canadian Radio-television and Telecommunications Commission, *CRTC Communications Monitoring Report 2012* (September 2012) 181 Fig 6.1.5. Note that mobile penetration estimates vary depending on the data sources and the types of connected devices counted. For example if mobile broadband-only devices such as laptop wireless cards are excluded then, relying on Australian-sourced official data, the Australian penetration rate is 107 per cent. See Australian Competition and Consumer Commission, 'Telecommunications Reports 2011–12: Report 1 – Telecommunications Competitive Safeguards for 2011–12' (Commonwealth of Australia, 2013) 11; Australian Bureau of Statistics, *Australian Demographic Statistics, June 2012* (18 December 2012) <http://www.abs.gov.au/AUSSTATS/abs@.nsf/Lookup/3101.0Main+Features1Jun%202012>.

[87] Canadian Radio-television and Telecommunications Commission, above n 86, 174, Table 5.5.11.

[88] For an explanation of Australia's policy, see Taylor, above n 61, 17–23.

[89] For an explanation of New Zealand's policy, see *Ultra-Fast Broadband Initiative* (25 June 2012) Ministry of Business, Innovation and Employment <www.med.govt.nz/sectors-industries/technology-communication/communications/broadband-policy/ultra-fast-broadband-initiative>.

[90] For an explanation of Singapore's policy, see *Next Gen NBN* Infocomm Development Authority <www.ida.gov.sg/Policies-and-Regulations/Industry-and-Licensees/Next-Gen-NBN>.

is inappropriate in those jurisdictions. Less controversially, most jurisdictions agree that from a regulatory policy perspective the ability to trade radio frequency spectrum on the market enables spectrum to move to its highest value use. Australia[91] and New Zealand[92] are world leaders in terms of allowing spectrum to be traded[93] (although the market appears to be largely illiquid for a variety of reasons). A best practice principle of permitting spectrum trading in TPP parties would be useful. Those countries still developing the mechanism for trading (which includes complex issues of licensing and radio communications technical planning) could deviate with the explanation that they were aiming at compliance within a period of time. The TPP would thus contain some form of institutional capacity-building as well as peer review in terms of what approaches to trading are successful.

B International Mobile Roaming

International mobile 'roaming' services are offered by telecommunications service suppliers to enable their subscribers travelling abroad to make and receive calls and SMS messages and to access data using their mobile telephones or other mobile devices, including their associated numbers.[94] International mobile roaming charges are of concern across the world and have drawn the attention of the WTO,[95] the OECD, the ITU, and domestic and regional regulators and policymakers. A decade ago, international roaming was promoted as a service offering unusual convenience (particularly for the business sector) and therefore justifying premium pricing. The rapid and ubiquitous adoption of mobile services,

---

91 *Radiocommunications Act 1992* (Cth) pt 3.2 div 5 (trading of spectrum licences) and pt 3.3 div 8 (transfer of apparatus licences).

92 Martin Cave, Chris Doyle and William Webb, *Essentials of Modern Spectrum Management* (Cambridge University Press, 2007) 97–99.

93 See also *Regulatory Issues in Sectors and Modes of Supply*, WTO Doc S/WPDR/W/48 (13 June 2012) (Note by the Secretariat) [94].

94 See Ministry of Economic Development of New Zealand and Department of Broadband, Communications and the Digital Economy of Australia, *Trans-Tasman mobile roaming: Discussion document* (May 2010) [1] <http://www.dbcde.gov.au/__data/assets/pdf_file/0008/127709/Trans-Tasman_mobile_roaming_discussion_ document.pdf>.

95 *Regulatory Issues in Sectors and Modes of Supply*, WTO Doc S/WPDR/W/48 (13 June 2012) (Note by the Secretariat) [97]; *International Mobile Roaming: Possible Implications for GATS*, WTO Doc S/C/W/337 (13 July 2011) (Note by the Secretariat).

dramatic increase of 'smartphones' and data services, consumer expectation to be 'always online', and steady expansion of international travel have rendered this approach to the pricing of roaming increasingly difficult to sustain. Various means by which governments could intervene to address roaming charges have been examined, including increased regulation, which, given how roaming works in practice, would need to be adopted on a bilateral or multilateral basis in order to be effective. Within the EU, for example, retail and wholesale charges for various roaming services are capped by regulation.[96]

Attempts by governments to intervene to address roaming charges on a bilateral basis create a potential conflict with WTO rules prohibiting discrimination against services and service suppliers from particular WTO Members in comparison with services and service suppliers from other countries. That is, for example, an agreement by a WTO Member to cap roaming charges imposed by its own telecommunications suppliers on travelling subscribers of telecommunications suppliers of another WTO Member, on the basis of reciprocity, discriminates against suppliers of other WTO Members not subject to the agreement.[97] This kind of discrimination appears contrary to the obligation in Article II:1 of the GATS to accord MFN treatment in the following terms:

> With respect to any measure covered by this Agreement, each Member shall accord immediately and unconditionally to services and service suppliers of any other Member treatment no less favourable than that it accords to like services and service suppliers of any other country.

Notably, this obligation applies generally rather than only to service sectors in which a Member has made specific commitments, except to the extent that the Member imposing the regulatory cap has listed MFN exemptions in its negotiated list annexed to GATS. As a cornerstone of trade liberalisation, the MFN obligation also appears in most PTAs (and, indeed, bilateral investment treaties).

As a result of the potential conflict between bilateral agreements to limit roaming charges and the MFN rule, international discussions of how to tackle high roaming charges on a cooperative basis have noted the limits imposed by international trade law. For example, the OECD

---

96 *Regulation (EC) No 717/2007 of the European Parliament and of the Council of 27 June 2007 on roaming on public mobile communications networks within the Community*, OJ L 171 (29 June 2007) 32, as amended.

97 For further elaboration of this point, see Tania Voon, 'Discrimination in International Mobile Roaming Regulation: Implications of WTO Law' (2013) 16(1) *Journal of International Economic Law* 91.

Council's recommendation on roaming services, which encourages bilateral and multilateral agreements, states: 'Members' trade obligations, including WTO provisions and principles, should be observed when assessing the possibility of reaching agreements on wholesale price regulation.'[98] Similarly, an ITU recommendation for regulatory intervention to lower international mobile roaming rates specifies that 'regulators and policy makers' should 'tak[e] into account specific national or regional conditions',[99] which would arguably include obligations under international agreements.

If governments determine that market failure exists in the provision of international mobile roaming services, how might they intervene on a bilateral or multilateral basis to regulate roaming rates? One answer is to rely on relevant exceptions in the GATS, namely the exception for measures necessary to secure compliance with other domestic laws (such as competition laws) in GATS Article XIV(c), or the exception for measures contained in economic integration agreements in GATS Article V:1. However, those exceptions contain stringent conditions that would not necessarily be satisfied by a reciprocal arrangement for roaming regulation.[100] Moreover, PTAs do not necessarily contain corresponding exceptions to the MFN obligation in the context of telecommunications, meaning that even if a country could show a discriminatory arrangement concerning roaming was justified under WTO law, the arrangements might not be justified under its other international trade agreements.

Ambitious plurilateral agreements such as the TPP may offer an opportunity to alleviate concerns about discrimination. If all relevant trading partners are included in the agreement, this may reduce the chance of a complaint at the WTO level or pursuant to another bilateral agreement. If all the parties to the agreement agree on how to address roaming, this may also minimise the distortions in trade that may result from discriminatory regulation of roaming charges. But what agreement could be reached regarding roaming in the TPP or any other major plurilateral treaty? A uniform approach, whereby every party's suppliers receive the same preferential rates and treatment, is unlikely to be feasible, given the wide variations in regulatory, market and institutional

---

98 OECD, *Recommendation of the Council on International Mobile Roaming Services*, C(2012)7 (16 February 2012) <http://webnet.oecd.org/OECDACTS/Instruments/ShowInstrumentView.aspx?InstrumentID=271&InstrumentPID=276&Book=False>.

99 ITU, *Recommendation ITU-T D.98: Charging in International Mobile Roaming Service* (September 2012) [4.3].

100 See Voon, above n 97.

structures in telecommunications in different countries. A more flexible approach, offering greater benefits to suppliers from those parties that wish to participate, may heighten concerns about discrimination, potentially threatening the protection provided by GATS Article V:1 against claims of MFN violation arising from the TPP itself. Leaving the discretion with telecommunications regulators to impose caps on roaming charges may also not satisfy all parties, since regulators in some parties are likely to be much harsher on their own suppliers than regulators in others. This is particularly a risk in relation to jurisdictions where the major mobile operators remain state-owned, for example in Vietnam.

Another option is, of course, to leave international mobile roaming charges to the market: that is, continue to allow suppliers to set their own roaming rates. Some evidence exists that roaming charges are falling, at least in some markets.[101] Further roaming charge decreases may be expected as a result of increasing consumer information, technological and regulatory developments allowing consumers to choose who supplies their roaming services rather than being tied to their primary telecommunications supplier, and greater competition from other sources such as pre-paid sim cards and mobile phone renting for travellers. Consumers are also increasingly communicating with social media and 'over-the-top' applications, which bypass traditional circuit-switched voice services.[102] These services can be facilitated by wifi and are not reliant on mobile roaming. Allowing roaming charges to fall naturally in response to market forces would avoid the problem of discrimination contrary to international trade law.

The problem of addressing high international mobile roaming charges while respecting the principle of non-discrimination pursuant to the MFN rule exemplifies other difficulties that may arise as countries proceed increasingly towards bilateral and plurilateral rather than multilateral approaches to liberalising trade in services. A positive solution in the context of roaming could therefore provide the basis for responding to analogous problems in other service sectors as they continue to arise.

---

101 New Zealand Ministry of Business, Innovation & Employment and Australian Department of Broadband, Communications and the Digital Economy, 'Trans-Tasman roaming: Draft report' (August 2012) 32–34.

102 Australian Communications and Media Authority, 'Communications report 2011–12 series: Report 3 – Smartphones and tablets: Take-up and use in Australia' (Commonwealth of Australia, 2013) 36 <www.acma.gov.au/WEB/STANDARD/pc=PC_600063>.

CONCLUSION

Telecommunications represents one of the most dynamic services sectors, presenting policymakers with a constant challenge to stay up to date with changes in technology and market practices. This factor creates a particular difficulty when it comes to agreeing international rules that will endure not merely for a year or two, covering the current generation of mobile devices but into the next decade. The value of agreed obligations, reflecting technology at a particular time, declines as technology changes. Plurilateral approaches such as the International Services Agreement and the TPP provide realistic avenues for updating and reinvigorating existing disciplines in the absence of greater widespread movement at the level of the WTO or the ITU. This chapter has raised issues for reflection on the specific question of international mobile roaming and the more general question of how to structure telecommunications chapters in PTAs. Recognising that these issues are unlikely to be wholly resolved in either the TPP or the International Services Agreement, members of the WTO and the ITU will need to continue to consider them in negotiating improvements to the GATS, the International Telecommunications Regulations, and future PTAs.

8. State–state dispute settlement under the Trans-Pacific Partnership Agreement

Andrew Mitchell and James Munro

INTRODUCTION

Most modern preferential trade agreements (PTAs) contain formal state–state dispute settlement mechanisms, and the Trans-Pacific Partnership Agreement (TPP) will be no exception.[1] The addition of Mexico and Canada to the TPP negotiations brings the total number of TPP parties to 11, encompassing Australia, New Zealand, the United States, Peru, Chile, Brunei, Malaysia, Singapore, and Vietnam. This chapter discusses a number of special legal issues facing the TPP parties as they seek to design a well-functioning dispute settlement mechanism to resolve their disputes under the TPP.

First, we discuss the implications of multiple overlapping trade treaties between various subsets of TPP parties, each containing their own dispute settlement systems, which raises questions in relation to conflicts of norms and conflicts of jurisdiction. Second, we consider the rules of interpretation that will be used by tribunals convened under the TPP to construe its terms and settle disputes, including a potential role for the jurisprudence of the World Trade Organization (WTO) dispute settlement system.

Although the TPP parties have not released a draft text of their dispute settlement mechanism, we draw on their rich body of precedents under past PTAs and evaluate their effectiveness in addressing these special legal issues. We find a remarkable degree of diversity and inconsistency

[1] Department of Foreign Affairs and Trade, Commonwealth Government, *Enhancing Trade and Investment, Supporting Jobs, Economic Growth and Development: Outlines of The Trans-Pacific Partnership Agreement* (12 November 2011) <http://www.dfat.gov.au/fta/TPP/111112-TPP-broad-outlines.html>.

in TPP parties' past practices, with some precedents substantially more effective than others in resolving particular legal problems.

I OVERLAPPING TREATIES AND DISPUTE SETTLEMENT MECHANISMS

All of the TPP parties are WTO Members,[2] and all have at least one existing PTA with another TPP party.[3] This means that, for each TPP party, the TPP represents (at least) a *third* trade agreement applicable in its relations with (at least) one other TPP party.

For example, Australia and Malaysia are both WTO Members, and hence the provisions of the WTO Agreement and its dispute settlement mechanism apply between them. They are also both parties to the *Agreement Establishing the ASEAN–Australia–New Zealand Free Trade Area* (AANZFTA), and hence its provisions and dispute settlement mechanism also apply in their trade relations. Further, Australia and Malaysia concluded their own bilateral PTA in 2012, which became their third trade agreement with a dispute settlement mechanism. Therefore, for Australia and Malaysia, the TPP will represent a fourth trade treaty covering largely the same core disciplines and subject matter. This situation is repeated over and over for a large number of subsets of TPP parties. At the most extreme end lie Singapore and New Zealand, between which the TPP will represent a *fifth* trade treaty.[4]

---

2 World Trade Organization, *Members and Observers*, <http://www.wto.org/english/thewto_e/whatis_e/tif_e/org6_e.htm>.

3 For example, Australia, New Zealand, Vietnam, Brunei, Malaysia and Singapore are all party to the *Agreement Establishing the ASEAN–Australia–New Zealand Free Trade Area*, signed 27 February 2009, [2010] ATS 1 (entered into force 1 January 2010). Canada, Mexico and the United States are all party to the *North American Free Trade Agreement*, signed 17 December 1992 (entered into force 1 January 1994). Chile and Peru have their own bilateral PTA: *Acuerdo de Libre Comercio Chile – Peru*, signed 22 August 2006 (entered into force 1 March 2009). These three existing PTAs alone cover all of the TPP parties.

4 The other four include: *Agreement between New Zealand and Singapore on a Closer Economic Partnership*, signed 18 August 2000 (entered into force 1 January 2001); *Trans-Pacific Strategic Economic Partnership Agreement*, signed 18 July 2005 (entered into force 28 June 2006); *Agreement Establishing the ASEAN–Australia–New Zealand Free Trade Area*, signed 27 February 2009, [2010] ATS 1 (entered into force 1 January 2010); *Marrakesh Agreement Establishing the World Trade Organization*, opened for signature 15 April 1994, 1867 UNTS 3 (entered into force 1 January 1995).

The presence of multiple overlapping treaties between TPP parties raises two complex questions. First, where the norms in two or more overlapping treaties are inconsistent or in conflict with one another, which norms prevail? Second, if the same set of factual circumstances, acts or omissions lead to contraventions of multiple treaties containing similar or divergent norms, which treaty's dispute settlement procedures may be activated? The past practice of TPP parties in their existing PTAs reveals a wide diversity of practice, and how these questions will be approached in the TPP is the subject of this section.

A Conflict of Norms

A Study Group of the International Law Commission has described a conflict of norms as 'a situation where two rules or principles suggest different ways of dealing with a problem'.[5] The swordfish dispute between the European Union (EU) and Chile provides a classic illustration of a 'conflict of norms'.[6] On the one hand, Chile banned EU fishing boats that had caught swordfish from docking at its ports. Chile argued this was justified under the *United Nations Convention on the Law of the Sea* (UNCLOS),[7] since swordfish are an endangered species whose catch is prohibited. For its part, the EU claimed that Chile was *obliged* to allow its boats to dock at Chilean ports under the freedom of transit rules of the WTO.[8] The EU initiated proceedings against Chile in the WTO, whereas Chile initiated proceedings against the EU under UNCLOS. While they ultimately reached a diplomatic settlement, this dispute between Chile and the EU reveals how the same factual circumstances can bring different norms under different treaties into conflict. It raises the question: which treaty's norms prevail? In order to address this question, TPP parties have frequently included 'Relation to other Agreements' provisions in their past PTAs. These provisions seek to set out a hierarchy

---

5 International Law Commission, *Fragmentation of International Law: Difficulties Arising from the Diversification and Expansion of International Law: Report of the Study Group of the International Law Commission*, authored by Chair Martti Koskenniemi, UN Doc A/CN.4/L.682 (13 April 2006) [25].

6 European Commission, 'EU and Chile reach an amicable settlement to end WTO/ITLOS swordfish dispute' (Media Release, IP/01/116, 25 January 2001).

7 *United Nations Convention on the Law of the Sea*, opened for signature 10 December 1982, 1833 UNTS 3 (entered into force 16 November 1994).

8 European Commission, 'EU and Chile reach an amicable settlement to end WTO/ITLOS swordfish dispute' (Media Release, IP/01/116, 25 January 2001).

between potentially conflicting norms in different treaties. However, they take varying approaches.

The approach taken by Australia and the United States in their bilateral PTA begins by affirming 'their existing rights and obligations with respect to each other under existing bilateral and multilateral agreements to which both Parties are party, including the WTO Agreement'.[9] This 'affirmation' appears to suggest that the PTA is not intended to trump or displace any existing rights and obligations. The practical legal effect of this provision appears to be the exclusion of the principles of *lex specialis* and *lex posterior* in respect of existing treaties, which supply the default rules for conflict resolution under general international law.[10] In very basic terms, those default rules provide that more specific and specialised norms trump more general norms, and norms agreed later in time trump norms agreed earlier in time.[11]

The Australia–United States PTA goes on to state expressly that:

> This Agreement shall not be construed to derogate from any international legal obligation between the Parties that entitles goods or services, or suppliers of goods or services, to treatment more favourable than that accorded by this Agreement.[12]

According to this provision, the norms in *other* agreements take priority, but only under certain circumstances. First, the norm in the other agreement must be an 'obligation', as distinct from a 'right' or 'permission' (although the obligation 'entitles' goods, services or suppliers of goods or services to certain treatment). Second, that obligation must accord 'more favourable treatment' than that provided under the present agreement. Peru and Singapore took the same approach in their bilateral PTA.[13] It therefore engages Article 30(2) of the *Vienna Convention on the*

---

[9] *Australia–United States Free Trade Agreement*, signed 18 May 2004, [2005] ATS 1 (entered into force 1 January 2005) art 1.1.2.

[10] International Law Commission, *Fragmentation of International Law: Difficulties Arising from the Diversification and Expansion of International Law*, Report of the International Law Commission on its Fifty-eighth Session, UN Doc A/CN.4/L.682 (13 April 2006) [56]–[87], [228]–[256].

[11] Ibid.

[12] *Australia–United States Free Trade Agreement*, signed 18 May 2004, [2005] ATS 1 (entered into force 1 January 2005) art 1.1.3.

[13] *Free Trade Agreement between Peru and Singapore*, signed 29 May 2008 (entered into force 1 August 2009) art 1.2.

Law of Treaties (VCLT),[14] (which provides: 'When a treaty specifies that it is subject to, or that it is not to be considered as incompatible with, an earlier or later treaty, the provisions of that other treaty prevail') but makes the relevant specification conditional on the existence of these two circumstances.

The approach taken by Australia and Malaysia in their bilateral PTA is much bolder in subordinating its norms to any other treaty to which they are party. In particular, it provides that '[n]othing in this Agreement shall be construed to derogate from any existing right or obligation of a Party under the WTO Agreement and other agreements to which the Parties are party'.[15] Unlike the Australia–United States PTA, the Australia–Malaysia PTA subordinates its own norms to 'rights' contained in other treaties to which they are party, including non-trade treaties, and it omits the condition that such norms must provide 'more favourable treatment'. As such, a right or permission to take certain measures under an environmental or cultural treaty that may be trade-restrictive and otherwise prohibited by the PTA appears to be effectively permitted by this provision.[16] This approach is mimicked by AANZFTA,[17] which covers the following TPP parties: Australia, New Zealand, Malaysia, Singapore, Vietnam and Brunei. Additionally, AANZFTA includes the *Trans-Pacific Strategic Economic Partnership Agreement*,[18] which includes TPP parties Chile, Singapore, Brunei and New Zealand.

In contrast, a number of TPP parties have taken a diametrically opposite approach. Canada and Peru,[19] Canada and Chile,[20] and Mexico, Canada and the United States,[21] provide the following in their respective PTAs:

---

[14] Opened for signature 23 May 1969, 1155 UNTS 331 (entered into force 27 January 1980).

[15] *Malaysia–Australia Free Trade Agreement*, signed 22 May 2012 (entered into force 1 January 2013) art 21.2.2.

[16] See, e.g., Tania Voon, 'UNESCO and the WTO: A Clash of Cultures?' (2006) 55 *International and Comparative Law Quarterly* 635, 642–3.

[17] *Agreement Establishing the ASEAN–Australia–New Zealand Free Trade Area*, signed 27 February 2009, [2010] ATS 1 (entered into force 1 January 2010) ch 18 art 2.2.

[18] *Trans-Pacific Strategic Economic Partnership Agreement*, signed 18 July 2005 (entered into force 28 June 2006) art 18.2.

[19] *Free Trade Agreement Between Canada and the Republic of Peru*, signed 29 May 2008 (entered into force 1 August 2009) art 102.2.

[20] *Canada–Chile Free Trade Agreement*, signed 5 December 1996 (entered into force 5 July 1997) art A-03.2.

[21] *North American Free Trade Agreement*, signed 17 December 1992 (entered into force 1 January 1994) art 103.2.

1. The Parties affirm their existing rights and obligations with respect to each other under the *Marrakesh Agreement Establishing the World Trade Organization* and other agreements to which such Parties are party.
2. In the event of any inconsistency between this Agreement and such other agreements, this Agreement shall prevail to the extent of the inconsistency, except as otherwise provided in this Agreement.

Despite the affirmation of existing rights and obligations, this provision provides that the PTA *prevails* to the extent of any inconsistency. In other words, in contrast to the other approaches discussed above, the provisions of the PTA *can* be construed to derogate from rights and obligations in other agreements under this approach.

A fourth approach adopted in some existing PTAs between TPP parties is to be silent on the issue of norm conflict[22] (in which case the general default rules under international law would apply),[23] or simply to 'affirm … existing rights and obligations' under other treaties.[24]

A variety of precedents thus exist for addressing the issue of 'conflicts of norms' in the TPP. A key question, however, is whether any of these precedents are effective or workable in practice. In particular, most of these approaches are invoked only in the event of an 'inconsistency' or 'derogation', but make no attempt to set out any test for what constitutes an 'inconsistency' or 'derogation'. This is important in light of a broader debate in international law on the very nature of 'conflicts of norms'.[25] On the traditional and arguably prevailing view, a conflict occurs only where a party cannot comply with its obligations under two treaties

---

[22] See, e.g., *Singapore–Australia Free Trade Agreement between the Government of Australia and the Government of the Republic of Singapore*, signed 17 February 2003, 2257 UNTS 103 (entered into force 28 July 2003) art 5.

[23] Andrew Mitchell and Tania Voon, 'PTAs and Public International Law' in Simon Lester and Bryan Mercurio (eds), *Bilateral and Regional Trade Agreements: Commentary and Analysis* (Cambridge University Press, 2009) 114, 134.

[24] See, e.g., *Australia–Chile Free Trade Agreement*, signed 30 July 2008, [2009] ATS 6 (entered into force 6 March 2009) art 1.2.

[25] See, e.g., Erich Vranes, 'The Definition of "Norm Conflict" in International Law and Legal Theory' (2006) 17 *European Journal of International Law* 395, 396–415; Tim Graewert, 'Conflicting Laws and Jurisdictions in the Dispute Settlement Process of Regional Trade Agreements and the WTO' (2008) 1 *Contemporary Asia Arbitration Journal* 287, 291–93; Gabrielle Marceau, 'Conflicts of Norms and Conflicts of Jurisdictions: The Relationship between the WTO Agreement and MEAs and Other Treaties' (2001) 35(6) *Journal of World Trade* 1081, 1084–1086; Claude Chase, 'Norm Conflicts between WTO Covered Agreements – Real, Apparent or Avoided?' (2012) 61(4) *International and Comparative Law Quarterly* 791, 800–803.

simultaneously.[26] This was the view of the panel in *Indonesia – Automobiles*, which stated:

> [i]n international law for a conflict to exist between two treaties … [their] provisions must conflict, in the sense that the provisions must impose mutually exclusive obligations … "[T]echnically speaking, there is conflict when two (or more) treaty instruments contain obligations which cannot be complied with simultaneously."[27]

A similar view was expressed by the Appellate Body in *Guatemala – Cement*, which defined a conflict as where 'adherence to the one provision will lead to a violation of the other provision'.[28] However, this view has been criticised as unduly narrow.[29] It acknowledges conflicts only between norms obliging a party to do an act and norms prohibiting that same act, while ignoring a whole category of other norms that *permit* certain acts.[30] These permissive norms often take the form of rights or exceptions. Under the narrow view, where one treaty contains a right (but not an obligation) to undertake a certain act whereas another treaty contains a prohibition against that act, there is no conflict because a party can comply with both treaties by not exercising the right in the first treaty. In other words, the permissive norm is effectively neutered and no real conflict ever arises.[31]

On a broader view, the very purpose of norms is to regulate behaviour.[32] Therefore, if certain behaviour is simultaneously permitted and prohibited, its regulation is contradictory, and therefore the norms are in

---

26 Marceau, above n 25, 1086; Vranes, above n 25, 395.

27 Panel Report, *Indonesia – Certain Measures Affecting the Automobile Industry*, WTO Doc WT/DS54/R, WT/DS55/R, WT/DS59/R, WT/DS64/R and Corr. 1 and 2, and Corr. 3 and 4 (adopted 23 July 1998) [14.28] n 649, quoting *Encyclopaedia of Public International Law* (North-Holland 1984) 468.

28 Appellate Body Report, *Guatemala – Anti-Dumping Investigation Regarding Portland Cement from Mexico*, WTO Doc WT/DS60/AB/R (adopted 25 November 1998) [65].

29 See, e.g., Vranes, above n 25, 396–415; Chase, above n 25, 805; Graewert, above n 25, 292–93.

30 Vranes, above n 25, 395–96, 402, 404.

31 Marceau, above n 25, 1086.

32 Vranes, above n 25, 404; Chase, above n 25, 805; Christopher Borgen, 'Resolving Treaty Conflicts' (2005) 37 *George Washington Law Review* 573, 581.

conflict.[33] This was the approach taken by the panel in *EC – Bananas III*.[34] It was faced with the question of construing this conflict provision:

> In the event of conflict between a provision of the General Agreement on Tariffs and Trade 1994 and a provision of another agreement in Annex 1A to the Agreement Establishing the WTO … the provision of the other agreement shall prevail to the extent of the conflict.

The panel found that the term 'conflict' referred not just to instances where 'obligations are mutually exclusive in the sense that a Member cannot comply with both obligations at the same time', but also to 'the situation where a rule in one agreement prohibits what a rule in another agreement explicitly permits'.[35]

The fact that the attempts to regulate conflicts of norms in many past PTAs by TPP parties do not address this underlying question could undermine their utility. While one party might seek to invoke the conflicts provision where there is a conflict between a right or exemption in one treaty and a prohibition in another, another party might dismiss this as a '*faux*' conflict, since a party can comply with both treaties by simply refraining from the act and not exercising the right. This effectively occurred in the *Canada – Periodicals* dispute, where the United States initiated and won a dispute in the WTO in relation to a Canadian measure that was otherwise expressly permitted under carve-outs for 'cultural products' in its PTA with the United States and Mexico.[36]

Given this broader debate on what constitutes a 'conflict of norms', it is unclear how an arbitral tribunal under a PTA would approach the issue when faced with the precedents of TPP parties discussed above. Indeed, it is unclear whether and how it could even be raised as an effective defence before a tribunal by a defendant party seeking to justify derogations from a TPP norm. This is because, notwithstanding the conflict rules discussed above, many past PTAs between TPP parties contain the additional following provision:

> In case of any inconsistency between this Agreement and any other agreement to which both Parties are parties, the Parties shall consult with each other with

---

33 Vranes, above n 25, 404.

34 Panel Report, *European Communities – Regime for the Importation, Sale and Distribution of Bananas, Complaint by Mexico*, WTO Doc WT/DS27/R/MEX (adopted 25 September 1997).

35 Ibid., [337].

36 Graewert, above n 25, 293.

a view to finding a mutually satisfactory solution in accordance with public international law.[37]

The presence of this kind of provision raises the question as to whether conflicts of norms and inconsistencies are even justiciable by a tribunal. Such provisions arguably reserve the resolution of conflicts to consultations between the parties, rather than before tribunals. Further, most dispute settlement mechanisms are limited in scope as follows: '*[e]xcept as otherwise provided in the Agreement*, the dispute settlement provisions of this Section shall apply with respect to the avoidance or settlement of all disputes'.[38] It is unclear whether the presence of a special consultation mechanism for conflicts of norms would make disputes over them 'otherwise provided in the Agreement' and therefore outside the purview of formal dispute settlement mechanisms.

Of course, as mentioned above, some TPP parties have taken a slightly less ambiguous approach in drafting provisions dealing with conflicts of norms. For example, the approach taken by Australia and the United States allows pre-existing treaties to take priority only with respect to

---

[37] See, e.g., *Singapore–Australia Free Trade Agreement between the Government of Australia and the Government of the Republic of Singapore*, signed 17 February 2003, 2257 UNTS 103 (entered into force 28 July 2003) art 5; *Australia–Thailand Free Trade Agreement*, signed 5 July 2004, [2005] ATS 2 (entered into force 1 January 2005) art 1906; *Free Trade Agreement between the Republic of Korea and the Republic of Peru*, signed 14 November 2010 (entered into force 1 August 2011) art 1.2.2; *Agreement Establishing the ASEAN–Australia–New Zealand Free Trade Area*, signed 27 February 2009, [2010] ATS 1 (entered into force 1 January 2010) ch 18 art 2.3; *Agreement between Japan and the Republic of Peru for an Economic Partnership*, signed 31 May 2011 (entered into force 1 March 2012) art 2.2; *Free Trade Agreement between Peru and Singapore*, signed 29 May 2008 (entered into force 1 August 2009) art 19.4; *Malaysia–Australia Free Trade Agreement*, signed 22 May 2012 (entered into force 1 January 2013) art 21.2.3.

[38] See, e.g., *Singapore–Australia Free Trade Agreement between the Government of Australia and the Government of the Republic of Singapore*, signed 17 February 2003, 2257 UNTS 103 (entered into force 28 July 2003) ch 16 art 1.1; *Free Trade Agreement between the Republic of Korea and the Republic of Peru*, signed 14 November 2010 (entered into force 1 August 2011) art 23.2; *Agreement Establishing the ASEAN–Australia–New Zealand Free Trade Area*, signed 27 February 2009, [2010] ATS 1 (entered into force 1 January 2010) ch 17 art 3; *Free Trade Agreement between Peru and Singapore*, signed 29 May 2008 (entered into force 1 August 2009) art 17.2; *Malaysia–Australia Free Trade Agreement*, signed 22 May 2012 (entered into force 1 January 2013) art 20.3.1 (emphasis added).

obligations that allow 'more favourable treatment' to goods, services or suppliers of goods or services. Even then, however, a degree of opacity remains. In particular, whether more stringent intellectual property or environmental protections constitute 'more favourable treatment' depends to some extent on a country's perspective and interests.

Therefore, even though TPP parties have strived to resolve conflicts of norms in past PTAs through 'Relation to Other Agreements' provisions, the considerable ambiguities surrounding their practical application substantially undermine their effectiveness. This could be improved by including an explicit standard for when a conflict of norms occurs. For example, Vranes has suggested that '[t]here is conflict between two norms, one of which may be permissive, if in obeying or applying one norm, the other is necessarily or possibly violated'.[39] While this particular formulation generates its own difficulties by introducing a vague and ambiguous concept of 'possible violations', it could be improved by using a clearer standard such as 'whose effectiveness or utility is materially impaired'. This would capture the situation where there is a norm permitting (but not requiring) a certain act, and another norm prohibiting that act. Further improvements could be made by clarifying the relationship between the consultation mechanisms to resolve inconsistencies and the formal dispute settlement procedure. For example, it could be more clearly specified whether, and to what extent, 'Relation to Other Agreements' provisions are justiciable as a defence to otherwise norm-violating conduct.

B Conflict of Jurisdiction

Conflicts of jurisdiction occur where two dispute settlement fora have competence over the same factual circumstances giving rise to a dispute.[40] The *Argentina – Poultry* dispute between Argentina and Brazil provides an archetypal example.[41] Brazil first challenged an Argentinian measure before a *Mercado Común del Sur* (MERCOSUR) tribunal and lost. Not content with that outcome, Brazil re-litigated the matter before a WTO panel and won.

---

39 Vranes, above n 25, 415.

40 Songling Yang, 'The Key Role of the WTO in Settling its Jurisdictional Conflicts with RTAs' (2012) 11 *Chinese Journal of International Law* 281, 282; Marceau, above n 25, 1108.

41 Panel Report, *Argentina – Definitive Anti-Dumping Duties on Poultry from Brazil*, WTO Doc WT/DS241/R (adopted 19 May 2003).

The past practice of TPP parties suggests that they share a concern about the potential for two international tribunals to adjudicate the same dispute in parallel or sequentially.[42] This concern is probably founded on the potential for the finality and certainty of a tribunal's decision to be called into question, since it may be effectively revisited by another tribunal. Parties may also be concerned about the potential for double jeopardy or double compensation, depending on the remedies awarded by different tribunals. Further, the potential for two tribunals to adjudicate the same dispute calls into question the legitimacy and stability of the broader system in which international tribunals function, since the outcome of one tribunal does not necessarily settle or resolve a dispute if another tribunal has the potential to re-arbitrate the matter and render an inconsistent finding.

That said, as will be shown, TPP parties have expressed differing degrees of concern through their past practice. While some have sought to prevent *any* potential for multiple proceedings in respect of the same factual circumstances, others have limited this to instances where the same norms or rules are at stake, thus permitting multiple proceedings where substantially different claims might be available under different treaties. We now survey this past practice of TPP parties in seeking to prevent conflicts of jurisdiction.

One particularly common approach is found in the PTA between Australia and Malaysia, which provides:

> Where a dispute concerning any matter arises under this Agreement and under another international agreement to which the Parties are party, the Complaining Party may select the forum in which to address that matter and that forum shall be used to the exclusion of other possible fora in respect of that matter.[43]

Under this approach, the complainant may select the forum in which the matter giving rise to the dispute is addressed. Once selected, however, that matter may not be raised in any other forum. A key benefit of this approach is its simplicity in preventing a given dispute from being re-litigated. It effectively eliminates the potential for two tribunals producing inconsistent outcomes in relation to the same issue, providing certainty and finality to the selected tribunal's decision.

---

[42] Joost Pauwelyn and Luiz Eduardo Salles, 'Forum Shopping Before International Tribunals: (Real) Concerns, (Im)Possible Solutions' (2009) 42 *Cornell International Law Journal* 77, 81–83.

[43] *Malaysia–Australia Free Trade Agreement*, signed 22 May 2012 (entered into force 1 January 2013) art 20.5.

However, a number of drawbacks are associated with this kind of provision. First, while it would prevent a party from bringing a claim under the subject PTA where that party has already initiated a claim elsewhere, it would not necessarily constrain a party from initiating a claim under other agreements having already initiated a claim under the PTA. That will depend on whether the tribunal under the other agreement (e.g. the WTO treaty) chooses to apply the PTA provision, which has no direct application beyond the PTA. A respondent might need to rely on equitable or good faith arguments, as Argentina did in *Argentina – Poultry*, to seek to prevent parallel claims or 'two bites of the cherry'.[44] Some argue that this would be a difficult argument to make if the other agreement has exclusive jurisdiction and is not empowered to recognise awards or disputes under other treaties, as is generally the case under the WTO Agreement.[45] However, notwithstanding the Appellate Body's apparent unease with the prospect of estoppel being used to condition the right to bring a claim, we believe a choice of jurisdiction clause may ground an estoppel at the WTO and potentially before other PTA dispute settlement bodies.[46]

In any case, this type of choice of forum clause is inflexible because it potentially locks parties into a particular avenue of dispute settlement at a relatively early stage. For example, Australia may be concerned about a Malaysian measure and initiate proceedings under the bilateral PTA. However, Peru might subsequently be concerned about the same measure and initiate proceedings under the TPP. Under this kind of provision, Australia would have no capacity to choose to consolidate its proceedings with those of Peru. In fact, that would be barred under the Australia–Malaysia PTA, since it would mean that Australia is effectively re-initiating a claim under another agreement.

This type of provision is also inflexible because it requires a complainant to choose between two potentially very different norms and rule-sets.

---

[44] Panel Report, *Argentina – Definitive Anti-Dumping Duties on Poultry from Brazil*, WTO Doc WT/DS241/R, adopted 19 May 2003, [7.17]–[7.23], [7.33]–[7.42].

[45] Jennifer Hillman, 'Conflicts Between Dispute Settlement Mechanisms in Regional Trade Agreements and the WTO – What Should the WTO Do' (2009) 42 *Cornell International Law Journal* 193, 205; Marceau, above n 25, 1101; Yang, above n 40, 286.

[46] See Andrew Mitchell and David Heaton, 'The Inherent Jurisdiction of WTO Tribunals: The Select Application of Public International Law Required by the Judicial Function' (2010) 31 *Michigan Journal of International Law* 559, 608–618.

For example, a decision by a party to repeal an emissions trading scheme could raise issues under both the Kyoto Protocol[47] and the TPP. An aggrieved party would need to foreclose one of those options, which protect different norms and values, under this choice of forum provision. That said, even if one TPP party forecloses its dispute settlement options under the TPP, it would be possible for another TPP party to initiate a dispute under the TPP in respect of the same matter.

Other approaches have sought to build in additional flexibilities to account for these problems.

The PTA between Australia and Chile limits the application of the exclusive choice of forum provision to 'other free trade agreements or the WTO Agreement'.[48] This means that a party is not prevented from pursuing a claim regarding the same matter under a non-trade agreement, such as UNCLOS or the Kyoto Protocol.

The Japan–Mexico and Australia–Thailand PTAs take an even broader approach, providing that the exclusive choice of forum provision 'does not apply if substantially separate and distinct rights or obligations under different international agreements are in dispute'.[49]

This could potentially allow the same matter to be challenged under different trade agreements, where those trade agreements provide 'substantially' separate and distinct rights. For example, part of a claim might be pursued under the WTO Agreement, but another part relating to investment chapter breaches or environment and labour standards might be pursued under a PTA.

Another approach could be for the TPP to allow proceedings in another forum to be pursued, as long as proceedings under the TPP are suspended. This would allow parties to return to the TPP if they consider it appropriate – but only if the dispute is not concluded under the other forum. This would at least give parties the option of using – or pausing – proceedings in the TPP if, for example, a similar dispute is being pursued

---

[47] *Kyoto Protocol to the United Nations Framework Convention on Climate Change*, opened for signature 10 December 1997, 2302 UNTS 108 (entered into force 16 February 2005).

[48] *Australia–Chile Free Trade Agreement*, signed 30 July 2008, [2009] ATS 6 (entered into force 6 March 2009) art 21.2.1.

[49] *Australia–Thailand Free Trade Agreement*, signed 5 July 2004, [2005] ATS 2 (entered into force 1 January 2005) art 1801; *Agreement between Japan and the United Mexican States for the Strengthening of the Economic Partnership*, signed 17 September 2004, (not yet in force) art 151.2.

in the WTO or under another PTA. This was the approach taken by Mexico and the EU in their PTA.[50]

Chile and the EU took an entirely different approach in their PTA, as follows:

> when a Party seeks redress of a violation of an obligation under this Part of the Agreement which is equivalent in substance to an obligation under the WTO, it shall have recourse to the relevant rules and procedures of the WTO Agreement, which apply notwithstanding the provisions of this Agreement.[51]

Under this approach, where an obligation under the PTA is 'equivalent in substance' to an obligation under the WTO, the dispute may *only* be pursued through the WTO. This is quite different from the other approaches discussed above, which usually confer discretion on the complainant to choose the forum of the dispute.

The fundamental issue in all of these approaches is striking the right balance between flexibility and certainty. On one hand, there is a need to prevent competing arbitral outcomes in the same dispute and to prevent a party from re-litigating a matter it has already lost. On the other hand, by leaving the choice of forum entirely in the hands of the complainant and barring further action in other fora, there is potential for complainants to 'forum shop' in a way that undermines delicately negotiated outcomes under another treaty. This was effectively the case in *Canada – Periodicals* as mentioned above, where the United States chose a forum and treaty where Canada would be unable to invoke certain cultural exemptions it had negotiated in another treaty.[52]

Perhaps a model approach that strikes a reasonable balance between these competing goals can be found in the very recent PTA between the EU and a group of Central American states:

> 4. The disputing Parties shall avoid bringing identical disputes in different fora when based on the same legal claims and measures.

---

50 *Economic Partnership, Political Coordination and Cooperation Agreement between the European Community and its Member States, of the one part, and the United Mexican States, of the other part*, signed 8 December 1997 (entered into force 1 July 2000), Decision No 2/2000 of the EC–Mexico Joint Council of 23 March 2000 (2000/415/EC) art 47.4.

51 *Agreement establishing an association between the European Community and its Member States, of the one part, and the Republic of Chile, of the other part*, signed 18 November 2002 (entered into force 1 March 2005) art 189.4(c).

52 Graewert, above n 25, 292–93.

5. In the case of non-identical disputes related to the same measure, the Parties shall refrain from initiating concurrent dispute settlement procedures.[53]

Under this approach, 'identical disputes' (disputes based on the same legal claims and measures)[54] are prohibited. This prevents multiple proceedings applying the same norms to the same set of facts, which precludes the potential for inconsistent outcomes on the same law and facts. However, where different norms apply to the same dispute, parties are only precluded from initiating *concurrent* disputes. Therefore, the potential for applying the different norm-set is not foreclosed but is simply paused until the other forum has considered the matter. This prevents the potential for tribunals concurrently considering the same matter and simultaneously rendering different opinions, as occurred in a particular international investment dispute.[55] It also reduces the potential for the 'tit-for-tat' initiation of disputes by different parties in different fora, as occurred in the swordfish dispute discussed above, as well as in *Mexico – Taxes on Soft Drinks*.[56]

A number of PTAs also seek to limit the potential for multiple disputes over the same matter by providing that measures of one party that have been authorised by the WTO Dispute Settlement Body cannot be challenged by the other party as a violation of the PTA, for example:

2. Nothing in Chapters 3, 7 and 8 shall be construed to prevent either Party from taking any necessary action as may be authorized by Article 22 of the Understanding on Rules and Procedures Governing the Settlement of Disputes in Annex 2 to the WTO Agreement, as may be amended.[57]

---

53 *Agreement Establishing an Association between Central America, on the one hand, and the European Union and its Member States, on the other*, signed 29 June 2012 (not yet in force) art 326.

54 Ibid., art 326.6.

55 *Lauder v Czech Republic (Final Award)* (Ad Hoc Arbitral Tribunal, UNCITRAL Rules, 3 September 2001); *CME Czech Republic BV v Czech Republic* (Ad Hoc Arbitral Tribunal, UNCITRAL Rules, Partial Award of 13 September 2001 and Final Award of 14 March 2003).

56 Appellate Body Report, *Mexico – Tax Measures on Soft Drinks and Other Beverages*, WTO Doc WT/DS308/AB/R, adopted 24 March 2006, [3], [10]–[11], [31].

57 *Agreement between Japan and the United Mexican States for the Strengthening of the Economic Partnership*, signed 17 September 2004 (not yet in force) art 167.2.

> Nothing in this Agreement shall preclude a Party from implementing the suspension of obligations authorized by the DSB ... [58]

However, these precedents will probably be insufficient in the TPP context without elaboration, since there is also the possibility for countermeasures to have been authorised under other bilateral and plurilateral PTAs.

II RULES OF INTERPRETATION

The importance of rules of interpretation cannot be overstated. As Van Damme states, '[p]rinciples of treaty interpretation push and pull a treaty in different directions and towards different meanings'.[59] The outcome of a dispute can hinge on the application (or non-application) by a tribunal of a given rule of interpretation. As such, the rules of interpretation used in the TPP will represent a key legal feature in its dispute settlement system. In this section, we evaluate the pros and cons of TPP parties' past practice, as well as a potential role for WTO jurisprudence in the interpretation of the TPP.

A Evaluating Past Practice of TPP Parties

A survey of TPP parties' past practice reveals a surprising level of diversity in the framing of provisions on rules of interpretation. A number of PTAs follow the approach taken in the WTO, requiring the agreements to be interpreted according to 'the customary rules of public international law'.[60] In a twist on this approach, Chile used a formulation in one of its PTAs requiring it to be interpreted 'in accordance with the

---

[58] *Free Trade Agreement between the European Union and its Member States, of the one part, and the Republic of Korea, of the other part,* signed 6 October 2010 (entered into force June 2010) art 14.16.

[59] Isabelle Van Damme, *Treaty Interpretation by the WTO Appellate Body* (Oxford University Press, 2009) 379.

[60] See, e.g., *Singapore–Australia Free Trade Agreement between the Government of Australia and the Government of the Republic of Singapore*, signed 17 February 2003, 2257 UNTS 103 (entered into force 28 July 2003) ch 16 art 1.5; *Free Trade Agreement Between Canada and the Republic of Peru*, signed 29 May 2008 (entered into force 1 August 2009) art 2110; *Agreement Establishing the ASEAN–Australia–New Zealand Free Trade Area*, signed 27 February 2009, [2010] ATS 1 (entered into force 1 January 2010) art 4; *Malaysia–Australia Free Trade Agreement*, signed 22 May 2012 (entered into force 1 January 2013) art 20.4.

applicable rules of international law'.[61] While drafted differently, this appears to have the same legal scope and effect as the approach taken in the WTO. In another innovation, Chile emphasised the principle of good faith in its PTA with the EU, providing:

> 3. Arbitration panels shall interpret the provisions of this Agreement in accordance with customary rules of interpretation of public international law, *due account being taken of the fact that the Parties must perform this Agreement in good faith and avoid circumvention of their obligations*.[62]

It is unclear what this additional clause on 'good faith' is designed to achieve. Article 31 of the VCLT, which reflects a customary rule of interpretation,[63] already includes a requirement that treaties be interpreted 'in good faith'. Indeed, despite the absence of this additional clause in the WTO Agreement, the Appellate Body has emphasised the role of good faith in informing treaty interpretation.[64] Perhaps it evinces a greater willingness of the parties to admit the application of principles such as collateral estoppel and *res judicata* in their disputes, but this is by no means clear.

The United States and Australia took a different approach in their PTA. They required it to be interpreted 'in accordance with applicable rules of interpretation under international law *as reflected in Articles 31 and 32 of the Vienna Convention on the Law of Treaties*'.[65] This direct reference to specific provisions of the VCLT may have been prompted by the fact that the United States is not a party to the VCLT. The parties may have been concerned that a tribunal could decline to apply those provisions of the VCLT on that basis. That said, this direct reference is probably

---

61 *Free Trade Agreement between the Republic of Korea and the Republic of Chile*, signed 15 February 2003 (entered into force 1 April 2004) art 1.2.2 (emphasis added).

62 *Agreement establishing an association between the European Community and its Member States, of the one part, and the Republic of Chile, of the other part*, signed 18 November 2002 (entered into force 1 March 2005) art 189.4(c) (emphasis added).

63 Appellate Body Report, *United States – Standards for Reformulated and Conventional Gasoline*, WTO Doc WT/DS2/AB/R (adopted 20 May 1996) [17].

64 See, e.g., Appellate Body Report, *United States – Anti-Dumping Measures on Certain Hot-Rolled Steel Products from Japan*, WTO Doc WT/DS184/AB/R (adopted 23 August 2001) [101].

65 *Australia–United States Free Trade Agreement*, signed 18 May 2004, [2005] ATS 1 (entered into force 1 January 2005) art 21.9 (emphasis added).

unnecessary since those Articles are widely recognised and applied as customary international law.[66]

Furthermore, a drawback of this 'direct reference' approach is that it limits tribunals to the rules contained in the specified provisions. As Van Damme states, 'treaty interpretation is not simply the application of Articles 31 to 33' of the VCLT, but instead involves a whole series of principles and rules found in general international law that are not necessarily codified in those provisions.[67] Indeed, the fact that the WTO Agreement provides for the WTO dispute settlement system to clarify the covered agreements 'in accordance with customary rules of interpretation of public international law'[68] rather than particular provisions of the VCLT has facilitated the use by those bodies of a wide variety of other codified and non-codified principles of interpretation.[69]

For example, the Appellate Body has frequently invoked *ut res magis valeat quam perea*, or the principle of effectiveness, as an interpretative aid.[70] Under this principle, '[a]n interpreter is not free to adopt a reading that would result in reducing whole clauses or paragraphs of a treaty to redundancy or inutility'.[71] Other uncodified rules and principles such as *ejusdem generis*,[72] *expressio unius est exclusio alterius*,[73] and state responsibility,[74] have also been referenced and applied in WTO jurisprudence when interpreting various provisions. Similarly, other provisions of

---

66 Appellate Body Report, *United States – Standards for Reformulated and Conventional Gasoline*, WTO Doc WT/DS2/AB/R (adopted 20 May 1996) 17.

67 Van Damme, above n 59, 49.

68 '*Marrakesh Agreement Establishing the World Trade Organization*, opened for signature 15 April 1994, 1867 UNTS 3 (entered into force 1 January 1995) annex 2 (*Understanding on Rules and Procedures Governing the Settlement of Disputes*) art 3.2.

69 Van Damme, above n 59, 380.

70 Appellate Body Report, *Japan – Taxes on Alcoholic Beverages*, WTO Doc WT/DS8/AB/R, WT/DS10/AB/R, WT/DS11/AB/R (adopted 1 November 1996) 12.

71 Appellate Body Report, *United States – Standards for Reformulated and Conventional Gasoline*, WTO Doc WT/DS2/AB/R (adopted 20 May 1996) 23.

72 Appellate Body Reports, *United States – Certain Country of Origin Labelling (COOL) Requirements*, WTO Doc WT/DS384/AB/R/WT/DS386/AB/R (adopted 23 July 2012) [442]–[444] n 897.

73 Panel Report, *China – Measures Affecting Trading Rights and Distribution Services for Certain Publications and Audiovisual Entertainment Products*, WTO Doc WT/DS363/R and Corr.1 (adopted 19 January 2010) nn 103, 124.

74 Panel Report, *Turkey – Restrictions on Imports of Textile and Clothing Products*, WTO Doc WT/DS34/R (adopted 19 November 1999) [9.9]–[9.12].

the VCLT related to interpretation, such as Article 28 on the non-retroactivity of treaties,[75] have been drawn upon in WTO jurisprudence. None of these interpretative aids would be captured under the Australia–United States approach, since it limits tribunals to Articles 31 and 32.

Peru's PTA with the EU takes a similar but slightly broader approach than the Australia–United States PTA, providing that:

> Any arbitration panel shall interpret the provisions [of this Agreement] in accordance with the customary rules of interpretation of public international law *included in the Vienna Convention on the Law of Treaties, done at Vienna on 23 May 1969.*[76]

Rather than limiting panels to specific provisions of the VCLT as in the Australia–United States PTA, this provision authorises the use of the VCLT more broadly. Any rule that is both customary and contained in the VCLT may be used under this approach. While this arguably captures interpretative tools outside Articles 31 and 32, such as the presumption against retroactivity and conflicts between successive treaties, it still limits tribunals to principles codified in the VCLT, and as Van Damme recalls, '[t]he ILC excluded many principles of interpretation from its codification exercise'.[77]

The approach taken by the EU and South Korea (neither of which is a TPP party) references the VCLT but also permits the use of customary rules found outside the VCLT:

> Any arbitration panel shall interpret the provisions referred to in Article 14.2 in accordance with customary rules of interpretation of public international law, including those codified in the Vienna Convention on the Law of Treaties.[78]

This approach is probably closest to the practical exercise of interpretation developed by the Appellate Body. While the VCLT is referenced as codifying some customary rules of interpretation, and provides a starting point for the exercise, a potentially wider toolbox of customary rules of

---

[75] Appellate Body Report, *Brazil – Measures Affecting Desiccated Coconut*, WTO Doc WT/DS22/AB/R (adopted 20 March 1997) 15.

[76] *Trade Agreement between the European Union and its Member States, of the one part, and Colombia and Peru, of the other part*, signed 26 June 2012 (not yet in force) art 317 (emphasis added).

[77] Van Damme, above n 59, 52.

[78] *Free Trade Agreement between the European Union and its Member States, of the one part, and the Republic of Korea, of the other part*, signed 6 October 2010 (entered into force June 2010) art 14.16.

interpretation under public international law is recognised. This formulation could therefore provide a useful precedent for TPP parties when drafting their 'rules of interpretation' provision.

Another option open to parties is to remain silent on the rules of interpretation. This was the approach taken by the parties to the *Trans-Pacific Strategic Economic Partnership Agreement*.[79] In practical terms, this option would likely have the same result as the approach taken by the EU and Korea, since the customary rules of interpretation under public international law would apply, including those contained in the VCLT.

B Harmonisation through Precedent?

Another pertinent question is the extent to which tribunals in the TPP will draw on WTO jurisprudence in interpreting the TPP. Of course, the absence of a formal legal hierarchy amongst the various permanent and ad hoc international dispute settlement bodies renders a strict doctrine of *stare decisis* unsuitable to public international law.[80] Even within the WTO dispute settlement system, WTO jurisprudence suggests that 'panels are not *bound* by previous decisions of panels or the Appellate Body even if the subject matter is the same'.[81] However, despite the absence of a formal system of binding precedent, the Appellate Body has emphasised the importance of 'taking into account' past jurisprudence with a view to avoiding 'inconsistent rulings'.[82] This approach has resulted in a *de facto* system of precedent, with panels and the Appellate

[79] See *Trans-Pacific Strategic Economic Partnership Agreement*, signed 18 July 2005 (entered into force 28 June 2006) ch 15 – it contains no rules of interpretation.

[80] Guido Acquaviva Fausto Pocar, 'Stare decisis', in R. Wolfrum (ed.), *The Max Planck Encyclopedia of Public International Law* (online) (Oxford University Press, 2008) <www.mpepil.com>.

[81] Panel Report, *India – Patent Protection for Pharmaceutical and Agricultural Chemical Products, Complaint by the European Communities and their member States*, WTO Doc WT/DS79/R (adopted 22 September 1998) [7.30] (emphasis in original).

[82] Appellate Body Report, *United States – Final Anti-Dumping Measures on Stainless Steel from Mexico*, WTO Doc WT/DS344/AB/R (adopted 20 May 2008) [145]–[162].

Body routinely citing and applying past conclusions and reasoning as authority to justify their findings.[83]

Tribunals under PTAs are not part of the WTO dispute settlement system, and they are required to interpret the terms of a PTA rather than the WTO Agreement. It might therefore appear *prima facie* inappropriate that they would apply the precedents and interpretations contained in WTO jurisprudence. However, PTAs are often drafted on the basis of the WTO Agreement and regularly incorporate its provisions directly. To the extent that the context of the PTA did not require an alternative interpretation, it would be appropriate for a PTA tribunal to apply WTO decisions in interpreting such provisions. Further, the jurisprudence of the WTO offers a rich body of legal reasoning that enjoys the substantial legitimacy associated with the WTO dispute settlement mechanism more generally. Aside from its legitimacy, that jurisprudence may usefully illuminate the object and purpose of PTA provisions (by analogy to similar WTO provisions) or show the object to which PTA provisions are directed (for example, where the PTA provisions address a gap in the WTO agreements revealed in dispute settlement proceedings).[84]

In this context, tribunals convened under PTAs have demonstrated a degree of willingness to draw on, and apply, WTO jurisprudence in order

[83] See further Meredith Kolsky Lewis, 'Dissent as Dialectic: Horizontal and Vertical Disagreement in WTO Dispute Settlement' (2012) 48 *Stanford Journal of International Law* 1.

[84] In this regard, it is worth noting that a desire to be consistent with, and build upon, the WTO Agreement is present in the text of the object and purpose of many PTAs. See, e.g., *Australia–United States Free Trade Agreement* (AUS-FTA), signed 18 May 2004, [2005] ATS 1 (entered into force 1 January 2005) art 1.1; *Free Trade Agreement between the European Union and its Member States, of the one part, and the Republic of Korea, of the other part,* signed 6 October 2010 (entered into force June 2010) art 55(c); *Free Trade Agreement Between Canada and the Republic of Peru*, signed 29 May 2008 (entered into force 1 August 2009) art 101; *Free Trade Agreement between the Republic of Korea and the Republic of Chile*, signed 15 February 2003 (entered into force 1 April 2004) art 1.1; *Free Trade Agreement between the Government of the People's Republic of China and the Government of the Republic of Chile*, signed 16 November 2005 (entered into force 1 October 2006) art 2; *Costa Rica–China Free Trade Agreement*, signed 8 April 2010 (entered into force 1 August 2011) art 1; *Peru–Singapore Free Trade Agreement,* signed 29 May 2008 (entered into force 1 August 2009) art 1; *Agreement Establishing the ASEAN–Australia–New Zealand Free Trade Area,* signed 27 February 2009, [2010] ATS 1 (entered into force 1 January 2010) art 2.

to construe the terms of their PTA.[85] This is despite the fact that they are neither expressly authorised, nor required, to do so. As an example, the tribunal in the *Broom Corn Brooms Case* cited WTO jurisprudence as authority when interpreting the term 'like products' under the *North American Free Trade Agreement*.[86] A number of the EU's recent PTAs take this one step further by requiring tribunals convened under the PTAs to apply WTO jurisprudence where the provisions under consideration are 'identical':

> Where an obligation under this Agreement is identical to an obligation under the WTO Agreement, the arbitration panel shall adopt an interpretation which is consistent with any relevant interpretation established in rulings of the WTO Dispute Settlement Body … .[87]

On the one hand, this should be an unsurprising rule of interpretation. It provides the parties with the certainty that identical provisions will be interpreted consistently across treaties. It does so by eliminating the possibility that an identical PTA provision will be given a different meaning from the corresponding WTO provision based on context, object or the structure of the PTA. It also clarifies and formalises the role of WTO jurisprudence in proceedings under a PTA. On the other hand, its systemic implications are remarkable. By including this rule, the parties are effectively setting up a normative system of binding precedent. As discussed above, not even the WTO dispute settlement system itself recognises a formal system of precedent. Indeed, the Appellate Body has expressly stated that it is the '*exclusive authority* of the Ministerial Conference and the General Council' rather than the Appellate Body or the Dispute Settlement Body 'to adopt … interpretations that are binding

---

[85] See, e.g., *Methanex Corporation v USA* (Final Award) (Ad Hoc Arbitration, UNCITRAL Rules, 3 August 2008) [6]; *In the Matter of the US Safeguard Action taken on Broom Corn Brooms From Mexico (Final Award)* (NAFTA Ch 20 Panel, USA-97-2008-01, 30 January 1998).

[86] *In the Matter of the US Safeguard Action taken on Broom Corn Brooms From Mexico (Final Award)* (NAFTA Ch 20 Panel, USA-97-2008-01, 30 January 1998) [61]–[70].

[87] *Free Trade Agreement between the European Union and its Member States, of the one part, and the Republic of Korea, of the other part*, signed 6 October 2010 (entered into force June 2010) art 14.16; *Agreement Establishing an Association between Central America, on the one hand, and the European Union and its Member States, on the other*, signed 29 June 2012 (not yet in force) art 322.2.

upon the WTO membership'.[88] As such, in a formal legal sense, the EU rule of interpretation accords WTO jurisprudence a higher status under these PTAs than it enjoys under the WTO itself.

That said, the scope of this rule is limited in its application to 'identical' obligations. The only truly 'identical' obligations will be those directly incorporated from the WTO Agreement, and those drafted with identical language. Many other obligations might be *very similar* to equivalents under the WTO Agreement, and will encompass the same concepts and disciplines, but are not strictly *identical*. A slightly broader formulation, such as 'identical or *substantially the same* obligation' could significantly enhance the application of this provision. In any case, this kind of provision should provide comfort to those who are dismayed at the so-called 'fragmentation of international trade law' through the proliferation of PTAs.[89] It demonstrates a deliberate effort to achieve harmony and consistency across different trade treaties, and, if appropriately drafted and tailored, should therefore be both welcomed and encouraged in the TPP.

CONCLUSION

Designing a state–state dispute settlement mechanism in the TPP raises a number of complex legal issues, on which the TPP parties have varied and divergent precedents. As we have shown, questions of conflict of norms of jurisdiction and the applicable rules of interpretation can have a material and determinative impact on the outcome of disputes. It is therefore of paramount importance that the TPP parties address these issues in a methodical and practical manner. While many of their (and other) precedents have significant shortcomings, some are both innovative and effective, and serve as a useful model for the TPP. It will be fascinating to observe how the parties conclude these issues in the final agreement and its subsequent effects.

---

88 Appellate Body Report, *United States – Final Anti-Dumping Measures on Stainless Steel from Mexico*, WTO Doc WT/DS344/AB/R (adopted 20 May 2008) [158] n 308 (emphasis added). See also *Marrakesh Agreement Establishing the World Trade Organization*, opened for signature 15 April 994, 1867 UNTS 3 (entered into force 1 January 1995) art IX:2.

89 See, e.g., Panagiotis Delimatsis, 'The Fragmentation of International Trade Law' (TILEC Discussion Paper No 2010-010, Tilburg Law and Economics Center, February 2010) <http://ssrn.com/abstract=1554909>.

9. Investor–state dispute settlement under the Trans-Pacific Partnership Agreement

Leon E. Trakman*

INTRODUCTION

The Trans-Pacific Partnership Agreement (TPP) is one of the most significant multilateral treaties to have been contemplated within the Asia Pacific region. Gantz observes that, '[s]hould Canada, Mexico and ultimately Japan be brought into the negotiations, the TPP would likely surpass that of any other regional trade agreement other than the European Union in total trade value.'[1] All three countries have since joined, affirming the economic importance of the impending treaty.

The potential growth of the TPP as a multilateral investment agreement is significant, both in the prospective size of its membership and its economic scope as a free trade and investment regime. TPP enthusiasts are likely to envisage it as the continuation of an evolving multilateral investment process, to replace in part the multilateral investment agreement that failed at the end of the 1990s and as a template for other

* I am indebted to colleagues at the Workshop on the International Center for the Settlement of Investment Disputes (ICSID) held in Xi'an Jiaotong University, in China on 25–30 June 2012, organised by Professor Wenhua Shan, for their insights; to colleagues at the Workshop on the TPP negotiations held at the Melbourne Law School on 18 August 2012 organised by Professor Tania Voon; and to Mark Feldman, Mark Kantor, Luke Nottage and Shiro Armstrong for their comments on a draft of this chapter. Particular thanks are owed to Kunal Sharma for his able research assistance.

[1] David Gantz, 'Trans-Pacific Partnership Negotiations: Progress, but no End in Sight' on *Kluwer Arbitration Blog* (22 June 2012) <http://kluwerarbitrationblog.com/blog/2012/06/22/trans-pacific-partnership-negotiations-progress-but-no-end-in-sight/>.

regions to replicate.[2] However, such optimism is arguably premature, going beyond the issue of the desirability and viability of a new multilateral investment agreement. What is relevant is that global foreign direct investment has grown geometrically since 1970, exceeding US$1.5 trillion in 2012.[3] Against this background, however one measures its economic significance, the impending TPP has the potential to have an enormous impact on global investment.

Nevertheless, there are many controversial aspects in the unfolding TPP negotiations. The first aspect relates to Australia's participation in the negotiations on the TPP's investment chapter, with its position being that it will not accept arbitration mechanisms for investor–state dispute settlement. The second aspect relates to the prospect of other Asia-Pacific Economic Cooperation (APEC) members joining later but with China not participating in TPP negotiations generally or in investment negotiations in particular.[4]

The prospect of Australia seeking an exemption from investor–state arbitration (ISA) within a TPP chapter on investment is probable at this time, following the Australian Labor government's policy statement in April 2011 that Australia would no longer enter into investment treaties that provided for ISA.[5] Australia's 2011 Policy Statement changes a

---

[2] See generally Stephan Schill, *The Multilateralization of International Investment Law* (Cambridge University Press, 2009) VI–VII: discussing non-ICSID methods of multilateralisation and investment jurisprudence; Steffen Hindelang, 'Bilateral Investment Treaties, Custom and a Healthy Investment Climate – The Question of Whether BITs Influence Customary International Law Revisited' (2004) 5 *Journal of World Investment and Trade* 789.

[3] See the United Nations Conference on Trade and Development, *World Investment Report 2012* (United Nations Publications, 2012) xi.

[4] On China's shifting position in regard to investment arbitration, see Vivienne Bath and Luke Nottage (eds), *Foreign Investment and Dispute Resolution Law and Practice in Asia* (Routledge, 2011).

[5] Department of Foreign Affairs and Trade (Cth), 'Trading Our Way to More Jobs and Prosperity' (Policy Statement, 12 April 2011) <http://www.dfat.gov.au/publications/trade/trading-our-way-to-more-jobs-and-prosperity.html#investor-state> (2011 Policy Statement). For a comment on the Australian government's 2011 Policy Statement, see Jürgen Kurtz, 'Australia's Rejection of Investor–State Arbitration: Causation, Omission and Implication' (2012) 27 *ICSID Review* 65; Luke Peterson, 'Australia Rejects ISA Provision in Trade Agreements' on *Don't Trade Our Lives Away* (19 April 2011) <http://donttradeourlivesaway.wordpress.com/2011/04/19/australia-rejects-investor-state-arbitration-provision-in-trade-agreements/>; Leon Trakman, 'Investor State Arbitration or Local Courts: Will Australia Set a New Trend?' (2012) 46 *Journal of World Trade* 83. See generally, Leon Trakman, 'Foreign Direct Investment:

course which Australia took in the past, since the early 1980s when it began concluding bilateral investment treaties (BITs), to include ISA provisions in its treaties, with the notable exception of the *Australia–United States Free Trade Agreement*.[6] The Australian government has since implemented its new policy in a free trade agreement (FTA) with Malaysia in May 2012 that does not include ISA provisions. The greatest uncertainty at this time is whether the new Liberal government (elected in September 2013) will endorse the policy statement adopted by the Labor government in 2011.

The issue of countries like Australia securing exemptions under the TPP's investment chapter tests the capacity of prospective investment agreements, such as the proposed TPP, to maintain both their authority and stability if they make country-specific concessions too readily. As a result, the exemption of Australia from ISA is significant for reasons well beyond Australia's global economic stature. First, such an exemption would be pervasive in exempting one country from the institution and process of enforcement that is embodied in the investment chapter. While the substantive provisions of the investment chapter could be enforced through state-to-state dispute settlement measures, investors would not be able to mount ISA claims directly. Second, the exemption could be replicated by other countries (although such replication may not be significant in itself). Third, general or specific exemptions from the TPP could lead to a two- or multi-tier regional investment agreement, heralding an assortment of BITs as signatories to the TPP seek to limit costs and maximise benefits arising from exemptions secured by some negotiating parties. Fourth, so long as there are exemptions from ISA under the TPP, there is always the prospect that country-specific annexes will grow, conceivably beyond workable limits. Insofar as there is longstanding concern about a 'spaghetti bowl' of free trade agreements, the negotiation of disparate side-agreements under the umbrella of the TPP may heighten

---

Hazard or Opportunity?' (2009) 41 *George Washington International Law Review* 1.

6 *Australia–United States Free Trade Agreement*, signed 18 May 2004, [2005] ATS 1 (entered into force 1 January 2005) (AUSFTA). The text of the AUSFTA is available at Department of Foreign Affairs and Trade (Cth), *Australia–United States Free Trade Agreement* <http://www.dfat.gov.au/fta/ausfta/final-text/>. See also Leon Trakman, 'Foreign Direct Investment: An Australian Perspective' (2010) 13 *International Trade and Business Law Review* 31, 79–81; Peter Drahos and David Henry, 'The Free Trade Agreement between Australia and the United States' [2004] *British Medical Journal* 1271.

doubts about a spaghetti bowl of BITs.[7] In addition, many of the TPP parties already have bilateral and multilateral FTAs with each other. For example, Australia already has two agreements with Malaysia[8] and two with New Zealand.[9] Any TPP will need a resolution on how to deal with existing FTAs and BITs that vary from it, notably in regard to dispute resolution measures. More important, therefore, than Australia's stance on ISA is the significance that its opting out of ISA can have for the TPP as a prospective investment agreement and its sequel in a complex array of country-specific annexes, exemptions and future BITs. It is in light of its potential impact on country-specific exemptions that Australia's probable exemption from ISA warrants consideration.[10]

That impact, however, ought not to be overstated. Australia is seeking an exemption from the ISA process only, not from substantive provisions in the TPP, such as from a fair and equitable treatment standard. Given this situation, Australia will need to propose an alternative dispute settlement mechanism, namely domestic courts, in order to make these substantive protections effective. The intended result will be that if Australia were to breach its obligations by denying substantive protection to a foreign investor, that investor presumably would be able to bring an action against Australia before Australian courts for violating its TPP obligations.

In light of these concerns, this chapter has two key objectives. The first is to examine Australia's 2011 Policy Statement rejecting investor–state arbitration in light of the dispute settlement provisions in the draft investment chapter of the TPP, leaked to the public in June 2012.[11] The second is to analyse the potential value of ISA as compared with other

---

[7] 'Swimming in the spaghetti bowl' is a phrase that is attributed to prominent Columbia University economist, Jagdish Bhagwati, to describe the economic effect of multiple 'free' trade agreements. See Jagdish Bhagwati, *Free Trade Today* (Princeton University Press, 2002).

[8] *Malaysia–Australia Free Trade Agreement*, signed 22 May 2012, [2012] ATNIF 9 (not yet in force); *Agreement Establishing the ASEAN–Australia–New Zealand Free Trade Area*, opened for signature 27 February 2009, [2010] ATS 1 (entered into force 1 January 2010) (*ASEAN–Australia–New Zealand FTA*).

[9] *Australia–New Zealand Closer Economic Relations – Trade Agreement*, signed 28 March 1983, [1983] ATS 2 (entered into force 1 January 1983); *ASEAN–Australia–New Zealand FTA*.

[10] On the background to the 2011 Policy Statement, see Trakman, 'Investor State Arbitration or Local Courts', above n 5.

[11] See Citizens' Trade Campaign, *Investment* <http://www.citizenstrade.org/ctc/wp-content/uploads/2012/06/tppinvestment.pdf>.

mechanisms of dispute settlement, notably resort to domestic courts of states parties, under a TPP framework.

I AUSTRALIA'S OBJECTION TO INVESTOR–STATE ARBITRATION

In a trade policy statement in April 2011 the Australian government enunciated that it 'does not support provisions that would confer greater legal rights on foreign businesses than those available to domestic businesses.'[12] In particular, it maintained that it will not:

> support provisions that would constrain the ability of Australian governments to make laws on social, environmental and economic matters in circumstances where those laws do not discriminate between domestic and foreign businesses.[13]

As a result Australia announced that it will 'discontinue' the practice of including investor–state dispute resolution procedures in trade agreements. Furthermore, '[i]f Australian businesses are concerned about sovereign risk in Australian trading partner countries, they will need to make their own assessments about whether they want to commit to investing in those countries.'[14] How significant this trade policy is in fact is the subject of a more detailed study by the author elsewhere.[15]

The result is that the Australian government has sought to be excluded from any ISA provisions under the TPP. It is also expected to provide that investor–state disputes be submitted to domestic courts for resolution, not unlike the dispute resolution provisions in the AUSFTA.[16]

Under the 2011 Policy Statement national law should govern the rights of foreign investors, particularly foreign investors filing claims against the Australian government, and the authority of domestic courts should prevail over other options, including resort to diplomatic channels. The

---

[12] See 2011 Policy Statement, above n 5.

[13] Ibid.

[14] Ibid., 1–2.

[15] See Trakman, 'Investor State Arbitration or Local Courts', above n 5; Leon Trakman, 'Choosing Domestic Courts over Investor–State Arbitration: Australia's Repudiation of the Status Quo' (2012) 35 *University of New South Wales Law Journal* 979.

[16] See Trakman, 'Foreign Direct Investment: Hazard or Opportunity?', above n 5, 48–53; Thomas Westcott, 'Foreign Investment Issues in the Australia–United States Free Trade Agreement' [2005] *Economic Roundup* 69.

jurisdictional rationale for this proposition is that investment disputes ought to be decided by the domestic courts of host states, not international tribunals.[17] The substantive rationale is that foreign investors should receive no better treatment than that accorded to local investors.[18]

The inference from these rationales is that were investor–state arbitration to privilege foreign investors it would not serve the national interest and, if it fails to service the national interest, domestic courts ought to replace it.

Thus far TPP negotiators appear to have provided Australia with an exemption from ISA provisions in the TPP and it is possible they will continue to do so, in a state-by-state negotiating process driven by the United States.[19] In support of this position is recognition that country-specific exemptions are part and parcel of the negotiations. In further support is the apparent dispelling of a one-size-fits-all TPP in recognition of local requirements of particular negotiating states on political, economic and social grounds.[20] On the other hand, the draft investment chapter text illustrates that the parties are not entirely in agreement over this issue. It is in no way settled, and the parties have not agreed definitively, that Australia should be exempt from investor–state dispute settlement obligations, as requested by it.

This current negotiating stance does not infer that exceptions to TPP provisions will be unrestricted, or even that current negotiation concessions will prevail. Exemptions from TPP provisions on investor–state dispute resolution will depend on the kind of cost–benefit analysis that

---

[17] On the significance of this view under the revitalised Calvo Doctrine, see Wenhua Shan, 'From "North–South Divide" to "Private–Public Debate": Revival of the Calvo Doctrine and the Changing Landscape in International Investment Law' (2007) 27 *Northwestern Journal of International Law and Business* 631; Bernardo Cremades, 'Resurgence of the Calvo Doctrine in Latin America' (2006) 7 *Business Law International* 53.

[18] For an analysis of the view that, if investment arbitration privileges foreign investors, it undermines the national interest and democracies' 'promise', see David Schneiderman, *Constitutionalizing Economic Globalization: Investment Rules and Democracy's Promise* (Cambridge University Press, 2008) chs 2, 6. See Trakman, 'Investor State Arbitration or Local Courts', above n 5.

[19] Ibid.

[20] At this time, Australia's unwillingness to agree to ISA under the TPP is not viewed as fatal to its involvement in TPP negotiations. See, e.g., Investment Treaty News, *Australia to Reject Investor–State Dispute Resolution in TPPA* (13 April 2012) International Institute for Sustainable Development <http://www.iisd.org/itn/2012/04/13/news-in-brief-7/>.

prevails at a changing negotiating table, in particular on whether the perceived benefit to the TPP membership at large outweighs the cost of exempting one or another TPP country from ISA. It is also conceivable that, following the recent election of a new federal government in Australia, it will withdraw Australia's objections to ISA. It is also possible the Australian government may use its stance on ISA as a bargaining chip in a trade-off for something it may want more, such as access to the United States' sugar market, so long as doing so would not appear as a backflip.[21]

There has been some resistance to Australia's policy shift. In response to the government's statement the Australian Chamber of Commerce and Industry, with the support of some lawyers and academics involved in international investment law, wrote to Prime Minister Gillard, urging reversion to Australia's longstanding treaty practice of including investor–state dispute settlement on a case-by-case basis.[22] Their further concern was that ISA provided protections for investors from court systems of treaty partners that lacked established rule of law traditions.[23]

The prospect of Australia modifying its position on ISA will likely also be influenced by whether it loses its ISA dispute with Philip Morris, or finds the cost exorbitant, arousing public sentiment against ISA.[24]

---

[21] This is speculative. Australia may adopt a variety of recourses, unrelated to access to United States' sugar markets, in possibly negotiating away its exemption from ISA.

[22] Letter from the Australian Chamber of Commerce and Industry to Prime Minister Julia Gillard, 13 July 2012 <http://acci.asn.au/Research-and-Publications/Media-Centre/Media-Releases-and-Transcripts/Global-Engagement/Australian-Foreign-Investment-Requires-Right-to-Su.aspx>.

[23] See Luke Nottage, 'Assessing Treaty Based Investor–State Dispute Settlement' on *Japanese Law in Asia-Pacific Socio-Economic Context* (28 July 2012) <http://blogs.usyd.edu.au/japaneselaw/2012/07/assessing_treatybased_investor.html>.

[24] See *Tobacco Plain Packaging Act 2011* (Cth). See Parliament of Australia, *Tobacco Plain Packaging Bill 2011* <http://parlinfo.aph.gov.au/parlInfo/search/display/display.w3p;query=Id%3A%22legislation%2Fbillhome%2Fr4613%22>: for the series of steps leading up to the passage of the Act. See also Simon Chapman and Becky Freeman, 'The Cancer Emperor's New Clothes: Australia's Historic Legislation for Plain Tobacco Packaging' [2010] *British Medical Journal* 340; Tania Voon and Andrew Mitchell, 'Implications of WTO Law for Plain Packaging of Tobacco Products' in Tania Voon et al. (eds), *Public Health and Plain Packaging of Cigarettes: Legal Issues* (Edward Elgar Publishing, 2012) 109. On Philip Morris's initiation of an action against Australia under the Australia–Hong Kong BIT, see Philip Morris International, 'Philip Morris Asia Initiates Legal Action Against the Australian Government Over Plain

Australia's faith in domestic courts over ISA may also be reinforced, given Philip Morris's unsuccessful constitutional challenge before the High Court of Australia to halt legislation requiring the plain packaging of cigarettes, although the Ukraine has since appealed Australia's legislation to the World Trade Organization.[25]

In order to analyse the implications of the current position, this chapter proceeds on the assumption that the policy adopted by the Gillard government will remain in place during the TPP negotiations, and that Australia will seek not to endorse ISA.

II CHALLENGES TO INVESTOR–STATE ARBITRATION

The TPP negotiators' preference for ISA over domestic courts is based neither wholly on precepts of objective rationality, nor upon pervasive notions of equality among states or their investors. It is about negotiating states calculating that their foreign investors are more likely to prevail before an investment arbitration tribunal than a foreign court. Such a 'win' is not grounded in objective economic rationality or dispassionate altruism. More often than not, states favour institutions for dispute resolution based on the capacity of those institutions to deliver results that treat their subjects abroad according to preferred 'home' rather than 'host' state standards.[26] It would be unrealistic to expect 'sovereign'

Packaging' (News Release, 27 June 2011) <http://www.pmi.com/eng/media_center/press_releases/pages/PM_Asia_plain_packaging.aspx>. On the Ukraine's appeal to the WTO see *Australia – Certain Measures Concerning Trademarks and Other Plain Packaging Requirements Applicable to Tobacco Products and Packaging*, WTO Doc WT/DS434/11 (17 August 2012) (Request for the Establishment of a Panel by Ukraine).

[25] On Philip Morris's unsuccessful constitutional challenge before the High Court of Australia, see *Case S389/2411*, High Court of Australia <http://www.hcourt.gov.au/cases/case-s389/2011>; *JT International SA v Commonwealth of Australia* (2012) 291 ALR 669. On Philip Morris's unsuccessful claim against the Prime Minister of Australia, see *Philip Morris Limited v Prime Minister* (2011) 12 ALD 619.

[26] See, e.g., Charles N. Brower and Lee A. Steven, 'NAFTA Chapter 11: Who then Should Judge? Developing the International Rule of Law under NAFTA Chapter 11' (2001) 2 *Chicago Journal of International Law* 193, 193–95; David A. Gantz, 'An Appellate Mechanism for Review of Arbitral Decisions in Investor–State Disputes: Prospects and Challenges' (2006) 39 *Vanderbilt Journal of Transnational Law* 39.

states to insist otherwise. Nor are TPP negotiating states blind to the pitfalls associated with ISA, even among ardent supporters. Recent model BITs, such as the United States' model bilateral investment treaty (BIT) adopted in 2012 and the Canadian model BIT, have restricted the scope of earlier model BITs, such as the United States' model BIT of 2004.[27] In doing so, they have implicitly limited the interpretative leeway of ISA tribunals by expanding on the scope of regulatory expropriation, eroding the link between the fair and equitable treatment of foreign investors and the minimum standard of justice, and modifying the national treatment standard accorded to foreign investors.[28] Recent model BITs include expanded subjective national security provisions and exempt measures taken by governments designed to protect domestic health, public morality, social welfare and sustainable development.[29] These recent developments are also reflected in recent agreements, such as the *United States–Peru Free Trade Agreement*[30] and the *Singapore–India Economic Cooperation Agreement*.[31]

Thus, notwithstanding the seemingly wide support for ISA among TPP negotiating states, the Australian government is not alone in its aversion to various aspects of investor–state arbitration. There is strong ideological

---

[27] See United States Department of State, *2004 Model BIT* <http://www.state.gov/documents/organization/117601.pdf> (*2004 US Model BIT*); see also Andrew Newcombe, *Canada's New Model Foreign Investment Protection Agreement* (August 2004) Investment Treaty Arbitration <http://ita.law.uvic.ca/documents/CanadianFIPA.pdf>.

[28] The 2012 United States Model Bilateral Investment Treaty is available at United States Department of State, *2012 U.S. Model Bilateral Investment Treaty* (20 April 2012) <http://www.state.gov/documents/organization/188371.pdf>. See also Kenneth J. Vandevelde, 'Model Bilateral Investment Treaties: The Way Forward' (2011) 18 *Southwestern Journal of International Law* 307. Cf *2004 US Model BIT*, above n 27.

[29] See Andrew Newcombe, 'General Exceptions in International Investment Agreements' (Draft Discussion Paper, BIICL Eighth Annual WTO Conference, 13–14 May 2008) 4, <http://www.biicl.org/files/3866_andrew_newcombe.pdf>.

[30] See *Peru Trade Promotion Agreement*, Peru–United States, signed 12 April 2006 (entered into force 1 February 2009) art 10.21; *US–Colombia Trade Agreement*, signed 22 November 2006 (entered into force 15 May 2012) art 10.21; *Free Trade Agreement Between the United States of America and the Republic of Korea*, signed 30 June 2007 (entered into force 15 March 2012) art 11.21.

[31] See *Comprehensive Economic Cooperation Agreement between the Republic of India and the Republic of Singapore*, signed 29 June 2005 (entered into force 1 August 2005).

and functional opposition to ISA, beyond the policy of a single state. In an open letter to the TPP negotiators, a group of influential lawyers wrote:

> As lawyers from the academy, bench and bar, legislature, public service, business and other legal communities in Asia and the Pacific Rim, we are writing to raise concerns about the Investment and Investor–State dispute arbitration provisions being considered in the on-going negotiations for a Trans-Pacific Partnership ... agreement.[32]

They raised a number of objections. Their first objection was to the broad definition of 'investment' because it did not require a foreign investor to make any contribution to the host state economy. Their second objection was to the breadth of the substantive obligations in the TPP including on grounds that they often grant foreign investors greater rights than those accorded to domestic investors under domestic law. Their third objection was to the grant of injunctive relief brought by foreign investors against host states on grounds that this would create 'severe conflicts of law'.[33] Their fourth objection was to the broad interpretation of a government 'measure' as including jury decisions in private contract litigation. Their fifth objection was to the use of most favoured nation (MFN) provisions to avoid 'the deliberate decision of governments to require investors to pursue remedies in the domestic courts of the host nation, at least initially'.[34] Their sixth objection was to the rotating roles of lawyers as arbitrators and advocates 'in a manner that would be unethical for judges'.[35] The final objection was to the exclusion of 'non-investor litigants and other affected parties' from participating in ISA proceedings, on the grounds that this was contrary to basic principles of 'transparency, consistency and due process'.[36]

Their emphatic conclusion was to call upon 'all governments engaged in the TPP negotiations to follow Australia's example by rejecting the Investor–State dispute mechanism and reasserting the integrity of our domestic legal processes.'[37]

---

[32] See *An Open Letter from Lawyers to the Negotiators of the Trans-Pacific Partnership Urging the Rejection of Investor–State Dispute Settlement* (8 May 2012) TPP Legal <http://tpplegal.wordpress.com/open-letter/>.

[33] Ibid.

[34] Ibid.

[35] Ibid.

[36] Ibid.

[37] Ibid.

In light of such views, Australia's 2011 Policy Statement against agreeing to ISA in its FTAs and BITs is not entirely unsubstantiated, given its own pre-existing treaty practices, not least under the AUSFTA in which ISA is excluded, and regional trade agreements in which ISA is restricted in its application.[38] As a result, the change in Australia's policy was not a bolt from the blue.

However, that is not to say that Australia's position is not anomalous. At the moment it appears that in the TPP negotiations over ISA Australia is the only negotiating party that is resisting ISA.[39] This raises important questions about the consequences of seeking an exemption: what are the costs and benefits of such an exemption? What direct and ancillary consequences are likely to flow from it, including in relation to other states? How might these consequences impact upon the TPP as a whole?

III THE COSTS AND BENEFITS OF INVESTOR–STATE ARBITRATION

Does the benefit of exempting Australia from investor–state arbitration outweigh the benefit of including it in the TPP? Included in this cost–benefit analysis is the political risk of other states opting out of ISA as well. This concern is supported historically by evidence of countries withdrawing from ISA, such as arbitrations administered by the International Centre for Settlement of Investment Disputes (ICSID), in reaction to an adverse ISA determination with nationwide political and economic consequences.[40] There is also evidence of states, particularly in

---

[38] See generally Drusilla K. Brown et al., 'Computational Analysis of the US FTAs with Central America, Australia and Morocco'(2005) 28 *World Economy* 1441: discussing the AUSFTA; Philippa Dee, 'The Australia–US Free Trade Agreement: An Assessment' (Pacific Economic Papers No 345, Australia–Japan Research Centre, Australian National University, 2005).

[39] See 2011 Policy Statement, above n 5, 1–2. On Australia's current and impending trade and investment agreements with Indonesia, Malaysia and Thailand, among other countries, see *About Free Trade Agreements*, Department of Foreign Affairs and Trade <http://www.dfat.gov.au/fta/index.html>.

[40] Venezuela, Bolivia and Ecuador are countries on point. See Bretton Woods Project, *ICSID in Crisis* (10 July 2009) <http://www.brettonwoodsproject.org/art-564878>; Leon Trakman, 'The ICSID in Perspective' in Leon Trakman and Nicola Ranieri (eds), *Regionalism in International Investment Law* (Oxford University Press, forthcoming 2013) ch 10: discussing the consequences of these comments for international investment law, ICSID, and the World Bank.

Latin America, favouring domestic courts over international tribunals resolving claims against states, including a return to the Calvo Doctrine enunciated by Argentina many decades ago.[41]

A further risk is that a two-tier system of ISA awards and domestic court decisions will lead to aberrant differences in ensuing TPP 'laws'. Such differences will highlight institutional divergences between domestic court decisions and ISA awards. They will accentuate investor forum shopping in pursuit of favourable investment decisions. They will undermine certainty, including the reasonable capacity to determine the nature and application of investment laws.[42]

A defence of a two-tier ISA–domestic court system is that it neither undermines nor dislocates the TPP, or the jurisprudence that evolves from it. First, ISA is an ad hoc dispute resolution process.[43] Second, the decisions of investment tribunals bind the direct parties only, and may well diverge from one ISA tribunal to the next.[44] This reasoning is, however, subject to challenge. The decisions of domestic courts as a matter of form are part of domestic investment law, whereas ISA decisions, formally at least, are part of international investment law. The inferred result is that, unlike ISA awards, decisions by national courts are not part of international investment jurisprudence. In addition, were domestic courts and investment tribunals both to decide disputes arising from the TPP, it would lead to institutionalised differences among different legal systems in the laws and processes that are applied to the TPP, beyond ad hoc differences of interpretation among ISA tribunals deciding particular cases.[45]

A substantive response is that domestic law itself is a material source of international investment law such as under Article 38 of the *Statute of the International Court of Justice*, even if it derives from the decisions of domestic judges. In effect, ISA tribunals can take into account the

---

[41] See generally Shan, above n 17; Cremades, above n 17.

[42] See Trakman, 'Investor State Arbitration or Local Courts', above n 5.

[43] See, e.g., Zachary Douglas, *The International Law of Investment Claims* (Cambridge University Press, 2009).

[44] While ISA awards are ad hoc and do not give rise to binding legal precedents, they are nevertheless part of the *opinio juris* of international investment law with sometimes significant persuasive authority: see Leon Trakman, 'The ICSID under Siege' (2012) 45 *Cornell International Law Journal* (forthcoming).

[45] See Leon Trakman, 'Australia and the Future of Investor State Arbitration' in Michael Legg (ed.), *The Future of Dispute Resolution* (LexisNexis Butterworths, 2012) 228.

decisions of domestic courts in making awards. Domestic courts, conceivably although not necessarily, can take account of ISA awards as well.

This substantive response is not altogether satisfying. At issue is not only that the substantive law of investment diverges among domestic legal systems and their courts. At issue is the fact that domestic courts, in common law systems at least, may be bound by precedent to apply domestic law governing investment that diverges from ISA jurisprudence, and from the investment law of other domestic legal systems. These differences may compound the perception that regional and bilateral investment treaties have produced not only a 'spaghetti bowl' of disparate treaty provisions, but also an incongruent body of investment laws and decisions.[46] The concern is that if the TPP is intended to level the playing field of investment laws among member states, that levelling would be somewhat undermined by inconsistencies in otherwise comparable issues between domestic judicial systems applying domestic investment laws and ISA awards predicated on a comparatively uniform body of investment treaty and customary law.[47]

Added to these differences is the observation that national legislation and executive orders may further differentiate national from international investment jurisprudence. If domestic states have sound economic, social and political reasons to ensure that their domestic courts implement those executive or legislative orders, the prospect of distinctive domestic laws governing investor–state disputes will grow ever more likely, and ever more formidable.[48]

---

[46] On the varied and inconsistent interpretations of investment treaties, see Jürgen Kurtz, 'Adjudging the Exceptional at International Investment Law: Security, Public Order, and Financial Crisis' (2010) 59 *International and Comparative Law Quarterly* 325, 325: Kurtz identifies three different methodologies of interpretation. But see William W. Burke-White and Andreas von Staden, 'Investment Protection in Extraordinary Times: The Interpretation and Application of Non-Precluded Measures Provisions in Bilateral Investment Treaties' (2008) 48 *Virginia Journal of International Law* 307.

[47] See Campbell McLachlan, 'Investment Treaties and General International Law' (2008) 57 *International and Comparative Law Quarterly* 361, 361. See generally Margrete Stevens, 'The ICSID Convention and the Origins of Investment Treaty Arbitration' in Albert Jan van den Berg (ed.), *50 Years of the New York Convention* (Kluwer Law International, 2009) 69: describing international investment law as a coherent system since the inception of the ICSID Convention.

[48] The suggestion is not that domestic states should forego their policy-making powers, including in relation to foreign direct investment. The suggestion

A converse objection is that, in an effort to avoid a fragmented body of international investment law, an investment *ius cogens* will emerge that accentuates the advantages enjoyed by wealthy investors from developed countries over developing countries and their investors. Given the institutional roots of ISA in textual methods of interpreting BITs,[49] there is a real risk of some ISA tribunals discounting the corrective justice claims made by developing countries. Their assumption will be that, unless the TPP expressly permits a developing state to restrict market access to foreign investors, an ISA tribunal ought not to impute a 'contextualised' meaning based on historical disadvantage into that text.[50] One response is that developing countries will either decline to conclude BITs or FTAs with developed countries such as under the TPP, or more probably, they will conclude such treaties in the somewhat adventitious hope of avoiding investor–state disputes. Serious problems inevitably arise when such hopes are disappointed.

These objections relate less to irredeemable flaws in ISA than to limitations in the treaty-making powers of developing countries under the TPP or any other bilateral or multilateral investment treaty. Even if treaty literalism sometimes impedes ISA proceedings, that does not in itself provide unqualified support for the contemplated alternative, namely, resort to domestic courts. Indeed, a preference for domestic litigation to resolve ISA disputes may protract more than it remedies deficiencies in ISA. The perception among some developing states is that the courts of wealthy developed states will rely on common or civil law traditions that, historically, were insulated from the plight of developing countries, and remain so today. The perceived harm is that the domestic courts in developed states that apply 'their' laws will discriminate against investors

---

is only that if domestic states do so disparately and inconsistently there would be no place left for international investment law. The nature and operation of foreign direct investment would depend on the nuanced proclamations of a myriad of domestic states. See further Leon Trakman and M. Sornarajah, 'A Polemic: The Case For and Against Investment Liberalization' in Trakman and Ranieri, above n 40, appendix.

[49] On textual methods of interpretation, see Clint Peinhardt and Todd Allee, 'Devil in the Details? The Investment Effects of Dispute Settlement Variation in BITs' in Karl Sauvant (ed.), *Yearbook on International Investment Law & Policy 2010–2011* (Oxford University Press, 2012); J. Romesh Weeramantry, *Treaty Interpretation in Investment Arbitration* (Oxford University Press, 2012).

[50] See August Reinisch, 'How Narrow Are Narrow Dispute Settlement Clauses in Investment Treaties?' (2011) 2 *Journal of International Dispute Settlement* 115: discussing the restrictive construction of investment agreements.

from developing states by failing to address the historical disadvantages faced by those investors and the absence of a level playing field today.

The choice of domestic litigation over ISA, or the converse, is contingent on the values the proponents of each ascribe to their preference. The proposition that domestic courts are subject to tried and tested domestic rules of evidence and procedure is offset by the fact that ISA arbitration, such as under ICSID, is guided by rules of procedure that seek to ensure that arbitration procedures are clear in nature and that an ICSID arbitrator's failure to apply them fairly can lead to annulment for non-compliance.[51] The rationale that domestic courts ought to accord no more than national treatment to foreign investors is countered by the argument that investment arbitrators are equally capable of subscribing to comparable standards of national treatment.[52] The supposed insularity of ISA from domestic law and procedure is also disputable on grounds that ISA arbitrators cannot summarily disregard domestic law if an FTA such as the TPP treats that domestic law as the applicable law.

Nor are domestic judicial systems invariably reliable in resolving investor–state disputes. It is realistic to expect that, in electing among domestic legal and judicial systems countries are likely to identify with legal and judicial systems of other countries whose substantive laws and procedures they perceive as being significantly comparable to their own and that are likely to lead to like results in like cases.[53] Countries are also

---

[51] See Trakman, 'The ICSID under Siege', above n 44.

[52] This proposition is complicated, particularly by the fact that different national legal systems have incorporated investment law differently. See M. Sornarajah, 'The Case Against International Investment Law' in Trakman and Ranieri, above n 40, ch 16.

[53] These observations are exemplified in Chapter 11 jurisprudence under the *North American Free Trade Agreement*, signed 17 December 1992, 32 ILM 289 (entered into force 1 January 1994) (NAFTA). See, e.g., *Mondev International Ltd v United States (Award)* (2004) 6 ICSID Rep 192, 57 [159] (*Mondev (Award)*); *Loewen Group, Inc & Anor v United States (Award)* (2003) 7 ICSID Rep 442 (*Loewen (Award)*); William Dodge, 'Loewen v. United States: Trials and Errors under NAFTA Chapter 11' (2002) 52 *DePaul Law Review* 563; Dana Krueger, 'The Combat Zone: Mondev International, Ltd v. United States and the Backlash against NAFTA Chapter 11' (2003) 21 *Boston University International Law Journal* 399: arguing that, but for a technical time bar, two tribunal decisions – *Mondev (Award)* and *Loewen (Award)* – might have prevailed over American judicial decisions.

readier to endorse a 'rule of law' culture with which they identify than a culture with which they do not.[54]

In addition, countries that uphold the principle of absolute immunity of sovereign states pose unique problems. The most important example is China.[55] Unless specific provision is made by agreement for waiver of immunity, Chinese courts will hold that China, as a sovereign state, is immune from suit by inbound investors. Nor will Chinese courts enforce arbitral awards made by commercial arbitration institutions against China. This issue will need to be specifically addressed in the TPP in respect of states that adhere to a conception of sovereign immunity comparable to that of China.

Ultimately, in terms of the general provisions, parties will need to make a choice. An appeal to a domestic court is desirable if the party seeks a final determination on jurisdictional and substantive grounds and considers that country's domestic court reliable. An annulment procedure on narrow jurisdictional grounds under Article 52 of the ICSID Convention[56] is preferable if the party considers those grounds suitable. Beauty lies in the eyes of the beholder.

One may well conclude that, as a practical solution, TPP negotiating countries should simply be left to decide whether or not to engage in negotiations and, if so, whether to seek country-specific exemptions under it or through bilateral treaty negotiations suppletive to the TPP. That would be consistent with state practice, such as the choice of domestic courts over ISA in resolving investor–state disputes under the AUSFTA.[57]

Opposition to ISA or, for that matter, to domestic courts deciding investor–state disputes is not exceptional. The United Nations Conference

---

[54] The AUSFTA empowers domestic courts in each signatory state to resolve investor–state disputes, rather than rely on investor–state arbitration. One of the rationales for this position was that the United States and Australia share a common 'rule of law' tradition. See Trakman, 'Foreign Direct Investment', above n 5.

[55] See *Democratic Republic of the Congo and Others v FG Hemisphere Associates LLC* [2011] HKCFA 31 (Hong Kong Court of Final Appeal). See also Simon McConnell et al., *Absolute State Immunity Prevents Enforcement of Arbitral Award in Hong Kong*, Singapore International Arbitration Centre <http://www.siac.org.sg/index.php?option=com_content&view=article&id=312:absolute-state-immunity&catid=56:articles&Itemid=171>.

[56] *Convention on the Settlement of Investment Disputes between States and Nationals of Other States*, opened for signature 18 March 1965, 575 UNTS 159 (entered into force 14 October 1966) (ICSID Convention).

[57] See AUSFTA ch 21.

on Trade and Development (UNCTAD) found resort to both ISA and domestic courts unduly costly, dilatory and as attenuating conflict.[58] Nor was UNCTAD's preference for conflict prevention and avoidance measures over both ISA and domestic courts itself exceptional in light of the sometimes intractable differences between state and foreign investor interests.[59]

ISA is not an elixir of perfection that ought to be perpetuated as of right. Like all institutions, it has its beauty spots and warts. What can be said is that a shift towards domestic courts resolving investment disputes is one alternative dispute resolution option to arbitration under the TPP. Were that choice to be based solely on the perceived quality of decision-making, one could attribute particular normative qualities to the effective and fair use of judicial or arbitral processes in discrete cases arising from the TPP. However, ascribing normative values to decision-making processes is unavoidably subjective. Specifically, an assessment of the economic rationale favouring domestic litigation over ISA reflects self-interested propositions, such as the perceived benefit of one's foreign investors making claims before a foreign court rather than an ISA tribunal. Moreover, the political reality is that, in exercising preferences, countries negotiating the TPP are more likely to trust the domestic courts of other countries with which they share common social and economic traditions than those with which they do not.[60] Countries are also readier to endorse a 'rule of law' culture with which they identify than a culture with which they do not.[61]

Given these imponderables, the result may be that the choice between some form of investor–state arbitration and litigation before domestic courts should be pragmatically determined on the basis of pre-existing experience, including prior cases. However, it is too early to arrive at a pragmatic conclusion about domestic judges deciding investment cases, except to acknowledge a shift to domestic courts deciding investment

---

[58] See United Nations Conference on Trade and Development, *Investor–State Disputes: Prevention and Alternatives to Arbitration* (United Nations Publications, 2010) xvi.

[59] Ibid.

[60] These observations are exemplified in relation to Chapter 11 of the NAFTA, see above n 53.

[61] The AUSFTA empowers domestic courts in each signatory state to resolve investor–state disputes, rather than rely on investor–state arbitration. One of the rationales for this position was that the United States and Australia share a common 'rule of law' tradition. See Trakman, 'Foreign Direct Investment: Hazard or Opportunity', above n 5.

disputes which began decades ago in Latin America with the once disavowed and now resurrected Calvo Doctrine.[62] Whatever the institution adopted to resolve investor–state disputes, not limited to litigation or arbitration, the imponderable is in determining how the rule of law should be defined, applied, and enforced in relation to such disputes.[63] There are no fixed or infallible answers to these intertwined questions.

These are delicate issues for TPP negotiators from both developed and developing countries, as addressed further below.

IV SUBMITTING A CLAIM TO ARBITRATION UNDER THE TPP

The TPP is virtually certain to provide expressly for ISA, including conceivably detailed ISA provisions, stipulations for the choice of institutions before which to bring ISA claims, and the terms and conditions governing ISA.[64] It is probable, too, that the TPP will provide for a range of dispute resolution avenues, recognising particularly the arbitration rules of ICSID[65] and the United Nations Commission on International Trade Law (UNCITRAL).[66] Draft Article 12.18(3) of the TPP provides that a:

> claimant may submit a claim … :
>
> (a) under the ICSID Convention and the ICSID Rules of Procedure for Arbitration Proceedings, provided that both the respondent and the Party of the claimant are parties to the ICSID Convention;

---

[62] See above n 17 (discussing the Calvo Doctrine).

[63] See, e.g., Brower and Steven, above n 26; Gantz, above n 26.

[64] See also Luke R. Nottage and Kate Miles, '"Back to the Future" for Investor–State Arbitrations: Revising Rules in Australia and Japan to Meet Public Interests' (2009) 26 *Journal of International Arbitration* 25.

[65] See International Centre for Settlement of Investment Disputes, *ICSID Rules of Procedure for Arbitration Proceedings (Arbitration Rules)* in ICSID Convention, Regulations and Rules, ICSID Doc ICSID/15 (2006) 99.

[66] On the distinctive attributes of the investment arbitration under the UNCITRAL arbitration rules, including that member states need not be parties to UNCITRAL proceedings, see *UNCITRAL Rules on Arbitration as Revised in 2010*, GA Res 65/22, UN GAOR, 6th Comm, 65th sess, 57th plen mtg, Agenda Item 77, UN Doc A/RES/65/22 (6 December 2010). See also Claudia M. Gross, *Current Work of UNCITRAL on Transparency in Treaty-Based Investor–State Arbitration*, Organisation for Economic Co-operation and Development <http://www.oecd.org/dataoecd/14/5/46770295.pdf>.

(b) under the ICSID Additional Facility Rules, provided that either the respondent or the Party of the claimant is a party to the ICSID Convention;
(c) under the UNCITRAL arbitration rules; or
(d) if the claimant and respondent agree, to any other arbitration institution … or under any other arbitration rules.[67]

This wide choice of arbitration institutions in the draft is likely to prevail, particularly given the consensual nature of arbitration in general and the likelihood that different disputing parties will opt for different arbitral options varying from institutional arbitration under ICSID to ad hoc arbitration under the UNCITRAL,[68] as well as resorting to various international and regional commercial arbitration centres. It is noteworthy, too, that comparatively recent amendments to arbitration rules, notably, the UNCITRAL arbitration rules, were influenced somewhat by the perceived needs of investor–state arbitration.[69]

In practice, either state or investor parties, or both, may diverge over submitting an investment dispute to international arbitration. Developing countries may resist this option on grounds that it is secretive, unduly costly and favours developed states. A related concern may be that it will imbed the commercial interests of investors at the expense of the public policy interests of host states.[70]

These concerns have some foundation. A functional challenge to institutional ISA, such as under ICSID, is the cost arising from the often

---

[67] See Investment Chapter, above n 11, art 12.8(3).

[68] Of note, the UNCITRAL Model Law is widely adopted globally, including in Australia. See, e.g., *International Arbitration Act 1974* (Cth) s 16. For the text of the UNCITRAL Model Law and, in particular, art 34 see *Revised Articles of the Model Law on International Commercial Arbitration of the United Nations Commission on International Trade Law, and the Recommendation Regarding the Interpretation of Article II, Paragraph 2, and Article VII, Paragraph 1, of the Convention and Enforcement of Foreign Arbitral Awards, Done at New York, 10 June 1958*, GA Res 61/33, UN GAOR, 6th Comm, 64th plen mtg, UN Doc A/RES/61/33 (18 December 2006).

[69] Some of the 2010 amendments to the UNCITRAL arbitration rules were inspired by the rising use of the UNCITRAL arbitration rules in investor–state arbitrations. See, for example, UNCITRAL, *2010 – UNCITRAL Arbitration Rules (as revised in 2010)* <http://www.uncitral.org/uncitral/en/uncitral_texts/arbitration/2010Arbitration_rules.html>.

[70] See Leon Trakman, 'Legal Traditions and International Commercial Arbitration' (2006) 17 *American Review of International Arbitration* 1, 119–20, 26–28.

complex nature of proceedings.[71] ISA proceedings are also perceived to be dilatory, difficult to manage, disruptive, unpredictable, and not subject to appeal.[72] Coupled with these challenges is the observation that low-income TPP parties may lack the resources to bear the legal fees and related costs of defending claims from well-resourced transnational investors.[73] Moreover, these countries also lack the econometric data to verify the adverse impact of foreign investment upon their local economies, such as upon the environment.[74]

Nor are cost hurdles limited to developing states negotiating the TPP and their investors. Studies on conflict resolution in international investor–state arbitration, notably by UNCTAD, level criticism at both investor–state arbitration and litigation on economic grounds, including the high cost of managing disputes generally.[75]

Nor are the metrics used to measure the performance costs of commercial or investment arbitration reliable in predicting costs and time in prospective cases. This is due, in part, to unanticipated contingencies, such as disruption costs and delays arising from a challenge to an arbitrator, the absence or illness of a party or arbitrator, managing third party interventions, and enforcing an award.[76] These costs and delays

---

[71] See International Centre for Settlement of Investment Disputes, *Schedule of Fees* (1 January 2013) <https://icsid.worldbank.org/ICSID/FrontServlet?requestType=ICSIDDocRH&actionVal=ShowDocument&ScheduledFees=True&year=2013&language=English> (*Schedule of Fees*): indicating the cost of an ICSID arbitration.

[72] On the absence of an appeal in ICSID arbitration, see ICSID Convention art 53(1): 'The award … shall not be subject to any appeal or to any other remedy except those provided for in this Convention.' The most significant remedy under the ICSID Convention is the annulment of an award under art 53.

[73] See *Schedule of Fees*, above n 71; see also International Centre for Settlement of Investment Disputes, *Memorandum on the Fees and Expenses of ICSID Arbitrators* (6 July 2005) <http://icsid.worldbank.org/ICSID/FrontServlet?requestType=ICSIDDocRH&actionVal=Memorandum>.

[74] See, e.g., Hillary French, 'Capital Flows and the Environment' (1998) 22 *Foreign Policy in Focus* 3: 'As investors search the globe for the highest returns, they are often drawn to places endowed with bountiful natural resources but are handicapped by weak or ineffective environmental laws.' See also 'Disadvantages of Foreign Direct Investment' on *Economy Watch* (30 June 2010) <http://www.economywatch.com/foreign-direct-investment/disadvantages.html>.

[75] United Nations Conference on Trade and Development, *Investor–State Disputes*, above n 58, xxiii.

[76] See, e.g., Susan D. Franck, 'Rationalizing Costs in Investment Treaty Arbitration' (2011) 88 *Washington University Law Review* 769, 789, 815–16: providing an economic rationalisation of the costs of arbitration under investment

arise in dispute resolution in general. However, they are accentuated in ISA disputes in which the economic stakes are often high, national sensitivities are at issue, and damage to the reputation of states and sometimes investors exceeds the already high costs of the dispute.[77] Public interest interveners sometimes can help to clarify at least some social costs of adverse ISA determinations, usually to the host state. However, these groups can do so only if they are privy to cost data, only if they can afford to petition to be heard, only if their petitions are granted, and only if their evidence is credible and material.

V EXEMPTIONS FROM INVESTOR–STATE ARBITRATION

In rejecting investor–state arbitration, Australia to date has adopted a stance that no other developed state has followed and none other appears to have endorsed in TPP negotiations yet. Australia's position is bold. As noted above, it is supported by a number of leading jurists in multiple common law jurisdictions. However, Australia's close economic partner, New Zealand, may fall short of following Australia's lead, although that is not certain.[78]

At its best, the attempt by Australia to negotiate an exemption from ISA in TPP negotiations is in the national interest. It protects Australia

---

treaties; Anthony Sinclair, Louise Fisher and Sarah Macrory, 'ICSID Arbitration: How Long Does It Take?' (2009) 4(5) *Global Arbitration Review* (online) <http://www.globalarbitrationreview.com/journal/article/19164/icsid-arbitration-long-does-take>.

[77] See, e.g., Bretton Woods Project, *ICSID – International Centre for Settlement of Investment Disputes* (14 July 2009) <http://www.brettonwoodsproject.org/item.shtml?x=537853>. On ICSID's figures, including that foreign investors have won 48 per cent of ICSID/Additional Facility cases, see International Centre for Settlement of Investment Disputes, *The ICSID Caseload – Statistics (Issue 2012-2)* (2012) 13, chart 9 <https://icsid.worldbank.org/ICSID/FrontServlet?requestType=ICSIDDocRH&actionVal=ShowDocument&CaseLoadStatistics=True&language=English32>.

[78] The fact that the jurists who have publicly opposed ISA in the TPP include a significant number of New Zealand jurists might suggest that New Zealand is more likely to oppose ISA. However, there are a number of contrary indications. New Zealand does not have an FTA or BIT with the United States and would undoubtedly wish to have one, not least of all to have access to the large United States market for its agricultural goods. Were New Zealand to resist ISA it may fear losing market access in the United States as elsewhere and having to make concessions on such access in a manner it would prefer to avoid.

from the volatility and the high cost of investor–state arbitration in which multinational companies such as Philip Morris are able to lodge challenges to Australia's domestic public policies under one or another free trade or investment treaty.[79] Australia also has good reason to try to protect its public interests from aggressive foreign investors and to preserve the integrity of its local laws.[80] Central to Australia's resistance to agreeing to ISA in TPP negotiations are its concerns about public health and environmental safety, since reaffirmed with the initiation of the ISA case brought against it by Philip Morris under the Australia–Hong Kong BIT. The setback for the tobacco industry to date is in losing its constitutional challenge to Australia's 'right' to require the plain packaging of cigarettes, in the High Court of Australia, although the legislation is now being challenged in the World Trade Organization.[81]

However, there are four key impediments to a country such as Australia achieving these very objectives by rejecting investor–state arbitration in TPP negotiations. First, Australia's reliance on domestic courts to resolve conflicts with inbound investors like Philip Morris does not provide the public policy protection a government in its position is likely seeking. Foreign investors may well mount expensive claims against Australia before domestic courts,[82] in Australia as elsewhere, as they would through investor–state arbitration. Australia has no reasonable assurance of prevailing over inbound investors before a domestic Australian court. It also has no reasonable assurance that its outbound investors would succeed before the domestic court of a host partner state. Second, Australia's insistence that it not be subject to investor–state arbitration in the TPP may isolate it from other negotiating states that adopt ISA, however reluctantly a few may be to do so. Third, Australia's rejection of investor–state arbitration may well expose Australian investors abroad to

---

79 See sources cited above nn 24 and 25.

80 See John Hilvert, *Aussie Negotiator Declines TPP Assurances* (8 March 2012) IT News <http://www.itnews.com.au/News/292937,aussie-negotiator-declines-tpp-assurances.aspx>; Mike Masnick, *Significant Concerns About TPP Raised Down Under* (6 June 2012) Techdirt <http://www.techdirt.com/articles/20120605/03172719203/significant-concerns-about-tpp-raised-down-under.shtml>.

81 See above n 24. See also Christine Kerr, 'Appeal to WTO May Yet Deliver Big Tobacco Victory', *The Australian* (online), 18 August 2012 <http://www.theaustralian.com.au/national-affairs/appeal-to-wto-may-yet-deliver-big-tobacco-victory/story-fn59niix-1226452794144>. See also Australian Minister for Trade and Competitiveness, 'High Court Ruling Bolsters Australia's WTO Case for Plain Packaging' (Media Release, 20 August 2012) <http://trademinister.gov.au/releases/2012/ce_mr_120820.html>.

82 See sources cited above nn 24 and 25.

foreign courts of host states whose procedures fall short of the standards of transparency not only of Australian courts, but also of investor–state arbitration tribunals.[83] It is noteworthy that approximately 76 per cent of the cases in which investment treaty awards were rendered up to June 2006 involved states that ranked at or below 50 on Transparency International's 2008 Corruption Perception Index (CPI). That number increased to 84 per cent when cases involving the United States and Canada were excluded. Over 69 per cent of the cases involved states that ranked at or below number 70 on the CPI.[84] The World Bank's Worldwide Governance Indicator (WGI) also indicated that 68 per cent of those states were in the bottom 60 per cent of the 'rule of law' indicator.[85] The inference is that foreign investors have good reason not to trust all domestic courts equally to apply the 'rule of law' or, in some cases, at all.

The fourth and final reason as to why the rejection of ISA under the TPP fails to protect Australia's national interests is based on the existence of preferable alternatives. Australia can try to negotiate bilateral caps on treaty protection to foreign investors set at Australia's domestic substantive law standards; or it could try to negotiate for broader general exceptions or exclusions of entire measures with existing or new treaty partners. In both cases such action would provide at least some protection to Australia's outbound investors. A tentative conclusion is that the choice of domestic litigation over investor–state arbitration is neither compelling in itself nor according to benchmark indicators of trustworthiness that are imputed to a significant number of domestic courts. As a result, the virtue of domestic litigation is contingent, not only on the value preferences of those who subscribe to it, but also on the trust placed in national courts in discrete jurisdictions. If a choice is made between domestic courts applying allegedly comparable standards of transparency and ISA, a domestic appeals process is ordinarily more

---

[83] See Trakman, 'Australia and the Future of Investor State Arbitration', above n 45.

[84] See Mark Kantor, *The Transparency Agenda for UNCITRAL Investment Arbitrations: Looking in All the Wrong Places* (22 January 2011) Institute for International Law and Justice, 10 <http://www.iilj.org/research/documents/IF2010-11.Kantor.pdf>. Kantor's calculations are based on information contained in the list of states in Susan Franck, 'Empirically Evaluating Claims about Investment Treaty Arbitration' (2007) 86 *North Carolina Law Review* 1, annex 1.

[85] See Daniel Kaufmann, Aart Kraay and Massimo Mastruzzi, *Worldwide Governance Indicators*, World Bank <http://info.worldbank.org/governance/wgi/index.asp>.

robust than an ISA annulment procedure.[86] For example, annulment under Article 75 of the ICSID Convention is limited to jurisdictional grounds. An appeal of a domestic court can be on both jurisdictional and substantive grounds.[87]

However, the benefits of resorting to domestic courts are offset by benefits arising under ISA. The proposition that appropriate domestic courts apply tried and tested domestic rules of evidence and procedure to disputes is offset by the fact that ISA, such as under the ICSID Convention, is guided by rules of procedure that seek to ensure that arbitration procedures are clear in nature; and that an ICSID arbitrator's failure to apply them fairly can lead to annulment for non-compliance.[88] The rationale that domestic courts ought to accord no more than 'national treatment' to foreign investors is countered by the argument that investment treaties may require ISA tribunals to subscribe to well-established international standards of 'national treatment'.[89] The supposed insularity of ISA arbitration from domestic law and procedure is also disputable on grounds that ISA arbitrators cannot summarily disregard domestic law.[90] A foreign investor that wins an ISA dispute, but cannot enforce it before a domestic court that denies such enforcement, ultimately wins nothing of substance.[91]

If choices between ISA and domestic courts are to be made, beauty will lie in the eyes of the beholder. However, careful research into whether domestic courts operate on a level playing field, including by enforcing ISA awards, will help to provide a clearer view.[92]

---

[86] On ICSID annulment proceedings, see Lise Johnson, 'Annulment of ICSID Awards: Recent Developments' (Background Paper, IV Annual Forum for Developing Country Investment Negotiators, International Institute for Sustainable Development, 27–29 October 2010) <http://www.iisd.org/publications/pub.aspx?id=1423>.

[87] While presented as an advantage, some TPP countries are likely to resist substantive review, not only under the TPP, but due to resistance to substantive review in administrative law more generally.

[88] On the ICSID Convention, see above n 65.

[89] This proposition is complicated, particularly by the fact that investment law is incorporated differently into different national legal systems. See especially Sornarajah, 'The Case Against International Investment Law', above n 52.

[90] See, e.g., Christoph Schreuer, 'Fair and Equitable Treatment in Arbitral Practice' (2005) 6 *Journal of World Investment and Trade* 357, 357.

[91] On difficulties arising in the recognition and enforcement of transnational arbitration, see Stevens, above n 47.

[92] For such a study, see Simon Butt, 'Foreign Investment in Indonesia: The Problem of Legal Uncertainty' in Vivienne Bath and Luke Nottage (eds), *Foreign Investment and Dispute Resolution Law and Practice in Asia* (Routledge, 2011) 112.

Despite the availability of preferable alternatives, Australia's unwillingness to submit to investor–state arbitration is not necessarily a death knell for Australian outbound investors. Australian outbound investors have several choices. They can engage in foreign direct investment in states that have BITs with Australia, such as the United States, and in whose courts Australian investors are reasonably comfortable. They can invest in countries in whose courts they do not trust by forging a link with an intermediary country and relying on a BIT between the host country and intermediary country that provides for ISA. Intermediary states, in turn, can provide foreign investors residential or domiciliary status that enables investors to lodge claims against an allegedly recalcitrant state under a BIT between that intermediary and recalcitrant state.

An incidental beneficiary of such investor resort to intermediary states is the Australian government, in not having to conclude BITs with ISA provisions with states that do not subscribe to the rule of law as conceived by Australian courts. The Australian government can also decline to intervene diplomatically on behalf of outbound Australian investors on grounds that those investors have lodged their claims through intermediary states, not Australia. There is also no shortage of potential intermediary states to which outbound investors may resort. Notable among these states are the Netherlands Antilles and Mauritius, which have stable financial systems and transparent and investor-friendly tax regimes.[93]

The practice of foreign investors bringing ISA or other claims through intermediary states is not unprecedented. Brazil has effectively insulated itself from investor–state arbitration by declining to ratify any of its investor–state treaties; its investors abroad have transacted through 'good governance' intermediary states. As a result, Brazilian companies have gained access to resource-wealthy countries such as Venezuela directly or through intermediary states without exposing Brazil to investor–state claims in respect of which Brazil has assumed no treaty obligations.[94]

---

[93] On the tax and related protection accorded foreign investors in the Netherlands Antilles, see, e.g., International Business Company Formation, *Netherland Antilles – Forming a Private, Limited Liability Company* <http://www.ibcf.com/jurisdiction.php?source=&country=Netherland%20Antilles>.

[94] See, e.g., Ricardo Ortíz, *The Bilateral Investment Treaties and the Cases at ICSID* (2006) Forschungs und Dokumentationszentrum Chile-Lateinamerika, table 2 <http://fdcl-berlin.de/fileadmin/fdcl/Publikationen/FOCO-ICSID-engl-2006.pdf>, which notes that Brazil had entered into 14 BITs by 2006, but had not ratified any of them.

However, investor treaty-shopping for intermediary states is not risk-free. In particular, treaty-shopping investors risk losing ISA claims on jurisdictional grounds, that their business connection to an intermediary state is insufficiently substantial to justify the ISA claim. That risk is conceivably accentuated as more states strive for intermediary status, seeking to resource investors with ever readier means of establishing business and legal connections domestically. Coupled with these risks is the prospect of regulators, including ISA tribunals, establishing rules to regulate such treaty shopping.

What is apparent is that even if Australia remains adamant in seeking an exemption from investor–state arbitration in the TPP, it may well remain as a negotiating party. The opportunity to participate in possibly the second largest global investment treaty after the European Union is too good to bypass.[95] However, over the longer term Australia may find itself in a lonely place at the end of a long table of contrary-minded states; and Australia's outbound investors may be exposed to the domestic courts of negotiating states that do not have the 'rule of law' traditions to which Australia subscribes.

CONCLUSION

The TPP is still in its early stages of development. At this stage it is difficult to anticipate how negotiations will impact on the nature of an already stratified body of international investment law and practice. It is also difficult to identify the extent to which the TPP will serve as an umbrella agreement on investment, mushrooming into a series of BIT side agreements that may diverge both *inter se* and from the TPP itself. It may be that such mushrooming of BITs may not eventuate, but that the TPP will address issues systematically such as by imposing uniform performance requirements[96] and by regulating non-conforming measures.[97] Alternatively, the TPP may include selective country-specific reservations.

---

[95] See, e.g., *Investor–State Arbitration Not Deal Breaker for TPP Negotiations* (11 May 2012) Chapman Tripp <http://www.chapmantripp.com/publications/Pages/Investor-state-arbitration-not-deal-breaker-for-TPP-negotiations.aspx>.

[96] See Investment Chapter, above n 11, art 12.7.

[97] Ibid., art 12.9.

What is reasonable to infer at this time is that the TPP will provide for investor–state arbitration from which only Australia will seek an exemption. What appears likely too is that this exemption will be permitted, although precisely how it will be framed remains unclear. What is probable, too, is that the TPP will include country annexes based on negotiated exemptions and exclusions for individual countries on a host of matters, not limited to exemptions for ISA.

Thus, more important than the purported exemption of one country from ISA is the prospect that negotiating states will seek a range of qualifications in the application of the TPP's investment chapter to them. The more diffuse these qualifications are, the more complex and also the more diluted the TPP is likely to become. If the TPP embraces high sounding requirements for states parties, which are followed by numerous country-specific exemptions, it may lose its legitimacy as an agreement. If it spurns a host of BIT side agreements between and among TPP signatories, it may lose its cogency as an umbrella agreement. In effect, the BITs that evolve out of the TPP may become more important to their signatories than the investment chapter in the TPP itself.

Regarding dispute resolution in particular, the choice of TPP parties is not solely between ISA and litigation. Conflict preventive and avoidance measures sometimes are preferable to both.[98] 'Multi-tiered' dispute resolution agreements can allow parties to agree upon a tiered process, varying from negotiating in good faith, to mediation, and failing both, to arbitration or litigation, or conceivably, to both.[99] It is noteworthy that UNCTAD considered conflict prevention and avoidance sufficiently important to devote a detailed study to it.[100]

Nor, too, is it persuasive to insist that ISA is inherently superior to, say, litigation because arbitrators are investment specialists, while domestic judges operate as courts of general jurisdiction. Neither resort to ISA under the TPP nor to litigation under any exemption or side agreements ensures equitable and transparent procedures or sound substantive determinations. Evidence of an unjust expropriation is both legally and

---

[98] United Nations Conference on Trade and Development, *Investor–State Disputes*, above n 58. For international investment claims and decisions see Oxford University Press, *Investment Claims* <http://www.investmentclaims.com>.

[99] See Klaus Peter Berger, *Private Dispute Resolution in International Business: Negotiation, Mediation, Arbitration* (Kluwer Law International, 2006) vol 2, 74–78.

[100] United Nations Conference on Trade and Development, *Investor–State Disputes*, above n 58.

factually informed: it calls for good judgement, along with investment expertise. It raises difficult questions of law, not least of all about the nature of an 'investor' and an 'investment' in respect of which states diverge, not only *inter se*, but in their own perspectives of it as well.[101]

What can be said in defence of ISA under the TPP is that, while it does not lead to judicial precedent as common lawyers conceive of it, reliance on ISA is more stabilising than reliance on a plethora of different local laws and procedures that domestic courts apply to foreign investment.[102] However fragmented different standards of treatment accorded to foreign investors may be under customary international law, and however difficult it may be to identify cohesive principles out of ad hoc and sometimes unpublished arbitration awards, an international investment jurisprudence does exist.[103]

---

[101] On the diverse nature of an 'investment', see Andrea K. Bjorklund, 'The Emerging Civilization of Investment Arbitration' (2009) 113 *Penn State Law Review* 1269; Joseph M. Boddicker, 'Whose Dictionary Controls?: Recent Challenges to the Term "Investment" in ICSID Arbitration' (2010) 25 *American University International Law Review* 1031; Julien Burda, 'A New Step Towards a Single and Common Definition of an Investment? – Comments on the Romak versus Uzbekistan Decision' (2010) 11(6) *Journal of World Investment and Trade* 1085; Julian Davis Mortenson, 'The Meaning of "Investment": ICSID's Travaux and the Domain of International Investment Law' (2010) 51(1) *Harvard International Law Journal* 257; Noah Rubins, 'The Notion of "Investment" in International Investment Arbitration' in Norbert Horn and Stefan Kröll (eds), *Arbitrating Foreign Investment Disputes* (Kluwer Law International, 2004) 283.

[102] On the development of international investment norms, see Foreign Investment Review Board, *OECD Investment Committee* <http://www.firb.gov.au/content/international_investment/current_issues.asp?NavID=60>.

[103] On such authorities, see for example, Rudolf Dolzer and Christoph Schreuer, *Principles of International Investment Law* (Oxford University Press, 2008). But see Sornarajah, 'The Case Against International Investment Law', above n 52.

10. The Trans-Pacific Partnership Agreement, the environment and climate change

Joshua P. Meltzer

INTRODUCTION

The trade and environment relationship is complex and presents both challenges and opportunities. For instance, trade can lead to increased economic efficiency, productivity and growth. But economic growth can result in increased consumption of non-renewable resources and greater environmental harms, such as increasing air pollution and worsening water quality. On the other hand, increased economic growth can generate the resources to address environmental damage and provide a pathway for countries to transition out of polluting industries into more service-oriented ones that are less polluting and damaging to the environment. Trade agreements can also strengthen the capacity for governments to respond to environmental concerns. For instance, reducing trade barriers on environmental goods can reduce the costs of green technologies, thereby supporting efforts to address global challenges such as climate change.

International trade can also be a pathway for the transmission of weaker environmental policies from one country to another. For instance, a country's lax environmental standards that fail to internalise the social costs of environmental harms, such as pollution from the production of goods, can provide an unfair competitive advantage to its exports, raising concerns that this will create economic and political pressures in the importing country to also lower their environmental standards. Additionally, a number of environmental harms, such as illegal logging and overfishing, can be magnified by international trade, which expands the market for these goods. Yet trade agreements can be used to reinforce existing rules prohibiting trade in these products, thereby strengthening conservation efforts. Trade agreements also raise concerns that a government's capacity to respond to environmental harms in ways that restrict trade will become constrained by trade rules that are enforced by legally binding dispute settlement procedures with penalties such as trade sanctions. Finding an appropriate balance between trade rules that promote liberalised trade and maintaining policy space for governments to respond to environmental concerns is another challenge.

As a twenty-first-century trade agreement, the Trans-Pacific Partnership Agreement (TPP) presents an important opportunity to address a range of environmental issues, from illegal logging to climate change and to craft rules that strike an appropriate balance between supporting open trade and ensuring governments can respond to pressing environmental issues. Moreover, the ambition of the TPP parties is for the TPP to become the building block for a Free Trade Area of the Asia-Pacific (FTAAP).[1] Accordingly, the rules that are agreed in the TPP could set the rules for trade and investment in the broader Asia-Pacific region for years to come.

The TPP is currently being negotiated by 12 countries, namely: Australia, Brunei, Canada, Chile, Japan, Malaysia, Mexico, New Zealand, Peru, Singapore, the United States (US), and Vietnam (TPP12). In March 2013 Japan announced its interest in joining the TPP and, following consultations between the US Administration and Congress, Japan joined the TPP negotiations in July. The total gross domestic product (GDP) of the current TPP parties is approximately $27.5 trillion, comprises 40 percent of global GDP and one third of world trade. Of this amount, the United States accounts for approximately $15.5 trillion, or almost 60 per cent of TPP GDP.[2] The United States' economic size and strategic importance for other TPP parties means that its approach to the TPP will be the starting point for the negotiations and will significantly influence the outcome.

The first part of this chapter provides an overview of the US approach to the environment in its most recent free trade agreements (FTAs) in order to understand the most likely US approach to environmental issues

---

1 2010 Asia-Pacific Economic Cooperation Leaders Declaration, *Yokohama Declaration – The Yokohama Vision – Bogor and Beyond* (13–14 November 2010) The 18th APEC Economic Leaders' Meeting, <http://www.apec.org/Meeting-Papers/Leaders-Declarations/2010/2010_aelm.aspx>; see also Carlos Kuriyama, 'The Mutual Usefulness between APEC and TPP' (APEC#211-SE-01.5, APEC Policy Support Unit, October 2011).

2 *Direction of Trade Statistics* and *World Economic Outlook*, International Monetary Fund (August 2013) <http://www.imf.org/external/data.htm>.

in the TPP. The second part of this chapter considers a range of environmental issues that have yet to be addressed comprehensively in FTAs but which could be addressed in the TPP, including climate change.

I HOW THE UNITED STATES ADDRESSES ENVIRONMENTAL ISSUES IN ITS FREE TRADE AGREEMENTS

A The Power to Negotiate Trade Agreements

Under the *US Constitution*, Article 1 Section 8 gives Congress the 'power to regulate commerce with foreign nations …', and Article II gives the President exclusive authority to negotiate treaties. Pursuant to legislation – referred to as Trade Promotion Authority (TPA) – Congress delegates trade negotiating authority to the President (which is exercised by the United States Trade Representative (USTR)) and maintains its authority over trade policy by defining the negotiating objectives. Congress also agrees to vote on trade agreements in an expedited manner and to refrain from seeking amendments to treaties negotiated by the USTR. In return, the President is required to consult with Congress during the negotiations and notify Congress 90 days prior to signing an agreement.[3] TPA was most recently granted in 2002 by the *Trade Act*, which expired in 2007.[4] Notwithstanding this, the USTR continues to follow the terms of this Act in the TPP negotiations.[5] Additionally, the negotiating objectives in the 2002 *Trade Act* were updated by the so-called 2007 Bipartisan Trade Deal, which on environmental issues envisions US FTAs including a list of multilateral environmental treaties that the FTA parties must enforce and which are subject to the FTA's dispute settlement mechanism. Moreover, some senators have urged the USTR to go beyond the Bipartisan Trade Deal and address other issues, such as the sustainability of trade in natural resources and wildlife.[6]

---

[3] J.F. Hornbeck and William Cooper, 'Trade Promotion Authority and the Role of Congress in Trade Policy' (CRS Report for Congress No RL33743, Congressional Research Service, 9 August 2012) <http://www.fas.org/sgp/crs/misc/RL33743.pdf>.

[4] HR 3009 Trade Act of 2002 (the '*Trade Act*').

[5] Hornbeck and Cooper, above n 3.

[6] Letter from Senators R. Wyden, J.F. Kerry, J.A. Merkley, K.E. Millibrand, B. Cardin, O. Snowe, B. Boxer, S. Brown, S. Whitehouse and T. Udall to United States Trade Representative Ron Kirk, 17 October 2012.

As discussed below, the TPP also presents an opportunity to address a range of climate change issues. Climate change was not part of the 2002 *Trade Act* or the Bipartisan Trade Deal and is a source of significant political division in Congress. Much of the resistance in Congress to addressing climate change, and in particular pricing carbon, has arisen from concern about the economic impacts on the US economy. In contrast, the TPP could include a number of provisions addressing climate change that would benefit the US economy, such as requiring reductions in trade barriers on environmental goods and services.

B Environment Chapters in US Free Trade Agreements: Implications for the TPP

The US has FTAs with six of the TPP countries, and each one includes an environment chapter. However, as these FTAs were finalised prior to the 2007 Bipartisan Trade Deal, their environmental provisions are less instructive for the TPP process. For instance, in the Australia–US FTA, the parties merely agreed to enforce their environmental laws and various transparency provisions, none of which are subject to the FTA's dispute settlement mechanism.[7]

The Korea–US FTA (KORUS), signed in 2010 and passed by the US Congress in 2011, entered into effect on 15 March 2012 and is the most recent FTA the US has completed. As an FTA with a country in the Asia-Pacific and potential future TPP member,[8] KORUS provides the most relevant insight into how the US has implemented the terms of the 2002 *Trade Act* and the Bipartisan Trade Deal and what types of environmental rules the US will likely seek in the TPP. As in previous US FTAs, KORUS includes a dedicated environment chapter. Consistent with the Bipartisan Trade Deal, a key element of this chapter is the commitment by the parties to adopt, maintain and implement laws and regulations to fulfil their obligations under seven Multilateral Environmental Agreements (MEAs) listed in an annex to the chapter.[9] Not all TPP parties are party to these MEAs, and the US will likely expect their eventual participation as part of a final agreement.

---

[7] *Australia–United States Free Trade Agreement*, signed August 2004 (entered into force 1 January 2005), ch 19.

[8] Jeffrey Schott, Barbara Kotschwar and Julia Muir, *Understanding the Trans-Pacific Partnership* (Peterson Institute for International Economics, 2013) 45.

[9] *United States–Korea Trade Agreement*, signed 30 June 2007 (entered into force 15 March 2012) (KORUS) ch 20, annex 20-A.

One of the main benefits of including these MEAs in the TPP will be access to the agreement's dispute settlement procedures to enforce compliance with these MEAs. But giving a panel under the TPP dispute settlement mechanism the authority to decide whether a party has failed to implement an MEA raises concerns about whether such panelists have the expertise to interpret MEAs and how this affects the development of international environmental law – particularly when MEAs lack similar types of judicial processes that can interpret MEAs.

The parties to KORUS were sensitive to this issue and agreed that a panel established to adjudicate a breach of an MEA commitment should consult with any entity with responsibility for addressing non-compliance with the MEA – such as the Permanent Court of Arbitration under the *Convention on International Trade in Endangered Species of Wild Fauna and Flora* (CITES)[10] – and to defer to any interpretative guidance this entity provides on the issue.[11] KORUS also addresses how the parties should respond to any inconsistency between a commitment in an MEA and in KORUS by balancing their obligations under both agreements. KORUS does not preclude a party from taking a measure to comply with an MEA provided that 'the primary purpose of the measure is not to impose a disguised restriction on trade'.[12] The parties to KORUS have also committed to enhance the mutual supportiveness of MEAs and trade agreements to which they are both parties.[13] This commitment complements work in the World Trade Organization (WTO) Doha Round addressing the relationship between the WTO and MEAs.[14] Including similar provisions in the TPP would strike a balance between using the more effective dispute settlement procedures that will be part of the TPP to ensure compliance with these MEAs while providing opportunity for international environmental law and the decisions of other competent institutions to be considered by a panel under the TPP.

KORUS also recognises that enforcing commitments under MEAs takes resources, and the question of how to allocate scarce resources amongst often competing environmental priorities remains a prerogative

---

[10] *The Convention on International Trade in Endangered Species of Wild Fauna and Flora*, signed 3 March 1973 (entered into force 1 July 1975) (CITES) art XVIII.

[11] KORUS arts 20.9.3(a)–(b), 20.9.6(a)–(c).

[12] Ibid., art 20.10.3.

[13] Ibid., art 20.10.1.

[14] *Ministerial Declaration*, WTO Doc WT/MIN(01)/DEC/1 (20 November 2001) (adopted 14 November 2001) [31(i)].

of the parties.[15] Including such flexibilities in the TPP will be particularly important for developing countries, which face greater resource constraints and will want to retain the ability to make decisions over which environmental challenges to resource. The parties to KORUS also agreed that 'it is inappropriate to encourage trade or investment by weakening or reducing the protections afforded in its environmental laws'.[16] In order to fulfil this goal, KORUS requires the parties to refrain from derogating from their laws in ways that weaken environmental protection and affect trade and investment between the parties.[17] This outcome is consistent with the Bipartisan Trade Deal and will be part of US demands for the TPP.

This non-derogation commitment responds to concerns that trade agreements lead to a race to the bottom. The concern is that liberalised trade with countries with lower environmental standards provides a competitive edge to imports from these countries, leading domestic businesses to seek lower environmental standards in order to compete. There is limited evidence that FTAs lead to a regulatory race to the bottom.[18] One reason is that environmental regulations are often a small cost compared with other larger determinants affecting competitiveness, such as labour, material and capital costs and exchange rates.[19] Additionally, to the extent that businesses do seek lower environmental standards, they have to contend with consumer and environmental groups mobilising in support of stronger environmental standards, and it is not necessarily the case that businesses always win.

From a developing country perspective, lower levels of environmental protection might be viewed as a competitive advantage that provides an opportunity to attract increased levels of foreign direct investment. As an empirical matter, there is little support for the view that weaker environmental laws affect patterns of investment.[20] Moreover, tolerating environmental degradation of natural capital such as water and air quality and

---

[15] KORUS art 20.3.1(b).

[16] Ibid., art 20.3.2.

[17] Ibid., art 20.3.2.

[18] Daniel W. Drezner, 'Globalization and Policy Convergence' (2001) 3(1) *International Studies Review* 53, 75.

[19] Gene Grossman and Alan Krueger, 'Environmental Impact of a North American Free Trade Agreement' (Working Paper No 3914, National Bureau of Economic Research, 1991).

[20] R.J.R. Elliot and K. Shimamoto, 'Are ASEAN Countries Havens for Japanese Pollution-Intensive Industries?' (2008) 31 *World Economy* 236; G.S. Eskeland and A.E. Harrison, 'Moving to Greener Pastures? Multinationals and the Pollution Haven Hypothesis' (2003) 70 *Journal of Development Economics* 1.

the related human health effects may not accurately account for the long run costs, such as from a less healthy population.[21] Additionally, there is evidence that tighter environmental regulations can act as incentives for firms to adopt the latest technologies, improve their efficiency and productivity and act as a spur towards greater environmental innovation.[22] Moreover, increased trade liberalisation – a key driver of technology diffusion and adoption – could magnify the impact of stricter environmental standards on the uptake by domestic firms of environmental technologies.

The KORUS environment chapter also includes transparency and due process provisions that have important implications for environmental regulation. For instance, each party has agreed that judicial or administrative proceedings will be available to sanction and provide remedies for violations of its environmental laws and these proceedings will be impartial and independent.[23] Moreover, persons with a legal interest in a matter relating to human health or the environment will be able to sue for damages and have access to a range of remedies including injunctive relief, monetary penalties and the ability to request a party to take appropriate action to enforce its environmental laws.[24] Additionally, KORUS requires the parties to promote public awareness of their environmental laws, including ways that interested persons can enforce compliance with these laws.[25] Public participation in the implementation of the KORUS environmental chapter is also encouraged by persons from the other party.[26] These provisions are in addition to the KORUS Transparency Chapter, which includes commitments to publish in advance any laws, regulations, and so on, affecting the agreement in order to provide opportunities for interested persons to comment on the proposed measures,[27] and a commitment to address substantive comments received and to explain any substantive revisions made to the proposed regulation.[28]

---

21 Brian Copeland, 'International Trade and Green Growth' (Policy Research Working Paper No 6235, World Bank, October 2012) 9.

22 M. Porter and C. van der Linde, 'Toward a New Conception of the Environment–Competitiveness Relationship' (1995) 9 *Journal of Economic Perspectives* 97.

23 KORUS art 20.4.

24 Ibid.

25 Ibid., art 20.7.

26 Ibid., art 20.7.2.

27 Ibid., art 21.1.

28 Ibid., art 21.1(4)(c).

The US will demand similar transparency and due process commitments in the TPP environment chapter. Such a position will likely be supported by those TPP parties who have already made similar commitments in their FTAs with the United States. Once a country has agreed to follow particular procedures for making and implementing laws and to provide access to independent and impartial judicial proceedings, these procedures are usually applied to all laws and not just those required by the FTA, as it is often too difficult to apply transparency and due process requirements to some laws only. In this sense, transparency commitments in FTAs are de facto multilateral commitments. This should lead Australia and Chile, which have made similar commitments on transparency and due process in previous FTAs with the US, to support similar rules in all future trade agreements.

Encouraging increased transparency in governments' development of laws and regulations and providing access to impartial and independent judicial systems that operate according to generally accepted norms of due process will provide additional legitimacy to environmental laws and regulations and to the balance struck in these laws between free trade and environmental protection. Additionally, environmental laws in particular are often viewed as reflecting a trade-off between businesses concerned about their costs and environmental and consumer groups, who are focused on the human and environmental health effects. Requiring governments to make the public aware of new environmental laws and provide opportunities to comment and reasons for substantive changes to these laws should explicate and make transparent where these trade-offs are being made and for what reasons. This will make back-room deals that produce outcomes that cannot be readily explained less easy to accomplish. It should also lead to greater public acceptance of environmental laws.

The role and impact of stakeholder participation in strengthening environmental laws is reflected in the environmental Kuznets curve, an inverted U-shaped curve that describes how developing countries initially focus on poverty reduction at the expense of environmental health, such as clean air and water.[29] As wealth increases, citizens demand a cleaner environment, leading to improved environmental standards and an upwards sloping Kuznets curve. For instance, Kruger and Grossman have estimated that emissions of sulfur dioxide increase until a country's population achieves an average per capita income of US$4,000–$5,000,

---

[29] World Bank, *World Development Report 1992: Development and the Environment* (Oxford University Press, 1992).

declining thereafter.[30] Others have argued that the empirical evidence for the claim that environmental health improves with economic growth is limited.[31]

From a political economy perspective, one of the criticisms of the environmental Kuznets curve is that people may not adequately account for the benefits of access to clean air and water.[32] Moreover, promoting development at the expense of environmental health may not reflect an accurate accounting of the costs and benefits. For instance, the health of the poorest citizens might not be accurately reflected in a decision to promote a particular development, especially where opportunities for input into the decision-making process are limited. Moreover, addressing environmental degradation only after a certain stage of development will be ineffective for environmental damage that is irreversible, such as loss of biodiversity or the extinction of species. In fact, there is evidence that there is no economic advantage to tolerating environmental damage as a byproduct of economic growth.[33]

Including the KORUS transparency and due process provisions in the TPP should go some way towards clarifying the costs and benefits of development. For instance, requiring TPP governments to make public any proposed environmental laws and provide opportunities for all citizens to contribute to the decision-making process will give greater voice to those communities whose interests would otherwise not be heard. It will also provide TPP governments with more information about the impact of proposed laws, which should allow for a more accurate accounting of their costs and benefits. This could also lead the TPP parties to grow their economies with lower levels of environmental degradation.[34]

KORUS also establishes a framework and commitment for future cooperation on environmental issues between the US and Korea. In this

---

[30] Gene Grossman and Alan Krueger, 'Economic Growth and the Environment' (1994) 110(2) *Quarterly Journal of Economics* 353, 367.

[31] Willam Harbaugh, Arik Levinson and David Molloy Wilson, 'Reexamining the Empirical Evidence for Environmental Kuznets Curve' (2002) 84(3) *The Review of Economics and Statistics* 541.

[32] Stephane Hallegatte et al., 'From Growth to Green Growth: A Framework' (Policy Research Paper No 5872, World Bank, November 2011).

[33] Susmita Dasgupta, Hua Wang and David Wheeler, 'Surviving Success: Policy Reform and the Future of Industrial Pollution in China' (Policy Research Working Paper No 1856, World Bank, 1997).

[34] Susmita Dasgupta, Benoit Laplante, Hua Wang and David Wheeler, 'Confronting the Environmental Kuznets Curve' (2002) 16(1) *Journal of Economic Perspectives* 152.

regard, KORUS references the US–Korea environmental cooperation agreement (ECA) that was negotiated in parallel with KORUS. The ECA provides a comprehensive framework for US–Korea cooperation on environmental issues, such as combating illegal logging,[35] protecting, conserving and managing ecosystems and wildlife,[36] reducing air and water pollution[37] and developing cleaner energy sources.[38]

There are, however, limits to the ECA. In particular, the KORUS dispute settlement mechanism is not available should either government fail to fulfil its commitments under the ECA. The USTR appears interested in addressing this by including in the TPP environment chapter commitments on trade in wildlife and illegally harvested timber and fisheries subsidies.[39]

II ADDITIONAL ENVIRONMENTAL CONCERNS FOR THE TPP ENVIRONMENT CHAPTER

A Trade in Illegally Harvested Timber

The TPP presents an important opportunity to develop rules that support efforts to conserve forests and prevent trade in illegal logs in a region that is responsible for 'the most intense deforestation in the world, with devastating and irreparable effects on its, and the world's forests and ecosystems'.[40]

US policy on combating trade in illegally harvested timber is based on the 2008 *Lacey Act* Amendments, which extended the Act's original prohibition on trade in wildlife and plants native to the US that have been illegally taken and listed in CITES, to include timber illegally harvested

---

35 *Agreement between the Government of the United States of America and the Government of the Republic of Korea on Environmental Cooperation*, signed 23 January 2012 (entered into force 15 March 2012) (*US–Korea Environmental Cooperation Agreement*) art 2(2)(f).

36 Ibid., art 2(2)(e).

37 Ibid., art 2(2)(g).

38 Ibid., art 2(2)(i).

39 'USTR Green Paper on Conservation and the Trans-Pacific Partnership', (December 2011) Office of the United States Trade Representative, <http://www.ustr.gov/about-us/press-office/fact-sheets/2011/ustr-green-paper-conservation-and-trans-pacific-partnership>.

40 Vanda Felbab-Brown, 'Not as Easy as Falling Off a Log: The Illegal Logging Trade in the Asia-Pacific Region and Possible Mitigation Strategies' (Foreign Policy Working Paper No 5, Brookings Institution, March 2011) 2.

in other countries and imported into the US.[41] Whether timber has been illegally harvested is determined according to the laws of the country of harvest. Under the *Lacey Act* Amendments, the importer is required to declare the value and quantity of the timber, the plant's name, and its country of origin.

The *Lacey Act* Amendments are a novel approach to addressing trade in illegally harvested timber products as they rely on the laws in the country of origin as determining whether an illegal harvest has occurred. And requiring TPP parties to fulfil their obligations under these MEAs, which include CITES, uses this treaty's internationally agreed understanding of which species of flora are endangered as a common starting point amongst TPP parties for determining which timber should be protected.[42] Moreover, placing responsibility on the importer to declare to US customs the wood type and country of export, alongside criminal penalties for knowingly making a false declaration, creates a strong incentive for the importer to source their wood from legally harvested timber products.

Reducing the access of illegally harvested wood to the US market should reduce the commercial incentive for illegal logging. The *Lacey Act* also implicitly recognises that the challenge to addressing illegal logging is less about the need for better conservation laws and more about the effective enforcement by wood-exporting countries of their current laws. In fact, efforts to regulate logging since the 1980s have led to increased illegal logging in TPP countries, such as Malaysia.[43] Consistent with this policy, the US has pursued international cooperation with other countries that emphasises exchanging information about trade in illegal logs and enhancing the capacity of law enforcement agencies in these countries. For instance, the US and Indonesia have a memorandum of understanding (MOU) under which their customs authorities have agreed to share information on trade in timber products and to cooperate in enforcing laws affecting trade in timber products.[44]

In 2009, this approach to international cooperation was expanded to an Asia-Pacific Initiative on Illegal Logging and Trade, which includes all the TPP countries in the Asia-Pacific region (except for New Zealand)

---

41 The *Lacey Act* 16 U.S.C. δδ 337–3378.

42 CITES appendices 1, II, III.

43 Vanda Felbab-Brown, above n 40, vi.

44 *Memorandum of Understanding between the Government of the United States of America and the Government of the Republic of Indonesia on Combating Illegal Logging and Associated Trade*, signed 17 November 2006 (entered into force on the date of signing).

and those TPP countries in the Western Hemisphere. Additionally, in 2011, Asia-Pacific Economic Cooperation (APEC) Trade Ministers directed their officials to find ways to address trade in illegally harvested timber products, leading APEC to create an Experts Group on Illegal Logging and Associated Trade tasked with developing ways to achieve this goal.[45] This work has set the scene for including the type of information-sharing and law enforcement cooperation outlined above in the TPP and would continue an approach that all TPP parties have become engaged with in other. The most controversial element to date has been the US insistence that the commitments are mandatory and subject to dispute settlement, which is a step further than the voluntary nature of APEC and the US–Indonesia MOU, which does not have a binding dispute settlement mechanism.[46]

B Fisheries Subsidies

According to a report by the World Bank and the Food and Agriculture Organization, 75 per cent of fish stocks are underperforming at a cost of $50 billion annually.[47] Addressing the unsustainable exploitation of fish stocks from fisheries subsidies is part of the WTO Doha Round.[48] Moreover, at the 2005 Hong Kong Ministerial Conference, WTO Members agreed to 'strengthen disciplines on subsidies in the fisheries sector, including through the prohibition of certain forms of fisheries subsidies that contribute to overcapacity and over-fishing'.[49] The Hong Kong Declaration also states that 'appropriate and effective special and differential treatment for developing and least-developed Members should be an integral part of the fisheries subsidies negotiations, taking into account the importance of this sector to development priorities, poverty reduction,

---

[45] APEC, *Experts Group on Illegal Logging and Associated Trade* <http://www.apec.org/Groups/SOM-Steering-Committee-on-Economic-and-Technical-Cooperation/Working-Groups/Illegal-Logging-and-Associated-Trade.aspx>.

[46] 'USTR Acknowledges Objections on Enforceability in TPP Environment Talks' (29 June 2012) 30 (26) *Inside US Trade* (online).

[47] Ragnar Arnason, Kieran Kelleher and Rolf Willmann, *The Sunken Billions: The Economic Justification for Fisheries Reform* (World Bank, 2009), p xvii (executive summary).

[48] *Ministerial Declaration*, WTO Doc WT/MIN(01)/DEC/1 (20 November 2001) (adopted 14 November 2001).

[49] *Doha Work Programme: Ministerial Declaration*, WTO Doc WT/MIN(05)/DEC (22 December 2005) (adopted 18 December 2005), annex D [9]–[11].

and livelihood and food security concerns'.[50] Following this mandate, WTO Members have focused on developing a set of specific rules for fisheries subsidies. Some progress has been made, though significant differences remain. The Chair of the WTO Rules Negotiating Group circulated a draft text in November 2007 that included a prohibition on subsidies affecting fish stocks already over-fished with exceptions linked to fisheries management and special and differential treatment for the least developed WTO Members.[51]

All of the key issues in the WTO Round fisheries subsidies negotiations are likely to play out in the TPP negotiations, which include a mix of developed and developing countries with various interests in this issue. For instance, for those countries with effective fish management regimes and where fishing is not a significant economic issue, the focus is on sustainability and conservation. In contrast, some developing countries are concerned that subsidies rules could constrain their ability to support what is often an important source of food, employment and economic growth.[52] For instance, a key sticking point in the current TPP negotiations is over some developing country demands for a carve-out that would allow subsidies for small-scale fisheries.[53] That said, this issue does not necessarily split along developed/developing country lines. For instance, in the WTO, the US is part of a negotiating group referred to as 'Friends of Fish', which includes both developed and developing TPP parties – namely, Australia, Chile, New Zealand and Peru, who are supportive of strong disciplines on fisheries subsidies with appropriately tailored exceptions.[54] In contrast, Korea, often with the support of Japan, has generally opposed WTO efforts to reach an ambitious agreement limiting fisheries subsidies.[55]

---

50 Ibid., annex D [9].

51 *Informal Open-Ended Meeting with Senior Officials*, WTO Doc TN/RL/W/246 (27 November 2009).

52 *Statement by the Chairman*, WTO Doc TN/RL/W/246 (27 November 2009) 6.

53 'Why Japan is lagging on the TPP' (30 May 2012) *East Asia Forum* <http://www.eastasiaforum.org/2012/05/30/why-japan-is-lagging-on-the-tpp>.

54 *Fisheries Subsidies: Communication from Argentina, Australia, Chile, Colombia, the United States, New Zealand, Norway, Iceland, Peru and Pakistan*, WTO Doc TN/RL/W/243 (7 October 2009).

55 *Framework of the Disciplines on Fisheries Subsidies: Communication from the Republic of Korea*, WTO Doc TN/RL/W/245 (24 November 2009).

III ADDRESSING CLIMATE CHANGE AND OTHER ENVIRONMENTAL CHALLENGES IN THE TPP: BEYOND THE ENVIRONMENT CHAPTER

The commitments countries make under the TPP's environment chapter will not be the only way that the TPP could affect environmental health. In fact, liberalised trade combined with new TPP rules could reinforce and help achieve a range of environmental goals.

As outlined in the introduction, the impact of trade liberalisation on environmental health will depend on the type of economic growth that follows. Where liberalised trade provides increased access to and competition amongst services providers, this can underpin a shift in the FTA party's economy away from heavy industry and towards less environmentally harmful service industries and lead to more efficient and environmentally friendly production processes.[56] FTAs can also lead to increased access to green technologies at lower cost, which increases the capacity of an FTA party to address environmental issues such as air and water pollution. The TPP can also support efforts by TPP parties to reduce their greenhouse gas (GHG) emissions. Similar to the way the TPP can help countries improve a broad range of environmental challenges by shifting their economies into cleaner, less polluting industries, the TPP can assist countries' transition on to low-carbon pathways by providing access to pertinent goods, services and investment.

A Environmental Goods

Reduced tariffs on environmental goods can support domestic efforts towards environmental conservation and reducing GHG emissions. In particular, for TPP developing economies whose average bound tariffs are higher than developed economies, the environmental gains from reducing tariffs on environmental goods are potentially significant.[57] As developed country tariffs on environmental goods are already low, reducing these tariffs further is unlikely to provide much incentive for

---

[56] Grossman and Krueger, above n 19, 4.

[57] Veena Jha, 'Trade Flows, Barriers and Market Drivers in Renewable Energy Supply Goods' (Issue Paper No 10, International Centre for Trade and Sustainable Development, December 2009) 13.

business in these countries to increase their levels of environmental conservation.[58]

At the 2011 APEC meeting in Honolulu, the TPP parties released an outline of the key goals for the TPP, which include eliminating tariffs and other barriers to trade in goods and services.[59] Reducing tariffs on all goods to zero would overcome the need to develop a separate list of environmental goods. However, in the event that the TPP parties do not reach this goal or agree instead to phase out tariffs on goods, then ensuring trade barriers are eliminated on an appropriate list of environmental goods should remain a priority.

Reducing tariffs on environmental goods has been an ongoing element of the WTO Doha negotiations, though progress has been frustrated by the challenge of agreeing a list of environmental goods. At the APEC Summit in Vladivostok in 2012, the APEC economies agreed on a list of 54 environmental goods on which they would cut tariffs to 5 per cent or less by the end of 2015.[60] Agreeing on this list of environmental goods is a good start but it is a limited list compared with lists of environmental goods developed by APEC and the World Bank; it could be expanded upon in the TPP.[61]

There are, moreover, limits to developing lists that largely define an environmental good based on its end-use.[62] This is particularly the case in the climate change context, where the way in which goods are produced and disposed of largely determines their GHG emissions lifecycle. For instance, in the US, the electricity sector produces 40 per cent of GHG emissions and the commercial and industrial sectors

---

[58] Robert Howse and Petrus van Bork, 'Options for Liberalising Trade in Environmental Goods in the Doha Round' (Issue Paper No 2, International Centre for Trade and Sustainable Development, July 2006) 5.

[59] *Enhancing Trade and Investment, Supporting Jobs, Economic Growth and Development: Outlines of the Trans-Pacific Partnership Agreement* (12 November 2011) Office of the United States Trade Representative <http://www.ustr.gov/about-us/press-office/fact-sheets/2011/november/outlines-trans-pacific-partnership-agreement>.

[60] 2012 Leaders' Declaration, *Vladivostok Declaration – Integrate to Grow, Innovate to Prosper* (8–9 September 2012) <http://apec.org/Meeting-Papers/Leaders-Declarations/2012/2012_aelm.aspx> annex C.

[61] See generally Ronald Steenblik, 'Environmental Goods: A Comparison of the APEC and OECD Lists' (Trade and Environment Working Paper No 2005-04, Organisation for Economic Co-operation and Development, 29 November 2005).

[62] Howse and van Bork, above n 58, 18.

produce approximately 20 per cent.[63] This has led countries to regulate goods' GHG lifecycle.[64] For instance, the US Renewable Fuel Standard, which requires fuel sold and imported into the US to have a specific quantity of renewable fuel, identifies four categories of renewable fuels based on their GHG lifecycle. European Union (EU) countries, such as Germany and the United Kingdom, have also adopted laws that regulate renewable energy and transportation fuels based on their GHG emissions lifecycle.[65]

The TPP parties should therefore consider defining environmental goods by their lifecycle or production process. Providing a tariff cut for such goods would create the strongest incentive for industry to use less carbon-intensive production processes and thereby contribute the most to reducing GHG emissions.[66]

It is also the case that more stringent environmental regulation will be required in order for reduced trade barriers on environmental goods to lead to better environmental outcomes.[67] This is because, in a perfectly competitive market, firms do not have an incentive to go beyond what the law requires them to do. However, to the extent that lower tariffs reduce the cost of complying with environmental or climate change laws, this could create political space for the adoption of even more stringent regulations.[68] Reducing the costs of green technologies should also provide opportunities for business to demonstrate corporate social responsibility by doing more to reduce their GHG emissions.

---

63 United States Energy Information Administration, *Emissions of Greenhouse Gases in the United States 2009* (United States Department of Energy, March 2011).

64 Edvokia Moise and Ronald Steenblik, 'Trade-Related Measures Based on Processes and Production Methods in the Context of Climate-Change Mitigation' (Trade and Environment Working Paper No 2011/04, Organisation for Economic Co-operation and Development, 3 August 2011).

65 Ibid., 18–21.

66 Howse and van Bork, above n 58, 12; Joshua Meltzer and Kathy Sierra, 'Trade and Climate Change: A Mutually Supportive Policy', *Harvard International Review*, 7 December 2011, <http://hir.harvard.edu/disease/trade-and-climate-change>.

67 Howse and van Bork, above n 58, 5.

68 Mary Lovely and David Popp, 'Trade, Technology, and the Environment: Does Access to Technology Promote Environmental Regulation?' (2011) 61 *Journal of Environmental Economics and Management* 16.

B Non-tariff Barriers to Trade in Environmental Goods

Non-tariff barriers are an increasingly important obstacle to reducing costs and increasing access to environmental goods.[69] Some of the key non-tariff barriers include technology-specific regulations and standards that manufacturers must meet as well as different testing and conformity assessment requirements.[70]

In the energy sector, for instance, energy-efficiency labels applied to all manner of goods, from washing machines to computers, have become a key means of informing consumers and incentivising industry to produce more energy-efficient products.[71] Countries have already taken steps towards harmonising their labelling schemes. For instance, TPP countries such as Australia and Canada base their energy-efficiency labels on the US Energy Star program. However, this is not the case for other developing country parties to the TPP, and developed country differences remain in areas such as the stringency of standards and the use of different energy test procedures. This suggests that there is considerable scope for the harmonisation of standards to increase efficiencies and reduce costs.[72] The environmental benefits will also be greatest where harmonisation is to the highest standard.

Including commitments in the TPP that parties will use common standards and labels that inform consumers of the environmental benefits of particular goods would reduce costs and should increase trade in those goods. Moreover, in the event that the TPP parties were to consider providing tariff preferences to goods produced using low-carbon production processes, labelling is one way that customs officials and consumers

---

[69] *Market Access for Environmental Goods: Communication from Canada, European Communities, New Zealand, Norway, Singapore, Switzerland, and the United States*, WTO Doc TN/MA/W/70 (9 May 2006) 3.

[70] Barbara Fliess and Joy Kim, 'Non-Tariff Barriers Facing Trade in Selected Environmental Goods and Associated Services' (2008) 42(3) *Journal of World Trade* 535; Ronald Steenblik and Joy Aree Kim, 'Facilitating Trade in Selected Climate Change Mitigation Technologies in the Energy Supply, Building, and Industry Sectors' (Trade and Environment Working Paper No 2009-02, Organisation for Economic Co-operation and Development, 4 May 2009).

[71] Rod Janssen, 'Harmonising Energy Efficiency Requirements – Building Foundations for Co-operative Action' (Issue Paper No 14, International Centre for Trade and Sustainable Development, November 2010).

[72] Paul Waide et al., 'What Is To Be Expected and Gained from International Harmonization of Equipment Energy Efficiency Requirements?' (Summer Study on Energy Efficiency in Buildings, American Council for an Energy-Efficient Economy, 2010) 8-376.

could identify these goods.[73] There are also more general non-tariff barriers such as inadequate protection of intellectual property rights and slow and costly customs procedures that affect trade in environmental goods, and these issues are being addressed in the Doha Round.[74] Good progress has been made on customs (otherwise known as trade facilitation) issues.[75] The TPP provides an opportunity to build on progress so far in the Doha Round by including commitments that reduce the time it takes to release goods through customs and increasing the transparency and efficiency of customs processes, such as by publishing customs procedures on the internet.

In addition to the TPP parties reaffirming their commitments under the WTO's *Agreement on Technical Barriers to Trade* (TBT Agreement),[76] the TPP should include additional commitments that encourage cooperation amongst the TPP parties' standards-setting bodies with the aim of developing common approaches to issues such as energy efficiency and the methodology for determining a good's GHG lifecycle. Additionally, enhanced processes for mutual recognition of the results of the conformity assessment procedures would reduce costs by avoiding the need for duplicate testing of products in each TPP market.

Lack of transparency about non-tariff barriers is another troubling issue and includes difficulties determining their existence and how they are applied.[77] These barriers are also particularly acute for small and medium enterprises, which have less capacity to absorb these costs and to hire lawyers or agents in the importing country to try and navigate these issues.

Greater transparency in the development of standards and technical regulations, and opportunities for interested parties in each TPP country to provide comments, should also help TPP parties avoid developing regulations that are discriminatory and create unnecessary barriers to

---

[73] Joshua Meltzer and Kathy Sierra, 'Trade and Climate Change' (7 December 2011) *Harvard International Review* (online).

[74] Peter Yu, 'TRIPS Enforcement and Developing Countries' (2011) 26 *American University International Law Review*, 727.

[75] *Draft Consolidated Negotiating Text*, WTO Doc TN/TF/W/165/Rev.14 (17 December 2012) 24.

[76] *Marrakesh Agreement Establishing the World Trade Organization*, opened for signature 15 April 1994, 1867 UNTS 3 (entered into force 1 January 1995) (*Marrakesh Agreement*) annex 1A.

[77] Steenblik and Kim, above n 70, 11.

trade.[78] In this respect, KORUS includes a range of transparency commitments that go beyond the TBT Agreement, which could be usefully included in the TPP Agreement. These include requirements to allow persons from other TPP parties to participate in the standard-setting process and to provide electronic notice of the proposed new standards and regulations, including an explanation of the regulation's objective.[79]

C Environmental Services

Services are increasingly a key part of the shift to a greener and low-carbon economy. Renewable energy from wind farms and solar facilities requires engineers to design and run these facilities, and the downstream end of the supply chain for renewable energy is heavily services-driven. For instance, wind power facilities require persons with expertise in marketing, sales, financing, transportation and logistics as well as wind park operations and maintenance.[80]

Moreover, the types of technologies that can be used to address environmental issues such as climate change are changing rapidly. Governments around the world are supporting research and development into a range of new technologies that will also require new skill-sets to implement and operate. The deployment of environmental and GHG mitigation technologies will rely on a broad range of services not directly related to the environmental sector.[81] For instance, the development of a wind farm will require access to consulting, telecommunications, transportation/logistics and financial services for the design, financing and execution of the project. This points to the need for the TPP to broadly reduce barriers to services trade. Additionally, scheduling services commitments in the TPP using a negative list approach means that new services will be automatically bound, ensuring that the TPP services

---

[78] Aaron Cosbey, *Lessons Learned on Trade and Sustainable Development: Distilling Six Years of Research from the Trade Knowledge Framework* (International Institute for Sustainable Development and International Committee for Trade and Sustainable Development, 2004) 18.

[79] See KORUS ch 9.

[80] Jacob Funk Kirkegaard, Thilo Hanemann and Lutz Weischer, 'It Should be a Breeze: Harnessing the Potential of Open Trade and Investment Flows in the Wind Energy Industry' (Working Paper No 09-14, Peterson Institute for International Economics, December 2009) 39.

[81] Ronald Steenblik and Massimo Geloso Grosso, 'Trade in Services Related to Climate Change: An Exploratory Analysis' (Trade and Environment Working Paper No 2011/03, Organisation for Economic Co-operation and Development, 26 May 2011) 7.

commitments remain relevant in a rapidly changing market for green technologies.

D Energy and Climate Change Subsidies

Developing low-carbon energy sources such as from renewables and nuclear power will be key to decoupling economic growth from GHG emissions. TPP parties have adopted a range of renewable energy subsidies. For instance, 29 US states have renewable portfolio standards,[82] and Australia has a renewable energy target of generating 20 per cent of electricity from renewable energy by 2020, in addition to government support for the development of renewable energy such as solar power and carbon capture and storage.[83] The TPP parties also subsidise research and development into green energy. For instance, the 2009 *American Recovery and Reinvestment Act* (ARRA) in 2009 increased spending on developing clean energy from $17.895 billion in 2007 to $37.16 billion in 2010.[84]

Subsidies to support climate change efforts raise concerns about their trade impact and WTO consistency. The WTO *Agreement on Subsidies and Countervailing Measures* (SCM Agreement)[85] disciplines WTO Members' use of subsidies. The SCM Agreement prohibits subsidies conditional on export and the use of domestic content. There are also actionable subsidies where it can be demonstrated that there is a subsidy (that is, it entails a financial contribution such as government assistance to firms), that it confers a benefit on an enterprise and the subsidy is de facto or de jure specific.

Any analysis of the implications of such subsidies on trade needs to be done in the context of a market that already includes significant fossil fuel subsidies, which the International Energy Agency estimates were worth over $400 billion in 2010 and, without reform, will increase to

---

[82] Galen Barbose, 'Renewables Portfolio Standards in the United States: A Status Update' (Paper presented at 2012 National Summit on RPS, Washington, DC, 3 December 2012) <http://www.cleanenergystates.org/assets/2012-Files/RPS/RPS-SummitDec2012Barbose.pdf>.

[83] *Renewable Energy Target*, Australian Government, Department of Climate Change and Energy Efficiency <http://www.climatechange.gov.au/government/initiatives/renewable-target.aspx>.

[84] Joshua Meltzer, *A Carbon Tax as an Incentive for Green Innovation and the Implications for International Trade* (November 2012) Alliance21 <http://alliance21.org.au/site/assets/media/docs/1211_Meltzer_Paper.pdf>.

[85] *Marrakesh Agreement* annex 1A.

$660 billion by 2020.[86] Government action to encourage clean energy is therefore not an intervention into an otherwise perfect market but should be understood as an attempt to offset existing market distortions. The G20 agreement to phase out inefficient fossil fuel subsidies should also be understood in this light.[87] Additionally, Joseph Stiglitz has argued that the fossil fuel sector is also a recipient of a negative subsidy stemming from the failure to correctly price carbon emissions to reflect their climate change impacts.[88] This suggests that, from a climate change perspective, not all energy subsidies are harmful, and some are necessary to overcome the path dependency created by technology lock-in – the dominance of a market by an inferior technology – such as coal-fired power stations.[89] Additionally, subsidies are often required to encourage an optimal level of research and development.[90]

The trade law impacts of government assistance for a range of energy sources played out in the recent WTO *Canada – Renewable Energy* case, where the Appellate Body recognised the legitimacy of government support for renewable energy. The Appellate Body went on to find that comparing renewable energy generation with conventional sources of energy requires a full consideration of all the costs associated with non-renewable energy as well as the positive externalities from renewable energy such as 'guaranteeing long-term supply and addressing environmental concerns'. This led the Appellate Body to conclude that whether a benefit had been conferred by Canada's feed-in-tariff for renewable energy should be compared with the market for wind and solar PV and not the wholesale market for electricity generated from all sources of energy.[91]

---

86 International Energy Agency, 'World Energy Outlook 2010' <http://www.worldenergyoutlook.org/media/weo2010.pdf>.

87 *G20 Leaders' Statement: The Pittsburgh Summit* (24–25 September 2009) G20 Information Centre, University of Toronto <http://www.g20.utoronto.ca/2009/2009communique0925.html>.

88 Joseph Stiglitz, 'A New Agenda for Global Warming' (July 2006) *Economists' Voice* (online).

89 Mark Dutz and Siddharth Sharma, 'Green Growth, Technology and Innovation' (Policy Research Working Paper No 5932, World Bank, January 2012) 13.

90 Ibid.

91 Appellate Body Report, *Canada – Certain Measures Affecting the Renewable Energy Generation Sector*, WTO doc WT/DS412/AB/R (adopted 6 May 2013) [5.186], [5.199].

The issue of climate subsidies also arises when governments offset the impact of a domestic carbon price on so-called energy-intensive trade-exposed industries to address the competitiveness and carbon leakage concerns that arise as a result of imports from countries not pricing carbon. For instance, the EU has offset the impact of its cap and trade system on these industries by providing a free allocation of permits.[92] Australia also mitigates the impact of its carbon price for its energy-intensive trade-exposed industry.[93]

A number of these subsidies might fall foul of the SCM Agreement. For instance, the *Canada – Renewable Energy* case demonstrates the instability of the electricity market as a benchmark for determining whether a 'benefit' exists, and China has requested WTO consultations with the EU over Germany's FIT program.[94] Moreover, allocating free allowances to offset a domestic carbon price on energy-intensive trade-exposed industry could constitute a financial benefit under the SCM Agreement, as the government has provided a right to emit carbon for free.[95]

The limits to the WTO subsidies rules as they apply to climate change and energy subsidies should be addressed in the TPP. This would not address the application of WTO rules, but action should be undertaken with an eye to expanding TPP membership to all APEC economies. Agreement reached here could build a foundation for reform of the WTO subsidies rules.

One approach the TPP could take would be to develop a list of subsidies that would be non-actionable. The WTO SCM Agreement Article 8 (now expired) contains a list of non-actionable subsidies, including subsidies for research and development and assistance to adapt to new environmental requirements. Rob Howse has proposed that any list of non-actionable subsidies be defined in terms of policies listed in

---

92 *Climate Action: The EU Emissions Trading System* (4 January 2013) European Commission <http://ec.europa.eu/clima/policies/ets/index_en.htm>.

93 Economist Intelligence Unit, *Cleaning Up: Australia's Readiness for a Low Carbon Future: A report from the Economist Intelligence Unit* (*The Economist*, May 2011).

94 See *European Union and Certain Member States – Certain Measures Affecting the Renewable Energy Generation Sector*, WTO Doc WT/DS452/1 (7 November 2012) (Request for Consultations by China).

95 Robert Howse, 'Climate Mitigation Subsidies and the WTO Legal Framework: A Policy Analysis' (International Institute for Sustainable Development, May 2010) 9; see also Gary Hufbauer, Steve Charnovitz and Jisun Kim, *Global Warming and the World Trading System* (Peterson Institute for International Economics, 2009) 62–64.

the Kyoto Protocol and require that they be consistent with WTO norms of non-discrimination and transparency.[96] Another approach would be to allow countries to justify subsidies under Article XX of the *General Agreement on Tariffs and Trade 1994*,[97] which includes an exception that would cover measures to reduce GHG emissions.[98]

Increasing the transparency of subsidies would also be an important step and would give TPP parties information on subsidies programs that are often difficult to identify. The WTO SCM Agreement requires WTO Members to report their subsidies to the WTO, but such reporting has been low, largely due to a lack of sanctions for non-compliance.[99] The TPP parties could begin to address this by requiring subsidies to be reported to all other TPP parties in a standard format, with sanctions for breach.[100]

CONCLUSION

International trade both reflects and facilitates economic connectedness. In so doing, it has the potential to underpin economic growth and raise living standards globally. International trade can also lead to more rapid rates of environmental depletion, as access to new markets encourages efficiencies and production at scale. But providing access to the goods and services used to develop economies in more efficient ways will reduce the environmental costs of growth. Additionally, greater trade can increase exposure to new technologies and ideas, which could increase innovation and be a catalyst for developing breakthrough green technologies.

International trade rules also reflect decisions that governments take about how to balance the growth-promoting aspects of international trade with the need for resource conservation. And as new environmental

---

96 Howse, above n 95, 21.

97 *General Agreement on Tariffs and Trade*, GATT Doc LT/UR/A-1/A/1/GATT/2, signed 30 October 1947, as incorporated in the *Marrakesh Agreement*, annex 1A.

98 Appellate Body Report, *Brazil – Measures Affecting Imports of Retreaded Tyres*, WTO Doc WT/DS332/AB/R (adopted 17 December 2007) [151].

99 Sadeq Bigdeli, 'Will the "Friends of Climate" Emerge in the WTO? The Prospects of Applying the "Fisheries Subsidies" Model to Energy Subsidies' (2008) 1 *Climate Change Law Review* 78, 85.

100 See Ronald Steenblik and Juan Simon, 'A New Template for Notifying Subsidies to the WTO' (International Institute for Sustainable Development, May 2011).

challenges have arisen, particularly climate change, new bargains need to be struck about how trade rules should be used to support efforts to address this challenge.

As a twenty-first-century trade agreement, the TPP is currently the best opportunity to address current environmental challenges. The TPP is also the first major plurilateral trade negotiation post the WTO Doha Round where both the impacts of climate change and the inability to make significant progress in the United Nations climate change negotiations are clear. This highlights the importance of using the TPP to develop new international trade rules that can enable countries to develop their economies in an environmentally sustainable manner.

Whether it is depleting fisheries, declining biodiversity or reduced space in the atmosphere for GHG emissions, the underlying issue is resource scarcity. And in a world where an additional 3 billion people are expected to enter the middle class over the next 15 years, countries need to find new and creative ways to cooperate in order to satisfy the legitimate needs of their population for growth and opportunity while using resources in a manner that is sustainable for current and future generations.[101] The TPP parties already represent a diverse range of developed and developing countries. Should the TPP become a free trade agreement of the Asia-Pacific region, it will include the main developed and developing countries and will be a strong basis for building a global consensus on these trade and environmental issues.

---

[101] Homi Kharas, 'The Emerging Middle Class in Developing Countries' (Working Paper No 285, Organisation for Economic Co-operation and Development, 2010).

11. The Trans-Pacific Partnership Agreement and regulatory coherence

Rodrigo Polanco*

INTRODUCTION

The inclusion of a chapter on regulatory coherence in the Trans-Pacific Partnership Agreement (TPP) represents a major development in the area of preferential trade agreements (PTAs). The stated regulatory coherence goals of the TPP negotiations are to eliminate unnecessary regulatory barriers and to make the regulatory systems of member countries more compatible and transparent.[1] The regulatory coherence chapter in the TPP will reportedly include mechanisms to achieve greater domestic coordination of regulations, increase transparency and stakeholder engagement, and improve competitiveness and the ability of small and medium businesses to engage in international trade.[2]

As we will see, the notion of regulatory coherence has emerged mainly within international networks of governance, especially in the Asia-Pacific Economic Cooperation (APEC) group and in the Organisation for Economic Co-operation and Development (OECD). Its introduction into an international treaty poses a series of questions without clear answers, the most essential being the definition of regulatory coherence. For some, regulatory coherence means substantive regulatory harmonisation. Others think that it means a harmonisation process by which regulations are

---

* Email rodrigo.polanco@wti.org. I am grateful to Felipe Ferreira for research assistance in preparing this chapter and to Tania Voon for her comments on earlier drafts of this piece. All errors and omissions are mine.

1 Ian Fergusson and Bruce Vaughn, 'The Trans-Pacific Partnership Agreement' (CRS Report for Congress No R40502, Congressional Research Service, 12 December 2011) 8 <http://www.fas.org/sgp/crs/row/R40502.pdf>.

2 Thomas Bollyky, 'Regulatory Coherence in the TPP Talks' in C.L. Lim, Deborah Elms and Patrick Low (eds), *The Trans-Pacific Partnership: A Quest for a Twenty-first Century Trade Agreement* (Cambridge University Press, 2012) 171, 171.

developed and adopted. For still others, it means mutual recognition of regulations or indulgences in the application of the law of a country to foreign producers, traders and investors. Until we have a more focused understanding of what we mean by regulatory coherence, it will be difficult to study and measure it as a distinct political phenomenon.[3]

While it is true that the lack of a definition is not an insurmountable obstacle in itself, this situation leaves room for uncertainty regarding some very important questions, including:

- What obligations does a state assume when signing an international treaty covering regulatory coherence?
- If the notion of regulatory coherence does not entail any obligations, why include those commitments in an international treaty?
- What should the state do to fulfil its international commitment? Is it necessary to amend domestic legislation to implement it?
- What kind of control may the parties to the treaty exercise in respect of the commitments made by other parties?

This chapter aims to answer such queries, with reference to the origins of regulatory coherence in an international context and its relationship with regional and international trade. We will address possible positive and negative effects of such a scheme, concluding that unless we have a proper understanding and definition of regulatory coherence, it will be difficult to implement without raising concerns about influence and legitimacy between 'regulation-importer' states and 'regulation-exporter' states.

I A BRIEF HISTORY OF REGULATORY COHERENCE

A Regulatory Coherence in the Transatlantic Economic Council

During 2007, in the process of forming the Transatlantic Economic Council (TEC), a political space created by the United States and the European Union in order to 'oversee and accelerate government-to-government cooperation in order to further economic integration',[4] both parties spoke for the first time of regulatory coherence as a tool the main

---

[3] Theodore Posner and David Wolff, *Making 'Regulatory Coherence' Coherent* (25 April 2011) Law360 <http://www.law360.com/articles/240689/making-regulatory-coherence-coherent> 3.

[4] Ibid., 2.

objective of which would be to 'remove unnecessary differences between its regulations and further economic integration'.[5] This commitment is embodied in a document entitled *Framework for Advancing Transatlantic Economic Integration between the European Union and the United States of America*, section II of which reads:

> **Fostering Cooperation and Reducing Regulatory Burdens**
>
> In light of our shared commitment to removing barriers to transatlantic commerce; to rationalizing, reforming, and, where appropriate, reducing regulations to empower the private sector; to achieving more effective, systematic and transparent regulatory cooperation to reduce costs associated with regulation to consumers and producers; to removing unnecessary differences between our regulations to foster economic integration; to reinforce the existing transatlantic dialogue structures in regulatory cooperation both by intensifying our sector-by-sector EU–U.S. regulatory cooperation and our dialogue between the European Commission services and the U.S. Office of Management and Budget on methodological issues: we resolve to achieve the goals set out in Annex 1 in a timely manner.[6]

Consequently a cooperation agenda between regulatory agencies of the various states was established within the TEC, proposing goals to advance particular regulatory integration in six specific areas: cosmetics, medical devices, pharmaceuticals, the automotive sector, electrical equipment and nanomaterials.[7] Planning for the development of methodological frameworks for specific sectors 'to help ensure the comparability of impact assessments, particularly risk assessments and cost–benefit analysis' was also encouraged.[8]

The TEC was aimed at avoiding increased costs in international trade produced by the duplication of regulation across countries. To meet these objectives two kinds of cooperative efforts were set out. First, advancing regulatory integration in specific sectors; and, second, promoting the exchange of experiences and information among regulators. To make that exchange possible, the TEC has tried to establish a methodological framework that allows comparison between regulatory impact declarations, risk assessments and cost–benefit analyses related to regulation.

---

5 Ibid.

6 *Framework for Advancing Transatlantic Economic Integration between the European Union and the United States of America*, signed 30 April 2007 <http://trade.ec.europa.eu/doclib/docs/2007/may/tradoc_134654.pdf> (emphasis added).

7 Ibid., annex 1.

8 Ibid.

Both mechanisms are different in nature and have different objectives. While the first is much closer to a process of rules standardisation and is not unknown in international trade, the second aims to be a cooperative effort, which does not seek to make the rules generated by regulators comparable, but rather seeks to change the processes used by regulators to produce a regulation.[9]

Therefore, the TEC alone does not define regulatory coherence, but the second form of cooperation described above could be considered as an approach to the notion of regulatory coherence. It links regulatory coherence with regulatory reform processes and identifies regulatory impact studies as an essential element of regulatory coherence.

B OECD Regulatory Coherence and Public Policy

OECD countries were the first to take steps to improve the quality of their regulatory systems. In this context, in 1997 the OECD made the following diagnosis:

> Improving the empirical basis for regulatory decisions through impact analysis of new regulatory proposals is a popular reform strategy in OECD countries. By 1996, more than half of OECD countries had adopted Regulatory Impact Analysis ... programmes, up from one or two in 1980, and an increasing proportion of laws and other regulations affecting citizens are being shaped in part by various forms of [Regulatory Impact Analysis] ...[10]

In 2009, the OECD noted the mainstreaming of the use of Regulatory Impact Analysis (RIA) in its countries and stated:

> As a governance process RIA now forms a core component of the regulatory management strategy of all governments throughout the OECD. As an integrated systemic procedure, it has become one of the most widely used processes for improving the quality of regulatory decision-making.[11]

---

9 Ibid.

10 Scott H. Jacobs, 'An Overview of Regulatory Impact Analysis in OECD Countries' in Organisation for Economic Co-operation and Development (ed.), *Regulatory Impact Studies: Best Practices in OECD Countries* (OECD Publishing, 1997) 13, 13.

11 Organisation for Economic Co-operation and Development, *Regulatory Impact Analysis: A Tool for Policy Coherence* (OECD Publishing, 2009) 13.

The same OECD report noted that RIA 'aims to be both a tool and a decision process for informing political decision makers on whether and how to regulate to achieve public policy goals'.[12]

Linking RIA with public policy development could be seen as a consequence of increased democratic control demanded by citizens who are usually motivated by a number of different interests, which have different stakes in, and approaches to, the regulatory processes. These groups can include: those concerned about the costs of regulation and the impact of regulations on business in an environment that is already perceived as complex; those who see regulation as a tool to promote values; and those concerned about the impact of regulation in other areas such as trade and job creation.[13] Different motivations to establish accountability systems have led to an RIA system that is not fully uniform – a phenomenon that has also helped to make regulatory coherence an elusive concept.

The OECD analyses the process of regulatory change in its countries and publishes reports on the approaches taken so that countries can learn from the experience of other jurisdictions. These reports contain models of implementation of best regulatory practices. The changes studied often arise from a request to a government official about the cost of a law.[14]

C The APEC–OECD Checklist

APEC economies have developed, in conjunction with the OECD, a program of cooperation on regulatory reform with a strong emphasis on openness and market competition. To advance in this field APEC members reached agreement at the ministerial conference in 2000 held in Brunei Darussalam to create the APEC–OECD Co-operative Initiative on Regulatory Reform (the Initiative). In 2005 the work of the Initiative resulted in the creation of the APEC–OECD Integrated Checklist on Regulatory Reform (the APEC–OECD Checklist).[15] The APEC–OECD Checklist is a voluntary tool:

> that member economies may use to evaluate their respective regulatory reform efforts. There is no single model of regulatory reform, but this does not mean

---

12 Ibid., 12.

13 Jacobs, above n 10, 15.

14 Ibid., 16.

15 *APEC–OECD Integrated Checklist on Regulatory Reform* (September 2005) Asia–Pacific Economic Cooperation <http://publications.apec.org/publication-detail.php?pub_id=1200> 1.

> that standards, goals and well-structured institutions do not matter. Based on the accumulated knowledge of APEC and the OECD, the Checklist highlights key issues that should be considered during the process of development and implementation of regulatory policy, while recognizing that the diversity of economic, social, and political environments and values of member economies require flexibility in the methods through which the checklist shall be applied, and in the uses given to the information compiled.[16]

The checklist comprises four pillars, namely: regulatory reform, regulatory policies, competition policy and market liberalisation policies.

1. *Regulatory reform*: The APEC/OECD report considers this a horizontal issue, to be developed at all levels of government as a 'reflection on the degree of integration of regulatory, competition and market openness policies across levels of government, and on the accountability and transparency mechanisms needed to ensure their success'.[17] The origin of the regulatory reform movement dates back to the domestic deregulation efforts of the 1970s and 1980s, which focused on improving regulatory agency rule-making and streamlining administration, mainly in the United States, Australia and New Zealand.[18]
2. *Regulatory policies*: these policies should be designed to maximise the efficiency, transparency and accountability of regulations based on an integrated approach to the process of making rules and the application of regulatory tools and institutions.[19]
3. *Competition policy*: refers to policies that promote economic growth and efficiency by eliminating or minimising the distorting impact of laws, regulations, and administrative policies, practices, and procedures relating to competition. They do so by preventing and deterring anti-privacy practices and promoting competition through effective enforcement of competition laws.[20]
4. *Market liberalisation policies*: these are aimed at ensuring that a country can obtain the benefits of globalisation and international competition by eliminating or minimising the distorting effects of border (and behind-the-border) regulations and practices. These policies influence the range of opportunities open to international

[16] Ibid.
[17] Ibid., 2.
[18] Bollyky, 'Regulatory Coherence in the TPP Talks', above n 2, 174–5.
[19] Ibid.
[20] Ibid.

suppliers of goods and services to compete with their domestic counterparts.[21]

To enable their members to evaluate their progress on these points, the APEC–OECD Checklist contains questions inviting each country to assess their compliance with a specific goal that advances a regulatory policy. A tool such as an RIA is needed to build a regulatory policy because it allows for comparisons between policies. The preparation of an RIA also involves a commitment to undergo procedures towards enhancing efficiency and promoting predictability.

RIAs alone cannot build a regulatory policy. Among other things, governments should define a starting point to move forward with the rest of the themes proposed by the APEC–OECD Checklist. Efforts should focus on achieving an integrated system, involving all sectors of the state acting in a coordinated and mutually supportive fashion. To achieve this coordination, the APEC–OECD Checklist proposes two mechanisms: either the creation of a central coordinating body or, at least, the establishment of a coordination mechanism. Both solutions should avoid the isolation of a regulator, because:

> It is often difficult for regulators to reform themselves. Special interests, close identification with the objectives of out-dated regulation, and countervailing pressures from different parts of society make such self-reform even more complex. In addition, modern regulations and regimes apply across multiple areas. Regulatory quality control and consistency may benefit when responsibility is shared between regulators and a central quality control entity.[22]

Once defined, regulatory policy can generate regulatory practices where government officials have strong guidance and direction. Citizens can also clarify what they can expect from the regulations, thus increasing the predictability of regulatory practices. Achieving these goals requires the implementation of high standards of transparency, which are applied on a non-discriminatory basis. This means that laws and regulations should not establish different procedures or rules depending on the company, product, service or country. The transparency of the rulemaking process allows a:

> clear system for rule making that is known to stakeholders and policies governing the enforcement of laws can ensure that stakeholders know and

---

21 *APEC–OECD Checklist*, above n 15, 2–3.

22 Ibid., 15.

> understand how the law affects them; furthermore, it ensures consistent application of laws.[23]

The APEC–OECD Checklist even addresses – in the context of transparency – participation in the creation of future regulations through public consultation that will promote an emphasis on the regulations being developed:

> with appropriate and well-publicised procedures for effective and timely inputs from interested national and foreign parties, such as affected business, trade unions, wider interest groups such as consumer or environmental organisations, or other levels of government. Public consultation should not be limited to insiders, such as already established businesses, but should be open to all interested parties. Consultation works in both directions and educates both stakeholders and officials. It improves the quality of rules and programmes and also improves compliance and reduces enforcement costs for both governments and citizens subject to rules.[24]

This concept of transparency, which is to be applied by the consultation mechanisms with a view to broadly identifying participants to include other governments and possible future stakeholders, is one of the most difficult points of regulatory coherence to understand, in terms of both its scope and its effects.

Finally, the APEC–OECD Checklist suggests a mechanism for the government to evaluate the conformity of its regulation with its international commitments, stating that:

> The Rule of Law means that all properly functioning regulatory systems and every regulatory action (which by definition intrudes on the activities of the others) must be based in law. Every well functioning rule-making process will have a procedure for examining the proposed regulatory action for legality and compliance with other requirements, such as adherence to WTO obligations.[25]

These procedures may be the responsibility of a central body or may be assigned elsewhere and may involve legislative bodies.

Creating a centralised organ of state to act as a regulator is a possible way of ensuring coherent action across the state as a whole, minimising duplication in regulation and subjecting regulation to cost–benefit analyses. Cost–benefit analyses grant legal certainty and allow, in conjunction

---

23 Ibid., 7.
24 Ibid., 17.
25 Ibid., 15.

with the implementation of RIA mechanisms and increased transparency, the generation of rules that imply a commitment to competition and market liberalisation.

II REGULATORY COHERENCE AND INTERNATIONAL TRADE

International trade and regulation are often seen as opposing forces in the context of trade barriers. Trade barriers can be broadly classified as either 'border measures' or 'behind-the-border measures'.

A Border Measures

Border measures hinder or prevent access to a particular market, for example custom duties (or tariffs) and quantitative import restrictions (or quotas). These two measures fall within this broad category because they are applied 'at the border', on either the importation or exportation of products.[26]

The *General Agreement on Tariffs and Trade* (GATT)[27] was originally launched in 1947 as a tariff agreement, and its early decades were focused on the negotiation and 'binding' of tariff reductions. This was done in an international context dominated by high tariff rates, which were the result of the widespread application of protectionist measures by individual countries.[28]

To address such 'border measures', the GATT provides, in Article I, for the principle of most-favoured nation treatment (a similar provision is enshrined in Article II of the *General Agreement on Trade in Services* (GATS));[29] and, in Article XI, a general elimination of quantitative restrictions (such as pre-set amounts of the maximum number of products that can enter into a country). The latter is an absolute prohibition, despite the exceptions contained in its second paragraph, the main

---

[26] Federico Ortino, *Basic Legal Instruments for the Liberalisation of Trade: A Comparative Analysis of EC and WTO Law* (Hart Publishing, 2004) 37.

[27] *Marrakesh Agreement Establishing the World Trade Organization*, opened for signature 15 April 1994, 1867 UNTS 3 (entered into force 1 January 1995) annex 1A (*General Agreement on Tariffs and Trade 1994*).

[28] World Trade Organization, 'World Trade Report 2012' (Report, World Trade Organization, July 2012) 39 ('*World Trade Report 2012*').

[29] *Marrakesh Agreement Establishing the World Trade Organization*, opened for signature 15 April 1994, 1867 UNTS 3 (entered into force 1 January 1995), annex 1B (*General Agreement on Trade in Services*).

purpose of which is to ensure market access. According to Trebilcock and Fishbein, if quantitative restrictions at the border could be avoided and trade barriers expressed only in the form of tariffs, the relative transparency of tariffs would allow for their reduction in subsequent rounds of negotiations.[30]

B Behind-the-Border Measures

'Behind-the-border' measures affect products or people once they are within the territory of the relevant country.[31] These measures have raised policy concerns since the establishment of the GATT. As such measures can dilute or even nullify the value of tariff bindings and affect trade, drafters of the GATT included general rules covering broad categories of such measures, notably the 'national treatment' obligation under Article III (granting imported products treatment no less favourable than 'like' domestic products). Over time, more specific disciplines were negotiated, such as those applying to technical barriers to trade (TBT) and sanitary and phytosanitary (SPS) measures (food safety and animal and plant health measures).[32] The GATS also distinguishes between limitations on market access and national treatment, on the one hand, and domestic regulation on the other.[33]

The WTO has increasingly recognised that the effective implementation of good regulatory practices is key to minimising unnecessary barriers to trade.[34] Once a product has crossed the border, regulatory protectionism may impose a disadvantage on imported products by discriminating against them in a manner that is not necessary for the attainment of a genuine public policy objective.[35]

The national treatment principle prohibits discrimination between domestic goods in the implementation of internal regulations and taxation, and therefore prevents countries from engaging in 'regulatory

---

[30] Michael Fishbein and Michael Trebilcock, 'International Trade: Barriers to Trade' in Andrew Guzman and Alan Sykes (eds), *Research Handbook in International Economic Law* (Edward Elgar Publishing, 2007) 1, 15.

[31] Azim Sadikov, 'Border and Behind-the-Border Trade Barriers and Country Exports' (Working Paper No WP/07/292, International Monetary Fund, December 2007) 11 <http://www.imf.org/external/pubs/ft/wp/2007/wp07292.pdf>.

[32] *World Trade Report 2012*, above n 28, 37.

[33] GATS art XVII.

[34] Bollyky, 'Regulatory Coherence in the TPP Talks', above n 2, 174–5.

[35] Alan O. Sykes, 'Regulatory Protectionism and the Law of International Trade' (1999) 66 *University of Chicago Law Review* 1, 3.

protectionism'. Consequently, any tax or regulation that has a discriminatory effect on imports may be suspect under the principle of national treatment.[36] However, suspicion of a regulation is not sufficient ground for determining that it violates the national treatment rule. The rule is infringed only if the requirements of the standard are not met: that is, if the regulation results in like or directly competitive products receiving discriminatory treatment and does not fall within any of the exceptions contained in Article XX of the GATT, or Article XIV of the GATS in the case of services.

How can we secure the benefits of trade liberalisation without infringing the freedom of governments to pursue legitimate regulatory objectives? One of the main problems lies in distinguishing between two different situations:

> In one, a non-protectionist government cannot prevent certain domestic policies from incidentally discriminating against foreign competitors. In the other, a protectionist government uses a legitimate objective as an excuse to design domestic policies that inhibit foreign competition. The challenge is to devise rules which are sensitive to the difference between these two situations, exonerating the former while preventing the latter.[37]

This is one driver for regulatory coherence, which may assist in minimising disguised protectionism.

Nevertheless, regulatory protectionism is a trade barrier that operates in a grey area, because it is not as easy to detect as the application of a tariff or quota. Areas such as food inspection, product labelling and safety guidelines are governed by internal health, safety and technical regulations and have the potential to raise costs for foreign firms in comparison with domestic firms, giving domestic firms and products an advantage.[38]

If a country were not constrained in its use of these measures, they could be widely used to manipulate the terms of trade. The most important agreements to constrain such discrimination are the *Agreement on Technical Barriers to Trade*[39] (TBT Agreement), which deals with

---

[36] Fishbein and Trebilcock, above n 30, 30.

[37] Aaditya Mattoo and Arvind Subramanian, 'Regulatory Autonomy and Multilateral Disciplines: The Dilemma and a Possible Resolution' (1998) 1(2) *Journal of International Economic Law* 303, 304.

[38] Fishbein and Trebilcock, above n 30, 37.

[39] *Marrakesh Agreement Establishing the World Trade Organization*, opened for signature 15 April 1994, 1867 UNTS 3 (entered into force 1 January 1995) annex 1A ('*Agreement on Technical Barriers to Trade*').

technical regulations, standards and procedures for testing and certification; and the *Agreement on Sanitary and Phytosanitary Measures*[40] (SPS Agreement), which deals with food safety and animal health.

As the WTO is not a standard-setting body, the principal means through which it promotes regulatory convergence is by encouraging its members to use international standards. Neither the TBT Agreement nor the SPS Agreement requires WTO members to use international standards. However, although WTO members may adopt SPS measures or technical regulations that depart from international standards,[41] in such cases the burden of proving the necessity of the measure may shift to the country that adopted the regulation that is different from the international standard.

The absence of enforceable international standards may create problems in a world where production is increasingly offshored and international trade flows are dominated by intermediate inputs.[42] Reduced trade barriers, improved communications, and better and cheaper transport have enabled the integration of processes in the production of goods and services. The supply chain is now divided into links to obtain the highest efficiency at each stage, building on the different comparative advantages that each market has. Today few goods and services originate from a single place or supplier, but instead consist of components and parts from multiple suppliers scattered around various countries. These global production models now dominate international trade in intermediate products, which comprise 56 per cent of global trade in goods and 76 per cent of global trade in services.[43]

The Director General of the WTO has also referred to this process, emphasising the ever-increasing integration of the world economy:

> triggered by many factors such as improvements in transportation, in communications and by technological progress. Improved infrastructures and logistics have helped to reduce trade costs and keep them low, thus contributing to the creation of global production networks where countries or industries specialize in tasks.[44]

---

[40] Ibid., annex 1A (‘*Agreement on the Application of Sanitary and Phytosanitary Measures*’).

[41] *World Trade Report 2012*, above n 28, 198.

[42] Ibid., 58.

[43] Thomas Bollyky, ‘Better Regulation for Freer Trade’ (Policy Innovation Memorandum No 22, Council of Foreign Relations, 19 June 2012) 1 <http://www.cfr.org/trade/better-regulation-freer-trade/p28508>.

[44] Pascal Lamy, ‘Global Supply Chains Underline the Importance of Trade Facilitation’ (Speech delivered at Revisiting Trade in a Globalized World –

The existence of this production model is supported by reducing barriers between the various links in the production chain. These production processes should be fully transparent. Predictable environments should be developed to facilitate the actors involved in the complex chain planning coordination, where the costs associated with each link are maintained within margins to maintain the efficiency of the process. Achieving this goal is directly linked with the regulatory policies developed in each country, because each regulatory decision has the potential to make an impact on the levels of competitiveness of the supply chain as a whole. If we suppose that an importing country requires all foreign goods to comply with its national TBT or SPS measures, since this normally would increase the fixed cost of exporting, less productive firms (especially from least developed countries) would not generate enough revenues to cover the higher fixed costs of accessing the foreign market and may therefore exit it.[45]

Thus, some regulations may unnecessarily raise production costs of goods and/or services, reducing efficiency. In a highly integrated market, as we have at present, the loss of competitiveness of a stage can motivate the transfer of production to another market that offers better conditions, which harms not only producers but also countries receiving investment. The effect of this capital flight in developing countries that are not able to access other markets can even lead them to abandon or postpone necessary regulations for the fear of discouraging investment in their country.

This provides another reason to push for regulatory coherence: to establish better or new regulatory policies that maintain or improve the level of competitiveness of an economy by achieving a balance between legitimate policy goals and the tool used to achieve them.

Stakeholders of the supply chain will seek access to the regulatory process and maintain a certain predictive capacity of regulatory changes, for that is required to establish efficient forms of participation, promote transparency, and create rules and regulations under technical criteria that are part of an integrated and consistent system.

Maintaining the benefits of global supply chains:

> will depend on the adequacy, predictability, and efficiency of the regulatory oversight in the countries involved. The mechanisms that ensured accountability for products in the past – tort liability and companies' investments in the

---

Global Value Chains and Their Impact, Chengdu, China, 18 October 2011) <http://www.wto.org/english/news_e/sppl_e/sppl210_e.htm>.

[45] *World Trade Report 2012*, above n 28, 59.

> good reputation of their brands – do not easily extend to intermediate suppliers in countries where access to courts can be limited. Regulation and product standards are essential tools for promoting public health and safety, safeguarding the environment and rights of citizens, and ensuring the proper functioning of markets. But regulating effectively is far more difficult in this new global market …[46]

This new situation has been the final trigger to establish a regulatory coherence process that incorporates tools such as RIAs and advances transparency, and promotes a new way of interacting so as to enable progress.

As we can see, the objectives of domestic regulation and international trade are difficult to reconcile. WTO rules have been effective in limiting discriminatory regulatory measures, but have done little to eliminate the inefficient, unclear, and redundant but non-discriminatory regulations that obstruct international trade. Until the TPP, trade agreements have not, for the most part, improved collaboration among regulatory agencies.[47]

III REGULATORY COHERENCE IN THE TPP: A NEW WAY OF ADDRESSING REGULATORY PROTECTIONISM AND SECURING GLOBAL SUPPLY CHAINS

The previous sections analysed the relationship between regulation and international trade and the evolution of trade barriers where measures such as tariffs and quotas have been replaced by the introduction of regulatory protectionism, which poses a threat to a global supply chain. This scenario has led parties to the TPP negotiations to promote a chapter on regulatory coherence to face these new challenges.

A The TPP and Regulatory Coherence: An Unfinished Chapter

In September 2012, the United States Congressional Research Service report noted that regulatory coherence:

> represents one of the new cross-cutting trade issues added to the TPP negotiations. The goal of regulatory coherence is to ease the conditions and

---

46 Bollyky, 'Better Regulation for Freer Trade', above n 43, 1.
47 Bollyky, 'Regulatory Coherence in the TPP Talks', above n 2, 173.

> costs of trade between TPP countries while affirming the rights of TPP countries to regulate their economies to promote legitimate policy objectives.[48]

The report continues to refer to the statement made by the United States Trade Representative (USTR), who noted that this initiative:

> stems from the proliferation of regulatory and non-tariff barriers, which have become a major hurdle for business gaining access to foreign markets. Some of the goals of the effort are to 'improve regulatory practices, eliminate unnecessary barriers, reduce regional divergence in standards, promote transparency, conduct regulatory processes in a more trade-facilitative manner, eliminate redundancies in testing and certification, and promote cooperation on specific regulatory issues.'[49]

In this sense it has been noted that the main objective of regulatory coherence is 'the harmonization (or at least mutual recognition) of regulatory measures that exert a major influence on international trade'.[50] As a way to put these efforts, negotiations include:

> procedural rules for transparency (public notice and consultation for new regulations); elimination of duplicative and overlapping regulations; rules against anticompetitive practices, particularly for government monopolies and enterprises; greater use of mutual-recognition agreements for services and health and safety regulation; and clear lines of administrative and judicial appeal.[51]

In this same vein, stakeholders such as the TPP Coalition, a group of United States corporations, have expressed in a report by its working group on regulatory consistency that the goal of regulatory coherence is to:

---

48 Ian Fergusson et al., 'The Trans-Pacific Partnership Negotiations and Issues for Congress' (CRS Report for Congress No R42694, Congressional Research Service, 15 April 2013) 41 <http://www.fas.org/sgp/crs/row/R42694.pdf>.

49 Ibid., quoting United States Trade Representative, 'Trans-Pacific Partnership (TPP) Trade Ministers' Report to Leaders' (Press Release, 12 November 2011) <http://www.ustr.gov/about-us/press-office/press-releases/2011/november/trans-pacific-partnership-tpp-trade-ministers'-re>.

50 Claude Bartfield, 'The Trans-Pacific Partnership: A Model for Twenty-First-Century Trade Agreements?' (International Economic Outlook No 2, June 2011, American Enterprise Institute for Public Policy Research) 7 <http://www.aei.org/article/economics/international-economy/the-trans-pacific-partnership/>.

51 Ibid.

> maintain transparent, effective, enforceable and mutually coherent regulatory systems which are both risk and science based, adhere to international best practices, and assure high levels of collaboration among TPP governments and their stakeholders.[52]

The United States government has made clear its interest in regulatory coherence. The Executive Order No. 12866 (EO 12866), issued on 30 September 1993 by President Clinton (Regulatory Planning and Review), includes all the discussed elements of regulatory coherence (although it never mentions that concept). According to the OECD, one of the many stated objectives of EO 12866 is to make the regulatory process more accessible and open to the public.[53] In May 2012, President Barack Obama issued an executive order entitled Promoting International Regulatory Cooperation. The executive order established the creation of an interagency working group, led by the White House Office of Information and Regulatory Affairs, to promote international cooperation in order to reduce unnecessary regulatory differences across borders.[54] Bollyky notes that to meet this objective the working group should engage in four areas of work:

> 1. Focus first on international standards and regulatory burden sharing in the sectors of food, drug and biotechnology. …
> 2. Use trade talks to drive adoption of international standards in these priority sectors. …
> 3. Increase the ability of U.S. regulators to engage in burden sharing with foreign counterparts. …
> 4. Focus on the regional level.[55]

Regarding the fourth point, Bollyky adds that the TPP negotiations provide an excellent opportunity for the aforesaid new working group to improve regulatory cooperation, in foods, drugs and biotechnologies.

---

52 TPP Coalition, 'Regulatory Coherence Working Group Paper', Washington International Trade Association <http://www.wita.org/attachments/calendar events/1130/US%20Chamber-%20PPRegulatoryCoherenceWorkingGroupPaper.pdf>.

53 Organisation for Economic Co-operation and Development, 'Regulatory Reform in the United States: Enhancing Market Openness through Regulatory Reform' (Report, 1999) 11 <http://www.oecd.org/regreform/2756360.pdf>.

54 Cass Sunstein, *Reducing Red Tape: Regulatory Reform Goes International* (1 May 2012) White House Office of Management and Budget <http://www.whitehouse.gov/blog/2012/05/01/reducing-red-tape-regulatory-reform-goes-international>.

55 Bollyky, 'Better Regulation for Freer Trade', above n 43, 2–3.

Since 'U.S. trade officials have already identified improving regulatory coherence as one of their TPP negotiation objectives … [and] TPP parties are also members of APEC, the reception to this model should be favourable',[56] thus establishing a clear link to the regulatory policy promoted by APEC.

An unauthenticated preliminary draft of the TPP's chapter on regulatory coherence – leaked among others by the non-governmental organisation (NGO) Citizens Trade Campaign[57] – starts with a general provisions section that includes several statements regarding the importance of regulation and regulatory process:

ARTICLE X.1: GENERAL PROVISIONS

1. Regulatory coherence includes: [TPP countries should discuss further the appropriate scope for a definition of regulatory coherence]
2. The parties affirm the importance of:
   a. sustaining the benefits of the Agreement through provisions on regulatory coherence, particularly in terms of facilitating increased trade in goods and services and increased investment among the Parties;
   b. ***each Party's sovereign right to identify its regulatory priorities and establish and implement regulatory measures to address these priorities, at the levels that a Party considers appropriate;***
   c. the role that regulation plays in achieving public policy objectives, such as protecting the environment, worker rights, and public and worker health and safety;
   d. a wide range of stakeholder input in the development and implementation of regulatory measures; and
   e. regional regulatory cooperation taking into account the Parties' international obligations.[58]

Significantly, the draft suggests difficulty in agreeing on the general scope of regulatory coherence. Nevertheless, Article X.2.1 of the leaked chapter confirms that the obligation of regulatory coherence is limited to certain regulatory measures ('covered regulatory measures') as defined by each country:

---

56 Ibid.

57 *Trans-Pacific Partnership (TPP) Regulatory Coherence* (4 March 2010) Citizens Trade Campaign <http://www.citizenstrade.org/ctc/wp-content/uploads/2011/10/TransPacificRegulatoryCoherence.pdf> (emphasis added).

58 Ibid., 2 (emphasis added, square bracketed text in original).

> The Parties recognize that regulatory coherence can be facilitated through domestic mechanisms that increase inter-ministerial consultation and coordination associated with processes for developing regulatory measures of general application. The Parties further recognize that engagement among Parties on regulatory matters can be enhanced through ensuring that information on regulatory measures is centrally collected and widely disseminated. Accordingly, each Party shall endeavour to ensure that it has a process or mechanism to facilitate central coordination and review of certain new regulatory measures ('covered regulatory measures') at the central level of government, and should consider establishing and maintaining a national coordinating body for this purpose.[59]

The requirement to subject these measures to the coordination process and to prioritise them lies with each party, which should 'ensure that coverage is significant and not arbitrarily limited in order to avoid application of this Chapter'.[60]

The OECD and APEC did not consider it necessary to specify limits on the measures covered, which is consistent with the voluntary nature of their regulatory proposals. Under the leaked chapter of the TPP, a party could choose to exclude certain rules from the coordination mechanism, in recognition that this mechanism forms part of a set of treaty obligations rather than recommendations. For Kelsey, the TPP proposal significantly transforms the voluntary character of the existing OECD/APEC 'best practices' documents to an apparently enforceable obligation to establish processes and mechanisms. This change is not immediately evident, as the text primarily uses hortatory language.[61]

Nonetheless, as in the APEC–OECD Checklist, presumably this chapter of the TPP will allow countries to choose between establishing mechanisms, processes or a central body for coordination. Whatever the final decision adopted by each state, the characteristics required to generate the efficiency of regulatory coherence in this regard would be as set out in Article X.2(2):

> a. Publicly-available legal or administrative documents that specify institutional elements, and that grant sufficient resources and stature to be credible within the government and with external stakeholders;

---

[59] Ibid.

[60] Ibid., 2–3.

[61] Jane Kelsey, *Preliminary Analysis of the Draft TPP Chapter on Domestic Coherence* (23 October 2011) Citizens Trade Campaign <http://www.citizenstrade.org/ctc/wp-content/uploads/2011/10/TransPacific_RegCoherenceMemo.pdf> 5.

b. the authority to review covered regulatory measures to determine the extent to which the development of such measures adheres to good regulatory practices, which may include but are not limited to those set out in Article X.3 [below], and make recommendations based on that review;
c. an important role in advancing the transparency disciplines set out in Chapter X of this Agreement;
d. the ability to strengthen coordination and consultation among ministries within the government so as to minimize overlap and duplication, prevent the creation of inconsistent requirements across ministries, and ensure development of coherent regulatory approaches by, inter alia, allowing all ministries with an interest in a particular covered regulatory measure to participate in its development;
e. the ability to make recommendations for systemic regulatory reform for consideration by decision-makers; and
f. a periodic public report on its activities, including with respect to specific regulatory measures reviewed, any proposals for systemic regulatory reform, and an update on its own institutional development.[62]

These minimum requirements set an institutional model very similar to that established by the APEC–OECD Checklist for the purposes of ensuring coherent acts by the states. This relationship goes further in the leaked text as Article X.3 has a lengthy description of RIAs:

IMPLEMENTATION OF CORE GOOD REGULATORY PRACTICES

1. Through its national coordinating body, process or mechanism, each Party, in carrying out responsibilities for reviewing covered regulatory measures, should generally encourage relevant regulatory authorities, consistent with domestic law, to conduct regulatory impact assessments (RIAs) when developing covered regulatory measures that exceed a threshold of economic impact established by a Party, to assist in designing a measure to best achieve the Party's objective.
   a. An RIA should identify, among other things:
      (1) the problem and the policy objective that the regulatory authority intends to address, including an assessment of the significance of the problem and a description of the need for regulatory action;
      (2) potentially effective and reasonably feasible alternatives to achieve the policy objective; and

---

[62] *Trans-Pacific Partnership (TPP) Regulatory Coherence,* above n 57, 3 (square bracketed text in original).

(3) where appropriate, the grounds for concluding that the selected alternative achieves the policy objectives in a way that maximizes net benefits, including qualitative benefits, while also considering distributional impact.

b. An RIA should include the following elements:

(1) a consideration of whether, for all aspects of the planned regulatory measure, there is a need to regulate to achieve the policy objective or whether an objective can be met by non-regulatory and/or voluntary means, consistent with domestic law;

(2) an assessment, to the extent feasible and consistent with domestic law, of the costs and benefits of each available alternative, including not to regulate, recognizing that some costs and benefits are difficult to quantify and monetize;

(3) an explanation why the alternative selected is superior to the other available alternatives identified, including, if appropriate, through reference to the relative size of net benefits of the available alternatives; and

(4) decisions based on the best reasonably obtainable scientific, technical, economic, and other information, within the boundaries of the authorities, mandates, and resources of the particular regulatory authority.[63]

The importance that RIAs play in the implementation of coherent regulation is consistent with the express recognition, made in the same provision, of the importance of certain instruments of governance:

> The Parties recognize that these and other Good Regulatory Practice concepts that may be relevant to an RIA analysis are reflected in the APEC–OECD Integrated Checklist on Regulatory Reform and the APEC Information Notes on Good Practices for Technical Regulation.[64]

RIA has been defined as 'a process of systematically identifying and assessing the expected effects of regulatory proposals, using a consistent analytical method, such as benefit/cost analysis'.[65] RIA is a comparative *ex ante* process: it is based on determining the underlying regulatory objectives sought and identifying all the policy interventions that are capable of achieving them. These 'feasible alternatives' must all be

---

[63] Ibid., 4.

[64] Ibid., 5.

[65] Organisation for Economic Co-operation and Development, *Introductory Handbook for Undertaking Regulatory Impact Analysis (RIA)* (October 2008) 3 <http://www.oecd.org/regreform/regulatorypolicy/44789472.pdf> ('*Handbook for RIA*').

assessed, using the same method, to inform decision-makers about the effectiveness and efficiency of different options and enable the most effective and efficient options to be systematically chosen.[66]

The use of RIA promotes informed consideration of the effects of regulations on the market and maximises stakeholder rationality of the decision-making processes on the part of regulators. Thus, the OECD noted 'RIA's most important contribution to the quality of decisions is not the precision of the calculations used, but the action of analysing – questioning, understanding real-world Impacts and exploring assumptions.'[67] This kind of evaluation may even demonstrate that the best decision is not to regulate because of negative externalities such as strong civil society opposition, market failure, or the opening of the country's economy beyond the threshold of what is tolerable.

However, the objective of RIA is not to reduce or minimise the burden of regulation, but to improve its efficiency and act as an aid to stop the tide of new and burdensome rules.[68]

There is no single methodology for RIA but all RIA are based on an analysis of minimum economic rationality, as the 'objective of conducting RIA is to try to ensure that regulation is only made when the benefits of the regulation are larger than the costs it imposes'.[69] It must be emphasised that these benefits and costs should have as a goal social welfare maximisation, which in turn is mutable in different countries using RIA. This has led to a variety of analytical methods that allow governments to better pursue their goals according to their own realities, resources and priorities. This has led to claims that there is no 'right' model of RIA but '[t]he Appropriate path to regulatory reform will depend on the political, cultural and social Characteristics of the Individual Concerned country'.[70] Within the methodologies used by OECD

---

[66] Ibid.

[67] Organisation for Economic Co-operation and Development, *Regulatory Policies in OECD Countries: From Interventionism to Regulatory Governance* (OECD Publishing, 2002) 47 ('*Regulatory Policies in OECD Countries*').

[68] Facultad de Derecho, Universidad de Chile – Centro de Regulación y Competencia [University of Chile School of Law – Centre of Regulation and Competition], *Minuta de Trabajo # 1: Criterios para la Evaluación de Impacto Regulatorio en el Sistema Chileno* [Working Minutes # 1: Criteria for Regulatory Impact Assessment System in Chile] <http://www.regcom.uchile.cl/assets/files/Informes%20y%20Papers/Minuta%20de%20trabajo%201.pdf>.

[69] Organisation for Economic Co-operation and Development, *Handbook for RIA*, above n 65, 10.

[70] Organisation for Economic Co-operation and Development, *Regulatory Policies in OECD Countries*, above n 67, 3.

countries we find the following: 'cost/benefit analysis, cost-effectiveness or cost/efficiency, tax and budget analysis, socio-economic impact analysis, consequence analysis, compliance cost analysis and business impact tests'.[71]

The methodology of cost–benefit analysis is the most widely distributed and also represents the best practice for RIA:

> [w]hat is based on the quantification of costs and benefits in monetary terms and compared in an acceptable time period as which provides a solid basis for comparison of alternatives and to guide decision makers of the potential implications of the different options.[72]

Besides, all the other methodologies recognise in their essence a cost–benefit analysis that has been complemented by specific goals depending on the applicable policy and/or mechanisms that allow comparison with elements that are difficult to assess in monetary terms (which will generate a cost–benefit analysis incomplete but with enough capacity to define the aspects to be taken into consideration by those responsible for public policy).

Governments using RIA, despite differences in methodology, have identified the following as targets of RIA:

1. Improving their understanding of the 'real-world impacts of government action': this obliges governments to weigh the whole dimension of regulatory decisions;[73]
2. 'Integrating multiple public policy objectives': using RIA demonstrates the links between public policy;[74]
3. Improving 'transparency and consultation': RIA processes should include, as a way to integrate all dimensions of regulatory policy, opinion and participation of stakeholders;[75] and
4. Improving 'government accountability': this enables the public to

---

[71] Delia Rodrigo, 'Regulatory Impact Analysis in OECD Countries: Challenges for Developing Countries' (Background Paper, Organisation for Economic Co-operation and Development, June 2005) 17 <http://www.oecd.org/gov/regulatorypolicy/35258511.pdf>.

[72] Organisation for Economic Co-operation and Development, *Handbook for RIA*, above n 65, 10.

[73] Rodrigo, above n 71, 7.

[74] Ibid.

[75] Ibid.

scrutinise government decisions and analyse whether or not these are geared to public welfare.[76]

For the purposes of regulatory coherence, considering the essential inputs of RIAs would lead governments to improve their decision-making processes in regulatory matters. The inclusion in administrative law of the test of economic rationality can increase cooperation between national regulatory agencies and promote international cooperation as it produces comparable models that facilitate the integration of regulatory practices from one country to another. The rational analysis of regulatory measures improves the competitiveness of the country, making it more attractive for foreign investment that consolidates and/or enhances their role in the global supply chain to improve a country's market opening rates.

Article X.3 of the leaked TPP chapter also discusses topics such as the need to promote public access to the rules under consideration, maintain review procedures to determine modifications to or repeal of existing rules, and advance cooperation mechanisms with other members. Article X.3(4) deals with transparency, one of the other declared goals of the TPP:

> Each Party should ensure that relevant regulatory authorities provide appropriate public access to covered regulatory measures and their supporting documentation, regulatory analyses, data, and, where practicable, make this information available online for viewing and reproducibility, in accordance with the transparency disciplines set out in Chapter X of this Agreement.[77]

Transparency and participation are usually associated with the consultation process on the implementation of an RIA. The consultation allows for an 'input' from stakeholders and therefore enables responsible agencies to have empirical data to incorporate into the RIA before implementing regulatory policies. Along with this, the information obtained from the RIA is made available to the public, giving a clearer picture of the regulatory landscape and a guide to understanding the evolution of regulation.[78] Both elements are vital to the decision-making of stakeholders who see the predictability and clarity of regulation essential to making investment decisions that ultimately maintain the functioning of the global supply chains.

---

76 Ibid.

77 *Trans-Pacific Partnership (TPP) Regulatory Coherence*, above n 57, 5.

78 Jacobs, above n 10, 16–19.

Within the context of the TPP negotiations, transparency poses an additional problem because there is no clear delineation of how these consultation processes operate, or if they could be opened to include other stakeholders and governments other than the one planning to regulate. As we will see, this has the potential to introduce distortions and transform regulatory coherence into a process of standards imposition for those countries that have greater bargaining power and turn national regulation into an inefficient mechanism for achieving its ultimate ends.

The final provisions of the leaked TPP chapter include a mechanism for conflict resolution in Article X.8:

> DISPUTE SETTLEMENT
>
> Application of Chapter X [Dispute Settlement] to this Chapter is limited to the obligation to have 'processes or mechanisms to facilitate central coordination and review of certain new regulatory measures.' To establish an actionable breach of this obligation by another Party for purposes of Chapter X, a Party must demonstrate that the other Party (1) violated the obligation and (2) that such violation adversely affected trade and investment between those Parties.[79]

On this point, a report of the United States Congressional Research Service has stated that '[i]t is unclear, how much, if any, of these provisions would be subject to dispute settlement.'[80] For others, subjecting this TPP chapter to dispute resolution would likely discourage participation and the inclusion of strong provisions in this area for the whole agreement.[81] However, the dispute settlement mechanism is – again – limited to the obligation of having processes or mechanisms to facilitate central coordination and review of *certain* new regulatory measures.

In sum, what we know about the proposal for a regulatory coherence chapter in the TPP would commit member states to establish a trading system that:

---

[79] *Trans-Pacific Partnership (TPP) Regulatory Coherence*, above n 57, 7 (square bracketed text in original).

[80] Fergusson et al., 'The Trans-Pacific Partnership Negotiations', above n 1, 37.

[81] Bollyky, 'Regulatory Coherence in the TPP Talks', above n 2, 180.

1. Avoids capricious regulations or merely protectionist endeavours through demanding cost–benefit studies that prove a regulation necessary and the most efficient option;
2. Reduces regulatory barriers that have their origin in the dual certification processes due to the increase of cooperation;
3. Strengthens market access by way of transparency; and
4. Enhances participation in the rule-making process.

For some, this is a less ambitious goal than it should be. The United States Congressional Research Service stresses that this chapter would merely recommend that TPP partner countries establish domestic regulatory structures similar to the United States Office of Information and Regulatory Affairs:

> a venue to vet proposed regulations, and their compliance with domestic law and policy, as well as with trade agreements and other international obligations. Aside from seeking to assure regulatory coherence among various domestic agencies, the proposed mechanism would be *encouraged* to conduct regulatory impact assessments … that would assess the need for a given regulation, conduct cost–benefit analysis, and assess alternatives to regulation.[82]

In the name of effectiveness in reducing unnecessary regulatory heterogeneity, Bollyky suggests an 'integrated approach for regulatory coherence' where regulators and trade officials do not perform their respective businesses in parallel.[83] Therefore, trade negotiators should look to reduce barriers and concern themselves with the adequacy of national regulation, its enforcement, or the need for international cooperation to achieve its objectives.[84] From Bollyky's point of view, the TPP's regulatory coherence chapter should establish a formal joint institute to promote regulatory convergence and cooperation (built on the Australia–New Zealand model). Such an institute would be in charge of preparing common technical regulations and standards, formulating conformity assessment mutual recognition arrangements, assessing and recommending the adoption of international standards, and promoting the sharing of surveillance data and inspection reports through the development of

---

[82] Fergusson et al., 'The Trans-Pacific Partnership Negotiations', above n 1, 37 (emphasis added).

[83] Bollyky, 'Regulatory Coherence in the TPP Talks', above n 2, 179–80.

[84] Ibid.

confidentiality arrangements.[85] The decision to adopt these recommendations would remain with the participating governments, but TPP 'members should commit to decide on whether to adopt these joint recommendations within a fixed period of time and to provide a written, detailed explanation when deciding not to do so'.[86]

The question arises whether this robust infrastructure with a strong mandate would be able to address the difference between development and resources between TPP countries, which could influence their ability to promote or reject a specific proposed standard or regulation.

However, some authors have even criticised the 'less ambitious' procedure on regulatory coherence described in the leaked TPP chapter, as discussed in the next section.

B Fears of Regulatory Coherence: The Problems of Regulatory Sovereignty, Control of State Obligations and Implementation

Referring to the problem of regulatory protectionism, Guzman and Pauwelyn mention that the WTO has faced the same problem and wisely decided not to enter the business of distinguishing good regulations from bad. For them, '[r]ather than demanding that states promote good policy reasons for its regulatory measures the WTO requires only that they be subject to the national treatment obligation. Thus, paragraph 4 of GATT Article III requires that imports receive treatment "no less favourable" than that accorded to like domestic products with respect to regulatory burdens.'[87]

However, public policy objectives are taken into account in WTO law as regards international trade in both goods and services. GATT Article XX and GATS Article XIV provide certain general exceptions from the usual disciplines for particular policy measures that 'are not applied in a manner which would constitute a means of arbitrary or unjustifiable discrimination' between countries where the same/like conditions prevail, 'or a disguised restriction' on international trade/trade in services. GATS Article VI and TBT Article 2.2 can also be regarded as assessing the effectiveness or validity of regulation apart from the question of discrimination in relation to domestic regulation.

The Panel in *EC – Sardines* referred to TBT Article 2.2, affirming that:

---

85 Ibid., 180.

86 Ibid.

87 Andrew Guzman and Joost Pauwelyn, *International Trade Law* (Aspen Publishers, 2009) 257.

> it is up to the Members to decide which policy objectives they wish to pursue and the levels at which they wish to pursue them. At the same time, *these provisions impose some limits on the regulatory autonomy of Members* that decide to adopt technical regulations: Members cannot create obstacles to trade which are unnecessary or which, in their application, amount to arbitrary or unjustifiable discrimination or a disguised restriction on international trade. Thus, the *TBT Agreement, like the GATT 1994, whose objective it is to further, accords a degree of deference with respect to the domestic policy objectives which Members wish to pursue*. At the same time, however, the *TBT Agreement, like the GATT 1994, shows less deference to the means which Members choose to employ to achieve their domestic policy goals*. We consider that it is incumbent upon the respondent to advance the objectives of its technical regulation which it considers legitimate.[88]

While the leaked TPP regulatory coherence chapter seemingly does not speak of 'good and bad' regulations, it still may characterise regulation as unnecessary or ineffective. However, regulatory coherence does not work in the same way as national treatment. National treatment usually requires an *ex post* infringement of the rules governing international trade, whereas regulatory coherence would allow an *ex ante* analysis of the rule, even before its legal existence, without necessarily examining the effects of the measure in a given market. It does this because regulatory coherence aims to judge a given process or tool in achieving an objective of public policy.

This has led to the emergence of voices criticising the incorporation of regulatory coherence into the TPP. These critics are of the view that regulatory coherence curtails the sovereignty of states to regulate domestically. In this sense, Kelsey points out that the above mentioned leaked chapter has nothing to do with trade. It targets the institutional and procedural approach of internal regulation of TPP members. Under the guise of 'coherence', internal regulatory decisions and choices of the state are affected. This is achieved by imposing disciplines on the state's bureaucratic structure, decision processes and evaluative criteria.[89]

Kelsey's objections apply to three key areas. First, the way regulatory coherence can affect other international obligations assumed by states. Second, the burden imposed on governments to pursue a reduction of

---

88 Panel Report, *European Communities – Trade Description on Sardines* ('*EC – Sardines*'), WTO Doc WT/DS231/R and Corr 1, [7.120] (adopted 23 October 2002) as modified by Appellate Body Report WTO Doc WT/DS231/AB/R (emphasis added).

89 Kelsey, 'Preliminary Analysis of the Draft TPP Chapter on Domestic Coherence', above n 61, 1.

regulatory burden on business, and third, the creation of an environment that facilitates the exercise of external pressure on regulators.

On the first point, Kelsey says there is a vast literature that documents the conflict between free trade obligations and state obligations in relation to human rights, the environment, and indigenous and labour rights. The TPP, and the leaked chapter in particular, may impose disciplines that extend beyond the boundaries of the agreement and create an even greater risk that states are unable to comply with these international obligations.[90]

On the second point, as Kelsey points out, preparation of the level of documents required for the RIAs and the publication obligations would impose burdens that can be huge in the budgetary context of low-income developing countries that have more pressing demands on their limited resources.[91] A true cost–benefit analysis should extend to costs imposed on government and not just examine the costs/benefits for businesses.

On the third point, Kelsey remarks that even if the Agreement promotes various ways to achieve 'successful collaboration among Parties and their respective stakeholders', if adopted, it would create diverse opportunities for foreign states, corporations and lobby groups to pressure national governments about proposed or existing domestic regulation.[92]

Notwithstanding the above-mentioned criticisms, neither the draft leaked TPP chapter nor the APEC–OECD Checklist defines an RIA methodology. Therefore it is up to each state to delineate its own RIA methodology and its costs. Plus, it seems inappropriate to establish *per se* a link between the establishment of a mechanism for regulatory coherence and a threat to the fulfilment of other international obligations. It must be recognised that the lack of a global mechanism for the resolution of conflicting international obligations is a problem that is pervasive in international law and does not originate from the implementation of regulatory coherence. In fact, a modern RIA methodology could be beneficial in this regard, to the extent that an RIA requires an analysis of current regulations to prevent the enactment of rules contrary to other standards and obligations.

---

90 Ibid., 2.
91 Ibid., 3.
92 Ibid., 5.

CONCLUSION: QUESTIONS LEFT UNANSWERED

We still do not know what will be contained in the final TPP chapter on regulatory coherence. It has been reported that it will probably focus on intra-government regulatory reform rather than inter-governmental regulatory coherence. This is likely a result of United States regulators having resisted allowing their domestic responsibilities to be subject to potentially increased restrictions in international trade agreements, and conversely, NGOs and other TPP members are suspicious of the negotiations in this new area.[93]

Nevertheless, we can conclude that regulatory coherence is a process to generate standards that meet the criteria of: economic rationality through participatory methods; coordination through an organisation, procedure or mechanism at a governmental level that checks the consistency of the proposed domestic rule with the regulatory system as a whole; and integration with international peers. The key elements of this 'regulatory coherence' would be economic rationality (regulatory impact assessment), transparency and participation, and governmental coordination and review.

The final TPP text will allow us to answer some very important questions: is this chapter intended to create 'regulatory coherence' or a 'regulatory network'? If the former, which degree or type of convergence?

Regarding network effects, Raustiala concludes that this concept:

> helps illuminate why both powerful and weak jurisdictions which are members of networks might, as a concomitant of cooperation with one another, engage in the export and import of regulatory frameworks. Networks are characterized by extensive sharing of information, coordinating enforcement efforts, and joint policymaking activities. These activities plausibly exhibit network effects: the more regulatory agencies that participate in coordinating and reciprocating enforcement efforts, for example, the better off are all the other agencies.[94]

On the other hand, what will be the role of regulatory 'importers' or 'exporters'? Will it be a form of cooperation or the dissemination of 'the

---

[93] Bollyky, 'Regulatory Coherence in the TPP Talks', above n 2, 180.

[94] Kal Raustiala, 'The Architecture of International Cooperation: Transgovernmental Networks and the Future of International Law' (2002) 43 *Virginia Journal of International Law* 1, 64.

regulatory gospel' of a 'regulation-exporting' state?[95] Kelsey calls attention to the fact that the genesis of the draft chapter in regulatory coherence is the Anglo-American model of deregulation ('light-touch pro-market regulation and self-regulation') prevailing in the United States, Australia and New Zealand since the 1980s.[96] A truly coherent approach would not allow those or any other country to promote requirements on all TPP parties without previously assessing if they effectively comply with those regulations. A reality check should be performed comparing proposed rules and current practice before determining if other TPP countries have regulations that do not comply with new regulatory requirements.

The notion of 'coherence' poses some questions of influence and legitimacy: which standard will dominate in a given situation and why? In a regulatory asymmetric world, will the standard of the most powerful actor always prevail? Will this increase the tendency towards convergence, harmonisation or a dominant regulatory standard?[97]

As Bollyky points out:

> WTO transparency obligations on services regulations have been largely ignored, with developed countries being the worst offenders. High-income countries have been slow in many sectors to adopt international standards. Limited adoption of international standards undermines their relevance, particularly in the low- and middle-income countries least equipped to develop their own standards. Businesses increasingly rely on private or non-profit organization standards, third-party certifications, and their own safety and quality management systems to regulate their suppliers. The resulting incoherence increases trade costs and undermines regulatory compliance and enforcement.[98]

Regulatory coherence could play a major role in a wide range of subject areas in the TPP including technical barriers to trade, intellectual property rights, financial services, investment, competition policy, consumer rights and recognition of professional services qualifications.[99]

---

95 See Anne-Marie Slaughter, *A New World Order* (Princeton University Press, 2004) 172–77.

96 Kelsey, 'Preliminary Analysis of the Draft TPP Chapter on Domestic Coherence', above n 61, 3.

97 Ibid., 66.

98 Bollyky, 'Regulatory Coherence in the TPP Talks', above n 2, 173.

99 See Andrew Stoler, Peter Pedersen and Sebastián Herreros, *Negotiating Trade Agreements for the 21st Century* (ECLAC – Division of International Trade and Integration, Serie Comercio Internacional No 116, Santiago, October 2012) 25–26.

If this agreement seeks to promote deep economic integration and support modern production-sharing supply chains in the region, parties must guarantee clarity on the nature of regulatory coherence and its effect on behind-the-border barriers to trade. Moreover, negotiators should bear in mind that coherence can be facilitated by a variety of devices, such as harmonised rules and regulations, mutual recognition agreements, and special provisions or institutions within the treaty. These devices should be carefully selected to prevent undue influence over national policy and regulatory decisions.

Bibliography

BOOKS

Antons, Christoph, Michael Blakeney and Christopher Heath (eds), *Intellectual Property Harmonisation with ASEAN and APEC* (Kluwer Law International, 2004).

Baldwin, Richard and Patrick Low (eds), *Multilateralizing Regionalism: Challenges for the Global Trading System* (Cambridge University Press, 2009).

Baldwin, Richard, Pertti Haaparanta and Jaakko Kiander (eds), *Expanding Membership of the European Union* (Cambridge University Press, 1995).

Bartels, Lorand and Federico Ortino (eds), *Regional Trade Agreements and the WTO Legal System* (Oxford University Press, 2006).

Bath, Vivienne and Luke Nottage (eds), *Foreign Investment and Dispute Resolution Law and Practice in Asia* (Routledge, 2011).

Berger, Klaus Peter, *Private Dispute Resolution in International Business: Negotiation, Mediation, Arbitration* (Kluwer Law International, 2006).

Bethlehem, Daniel et al. (eds), *The Oxford Handbook of International Trade Law* (Oxford University Press, 2009).

Bhagwati, Jagdish, *Free Trade Today* (Princeton University Press, 2002).

Bhagwati, Jagdish and Arvind Panagariya (eds), *The Economics of Preferential Trade Agreements* (AEI Press, 1996).

Burri, Mira and Thomas Cottier, *Trade Governance in the Digital Age* (Cambridge University Press, 2012).

Cadot, Oliver et al. (eds), *The Origin of Goods* (Oxford University Press, 2006).

Capling, Ann, *All the Way with the USA* (University of New South Wales Press, 2005).

Cave, Martin, Chris Doyle and William Webb, *Essentials of Modern Spectrum Management* (Cambridge University Press, 2007).

Charlesworth, Hilary et al., *No Country is an Island: Australia and International Law* (University of New South Wales Press, 2006).

Conradi, Mike (ed.), *Communications Law Handbook* (Bloomsbury Professional, 2009).

Crawford, Susan, *Captive Audience – The Telecom Industry and Monopoly Power in the New Gilded Age* (Yale University Press, 2013).
de Melo, Jaime and Arvind Panagariya (eds), *New Dimensions in Regional Integration* (Cambridge University Press, 1993).
Destler, I.M., *American Trade Politics* (Institute for International Economics, 2005).
Dolzer, Rudolf and Christoph Schreuer, *Principles of International Investment Law* (Oxford University Press, 2008).
Douglas, Zachary, *The International Law of Investment Claims* (Cambridge University Press, 2009).
Drahos, Peter and John Braithwaite, *Information Feudalism: Who Owns the Knowledge Economy?* (Earthscan, 2002).
Elms, Deborah, *The Trans-Pacific Partnership: The Challenges of Untangling the Noodle Bowl* (International Negotiation, forthcoming 2013).
Guzman, Andrew and Alan Sykes (eds), *Research Handbook in International Economic Law* (Edward Elgar Publishing, 2007).
Guzman, Andrew and Joost Pauwelyn, *International Trade Law* (Aspen Publishers, 2009).
Heath, Christopher and Anselm Kamperman Sanders (eds), *Intellectual Property and Free Trade Agreements* (Hart Publishing, 2007).
Horn, Norbert and Stefan Kröll (eds), *Arbitrating Foreign Investment Disputes* (Kluwer Law International, 2004).
Hufbauer, Gary and Jeffrey Schott, *NAFTA Revisited: Opportunities and Challenges* (International Institute for Economics, 2005).
Hufbauer, Gary, Steve Charnovitz and Jisun Kim, *Global Warming and the World Trading System* (Peterson Institute for International Economics, 2009).
Jan van den Berg, Albert (ed.), *50 Years of the New York Convention* (Kluwer Law International, 2009).
Kelsey, Jane (ed.), *No Ordinary Deal. Unmasking the Trans-Pacific Partnership Free Trade Agreement* (Allen & Unwin, 2010).
Legg, Michael (ed.), *The Future of Dispute Resolution* (LexisNexis Butterworths, 2012).
Lester, Simon and Bryan Mercurio (eds), *Bilateral and Regional Trade Agreements: Case Studies* (Cambridge University Press, 2009).
Lester, Simon and Bryan Mercurio (eds), *Bilateral and Regional Trade Agreements: Commentary and Analysis* (Cambridge University Press, 2009).
Lim, C.L., Deborah Elms and Patrick Low (eds), *The Trans-Pacific Partnership: A Quest for a Twenty-first Century Trade Agreement* (Cambridge University Press, 2012).

Litan, Robert and Hal Singer, *The Need for Speed – a New Framework for Telecommunications Policy for the 21st Century* (Brookings Institution Press, 2013).

Low, Patrick and Andrew Stoler (eds), *Managing the Challenges of WTO Participation* (Cambridge University Press, 2005).

Macrory, Patrick, Arthur Appleton and Michael Plummer (eds), *The World Trade Organization: Legal, Economic and Political Analysis* (Springer, 2005).

Marchetti, Juan and Martin Roy (eds), *Opening Markets for Trade in Services: Countries and Sectors in Bilateral and WTO Negotiations* (Cambridge University Press, 2008).

Ortino, Federico, *Basic Legal Instruments for the Liberalisation of Trade: A Comparative Analysis of EC and WTO Law* (Hart Publishing, 2004).

Raworth, Philip, *Trade in Services: Global Regulation and the Impact on Key Service Sectors* (Oceana Publications, 2005).

Ricketson, Sam, *The Berne Convention for the Protection of Literary and Artistic Works: 1886–1986* (Kluwer, 1987).

Sauvant, Karl (ed.), *Yearbook on International Investment Law & Policy 2010–2011* (Oxford University Press, 2012).

Schill, Stephan, *The Multilateralization of International Investment Law* (Cambridge University Press, 2009).

Schneiderman, David, *Constitutionalizing Economic Globalization: Investment Rules and Democracy's Promise* (Cambridge University Press, 2008).

Schott, Jeffrey, Barbara Kotschwar and Julia Muir, *Understanding the Trans-Pacific Partnership* (Peterson Institute for International Economics, 2013).

Slaughter, Anne-Marie, *A New World Order* (Princeton University Press, 2004).

Steger, Debra (ed.), *Redesigning the World Trade Organization for the Twenty-first Century* (Centre for International Governance Innovation, 2010).

Trakman, Leon and Nicola Ranieri (eds), *Regionalism in International Investment Law* (Oxford University Press, forthcoming 2013).

Van Damme, Isabelle, *Treaty Interpretation by the WTO Appellate Body* (Oxford University Press, 2009).

Voon, Tania et al. (eds), *Public Health and Plain Packaging of Cigarettes: Legal Issues* (Edward Elgar Publishing, 2012).

Weber, Rolf and Mira Burri, *Classification of Services in the Digital Economy* (Springer, 2012).

Weeramantry, J. Romesh, *Treaty Interpretation in Investment Arbitration* (Oxford University Press, 2012).

Weiss, Linda, Elizabeth Thurbon and John Mathews (eds), *How to Kill a Country: Australia's Devastating Trade Deal with the United States* (Allen & Unwin, 2004).

Winham, Gilbert, *International Trade and the Tokyo Round Negotiation* (Princeton University Press, 1986).

Wolfrum, R. (ed.), *The Max Planck Encyclopedia of Public International Law* (online) (Oxford University Press, 2008).

World Bank, *World Development Report 1992: Development and the Environment* (Oxford University Press, 1992).

JOURNAL ARTICLES

Adlung, Rudolf and Sébastien Miroudot, 'Poison in the Wine? Tracing GATS-Minus Commitments in Regional Trade Agreements' (2012) 46(5) *Journal of World Trade* 1045.

Baldwin, Richard, 'Multilateralizing Regionalism: Spaghetti Bowls as Building Blocks on the Path to Global Free Trade' (2006) 29(11) *The World Economy* 1451.

Bartels, Lorand, 'The Trade and Development Policy of the European Union' (2007) 18 *European Journal of International Law* 715.

Benkler, Yochai, 'Wikileaks and the PROTECT-IP Act: A New Public-Private Threat to the Internet Commons' (2011) 140 *Daedelus* 154.

Bigdeli, Sadeq Z., 'Will the "Friends of Climate" Emerge in the WTO? The Prospects of Applying the "Fisheries Subsidies" Model to Energy Subsidies' (2008) 1 *Climate Change Law Review* 78.

Bjorklund, Andrea, 'The Emerging Civilization of Investment Arbitration' (2009) 113 *Penn State Law Review* 1269.

Boddicker, Joseph, 'Whose Dictionary Controls?: Recent Challenges to the Term "Investment" in ICSID Arbitration' (2010) 25 *American University International Law Review* 1031.

Borgen, Christopher, 'Resolving Treaty Conflicts' (2005) 37 *George Washington Law Review* 573.

Brower, Charles N. and Lee A. Steven, 'NAFTA Chapter 11: Who then Should Judge? Developing the International Rule of Law under NAFTA Chapter 11' (2001) 2 *Chicago Journal of International Law* 193.

Brown, Drusilla K. et al., 'Computational Analysis of the US FTAs with Central America, Australia and Morocco' (2005) 28 *World Economy* 1441.

Burda, Julian, 'A New Step Towards a Single and Common Definition of an Investment? – Comments on the Romak versus Uzbekistan Decision' (2010) 11(6) *Journal of World Investment and Trade* 1085.

Burke-White, William W. and Andreas von Staden, 'Investment Protection in Extraordinary Times: The Interpretation and Application of Non-Precluded Measures Provisions in Bilateral Investment Treaties' (2008) 48 *Virginia Journal of International Law* 307.

Burrell, Robert and Kimberlee Weatherall, 'Exporting Controversy? Reactions to the Copyright Provisions of the US–Australia Free Trade Agreement: Lessons for US Trade Policy' (2008) 2 *University of Illinois Journal of Law, Technology and Policy* 259.

Chapman, Simon and Becky Freeman, 'The Cancer Emperor's New Clothes: Australia's Historic Legislation for Plain Tobacco Packaging' [2010] *British Medical Journal* 340.

Chase, Claude, 'Norm Conflicts between WTO Covered Agreements – Real, Apparent or Avoided?' (2012) 61(4) *International and Comparative Law Quarterly* 791.

Choi, Won-Mog, 'Aggressive Regionalism in Korea–U.S. FTA: The Present and Future of Korea's FTA Policy' (2009) 12(3) *Journal of International Economic Law* 595.

Choi, Won-Mog, 'Defragmenting Fragmented Rules of Origin of RTAs: A Building Block to Global Free Trade' (2010) 13(1) *Journal of International Economic Law* 111.

Cremades, Bernardo, 'Resurgence of the Calvo Doctrine in Latin America' (2006) 7 *Business Law International* 53.

Dodge, William, 'Loewen v. United States: Trials and Errors under NAFTA Chapter 11' (2002) 52 *DePaul Law Review* 563.

Drahos, Peter, 'BITs and BIPs: Bilateralism in Intellectual Property' (2001) 4 *Journal of World Intellectual Property* 791.

Drahos, Peter and David Henry, 'The Free Trade Agreement between Australia and the United States' [2004] *British Medical Journal* 1271.

Drezner, Daniel, 'Globalization and Policy Convergence' (2001) 3(1) *International Studies Review* 53.

Driessen, Bart and Folkert Graafsma, 'EC's Wonderland: An Overview of the Pan-European Harmonized Origin Protocols' (1999) 33 *Journal of World Trade* 19.

Elliot, R.J.R. and K. Shimamoto, 'Are ASEAN Countries Havens for Japanese Pollution-Intensive Industries?' (2008) 31 *World Economy* 236.

Eskeland, G.S. and A.E. Harrison, 'Moving to Greener Pastures? Multinationals and the Pollution Haven Hypothesis' (2003) 70 *Journal of Development Economics* 1.

Estevadeordal, Antoni, 'Negotiating Preferential Market Access: The Case of the North American Free Trade Agreement' (2000) 34(1) *Journal of World Trade* 141.

Estevadeoral, Antoni and Kati Suominen, 'Rules of Origin in Preferential Trading Agreements: Is All Well with the Spaghetti Bowl in the Americas?'(2005) 5(2) *Economía* 63.

Fliess, Barbara and Joy Kim, 'Non-tariff Barriers Facing Trade in Selected Environmental Goods and Associated Services' (2008) 42(3) *Journal of World Trade* 535.

Flynn, Sean et al., 'The US Proposal for an Intellectual Property Chapter in the Trans-Pacific Partnership Agreement' (2012) 28 *American University International Law Review* 105.

Franck, Susan, 'Empirically Evaluating Claims about Investment Treaty Arbitration' (2007) 86 *North Carolina Law Review* 1.

Franck, Susan, 'Rationalizing Costs in Investment Treaty Arbitration' (2011) 88 *Washington University Law Review* 769.

Freeman, Becky, Simon Chapman and Matthew Rimmer, 'The Case for the Plain Packaging of Tobacco Products' (2008) 103(4) *Addiction* 580.

French, Hillary, 'Capital Flows and the Environment' (1998) 22 *Foreign Policy in Focus* 3.

Gantz, David, 'An Appellate Mechanism for Review of Arbitral Decisions in Investor–State Disputes: Prospects and Challenges' (2006) 39 *Vanderbilt Journal of Transnational Law* 39.

Gathii, James Thuo, 'Process and Substance in WTO Reform' (2004) 56 *Rutgers Law Review* 885.

Ginsburg, Jane, 'International Copyright: From a "Bundle" of National Copyright Laws to a Supranational Code?' (2000) 47 *Journal of the Copyright Society of USA* 265.

Graewert, Tim, 'Conflicting Laws and Jurisdictions in the Dispute Settlement Process of Regional Trade Agreements and the WTO' (2008) 1 *Contemporary Asia Arbitration Journal* 287.

Grossman, Gene and Alan Krueger, 'Economic Growth and the Environment' (1994) 110(2) *Quarterly Journal of Economics* 353.

Harbaugh, William, Arik Levinson and David Molloy Wilson, 'Reexamining the Empirical Evidence for Environmental Kuznets Curve' (2002) 84(3) *The Review of Economics and Statistics* 541.

Hillman, Jennifer, 'Conflicts Between Dispute Settlement Mechanisms in Regional Trade Agreements and the WTO – What Should the WTO Do' (2009) 42 *Cornell International Law Journal* 193.

Hindelang, Steffen, 'Bilateral Investment Treaties, Custom and a Healthy Investment Climate – The Question of Whether BITs Influence Customary International Law Revisited' (2004) 5 *Journal of World Investment and Trade* 789.

Kelsey, Jane, 'New-Generation Free Trade Agreements Threaten Progressive Tobacco and Alcohol Policies' (2012) 107(10) *Addiction* 1719.

Krueger, Dana, 'The Combat Zone: Mondev International, Ltd v. United States and the Backlash against NAFTA Chapter 11' (2003) 21 *Boston University International Law Journal* 399.

Kurtz, Jürgen, 'Adjudging the Exceptional at International Investment Law: Security, Public Order, and Financial Crisis' (2010) 59 *International and Comparative Law Quarterly* 325.

Kurtz, Jürgen, 'Australia's Rejection of Investor–State Arbitration: Causation, Omission and Implication' (2012) 27 *ICSID Review* 65.

Kwakwa, Edward, 'Reflections on "Development," "Developing Countries" and the "Progressive Development" of International Trade and Intellectual Property Law' (2011–12) 40 *Denver Journal of International Law and Policy* 221.

Levine, David, 'Transparency Soup: the ACTA Negotiating Process and "Black Box" Lawmaking' (2011) 26 *American University Law Review* 811.

Lewis, Meredith Kolsky, 'Expanding the P-4 Agreement into a Broader Trans-Pacific Partnership: Implications and Opportunities' (2009) 4 *Asian Journal of WTO and International Health Law and Policy* 401.

Lewis, Meredith Kolsky, 'The Trans-Pacific Partnership: New Paradigm or Wolf in Sheep's Clothing?' (2011) 34 *Boston College International and Comparative Law Review* 27.

Lewis, Meredith Kolsky, 'Dissent as Dialectic: Horizontal and Vertical Disagreement in WTO Dispute Settlement' (2012) 48 *Stanford Journal of International Law* 1.

Lovely, Mary and David Popp, 'Trade, Technology, and the Environment: Does Access to Technology Promote Environmental Regulation?' (2011) 61 *Journal of Environmental Economics and Management* 16.

Marceau, Gabrielle, 'Conflicts of Norms and Conflicts of Jurisdictions: The Relationship between the WTO Agreement and MEAs and Other Treaties' (2001) 35(6) *Journal of World Trade* 1081.

Mattoo, Aaditya and Arvind Subramanian, 'Regulatory Autonomy and Multilateral Disciplines: The Dilemma and a Possible Resolution' (1998) 1(2) *Journal of International Economic Law* 303.

McLachlan, Campbell, 'Investment Treaties and General International Law' (2008) 57 *International and Comparative Law Quarterly* 361.

Mitchell, Andrew, 'Towards Compatibility: The Future of Electronic Commerce Within the Global Trading System' (2001) 4 *Journal of International Economic Law* 663.

Mitchell, Andrew and David Heaton, 'The Inherent Jurisdiction of WTO Tribunals: The Select Application of Public International Law Required by the Judicial Function' (2010) 31 *Michigan Journal of International Law* 559.

Mortenson, Julian Davis, 'The Meaning of "Investment": ICSID's Travaux and the Domain of International Investment Law' (2010) 51(1) *Harvard International Law Journal* 257.

Nottage, Luke and Kate Miles, '"Back to the Future" for Investor–State Arbitrations: Revising Rules in Australia and Japan to Meet Public Interests' (2009) 26 *Journal of International Arbitration* 25.

Outterson, Kevin, 'Smoking and the First Amendment' (2011) 365 *The New England Journal of Medicine* 2351.

Pauwelyn, Joost and Luiz Eduardo Salles, 'Forum Shopping Before International Tribunals: (Real) Concerns, (Im)Possible Solutions' (2009) 42 *Cornell International Law Journal* 77.

Porter, M. and C. van der Linde, 'Toward a New Conception of the Environment–Competitiveness Relationship' (1995) 9 *Journal of Economic Perspectives* 97.

Raustiala, Kal, 'The Architecture of International Cooperation: Transgovernmental Networks and the Future of International Law' (2002) 43 *Virginia Journal of International Law* 1.

Reinisch, August, 'How Narrow Are Narrow Dispute Settlement Clauses in Investment Treaties?' (2011) 2 *Journal of International Dispute Settlement* 115.

Schreuer, Christoph, 'Fair and Equitable Treatment in Arbitral Practice' (2005) 6 *Journal of World Investment and Trade* 357.

Shan, Wenhua, 'From "North–South Divide" to "Private–Public Debate": Revival of the Calvo Doctrine and the Changing Landscape in International Investment Law' (2007) 27 *Northwestern Journal of International Law and Business* 631.

Sykes, Alan, 'Regulatory Protectionism and the Law of International Trade' (1999) 66 *University of Chicago Law Review* 1.

Trakman, Leon, 'Legal Traditions and International Commercial Arbitration' (2006) 17 *American Review of International Arbitration* 1.

Trakman, Leon, 'Foreign Direct Investment: Hazard or Opportunity?' (2009) 41 *George Washington International Law Review* 1.

Trakman, Leon, 'Foreign Direct Investment: An Australian Perspective' (2010) 13 *International Trade and Business Law Review* 31.

Trakman, Leon, 'Choosing Domestic Courts over Investor–State Arbitration: Australia's Repudiation of the Status Quo' (2012) 35 *University of New South Wales Law Journal* 979.

Trakman, Leon, 'Investor State Arbitration or Local Courts: Will Australia Set a New Trend?' (2012) 46 *Journal of World Trade* 83.

Trakman, Leon, 'The ICSID under Siege' (2012) 45 *Cornell International Law Journal* (forthcoming).

Vandevelde, Kenneth, 'Model Bilateral Investment Treaties: The Way Forward' (2011) 18 *Southwestern Journal of International Law* 307.

Voon, Tania, 'UNESCO and the WTO: A Clash of Cultures?' (2006) 55 *International and Comparative Law Quarterly* 635.

Voon, Tania, 'Discrimination in International Mobile Roaming Regulation: Implications of WTO Law' (2013) 16(1) *Journal of International Economic Law* 91.

Voon, Tania and Andrew Mitchell, 'Open for Business? China's Telecommunications Service Market and the WTO' (2010) 13(2) *Journal of International Economic Law* 321.

Voon, Tania and Andrew Mitchell, 'International Trade Law Implications of Australia's National Broadband Network' (2011) 35(2) *Melbourne University Law Review* 578.

Voon, Tania and Andrew Mitchell, 'Time to Quit? Assessing International Investment Claims Against Plain Tobacco Packaging in Australia' (2011) 14(3) *Journal of International Economic Law* 1.

Vranes, Erich, 'The Definition of "Norm Conflict" in International Law and Legal Theory' (2006) 17 *European Journal of International Law* 395.

Weatherall, Kimberlee, 'ACTA as a New Kind of International IP Lawmaking' (2011) 26(3) *American University International Law Review* 839.

Weatherall, Kimberlee, 'Politics, Compromise, Text, and the Failures of the Anti-Counterfeiting Trade Agreement' (2011) 33 *Sydney Law Review* 229.

Weatherall, Kimberlee 'Evaluating SOPA: Who Should Enforce IP Online?' (2012) 62(4) *Telecommunications Journal of Australia* 59.1.

Weatherall, Kimberlee, 'Three Lessons from ACTA and its Political Aftermath' (2012) 35 *Suffolk Transnational Law Review* 575.

Weber, Rolf, 'Digital Trade in WTO-Law – Taking Stock and Looking Ahead' (2010) 5 *Asian Journal of WTO & International Health Law & Policy* 1.

Westcott, Thomas, 'Foreign Investment Issues in the Australia–United States Free Trade Agreement' (2005) *Economic Roundup* 69.

Yang, Songling, 'The Key Role of the WTO in Settling its Jurisdictional Conflicts with RTAs' (2012) 11 *Chinese Journal of International Law* 281.

Yu, Peter, 'Currents and Cross-Currents in the International Intellectual Property Regime' (2004) 38 *Loyola of Los Angeles Law Review* 323.

Yu, Peter, 'TRIPS Enforcement and Developing Countries' (2011) 26 *American University International Law Review* 727.

Yu, Peter, 'Six Secret (and Now Open) Fears of ACTA' (2011) 64 *Southern Methodist University Law Review* 975.

Yu, Peter, 'The Alphabet Soup of Transborder Intellectual Property Enforcement' (2012) 60 *Drake Law Review Discourse* 16.

Index

agriculture 106–130, 114–16, 118, 126
  see also WTO: *Agreement on Agriculture*
Agreement on the Application of Sanitary and Phytosanitary Measures
  see SPS Agreement
Agreement on Subsidies and Countervailing Measures
  see SCM Agreement
Agreement on Technical Barriers to Trade
  see TBT Agreement
Albania 14
Almeida, Juliana 118
APEC 3, 46, 128–9, 180, 218, 221, 231, 235–8, 247–50, 258
APEC–OPEC Integrated Checklist on Regulatory Reform 235–8, 248–9, 258
Argentina 24, 165, 167, 190, 196
ASEAN 13, 38, 45–7, 61–4, 72, 157
  ASEAN–Australia–New Zealand Free Trade Agreement 64, 157, 160
  ASEAN–China Regional Trade Agreement 17, 20
  ASEAN Free Trade Area 17–18, 25
  ASEAN–Korea Regional Trade Agreement 17
  Free Trade Agreement of the Asia-Pacific 46
  Regional Comprehensive Economic Partnership 3
Association of Southeast Asian Nations
  see ASEAN
Asia-Pacific Economic Cooperation forum
  see APEC
Australia 51, 61, 63, 66, 87–9, 107–8, 128, 135, 137, 150–151, 156, 159, 164–8, 208, 219, 223, 226, 228, 236, 255, 260
  ASEAN–Australia–New Zealand Free Trade Agreement 64, 157, 160
  Australia–Chile Free Trade Agreement 168
  Australia–Hong Kong Agreement on the Promotion and Protection of Investments 89, 200
  Australia–Malaysia Free Trade Agreement 146–7, 157, 160, 166–7, 181–2
  Australia–New Zealand Free Trade Agreement 17, 64
  Australia–Singapore Free Trade Agreement 17
  Australia–Thailand Free Trade Agreement 168
  AUSFTA 5, 16, 46, 65, 86, 119–20, 133, 159–60, 172, 174, 181, 183, 189, 194, 210, 214
  investor-state dispute settlement 89–93, 180–89, 199–201, 203–205,
  RCEP 47
  tobacco 75–7, 82–6, 89–90, 95, 103

Bahrain 16
Berne Convention 68–70
bilateral investment treaties
  see international investment law
Bollyky, Thomas 246–7, 255, 260
Bosnia and Herzegovina 14
Brazil 24, 70, 77, 165, 203
Brunei 45, 52, 107, 116, 119, 156, 160, 208

Canada 19, 24, 52, 108, 112, 120, 123, 133, 137, 150–151, 156, 163, 179, 187, 201, 208, 223
  Canada–Chile Free Trade Agreement 15, 160–61
  Canada–Peru Free Trade Agreement 160–61
  NAFTA 13, 14, 15–16, 38, 77, 119, 122, 160–61
Chan, Margaret 102
Chile 14–15, 24–5, 40, 43–5, 77, 107, 115, 119, 133, 156, 158, 168–9, 208, 214, 219
  Australia–Chile Free Trade Agreement 168
  Canada–Chile Free Trade Agreement 15, 160–61
  Chile–China Free Trade Agreement 25
  Chile–EU Free Trade Agreement 18, 169, 172
  Chile–Japan Free Trade Agreement 16
  Chile–Korea Free Trade Agreement 171–2
  Chile–United States Free Trade Agreement 15, 44, 145–6
China 20, 25, 45–7, 60–61, 63–4, 70, 77, 144, 180, 194, 228
  ASEAN–China Regional Trade Agreement 17, 20
  Chile–China Free Trade Agreement 25
  China–Singapore Free Trade Agreement 144
Chinese Taipei 133
climate change
  see environment
Colombia 15, 24, 42, 57, 133
Costa Rica 133
COMESA 17–18
CITES 211, 216–17
Crawford, Jo-ann 116
Croatia 14
Cuba 85

developing countries 7, 24, 28–49, 192–3, 197–8, 212–15, 218–19, 243
Doha Development Round
  see WTO: Doha Round
Dominican Republic 85

ECOWAS 17–18
Ecuador 24, 94
environment 44, 47, 207–230
European Union (EU) 3, 4, 13, 14–15, 51, 70–71, 133–4, 137, 142–3, 152, 158, 177–9, 222, 227–8, 232–3
  Central America–EU Free Trade Agreement 169–70
  Chile–EU Free Trade Agreement 18, 169, 172
  EU–Mexico Free trade Agreement 18, 169
  European Parliament 66, 87
  EU–Peru Free Trade Agreement 174
  EU–South Korea Free Trade Agreement 18, 174–5
  Generalized System of Preferences 14

Faunce, Thomas 92
Fishbein, Michael 240
fisheries 218–9
Flynn, Sean 87
France 151
free trade agreements 11–12, 15, 25–6, 28, 37–9, 48, 88, 106, 114–18, 124, 126, 131, 135, 138, 141, 143–5, 147–9, 153–5, 158–9, 163–5, 171–4, 176–7, 193, 209–12, 220
  ASEAN–Australia–New Zealand 64, 157, 160
  ASEAN–China Regional Trade Agreement 17
  ASEAN Free Trade Area 17–18, 25
  ASEAN–Korea Regional Trade Agreement 17
  Australia–Chile 168
  Australia–Malaysia 146–7, 157, 160, 166–7, 181–2

Australia–New Zealand 17
Australia–Singapore 17
Australia–Thailand 168
Australia–United States 5, 16, 46, 65, 86, 119–20, 133, 159–60, 172, 174, 181, 189, 194, 210
Bangkok Agreement 17
Canada–Chile 15, 160–1
Canada–Peru 160–1
Central America–EU 169–70
Central America–United States 15–16
Chile–China 25
Chile–EU 18, 169, 172
Chile–Japan 16
Chile–Korea 171–2
Chile–United States 15, 44, 145–6
China–Singapore 144
dispute settlement 157–61, 163–71, 179–4
EU–Mexico 18, 169
EU–Peru 174
EU–South Korea 174–5
Free Trade Agreement of the Asia-Pacific 45–7, 60–63, 73, 129, 208, 230
Japan–Singapore 144
Mexico–Japan 16, 168
NAFTA 13, 14, 15–16, 38, 77, 119, 122, 160–61
P4
  see Trans-Pacific Strategic Economic Partnership Agreement
Peru–Singapore 159
Peru–Thailand 16
Peru–United States 15, 43, 124–5, 187
RCEP 3, 46–7, 61–4, 72
Singapore–India 187
South Korea–US 16, 56, 64, 210–1, 212–3, 215–6, 225
South Pacific Regional Trade and Economic Cooperation Agreement 17
spaghetti/noodle bowls 19–21, 60, 118, 181–2, 191
  WTO negotiations, compared to 34–8, 48–9
Fulponi, Linda 118

Gantz, David 179
GATS 131–5, 138–49, 152–5, 239, 241, 256
GATT 28, 30–1, 106, 109, 124, 228–9, 239–41, 156
Gauzman, Andrew 256
Germany 94, 151, 222, 228
Grossman, Gene 214–15

Harmonized System 108–109, 116, 126
health 44, 52, 55–9, 64, 69, 88
Honduras 85
Hong Kong 133, 189
  Australia–Hong Kong Agreement on the Promotion and Protection of Investments 89, 200
Howse, Rob 228

Iceland 133
ICSID 189, 193–4, 196–7, 202
India 20, 47, 60–61, 63–4, 70, 84, 137
  Singapore–India Free Trade Agreement 187
Indonesia 47, 85, 217
international investment law 187, 192–3, 198–9, 202–204
  Australia–Hong Kong Agreement on the Promotion and Protection of Investments 89, 200
  Calvo Doctrine (Argentina) 180, 196
  fragmentation 192, 206, 211
  investor-state arbitration 179–206
intellectual property 39, 52–7, 64–6, 69–70, 74, 81–9, 91, 132, 224
  Anti-Counterfeiting Trade Agreement 58–9, 66, 70, 72–3, 76, 86–8
  pharmaceuticals 52–3, 55–9, 64, 69–70
  TPP 42–4, 47, 50–74, 86–7, 132
  see also TRIPS
international law, fragmentation of 157–165, 192, 206, 258
International Court of Justice

Statute of the International Court of Justice 190
International Telecommunication Union 136–7, 148, 152–3, 155
Israel 133
Italy 16, 151

Japan 20, 24, 46, 61, 66, 77, 127–30, 133, 151, 179, 208, 219
Chile–Japan Free Trade Agreement 16
Japan–Singapore Free Trade Agreement 144
Mexico–Japan Free Trade Agreement 16, 168
Jordan 16

Kawai, Masahiro 114
Kelsey, Jane 93, 248, 257–8, 260
Korea
see South Korea
Kruger, Alan 215
Kyoto Protocol 168, 228

Macedonia, former Yugoslav Republic of 14
Malaysia 24, 40, 44, 52, 77, 108, 156–7, 208, 217
Australia–Malaysia Free Trade Agreement 146–7, 157, 160, 166–7, 181–2
market access 40–41, 43, 48, 61, 106, 109–14, 117–23, 129–31, 135, 192, 221, 239–40
Mauritius 203
McGrady, Benn 90, 100
Mercado Común del Sur (MERCOSUR) 165
Mexico 14, 19, 40, 45, 77, 112, 122–3, 133, 156, 163, 168–9, 179, 208
EU–Mexico Free Trade Agreement 18, 169
Mexico–Japan Free Trade Agreement 16, 168
NAFTA 13, 14, 15–16, 38, 77, 119, 122, 160–61
MFN 29, 44, 108–109, 113, 132, 134, 152–5, 188
Montenegro 14
Morocco 16

national treatment 135, 187, 193, 202, 240–41, 256–7
Netherlands Antilles 203
New Zealand 40, 45–7, 52–3, 61, 64, 77, 84, 87, 93–5, 107, 119–23, 128, 133, 146, 151, 156–7, 160, 182, 199, 208, 219, 236, 255, 260
Australia–New Zealand Free Trade Agreement 17
Norway 84, 103, 133

Oman 16
OECD 152–3, 231, 234–5, 248, 251–2

P4
see Trans-Pacific Strategic Economic Partnership Agreement
Pakistan 133
Panama 42, 57, 133
Paris Convention 69–70
Paraguay 24
Pauwelyn, Joost 256
Peru 24, 40, 42, 44, 52–3, 57, 77, 94, 107–108, 117, 122, 133, 156, 159–60, 167, 208, 219
EU–Peru Free Trade Agreement 174
Peru–Singapore Free Trade Agreement 159
Peru–Thailand Free Trade Agreement 16
Peru–United States Free Trade Agreement 15, 43, 124–5, 187
Petri, Peter 127
Philip Morris 76, 82–4, 86, 89–92, 185–6, 200
Philippines 43, 47
Plummer, Michael 127
preferential trade agreements
see free trade agreements
Pryles, Michael 91

Raustiala, Kal 259
Regional Comprehensive Economic Partnership

see free trade agreements, RCEP
regional trade agreements
see free trade agreements
regulatory autonomy 5, 90, 142, 214, 241, 257
regulatory coherence 231–61
regulatory transparency 213–15, 224–5, 229, 236–8, 244, 253
rules of origin 13, 14, 15–18, 19–26, 44–5, 125–6

SCM Agreement 226–8
Serbia 14
Shearer, Matthew 118
Sherman, Laura 146
Singapore 15, 24, 45, 51, 77, 86–7, 107–108, 116, 119, 151, 156–7, 208
Australia–Singapore Free Trade Agreement 17
China–Singapore Free Trade Agreement 144
Japan–Singapore Free Trade Agreement 144
Peru–Singapore Free Trade Agreement 159
Singapore–India Free Trade Agreement 187
SPS Agreement 27, 242–3
South Africa 14, 24
South Korea 16, 20, 42, 46–7, 54, 56–7, 60–61, 64, 115, 133–4
Chile–Korea Free Trade Agreement 171–2
EU–South Korea Free Trade Agreement 18, 174–5
South Korea–US Free Trade Agreement 18, 210–13, 215–16, 225
Stiglitz, Joseph 227
Switzerland 133

TBT Agreement 27, 76, 85, 224–5, 241–3, 256–7
Thailand 24, 43, 47, 77
Australia–Thailand Free Trade Agreement 168
Peru–Thailand Free Trade Agreement 16
tobacco 75–105, 200
see also Philip Morris; WHO Framework Convention on Tobacco Control
TPP 24, 40–41, 44, 47, 55, 61, 75–81, 126, 149–50
21st century agreement 107, 125, 130, 208, 230
agriculture 106–108, 111, 116–122, 125–30
confidentiality of negotiations 5–6, 103, 118
developing countries 38–45, 49, 192, 197–8, 212, 219–20
economic benefits 2–3, 60, 107, 127, 179–80, 208
environment 44, 47, 168, 208, 210–12, 215–26, 258
future members 60–3, 71, 73, 179–80, 228
health 44, 52, 57–9, 69–70, 90, 92–3, 103
intellectual property 42–4, 47, 50–74, 77–9, 86–7, 132
investment law 184, 191, 204–5
investor-state dispute settlement 89–95, 119, 180–81, 184–91, 193–4, 196–7, 199–201, 204–205, 254
market access 43, 106, 129–31, 192, 221
negotiations 51–3, 72, 88, 118, 121, 123, 125, 141, 184–5
other agreements 61, 70–71, 110–11, 115–17, 121–3, 125, 127, 131, 133–4, 136, 154, 157–8, 161–5, 182, 228
precedent for future agreements 39, 49, 71, 180, 208
regulatory autonomy 90, 215, 257
regulatory coherence 43, 223–4, 231, 244–56, 258–60
rules of interpretation 171, 173–5, 178
rules of origin 21–2, 45, 125–6
services 131–4, 138, 225–6

state-state dispute settlement 156, 163–6, 168–9, 178, 181
telecommunications 138, 141, 148–51, 154–5
tobacco 75, 79–81, 86–89, 99–105, 185–6
Trade Enhancing Access to Medicines 55–7, 64
Trakman, Leon 91
Transatlantic Trade and Investment Partnership
see TTIP
Trans-Pacific Partnership Agreement
see TPP
Trans-Pacific Strategic Economic Partnership Agreement 1, 16, 45–6, 119, 160, 175
Trebilcock, Michael 240
TRIPS 51–2, 68, 76, 85
TRIPS-plus 39, 43–4, 47–8, 62–4, 69–70, 86, 103
TTIP 3
Turkey 133
Tuthill, Lee 146

Ukraine 85, 186
UNCITRAL 196–7
UNCTAD 30, 194–5, 198, 205
United Kingdom 84, 144–5, 151, 222
Uruguay 84, 90, 92, 103
United States of America 3, 24, 39–40, 42–6, 48–9, 51–61, 63–73, 77–9, 93, 96–101, 107–108, 117–23, 128, 137, 141–6, 151, 156, 159–61, 163–5, 184–5, 187, 201, 203, 208–217, 219, 221–3, 226, 232–3, 236, 246, 259–60
AUSFTA 5, 16, 46, 65, 86, 119–20, 133, 159–60, 172, 174, 181, 183, 189, 194, 210, 214
Central America–United States Free Trade Agreement 16
Chile–United States Free Trade Agreement 15, 44, 145–6
NAFTA 13, 14, 15–16, 38, 77, 119, 122, 160–61
Peru–United States Free Trade Agreement 15, 43, 124–5
Singapore–United States Free Trade Agreement 16
South Korea–United States Free Trade Agreement 16, 18, 56, 64, 210–1, 212–3, 215–6, 225
Central America–United States Free Trade Agreement 16

Van Damme, Isabelle 173–4
VCLT 139, 142, 159–60, 172–5
Venezuela 24, 203
Vietnam 40, 43, 45, 52, 77, 107, 154, 156, 160, 208
Vranes, Erich 165

Wignaraja, Ganeshan 114
World Bank 35, 201, 218, 221
World Health Organization 78, 102
WHO Framework Convention on Tobacco Control 80–83, 87, 93, 102–104
World Intellectual Property Organization 50, 71
WTO 14, 22, 32, 34–5, 34–9, 47–9, 50, 62–4, 75, 85, 100, 106, 112–3, 118, 127, 131, 171–8, 186, 200, 240, 242, 244, 256–7
Agreement on Agriculture 109–110, 124
Agreement on the Application of Sanitary and Phytosanitary Measures see SPS Agreement
Agreement on Technical Barriers to Trade
see TBT Agreement
Agreement on Trade-Related Aspects of Intellectual Property
see TRIPS
developing countries 28–38, 218–19
dispute settlement 158, 162–3, 165, 167, 168–71, 173, 175–8
Doha Round 11–12, 33–7, 48, 111–14, 136, 211, 218, 221, 224, 230
General Agreement on Tariffs and Trade
see GATT

General Agreement on Trade in Services
see GATS
Kennedy Round 31
plurilateral agreement on services 4, 133–6, 155
Tokyo Round 31
Uruguay Round 33, 69, 109, 139

Yu, Peter 88

Zhai, Fan 127